Trumpets in the Mountains

Laurie A. Frederik

TRUMPETS IN THE MOUNTAINS

Theater and the Politics of National Culture in Cuba

Duke University Press   Durham and London   2012

© 2012 Duke University Press
All rights reserved
Printed in the United States of America
on acid-free paper ⊖
Designed by C. H. Westmoreland
Typeset in Minion Pro by Keystone Typesetting, Inc.
Library of Congress Cataloging-in-Publication Data
appear on the last printed page of this book.

DEDICATED TO

Nena, la viajera & Mom, la teatrista

CONTENTS

LIST OF ILLUSTRATIONS   ix

ACKNOWLEDGMENTS   xi

Prologue: The Red Blood of Cuban Identity   xix

Introduction: More than Just Scenery   1

1. Revolution and Revolutionary Performance
*or, what happens when el negrito, la mulata, and el gallego
meet el Hombre Nuevo*   41

2. Artists in the Special Period, Option Zero, and the Hombre Novísimo
or, the heroic rescue of Liborio and Elpidio Valdés   76

3. Creative Process and Play Making in Cumanayagua
or, waiting for Atilio on the side of a country road   111

4. The Inundation of Siguanea and Cuba
or, the near drowning and rescue of Cuba's Godot   142

5. Cultural Crusades and the Unsung Artists of Guantánamo
or, how Don Quixote saves humble Harriero from the devil   175

6. Storytellers and the Story Told:
Voices and Visions in the Zones of Silence
or, who wins the wager if the cockfight ends in a draw   218

7. Dramatic Irony and Janus-Faced Nationalism
or, the triumphant stage return of el negrito and míster Smith   259

NOTES   279

GLOSSARY   291

SOURCES CITED   297

INDEX   325

LIST OF ILLUSTRATIONS

MAPS

1. Cuba and Cuban provinces after 1976   xvi
2. Cienfuegos and Villa Clara Provinces, including Cumanayagua, Manicaragua, and the Escambray Mountains   xvi
3. Guantánamo Province, including the traveling route for La Cruzada Teatral   xvii

FIGURES

1. Liborio the guajiro, classic drawn image by Ricardo de la Torriente, 1920s   109
2. Liborio cartoon with Fidel Castro, by the cartoonist Alfredo Pong, 1991   109
3. Campesino crushing coffee beans, Escambray Mountains   126
4. Teatro de los Elementos in "training" and "saludando el sol" (greeting the sun) in the countryside, Cumanayagua   131
5. Rural theater audience in Cuatro Vientos, Escambray Mountains   136
6. Rural theater audience in Dos Brazos, Guantánamo Province   136
7. Atilio Caballero interviewing Wansa Ramos, Cumanayagua   145
8. Macías with his oxen in Siguanea, Escambray Mountains   148
9. Macías and José Oriol by the lake in Siguanea, Escambray Mountains   154
10. Scene from *Ten mi nombre como un sueño*: the Poeta Loco (Isnoel) cutting through the words of the capitalist, Pepillo Hernández (Lexis), Cumanayagua   157
11. Scene from *Ten mi nombre como un sueño*: the Guajiro in Love (Hector) and the Señorita (Kirenia), Cumanayagua   166
12. Scene from *Ten mi nombre como un sueño* with full cast, Cumanayagua   166
13. La Cruzada Teatral puppet performance for rural school children, Guantánamo Province   184
14. Tío Tato (Carlos) performing in Yumurí, Guantánamo Province   185
15. Bohío and campesino family in Dos Brazos, Guantánamo Province   194
16. Corina, campesina in her bohío, Dos Brazos, Guantánamo Province   194

17. La Cruzada Teatral members and the author on the truck at Punta de Maisi, Guantánamo Province   196

18. La Cruzada Teatral, rowboat ride to next performance in Boma II, with two of the actors, Edilberto and Pindi, and a campesino rower, Guantánamo Province   196

19. La Cruzada Teatral, Don Quixote (Carlos), Sancho Panza (Juan Carlos), and guajiro characters (Maruha and Edilberto) in *La muerte juega el escondido*, Guantánamo Province   202

20. Grupo Lino Álvarez de Realengo 18, the Baratute family, other theater company members, and the author, El Lechero, Guantánamo Province   222

21. Espiritista and her altar, Dos Brazos, Guantánamo Province   226

22. Musicians preparing to perform in *Guajiros a los cuatro vientos*, Dos Brazos, Guantánamo Province   226

23. Impromptu cockfight held before the official demonstration, Dos Brazos, Guantánamo Province   227

24. Virginia and Ury interviewing campesinos in Dos Brazos, Guantánamo Province   227

25. Altar de Cruz ritual, the *madrina* (godmother or ritual hostess) sits by the altar and judges the campesinos singing improvisational choruses, Dos Brazos, Guantánamo Province   234

26. Altar de Cruz ritual, one of the competing choruses sings to the altar, Dos Brazos, Guantánamo Province   234

27. El Laboratorio de Teatro Comunitario director Ury Rodríguez directs Rey, a campesino actor, the soon-to-be abandoned script in Ury's hand, Dos Brazos, Guantánamo Province   237

28. *Guajiros a los cuatro vientos* set and rehearsal, Dos Brazos, Guantánamo Province   239

29. During the performance of *Guajiros a los cuatro vientos*, with El Laboratorio co-director, Virginia, acting in the scene, Dos Brazos, Guantánamo Province   239

30. *Guajiros a los cuatro vientos*, full cast, Dos Brazos, Guantánamo Province   240

31. Teatro de los Elementos actors walk thorough Cuban countryside en route to Siguanea, Escambray Mountains   277

ACKNOWLEDGMENTS

The making of a book requires the participation of many people. I wish to first thank my longest-standing inspiration, my grandmother, Mildred Frederiksen ("Nena"). The stories and photographs from her international travels with my grandfather, John Frederiksen, set the spark inside of a small girl's imagination and ignited the wanderlust that would last a lifetime. I must also thank my extremely talented and artistic mother, Karen Frederiksen, who first put me up on a proscenium stage in my debut role as "Scarlet" in the play *Li'l Abner* when I was eight years old. Without a doubt, the ghosts of those theatrical hillbillies from Dogpatch USA hover over these pages. The music and theater people filling our house throughout the years also gave me a gentle nudge in the direction of art and performance—as a practicing artist and in my anthropological research.

If not for Professor Frederick Damon at the University of Virginia, a cultural anthropologist who motivated me to shift from nonhuman to human primates, this book might instead be titled: *Chimpanzees in the Mountains*. Professor Damon also introduced me to Karl Marx by forcing his senior seminar class to read *Das Capital*, vol. 1 in its entirety, which, without a doubt, contributed to my interest in socialism and communist revolutions. Faculty in the Department of Social Anthropology at the University of Cape Town—especially David Coplan, John Sharpe, Mamphela Ramphele, Andrew Spiegel, Linda Waldman, and Fiona Ross—were key influences when I first began to connect politics and social protest to artistic performance. Upon my arrival at the University of Chicago, my tentative plan to continue to pursue theater as a site of anthropological investigation was encouraged by Andrew Apter, Jean Comaroff, and John Comaroff. When my regional focus shifted from Africa to Latin America, these mentors were joined by what ultimately became my Ph.D. dissertation committee: James Fernandez, Claudio

Lomnitz, Loren Kruger, Susan Gal, and Stephan Palmié. Each one of these brilliant individuals helped me in distinct yet immeasurable ways to make theoretical sense of the ethnographic data and to present my analysis in a coherent form that contributes to different bodies of knowledge. Their expertise and guidance—in ritual and the African diaspora; narrative, performance, and the "inchoativity" of metaphor; Latin American intellectuals and nationalism; political theater; and language ideology—were essential to the completion of this book. James Fernandez, Claudio Lomnitz, and Loren Kruger were my closest readers and provided valuable comments on early chapter drafts. I greatly appreciate the extent to which they gave me their time, moral support, and friendship. An extra note of special thanks to both James and Renate Fernandez for their ongoing support of the nonacademic sort—delicious homemade gazpacho, Spanish wine and cheese, sunny afternoons in *el jardín*, and lighthearted conversation kept me sane during the more frustrating moments of "moodling and puttering."

I am indebted to many others at the University of Chicago who provided feedback on ideas or chapter versions on an ongoing basis, and who were motivational in some crucial way: first and foremost, Greg Downey, along with Ariana Hernández-Reguant, Paul Ryer, Laura-Zoe Humphreys, Matthew Hill, Jesse Shipley, Alex Dent, Liz Garland, Michael Madero, and João Felipe Gonçalves. Outside of Hyde Park and at other institutions I thank Denise Blum, who has been an ongoing voice of encouragement and who willingly provided feedback well beyond the call of collegial duty. José B. Álvarez IV, who became my cultural mentor, Spanish teacher, and close friend on my very first plane ride to Cuba in 1997, was gracious enough to check all of my Spanish translations over a decade later—*gracias Pepe*. And finally, my sincere thanks to Elizabeth Ruf, a fellow *teatrista* who understands more than anyone what it took to do research on Cuban theater in the 1990s and who has been a constant source of inspiration in *la lucha*.

Preliminary research trips to Cuba in 1997 and 1998 were provided by grants from the John D. and Catherine T. MacArthur Foundation, Spencer Foundation, Tinker Foundation, and Hewlett Foundation. My first year of fieldwork (1999) was funded by the Wenner-Gren Anthropological Foundation, and my second year (2000) by a Fulbright-Hays Doctoral Research Grant. After returning from "the field," the Department of Anthropology at the University of Notre Dame supported a large part of the dissertation-writing phase with a Pre-Doctoral Fellowship (2002–4) and subsequent employment as visiting assistant professor (2005). The Notre Dame faculty accepted me into the department as a colleague, providing me with a quiet space to write, the opportunity to teach, and a positive and nurturing environment. Thank you in particular to James McKenna, Carolyn Nordstrom, Victoria Sanford, Greg Downey (again), Karen Richman, James Bellis, Susan Blum, and Kimbra Smith. At the University of Maryland I thank Catherine Schuler, Faedra Carpenter, Heather Nathans, and the graduate students present at my "Rough Drafts" session for their valuable commentary on early chapters. A generous research grant from the University of Maryland (GRB) permitted me to update my ethnographic research and begin manuscript preparation during the summer of 2008. Thanks also to Dan Wagner and the APT committee in the School of Theatre, Dance, and Performance Studies for giving me a semester-long teaching-release to finish this manuscript. Vicki Hynes was kind enough to advise me on map making in the eleventh hour.

While living in Cuba, many people helped me adapt to daily life and treated me as one of the family, including Lola, Lisbet, Estelita, Oscar, Zoila, Juan, Anissa, Alejandro, Mario, Martha, Cecila, Gabriela, and especially Isnoel and Ury. Sociologist and *teatrista* Esther Suárez Durán has been an invaluable teacher who has patiently and thoroughly answered my incessant questions for over a decade. Esther has also been a very dear friend and I look forward to our future collaborations. The Centro Nacional de Investigaciones de Artes Escénicas officially supported my work, and gave me the opportunity to share my findings with them and receive feedback from the Cuban perspective. Thank you to CNiAE director Haydeé Santa Sálas and researchers Miquel León Sánchez, Roberto Gácio, and Nancy Benítez Trueba. The directors and staff at the Consejo Nacional de Artes Escénicas and the Centro de Cultura Comunitaria in Havana, especially Alexis Abreu Baez and René Cardona, were also important supporters of and informants for my research.

Most of all—I am ever thankful for the support and friendship of the very talented artists who allowed me to live, work, and perform with them in their home bases and also to travel with them into the most isolated mountain communities of Cuba. In Cumanayagua, the director of Teatro de los Elementos, José Oriol González, welcomed me into the group's daily activities, provided me with a place to stay, and gave me access to all of the group's archives. I would never have been able to carry out this research without his blessing and those of the theater group members: Isnoel Yanes, Lexis Pérez Hernandez, Hector Castellanos Sobrino, Kirenia Macías, "Lolo" Ramón Ojeda, Freddy Pérez Romero, Joel Ramón Pérez, and Atilio Caballero, along with the friends of Los Elementos and residents of Cumanayagua (including Danilo, Nego, Kelly, Luisito, Rafael, Abelito, Yamilé, Sabina, Milagro, the folks at the Casa de Prado and Casa de Cultura). I am also grateful to the *campesinos* of Siguanea and the Escambray Mountains for accepting the strange *yanqui* as part of the theater group.

I am extremely grateful to Maribel Lopez Carcassés and all the members of La Cruzada Teatral of Guantánamo: Ury, Virginia, Edilberto, Carlos, Tula, Emilio, Pindi, Rafael, Eldis, Maruha, Liuba, Lula, Juan Carlos, Norma, and "El Mago" along with *Bohemia* journalists, Tomás Barceló and Jorge Ignacio Pérez) who allowed me to share their travel space on a crowded truck, in camping areas, and subsisting on very limited resources. It was an amazing experience that introduced me to communities of Cuba to which I would have never gained access otherwise. Their talent, hard work, endurance, and motivation were truly inspirational.

After La Cruzada had ended for the year, Ury Urgelles Rodríguez invited me to participate in his new project, El Laboratorio de Teatro Comunitario in Dos Brazos, Guantánamo. Asking an American anthropologist to join a new theater project yet to be formally approved was not an endeavor most Cuban artists would risk, and I appreciate the trust that Ury demonstrated. My understanding of rural Cuba and Cuban theater would have suffered greatly without this final stage of fieldwork and without knowing Ury and his professional partner Virginia. My thanks also goes out to Abel, the town doctor, and all the *campesinos* of Dos Brazos who so openly and affectionately welcomed me into their homes for *cafecitos*, *tragos de ron*, and candid conversation. While working in Guantánamo and Dos Brazos, I was also introduced to El Grupo Lino Álvarez de Realengo 18—the "lost theater group." Thanks to the Baratute family and group members, especially Regino, Julio, Graciano, Mercedes, Gricelda, Ernestina, David, and Luis. These generous people had nothing, yet they provided me with meals and a bed, and took time away from their extensive list of chores to talk with me about El Lechero and the long history of their theater group.

Finally, to my best friend and husband, Jehangir Meer, who I was fated to meet in a Cuban *rueda* dance class in Chicago after returning from over two years of fieldwork. I am now very glad I did not learn rueda sufficiently while living in Cuba. Thank you for sticking by me and for large measures of patience and love.

MAP 1. Cuba and Cuban provinces after 1976 (map by George Chakvetadze, Alliance USA, 2011)
(below) MAP 2. Cienfuegos and Villa Clara Provinces, including Cumanayagua, Manicaragua, and the Escambray Mountains (map by George Chakvetadze, Alliance USA, 2011)

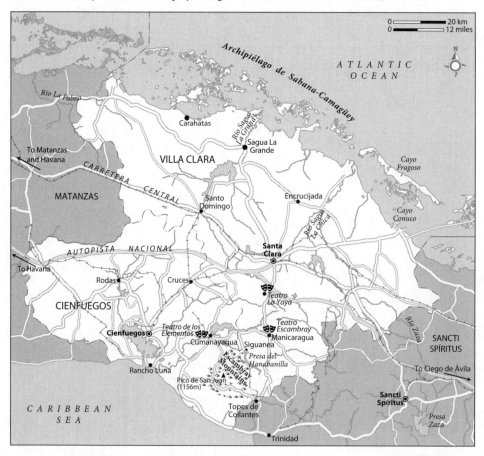

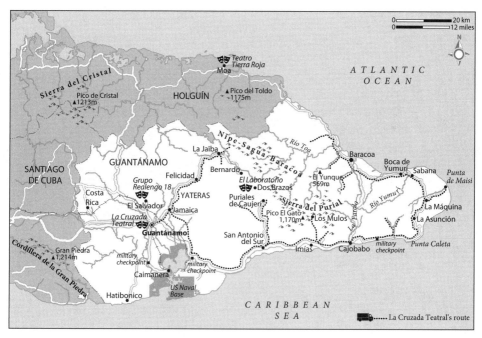

MAP 3. Guantánamo Province, including the traveling route for La Cruzada Teatral (map by George Chakvetadze, Alliance USA, 2011)

PROLOGUE

The Red Blood of Cuban Identity

In the spring of 2000, I traveled through Cuba's rural Guantánamo Province on the back of a Russian flatbed truck with twenty-four Cuban artists and theater performers. Holding on for dear life as the ancient machine thundered through rocky mountain passes, hats tied down tight so gusts of wind and dust did not blow them off onto the dusty roads, we took in the *paisaje*—the beautiful scenery of the most distant points from Cuba's capital city of Havana. At the Punta de Maisí, the absolute eastern endpoint of the island, we jumped down from the truck and looked out over the ocean toward Haiti, conscious of our position on the map and of the vastness of the ocean that surrounded the island. An eerie graveyard of shipwreck victims was haunting, reminding us of the ultimate fragility of human life and the risks some take to chase a faraway dream.

The group that disembarked from the truck that afternoon was called *La Cruzada Teatral* (the Theater Crusade), and it trekked—loaded with bedding, cooking supplies, and the group's puppets, costumes, and stage props—into the farthest, most isolated reaches of rural Cuba called the *zonas del silencio* (zones of silence). Considered *inculto* (uncultivated, uneducated), even fifty years after a revolution that promised equality, education, and "cultural development" for all, many Cuban *campesinos* (farmers, once rural peasants) still had never had access to professional artistic performances. Their exposure to the performing arts and to what urban Cubans considered "culture" was limited to local amateurs—guitar trios and folk singers who practiced on front porches, bartering their music for bottles of rum and pork sandwiches at neighbors' *fiestas*. La Cruzada's old truck rumbled through the small mountain communities once a year, performing in local schools by day and in town plazas at night, actors and audience congregating under and around a single spotlight powered by a small, humming generator.

The members of La Cruzada claimed that during the first years of the trek, some campesinos did not understand the difference between the character and the real individual and were confused to see the actors walking around town in their normal clothing without the make-up and puppets that had accompanied them on stage the night before. Disturbed by this, the campesinos were initially hesitant to socialize with the visitors. The children of these isolated caseríos (small village-like communities with a scattered handful of dwellings) feared the small and unnatural-looking puppets even more than the costumed humans, since they had been warned by their parents and local pastors that the colorful figures with large heads mounted on sticks were unnatural, even demonic. However, after ten years of annual mountain crusades, these hesitations and suspicions were gone among those living in the visited areas, even though "selective inattention" still seemed to be their natural mode of behavior for theater-watching—conversing openly during the performance, coming and going, sometimes watching and sometimes not, often dispersing without applause or the usual formalities of exiting a conventional performance space.

In 2000, residents welcomed the itinerant actors by lining up along the narrow roads leading to the central plaza. They sang, cheered, and threw small white flowers. I caught one of the airborne flowers, tucked it into my field notebook, and took in the scene. I was thankful to be able to blend in with the Cuban artists, rolling into each location on what could have been a magnificent white stallion donned with red feathers instead of a huffing, puffing, smoke-spitting, and rusted-out blue truck. Tired travelers were offered tangerines and sweet coconut candy called *cucurucho*. They were hugged and greeted by name. Carlos, whose clown character, Tío Tato (Uncle Tato), was by then a Cruzada favorite, had changed his act entirely to dispel the type of fear demonstrated in the first mountain treks. Instead of entering as a made-up character, he began calmly seated, dressed in his own clothes, and introduced himself as Carlos. He pointed to a big backpack, inside which, Carlos claimed, was his good friend Tío Tato, who happened to be sleeping. He invited the children to "wake up" Tato and pulled out the clown outfit, piece by piece, putting each article on a different child. At the end, Carlos took the clothes back from the children and put them on himself, thus becoming his character and dispelling the theatrical mystery. He applied his clown make-up in the same fashion, pulling out his make-up kit and telling the children it was Tato's "face."

Once the conversion was complete, Carlos then asked: "What color is Tato's face most made up of?" to which the children answered loudly and in unison, "yellow!"

"What does the color stand for?"

"The sun!"

"And blue?"

"The sky!"

"And red?"

"Blood!"

Carlos corrected them on the last point: "No, no, not blood. Red stands for the Caribbean culture." In this way he subtly sidestepped Cuba's preoccupation with the struggle, *la lucha*, and the blood shed by revolutionary heroes, which were so prominent in the children's education. "They always yell *sangre* when I say red," Carlos told me afterward, perturbed and shaking his head.

Watching Carlos and Tío Tato and listening to the reactions of the children and their parents in the audiences revealed the extent to which politics and metaphors of the Cuban Revolution had infiltrated the consciousness of the population, even those without electricity, television, and radio. In these zones of silence, campesinos relied on their teachers, on the locally appointed Communist Party delegates, and on older residents for guidance and ideological modeling. When La Cruzada came to town, the artists were given temporary cultural authority in the community. They became the town storytellers and familiar national tales were retold in new ways—by enacting fables, legends, and poetic histories.

In Cuba, the color red symbolized blood, war, the Revolution and la lucha, and children as young as four recognized the semiotic system set so firmly into place. Although red also symbolized the Caribbean—the perceived redness of indigenous skin, the warmth of the tropical sun setting over the ocean, or the fiery spirit of the culture—the association took a back seat to the all-pervasive propaganda in the schools and mass media calling for sacrifice and *"¡Patria o Muerte!"* (Fatherland or Death!). In contrast, little American children asked to call out associations for red might come up with red apples and Mom's apple pie (honesty, security, love), or red cherries and Washington's cherry tree ("I cannot tell a lie"). Although weakened by national controversy, perhaps some would still point to the red stripes of the American flag ("I pledge allegiance" and "liberty for all"). National narratives are guided by our national symbols and key metaphors and shaped by the political history read to us repeatedly throughout our lifetime. The moment when Carlos shakes his head at the children yelling "¡sangre!" emerges as a familiar motif throughout this Cuban story I am about to tell.

Living in the rural regions of Escambray and Guantánamo with the campesinos, their *buey* (oxen) and *gallos finos* (fancy roosters), under the thatched roofs of their small *bohíos* (huts), amidst the mountains and winding rivers and where salsa music and the Afro-Cuban religion Santería were out of place as "too urban," I learned about a part of Cuba that was not seen in tourist brochures and was not for sale. I would never have understood the complexities of *cubanía* without having woken up, day after day, to its dewy morning sunlight and the sound of campesinos calling " heetoow" to their animals in the fields. Yet romantic and isolated as it may have appeared, the countryside was still a place where red meant blood and revolution, and where "¡Viva la Revolución!," "¡Patria o Muerte!," "¡Salvamos a Elián!," and other political messages were spelled out in white stones and coconut shells placed upon a hill.

Sonido de trompetas en las montañas
tocan a nacimiento
Siguanea como el Tibet, el universo
como un reloj de bolsillo
y mi alma como un jarrón
donde florece el mundo
que mañana no será más.

Sounds of trumpets in the mountains
marking a birth
Siguanea, like Tibet, the universe,
like a pocket watch,
and my soul like a vase
where the earth blossoms,
but that will not exist tomorrow.

Décima sung by campesino during
interview with actors, Siguanea, 1999

INTRODUCTION:
MORE THAN JUST SCENERY

Campesinos in rural Cienfuegos and Guantánamo claim that Havana is not the "real" Cuba, for it is a cosmopolitan city that has always been exposed to international influences. The real Cuba is in the countryside, they argue, where the culture has developed in its own uncontaminated way and where the *pura cepa* (pure stock or root) is still alive and thriving. The president of the National Theater Board, Julián González, also told me this when he met up with La Cruzada Teatral in Holguín for one of its performances. As an urban dweller (he admitted), but also a cultural specialist, he conceded, "Laura, mira," waving his hand to indicate the green hills lying for miles before us, "*esto* es Cuba de verdad, ya te das cuenta" (Look, Laurie, *this* is the real Cuba, as I'm sure you realize by now). This Cuba *de verdad* (real, true), according to its residents and proponents, is a "pure" and noble face of Cuba whose spirit is not yet "contaminated" by the commercial market in the cities, the discontent of fleeing rafters, or dissident Damas de Blanco (Ladies in White) posing for foreign cameras. Conversely, urban residents say that Havana is, indeed, the real Cuba, and that *todo el resto* (the rest) is *sólo paisaje* (just scenery). After all, Havana is where the majority of Cubans live or want to live; it is "where everything happens." This popular jab extends to theoretical debates in artistic and academic communities both inside and outside of Cuba. Most stories about Cuban national and cultural identity have been told from the perspective of the intellectual and urban center, neglecting the other voices that have actively participated in conversations about *cubanía* (Cubanness). At various academic conferences between 2001 and 2009, I was bewildered by what some of my fellow scholars had to say; it was as if we had been conducting research in entirely different countries. According to many of these scholars, "Cubans" (without qualification) during and after the economic crisis of the 1990s had begun to see themselves as active agents in the international system, comfortably participating in the capitalist market. They were firmly on the road to socioeconomic transition and would inevitably proceed to political transition as well. Capitalism was teleologically inevitable; in fact, much of the analyses of this period were referred to as "transition literature."[1] The *campesino*, or small-town Cubans, were nowhere to be seen in these narratives. The voices presented were urban, racially politicized, and dollar-savvy.[2]

Trumpets in the Mountains takes the reader far away from the urban and cosmopolitan cultures of Havana and Santiago de Cuba to reveal a face of Cuba that has had great cultural and political significance in the history of the nation. It is the Cuba that thrives in the countryside, in the nooks and crannies of the rocky mountain regions. These seemingly faraway places are referred to as Cuba's *áreas de acceso difícil* (areas of difficult access) or *zonas de silencio* (zones of silence), for they are far off the beaten track and one must be determined (and in good physical shape) to reach them. A distinct interpretation of national identity is presented through the eyes of these rural folk and the performing artists living among them. Unlike in Havana, rural storytellers and theater people draw creative inspiration from the religious rituals of *espiritismo* (spiritism) and *cruzados* (crossed or mixed religions), not Santería, and they ride on horses and mules, not in crowded buses or '57 Chevys. Rural folk dance *danzón* and *son* instead of salsa and they rap to traditional *décimas* (improvisational sung verse) rather than hip-hop. In the countryside, artists and local residents assert that Cuba is inaccessible and thus safe from the contaminated *pseudo-cultura* (pseudo-culture) of global culture and capital that seeps into the cities (cf. Adorno 1993). The process that creates pseudo-culture has also been referred to as "folklorization" "folkloricization," where what is supposedly "authentic" folklore (spontaneously generated and orally passed down) is redesigned and marketed (cf. Hagedorn 2001; Mendoza 2008; Olson 2004). The distinction between pure culture and pseudo-culture was the underlying dichotomy in many ideological conflicts in Cuba during the period of my fieldwork. As one might expect, such divisions were never cleanly delineated or collectively understood, and one of the more fascinating parts of this ethnographic research was to see how Cubans, particularly Cuban artists living outside the cultural capital of Havana, dealt with inconsistencies and contradictions. The comedies and tragedies of a society adapting to crisis were revealed during the creative processes of artistic production.

I first arrived in Havana in 1997 during what Fidel Castro termed the "Special Period in Time of Peace," the severe economic crisis Cuba suffered after the fall of the socialist block in Eastern Europe. Castro explained that it was to be a "special period" rather than an emergency, since it was not acute (at least not yet) and would be temporary, not then predicting ten-plus years. It was not a war or a revolution (or perhaps more accurately, not a counter-revolution); therefore it was to be a difficult but passing phase "in time of peace." Although the Special Period was still in full force in 1997, it was much improved compared to its direst era: from 1990 to 1995. Memories of near starvation, immobility, and utter desperation were still fresh in the minds of the population, and both rural and urban citizens of Cuba often categorized their social realities as *antes* (before 1990) and *ahora* (now, after 1995). My first impressions of Cuba were similar to those of my academic colleagues. For this initial three-month visit, I stayed mostly in Havana with just a couple of short trips to the cities of Santa Clara and Santiago de Cuba, seeing for myself what Katherine Verdery calls an "economy of shortage" (Verdery 1996). Describing primarily Romania and other socialist countries in Eastern Europe, she explains that an economy of shortage occurs when economic decline, product scarcity, and hoarding (company and individual) produce an imbalance in the access to goods. "It was a scarcity primarily of supplies rather than demand (the scarcity central to capitalism)" (ibid.: 42–43). I observed and experienced the daily blackouts and lengthy queues to buy bread, milk, and cooking oil, and the endless waits for buses impossibly stuffed with sweaty bodies. With a ridiculous level of determination and American obstinacy and used to a country of overabundance, I would sometimes set off on a day-long mission to find the toilet paper rumored to be on sale somewhere in the city or the ever-elusive loaf of whole wheat bread I periodically found in the *shopping* (dollar stores) out in Miramar, which was an hour-long bike ride each way.

I was fascinated by the endurance of Afro-Cuban religions: the historical process of Yoruba-Catholic syncretism, rich symbolism and dynamic ritual performances, mystery and magic of *consultas* (consultations with Santeria priests), and powerful drums and music of *toques de santo* (ritual and festive gatherings to give homage to the *orishas*). The loosening of the restrictions on the religious rituals and artistic performances sent syncopated rhythms and dancing bodies pulsing into the street—invisibly drifting through open apartment windows or thrust out into the public spaces. As a dancer and musician, these vibrant and performed elements of Cuban culture were very seductive to me. I spent many an afternoon watching rumba and drumming performances and taking classes with area dance companies in the hopes that my body, trained in ballet and gymnastics, might yield to Caribbean movements and rhythms.

Havana was a captivating city, full of dynamic cultural production, revolutionary ghosts, and political importance, and there were research themes aplenty for patient and persistent ethnographers. However, it was not the only face of Cuba, and my love of the mountains and an interest in nontraditional theater and performance sent me on a quest to find an alternative to the noise, bustle, and internationalism of the city. I began by investigating the different sorts of theater groups based in rural locations, traveling out to see them rehearse and perform, and to talk with the artists. Social life in rural Cuba was similar to most "country" cultures around the world in that it moved at a much slower pace and was far less densely populated than the urban centers. The days began before sunrise, when it was still cool enough to work the land, and ended at sunset, when it was difficult to see much beyond the circular glow of the lantern. One had to walk many hours through mountain paths and pastures to reach a village or even a single family dwelling, which were easily missed if not situated on the main path or if one did not know the subtle landmarks of the trails heading elsewhere. Since rural *bohíos* (rural huts, small rural houses) were built from the land—earth, wood, and palm leaves—they were often camouflaged by the shade of the trees or tucked into the side of a hill. The richness and uniqueness of rural culture was found along those long, quiet walks through the mountains as well as in the peopled destinations. The network of households and the periodic passing of ox carts or men on horseback along the path took longer to map out, but were ultimately just as identifiable as a square community block in one of Havana's neighborhoods. My understanding of these relationships and their connection to urban cultural practices were made visible, not through architectural proximity, agricultural trade relations, or kinship structures, but along the waving and creative connective lines of theater, music, and storytelling.

I did not set out to study campesinos; nor did I expect them to be such an important part of studying artists and national politics, but the contrast between the reality and the mythical conception of the Cuban rural peasant and farmer soon became a central theme in my fieldwork. Concentrated in the figure of the campesino were nostalgia (Boym 2001; Dent 2009; Stewart 1996; Williams 1972), notions of purity and contamination (Douglas [1966] 2003), and the maintenance of cultural authenticity and national heritage (Dávila 1997, 2001; Handler 1988; Handler and Gable 1997; Herzfeld 1982). The relationship between nature and national identity, as well as between nature and tourism (Desmond 1999) greatly influenced the ways in which both intellectuals and everyday citizens were discussing nationalism in twenty-first-century Cuba. Connections to nature and *la tierra* (land) became popular and safe, seemingly apolitical ways to narrate the nation after 1990 (cf. Bhabha 1990; Sommer 1991). The distinctive language of the Revolution (the people's struggle) and the revolutionary citizen (humble, modest, with a socialist consciousness and morality) played a crucial role in the development of notions of Cuba's pura cepa and the fight against imperialism and globalization.

The campesino was largely isolated in a geographic sense from the majority of Cuba's population living in urban or semiurban areas. Historically, the campesino had been conspicuously persistent in the popular imagination and in artistic representation; although the campesino's symbolic power had fluctuated over the years. Rural folk were talked about, sung about, and represented in dance and theatrical demonstrations of what was labeled "traditional" life. The stereotypical campesino (also popularly called the *guajiro*, akin to "hillbilly") still made an appearance in modern productions of a prerevolutionary blackface vernacular theater called Teatro Bufo where his character (usually male) continued to appear as brutish, illiterate, and shoeless, in spite of the ubiquitous propaganda about the social advancement of the rural populations after the Revolution.

The image of the campesino as a national icon that also represented a distinct population was conceptualized differently in space and time—the most marked shift in this trope occurring just after Fidel Castro's Revolution in 1959. Although the campesino appeared on a superficial visual level much the same as in the rural imagery of the nineteenth century and early twentieth, people understood the meaning and actuality of the post-Revolution Cuban campesino in a very different way. One distinct example was Carlos Enríquez's well-known painting, *Campesinos felices* (*Happy*

Peasants, painted in 1938), which could never be mistaken for modern-day rural reality. The long, scrawny, sickly faces, the ragged clothing and destitute surroundings ironically labeled "happy" made a clear statement about the condition of prerevolutionary campesinos. Cubans recognized the difference between *antes* (before) and *después* (after), and so did the campesinos themselves, even if the living conditions for some were not very much better than what they were prior to 1959. Interestingly, the contemporary (albeit contradictory) movement for Cuba's pura cepa, did, in fact, lend a degree of cultural coherence to the campesino image through the generations.

Campesino conceptualizations—both antes and después—were guided, in large part, by the political maneuverings of Cuban artists and intellectuals, especially those who went out to live and work among the campesinos themselves. The campesino's renewed popularity developed as the result of an almost universal attempt by urban society to return to what was simple and pure, unsullied by individual greed and capitalist materialism. This shift occurred both out of practical need and ideological idealism. Anthropological scholarship has played a distinct role in the construction of this image, for critiques of colonialism, modernism, and the nation-state seem to leave people no other choice but to construct nostalgic narratives about tribes (or theater groups) not yet "discovered" and the humble folks still living off the land. Given the primacy of urban culture, these rural folk sometimes seem to have become exotic strangers (see Ching and Creed 1997). During times of crisis, society frequently turns to the idea of a past it believes to have been better than its present, often reinterpreting details in the retelling of its history, cleaning it up and making it more attractive. Richard Handler and Eric Gable argue that the images that make up an "authentic" history can actually be represented by "mutually contradictory paradigms of a collective past." They explain that icons may have contrasting meanings, because they express "the struggle between critical history and celebratory history" (1997:7). The juxtaposition between the narrative of nostalgia (rural past) and progress (urban future) was clearly visible in contemporary Cuba, especially in the 1990s, when a national image was promoted (the noble campesino as idealized representative of the "folk") in much different form than the image of Cuba that was being marketed internationally and for commercial audiences (salsa music and Afro-Cuban "folklore"). Some tourist packages in Cuba included a trip to an authentic *casa del campo* (rural house) to meet real-life campesinos and share a meal of traditional rural cuisine. But most tourists were encouraged to remain in the cities or on the beaches, and such casa del campo visits were usually set up as a stop on the way to or from other tourist destinations, such as Trinidad, Cienfuegos, or Varadero.

In Havana, the general image of the campesino or guajiro often remained one of backwardness and primitiveness, but *habaneros* (Havana residents), along with the theater groups I worked with in the rural areas, also saw the campesino as romantic, humble, noble, intelligent, strong, and resilient: this image served as the basis for their understanding of "pure" Cuban culture and identity. The term *guajiro* was used periodically by the actors I worked with, but in affectionate rather than derogatory terms. Rural performances were raw and gritty, performed for the entertainment of the campesinos themselves and not beholden to the usual aesthetic standards of urban, Western-style, "conventional," and intellectually judged theater. Theatrical success was measured by attendance, decibel level of audience laughter, and the fact that residents lingered late into the night, grudgingly mounting their horses for home only when it became too dark to see. There were no local newspaper reporters to critique the production based on artistic interpretation, no high-tech set design or identifiable acting technique. There were no theater house managers to pay or national reputations to uphold: the rural audience did not know who the stars actors or directors were, nor did they care. All that was necessary was a relatively flat clearing and space for people to sit, preferably out of the glare of the sun. Rural performers felt fulfilled and successful with their productions until confronted with cultural elites from Havana during festivals and national tours, at which time the "expert" assessment of urban intellectuals rocked the fragile balance of artistic confidence.

Crisis and Creativity: Old and New Revolutions

New artistic genres and styles are often born when a society is undergoing crisis and traumatic transformation; when desperate times force artistic minds to bend a philosophy, to adapt to the new social, political or economic situation, and to paint the picture of reality from different angles. In theater and performance this type of creative surge is especially apparent, given the immediacy and ephemerality of the medium: controversial issues can be incorporated on the spot, without waiting for resources, production permissions, publication and distribution. Cuba's moments of social, political, and economic crisis have been frequent, if not constant. Yet while there have been times of physical hunger and material deprivation among the population, the theater has always been well fed, never short of polemic or paradox. The Cuban playwright and sociologist Esther Suárez Durán believes that theater is an art that lives in a permanent state of crisis and that ongoing debate and social tension serve as useful provocations for artists to reflect upon, helping them to "shake out" their axiology and subjectivity (interviewed in González Rodríguez 1996:45). Theater and literary critic Rosa Ileana Boudet agrees, adding that theater lives and creates from within each new crisis (ibid.:44). In 1990, Cuba entered the Special Period in Time of Peace, and Castro spoke frankly to the Cuban citizens:

> *Debemos estar preparados para las peores circunstancias [. . .] Nos llevaría a un período especial en época de paz si surgen problemas muy serios en la URSS y nosotros no podamos recibir los suministros que recibimos de la URSS, entre otros, los suministros energéticos que son tan importantes, en un país donde ya el nivel de vida y desarrollo se basa en un consumo de 12 millones de toneladas de petróleo. [. . .] ¿Qué pasaría si de repente nosotros no tenemos 12 millones? Tenemos que saber que hacemos si hay 10, si hay 8, si hay 6, si hay 5, si hay 4, tenemos que saberlo.* (Fidel Castro, speech printed in *Granma*, March 10, 1990)

> We must prepare ourselves for the worst circumstances. [. . .] We might be entering a special period in time of peace if the serious problems in the USSR escalate and we are not able to receive the supplies we now receive from the USSR, among others, the energy supplies so important to a country where the standards of living and development are based on the consumption of 12 million tons of petroleum. What will happen if suddenly we do not have 12 million tons? We have to know what to do if there are 10, if there are 8, if there are 6, if there are 5, if there are 4; we have to know what to do.

And the problems in the USSR did escalate, just as Castro predicted, for soon after this speech, billions of dollars in aid and resources to Cuba were cut off.

Many Cuban artists and intellectuals remember the ideological oppression of 1968–76 as the last decisive crisis to hit their community before the Special Period. The era had various names, including the Quinquenio

Gris (Five Gray Years, attributed to Ambrosio Fornet; see Fornet 2007), Década Negra (Black Years), Años Oscuros (Dark Years), and also the Pavonato (literally "peacockery," referring to the persecutions of then minister of culture, Luis Pavón Tamayo). While both times of crisis were serious enough to threaten faith in the intended goals of the Revolution, the two were different in underlying causes and in the populations they affected. During the Gray Years, the state made a focused attempt to suppress dissident artists and intellectuals, homosexuals unwilling to "reform" themselves, and suspected counter-revolutionaries. In contrast, the crisis which began in the 1990s affected the entire Cuban population—artists, teachers, students, factory workers, administrators, doctors, and housewives, as well as elite Communist Party members. This time, the state's response to the crisis was not to create hidden labor camps to instill proper socialist *conciencia* into ideological dissenters (UMAP camps and their successors, see glossary and chapter 1), but rather to mobilize the masses to actively defend the integrity of their national culture. The Gray Years marked the Revolution's ideological crisis regarding ideas of freedom—the artistic community's calls for freedom of expression and socially critical art battling head-to-head with the collectivism of socialist philosophy and the Communist Party's claims to speak for the masses. But the catalyst that stimulated the Special Period was economic. The initial suffering and anxiety were based on a marked decrease in the availability of basic resources that affected all segments of society, producing a greater potential for mass resistance. Crisis in the country's political ideology and national identity were bound to follow. Although different in many ways, both the Gray Years and the Special Period provided artists with new creative impulses, motivated by the confrontation with a dangerous "enemy," regardless of whether the enemy was considered to be one of *los gusanos* (worms, traitors) within society's own ranks or *más allá* (farther away, beyond) and off the shores of the island altogether.

Theatrical performance and artistic representation have provided a rich vantage point from which to look at how contemporary Cubans interpret and deal with crisis and social transformation, for dialogue, paradox, and contradiction can be found at every level of production, effectively reflecting the complexity of the larger situation. At the same time, as is well known among the artists themselves, crisis often drives creativity and gives social urgency and political meaning to art. Crisis leads to a rupture between two states of perceived tranquility that opens up a space for new meaning making, as well as for the reinterpretation or recontextualization of old meanings (see Turner 1969 [social drama, liminality] and Taylor 1991 [theater of crisis]). I look at how these reinterpretations and recontextualizations of meanings in contemporary Cuba are interwoven with political structure and socialist ideology, and I analyze how national images are maintained and manipulated in both official rhetoric and popular consciousness.

Since the Revolution, Cuba has been in a perpetual state of self-defined crisis, of struggle, of lucha, and ideologically, these crises have been partially responsible for the defensive stance so pervasive in the rhetoric of daily life. "Ay, la lucha" (Ah, the struggle) and "Hay que luchar" (One must fight, keep up the struggle) have been popular refrains referring to a range of daily problems; from avoiding dissident imprisonment, to frustrations having to do with the workplace, *apagones* (blackouts), waiting for the bus, or even running out of milk. Much has been written about the development of Cuba's particular consciousness of struggle and *luchar* (see Blum 2011; Bunck 1994; Fagen 1969; Medin 1990; Pérez-Stable 1999, among others). Many writers have traced the phenomenon back to Ernesto "Che" Guevara and his emphasis on "assiduity and sacrifice" in the development of the "new socialist being," more popularly known as the *Hombre Nuevo* (Guevara 1965). In "Man and Socialism in Cuba," Guevara laid out the ideals and goals of the new revolutionary and socialist society and the inevitable difficulties along the way. The road is long and full of difficulties, he warned:

> We can see the new man who begins to emerge in this period of the building of socialism. His image is as yet unfinished. In fact it will never be finished, since the process advances parallel to the development of new economic forms. [. . .] What is important is that people become more aware every day of the need to incorporate themselves into society and of their own importance as motors of that society. They no longer march in complete solitude along lost roads toward far-off longings. They follow their vanguard, composed of the party, of the most advanced workers, of the advanced men who move long bound to the masses and in close communion with them. The vanguards have their eyes on the future and its recompenses, but the latter are not envisioned as something individual; the reward is the new society, where human beings will have different characteristics: the society of communist man. (Guevara 1965, full text in López Lemus 1980:39–40, translated in Gerassi 1968:392)

Accompanying the Hombre Nuevo was the development of a distinct "revolutionary consciousness," or *conciencia*—a political concept that would dominate state propaganda and artistic creation for the next four decades. Cooperation, sacrifice, struggle, political loyalty, and dedication to revolutionary heroes and legends became the backbone of national identity. Revolutionary metaphors were created and instilled in ideology and popular discourse, and thus, also perpetuated in theater and art. Regarding artists, Guevara stated:

> In the field of ideas that lead to nonproductive activities, it is easier to see the division between material and spiritual needs. For a long time man has been trying to free himself from alienation through culture and art. He dies daily in the eight and more hours during which he performs as a commodity to resuscitate in his spiritual creation. [...] Artistic experimentation is invented and is taken as the definition of freedom, but this "experimentation" has limits which are imperceptible until they are clashed with, that is, when the real problems of man and his alienated condition are dealt with. Senseless anguish or vulgar pastimes are comfortable safety valves for human uneasiness; the idea of making art a weapon of denunciation and accusation is combated. (Ibid.:42–43, translated in Gerassi 1968:395)

The new man and the new artist were to be at the frontlines of the revolutionary struggle, standing up for the masses and for Cuba. Freedom was not to be defined according to "bourgeois idealism" as a "concept of flight." Freedom had to be earned and would come with the successful building of socialism: "Our freedom and its daily sustenance are the color of blood and swollen with sacrifice" (ibid.:48, translated in Gerassi 1968:399).

From Marx to Martí

Economic crisis in Special Period Cuba ushered in an ideological crisis in which questions were raised about the competence of socialist politics and economy, alongside deeper questions about the true nature of cubanía.[3] Cuba's identity after 1959 was based on Marxist and Leninist philosophies, as well as modernization, socialist development, and a particular political consciousness created largely by Fidel Castro himself: a "Fidelismo" created, in part, by thousands of hours of his speeches and their published transcripts. But the events of 1989 proved a turning point in the trajectory of Cuban history. The desperation of the Special Period led to the legalization of the enemy currency (U.S. dollars) in 1993 and an open invitation to Western tourists. Together, these released a deluge of popular global trends and products into the country, leaving behind a distinctly capitalist flavor (see Corrales 2004; Palmié 2004; Wirtz 2004). A heightened questioning of the socialist political structure ensued, and Cuban intellectuals began to return to a national identity and heritage rooted in culture—expressive and artistic culture, as well as linguistic, idiosyncratic, and quotidian. The Cuban state aggressively promoted a *batalla* (battle) against the imperial enemy to "defend" its identity and to "rescue" cultural traditions it considered to be key. This enemy was no longer depicted solely in terms of a demonic Uncle Sam and the antagonism of the United States government, but as something that was broader, more evasive, more dangerous: cultural imperialism and globalization. The Cuban state sought to defend Cuban culture *de verdad* from this perceived threat.

Throughout his fifty years as president, Fidel Castro repeatedly reminded artists and intellectuals of their crucial role in cultivating revolutionary ideology. As Cubans, they were to be loyal to Fidel and the Revolution. As artists, they were responsible for the moral development of the country and the healthy maintenance of cubanía. "Without culture, there is no development," Castro repeatedly exclaimed, reminding members of UNEAC (*Unión Nacional de Escritores y Artistas de Cuba*, or the National Union of Writers and Artists of Cuba) that Cuba was immersed in a battle for "spiritual" literacy, which was one of the most noble goals of socialism to date. "We have to create things that have value and that millions of people read," said Castro, not just a few thousand (Castro 2000:1).[4] Thus, he called for more cultural specialists to create "valuable" culture and to combat neoliberal globalization:

> *Hace poco estábamos aterrorizados tratando de saber como podíamos salvar nuestra identidad. Ya no es una lucha defensiva, sino un contraataque. La cultura tiene no solo un valor en si misma, sino como formidable instrumento de liberación y de justicia. Es la manera de inculcar ideas, conceptos, de una sociedad humana, fraternal, solidaria.* (Castro 2000:1)

> Not long ago, we were terrorized when trying to figure out how we could save our identity. It is no longer a defensive fight, rather, a counterattack. Culture not only has value in itself, but rather as a formidable instrument of liberation and justice. This is the way to inculcate ideas, concepts, of a society which is human, fraternal, and which has solidarity.

However, the definition of true Cuban culture actually remained in a state of negotiation and flux, particularly among cultural officials, writers, artists, and other scholars, who championed the need to locate and rescue the pura cepa of Cuban culture. True cubanía and pura cepa were elusive concepts in the 1990s and early 2000s, caught in a whirl of economic crisis and ideological change, and agitated by the growing international presence and spread of globalized popular culture.

A dialogue began among artists and intellectuals about precisely which aspects of Cuban culture should be represented and maintained and which practices should be used to ward off external contamination to ensure the growth of a new, modern nation. Since Marxism-Leninism was no longer a tenable ideology in Cuban society, state administrators focused on cultural nationalism to justify the maintenance of the existing regime and rule. Contradictions inevitably arose when the nation came to be seen as a set of diverse groups, regions, and religions instead of a homogeneous mass of revolutionary loyalists in khaki, each calling the other *compañero* (comrade). As previously described, urban residents claimed that Havana was the core of Cuban culture and that the countryside was "just scenery," while rural campesinos claimed precisely the opposite. Given the difficulties of travel around the island, it was not surprising to hear such divergent opinions, for the center of one's world depended greatly on where one had been born or assigned to a job. Globalization notwithstanding, the search for pure cubanía was an increasingly complicated endeavor even within the island's own national boundaries.

Preemptive Nostalgia for the Pure Cuban

Listening to the different forms of national storytelling in Cuba over the past decade makes one able to fully appreciate the extent to which official voices—largely governmental, intellectual, artistic, and mass media—interact, and together develop an idea of national identity that appears to be natural and organic. In the last 100 years, the definition of the national Cuban character has gone from Caliban, the colonized victim, to Creole nationalist, to bearded revolutionary fighter, to khaki-clad socialist Hombre Nuevo, and now, after the crisis of the Special Period, to what I call a *Hombre Novísimo* (even newer man) living in a "para-socialist" society: still socialist, but not necessarily on its way to capitalism. In the 1960s, the characteristic qualities of the Hombre Nuevo were embodied in a worker's humility and stamina, coupled with urban savvy, progressive education, and communist ideology. However, the Hombre Novísimo of the twenty-first century is conceived as an urban man with campesino morals and a campesino soul; still communist in his humility and loyalty to the nation, but less aligned with a political party and more cognizant of a general *martiano* (José Martí centered) and nationalist philosophy of patriotism and of the united Latin American struggle against imperialist domination.[5]

Like the Hombre Nuevo, the Hombre Novísimo upholds a moral stance against capitalist greed and domination and fights against those who challenge the Revolution and contaminate the pura cepa of Cuban identity. But unlike the Hombre Nuevo, the Hombre Novísimo battles an enemy of ambivalent status in Cuban society—one that is condemned but also marketed by the state; one that is resented and simultaneously desired by many Cuban citizens. This contemporary foe takes the form of "pseudo-culture," "anti-culture," or, increasingly, "global culture," which is essentially understood in this socialist society as anything motivated by money or individual gain. Capitalism in any form symbolically and psychologically conflicts with Cuba's pura cepa. To the dismay of bureaucrats committed to the regime, the economic crisis justified the state's move to allow the sale of Coca-Cola (albeit made in Mexico), and to hire Santería priestesses, dancers, and drummers to entertain tourists in Old Havana. Fake Tommy Hilfiger T-shirts and jeans, and American rap music became all the rage in both the *occidente* (west) and *oriente* (east) regions of the island. The Cuban artists I worked with in Cumanayagua and Guantánamo generally shunned "places of consumption" where dollars were exchanged, such as hotels, non-peso restaurants, luxury stores, and tourist shows. Other Cubans I met who were Communist Party members or critical of capitalism and "cultural imperialism" shared this aversion. But such places were increasingly prevalent, especially in urban areas, and many residents, regardless of political philosophy, confessed to a covert fascination with foreign goods, not to mention the air conditioning. Sometimes, I was told, a single hour of cool air was worth the hefty price for a cola. I also avoided places of consumption whenever accompanied by my informants, and avoided them just in principle, trying to be a good ethnographer. But I confess that I did periodically succumb to the seductive lure of the old Russian air conditioners advertising their luxurious icy blasts with loud buzzing and water that dripped into the street.

One of the enduring issues in contemporary Cuba has been the question of what is *de verdad*, or authentically Cuban, in a society increasingly affected by consumerism and global cultural and political-economic trends. What was once the image of the progressive Hombre Nuevo has now become that of an *Hombre Viejo* (Old Man), reflected in Fidel Castro himself, symbolizing a dying past, old legends, and dead heroes (and to a lesser extent, this is also true of Fidel's younger brother and presidential successor, Raúl Castro). No longer able to rely on traditional keywords such as *sacrifice* and *struggle* or to rouse support through references to Marx or Lenin, state propaganda, assisted by cooperative artists, turned to cultural heritage and values, scolding the younger generation for its shallow materialism and greed and rewarding those who continued to represent the characteristics of Cuba's noble (and still socialist) campesino.

Many of the traditions that state officials and intellectuals preferred and thought of as ideally *cubano* after the onset of the Special Period were characteristic of the campesino, a pure and humble Cuban who was still morally unsullied thanks to the geographical isolation of the rural areas. The Cuban campesino played an important role in the history of the Cuban Revolution, not only fighting alongside the rebels, but also feeding and hiding them, risking their own and their families' lives. Following the Revolution, the initial successes of Cuba's agricultural transformation and the massive literacy movement were most apparent in the rural populations, which were largely destitute and uneducated before 1959 (remember Enríquez's *Campesinos felices*). Therefore, the ideal campesino after 1959 was not modeled on the *first* Cuban campesino (prerevolutionary peasant or *guajiro*/hillbilly), but rather on the first *socialist* campesino (enlightened worker), an image produced largely by early revolutionary crusades for literacy and education, along with the widespread agricultural reforms that had turned most individual farmers into collective farmworkers. When this particular prototype began to appear on the theater stages, in stories, and on painters' canvases, it was blended with individual creativity and artistic interpretation. These individual contributions, in turn, channeled ideas back into the official conception of the campesino through the mediation of cultural institutions that sponsored national festivals and academic events. In this way, embodiment, enactment, and representation led to the refashioning of the new twenty-first-century campesino, and, by extension, to a new twenty-first-century Cuban—the Hombre Novísimo.

After 1989, Cuba was struggling with its political and cultural identity, for if socialism was no longer the ideal, what was? "Revolution" was still a strong national signifier, but it could no longer be labeled a socialist or communist revolution. How would *revolutionary* be defined after 1990? Before Cuba could fight against any new Goliaths from foreign lands, it first had to define a new David. In the midst of crisis, Cuba was particularly vulnerable. Faced by the erosion of socialist norms, it had to hastily build up a new ideological fortress before the next battle. Those facing identity crisis often look nostalgically back to their roots, to their cultural core. Nostalgia is omnipresent in all cultures, especially in times of rapid change when we long for the simplicity and modesty of yore. What was distinctive about the Cuban case, however, was that this nostalgic yearning was not a simple matter of feeling a loss that called for a recovery. Instead, it was evoked by the impending threat of a loss—*preemptive nostalgia* for a loss that had not yet occurred.

The traditions in question did not somehow fade away over time; nor were they only alive in memory or otherwise out of reach. Cubans traced their current crisis to a set of particular historical moments—the fall of the Socialist Bloc, the withdrawal of Soviet funding, the Special Period, and the tightening of the U.S. blockade. The reaction was not one of melancholy and longing, but of self-righteous fortitude and a determination to reinstate and perpetuate cubanía. It was a counterattack, preemptive in nature, and it called on all citizens to do their part. Yet despite the so-called contaminating influences coming into the country from abroad, the preemptive strike was an internal movement, aimed at Cubans themselves. It was nostalgia for a Cuban ideal that had never existed in practice, but which the culture keepers were intent on keeping alive. It was nostalgia for the ever-hopeful "¡hasta la victoria siempre!" (ever onward toward victory). It was nostalgia for a *Hombre Novísimo* who would never be born if the battle were lost.

La Lucha

As metaphors of struggle and fight (*lucha*) were already omnipresent in revolutionary Cuban language and culture, such a reaction was not surprising. This defensive sentiment was directly imposed onto the Cuban population itself, especially in intellectual circles, the members of which were considered responsible for the expression and representation of the nation, as well as for the reproduction of its token symbols and metaphors. What Cubans longed for was not fully gone yet; thus they did not look back for it. If anything, Cubans in the late 1990s and early 2000s were looking forward, grabbing onto the essential nugget of the Hombre Nuevo and refashioning it in the context of the Special Period. Throughout their lives, Cubans had learned that la lucha was ongoing and that they had to fight for the Revolution and to defend all that was revolutionary. The late twentieth-century lucha called for similar techniques as those used directly following the Revolution. The weapons had changed, but the strategies remained the same.

Nationalistic campaigns were promoted on television, radio and billboards, and through a growing number of national conferences and cultural events. There was resurgence in images of old men with straw hats playing décimas under studio lights. The media celebrated the accomplishments of provincial farmers in the Cuban countryside. In general, campesino imagery was not new in Cuba. It had always been an important part of the nation's cultural identity, as was seen, for example, by a long-running television program called *Palmas y Cañas* (Palm Trees and Sugarcane), showcasing rural and traditional culture—mainly music, dance, and performance. However, a distinct resurgence of the campesino image in the 1990s manifested itself in new forms, with increased intensity and with a new message, especially in theater outside of Havana. State artists were encouraged to adopt this rhetoric, reinforced in special meetings with the heads of the provincial culture boards. In this way, they hoped to win national awards and garner funding for their projects. The new revolutionary armies, the modern *brigadistas*, were actors and performers who set out on crusades to find and rescue the noble campesinos, reminding them of their national value, their pure souls, and the importance of their maintaining a humble (socialist) lifestyle. Performing groups emerged to represent, *rescatar* (rescue), and give voice to the campesino, utilizing the romantic imagery inspired by the Cuban countryside. In the process, they made a name for themselves in professional theater, won awards, and secured resources from the state for their exemplary revolutionary and community work. Official recognition for good moral deeds was accompanied by material rewards (sometimes even in

U.S. dollars)—an unusual combination in socialist Cuba, but increasing in frequency after 1990.

In Cuba, theater artists have long played pivotal roles in retelling Cuban history and in developing national imagery and political consciousness. This has been especially true since the Cuban Revolution in 1959 and the turn to socialism in 1961. Artists funded and trained by the state occupied a position of middlemen, as vehicles of communication between people and state. They worked with "the people," the masses, who told them their own stories of everyday life, of Cuba as lived. These real-life experiences were first interpreted as oral data by the individual artists who collected it, then reinterpreted during the collective discussions that followed. Such discussions among theater groups wavered between daring critique of the present situation of the country and rigid self-censorship, which was a result of years of formal education in state schools and daily living experiences in socialist Cuba. The real-life story told in public had to be aligned with the state's version of reality. It could critique it but not contradict it, at least not directly. A synthesis of ideas was created and represented on stage, telling the story (in its artistic form) back to the people who inspired it, yet also back to the state—ever watchful in the wings.

The power of narrative and language used to tell the national story during the Special Period was distinct from earlier years of the revolutionary era. Socialist modernity and progress were the key drivers of political discourse from the 1960s into the 1980s, but when dreams of economic development were crossed with the withdrawal of essential resources for survival, the state was forced to rethink its strategy. Bourdieu states that "The constitutive power of (religious and political) language, and of the schemes of perception and thought which it procures, is never clearer than in situations of crisis: these *paradoxical* and *extra-ordinary* situations call for an extra-ordinary kind of discourse, capable of raising the practical principles of an ethos to the level of explicit principles which generate (quasi-) systematic responses, and of expressing all the unheard-of and ineffable characteristics of the situation created by the crisis" (Bourdieu 1983:129). Indeed, in Cuba, many mundane principles were made explicit, even sacred, in the attempt to redirect and reinvigorate *la lucha nacional*. However, the new discourse did not develop overnight; nor had it reached a conclusive end by 2010. From my first visit to Cuba in 1997 to my most recent, the "characteristics of the situation" were still being sorted out and decided upon, but the one essential component that surfaced, without a doubt, was the distinction between pure and contaminated, a dichotomy directly reminiscent of Mary Douglas's classic observations in *Purity and Danger* (1966). Douglas discusses the ways that perceptions of "dirt" and pollution in a society affect social ritual and behavior. She asks how to position pollution "in the contrast between uncontrolled and controlled power, between psyche and symbol" and continues: "As I see it, pollution is a source of danger altogether in a different class: the distinctions of voluntary, involuntary, internal, external, are not relevant. It must be identified in a different way" (Douglas 2003:100 [1966]). In Cuba, the idea of cultural and national pollution was complex and ambivalent, not lending itself to simple structuralisms. It would have to be "identified in a different way" as well.

By the late 1990s, the notion of pura cepa was central to nationalist rhetoric; to official and popular measurements of good or bad people, or to assess whether cultural actions or performed traditions were Cuban or pseudo-Cuban (polluted, contaminated). The "systematic response" to the idea of cultural and moral purity was often to point to the rural campesino. The importance of the artists' role in the perpetuation of the campesino figure throughout history was especially evident in the Cuban case, as one traces how the image emerged and was represented in theatrical performance, and how the campesino figure was theorized and guided by cultural critics and scholars. The campesino was a hero in time, if not in space. His humble, nonmaterialistic image and his supposed moral ideals were to be upheld, even if physically he remained isolated in inaccessible regions of the country and invisible to the majority of the population living in urban areas.

In my examination of theater groups in rural areas of Cienfuegos and Guantánamo Provinces, I came to doubt that this cultural movement was just a nostalgic attempt to repossess selected elements from the past, as it first appeared. Instead, I came to believe that it was actually an attempt to construct some kind of imaginary, a metaphysical reality—an officially sanctioned bricolage of past and future, of all the most distinctive and desirable attributes that officials sought to preserve: preemptive nostalgia for the Hombre Novísimo. My research goal was not to reiterate what other scholars have already documented about the image of the campesino as an icon of the rural past and his or her role in the construction of national identity (Boyer 2003; Dávila 1997; Dent 2009; Guerra 1998; Williams 1973), nor to delve into the representations and inventions of history as it related to that identity (Badone 1991; Bauer 1992; Handler 1988; Handler and Linnekin 1984; Herzfeld 1982; Hobsbawm and Ranger 1983; Ivy 1995; Lowenthal 1985, 1996; Tonkin 1992). Rather, I traced how this rural image had been appropriated by state officials, professional artists, everyday people on the street, and ultimately by the actual humble folk about whose traditions careers were being made.

Fieldwork with Cuban "Theater People"

The central goals of my research were to (1) understand how the onset of the "Special Period" economic crisis led to an ideological crisis that transformed notions of cubanía; (2) examine the process through which professional artists, their audiences, and communities reinterpreted what it meant to be "revolutionary" and socialist at the beginning of the twenty-first century; (3) examine the communicative, creative, and power relationships between rural theater artists, rural residents, urban intellectual elites, and the socialist state; and finally, (4) pose a question inspired by Gayatri Chakravorty Spivak (1988): "Can the *campesino* speak?" Or were they still spoken *for* in spite of the best intentions of the Revolution and of revolutionary artists? I was interested in exploring how the campesino was an example of a subaltern figure in Cuba—one that was being thrust onto the main stage, yet one that was still without a microphone and speaking role.

To address these questions, I conducted an ethnographic study of three professional companies of "theatre people" (*teatristas*) in context; professional troupes composed of actors, writers, musicians, dancers, producers, and designers. On such a small island, the professional network of artists and performers was small and intimately connected—in other words, everyone knew everyone. Teatro de los Elementos (Theater of the Elements) resided in the small town of Cumanayagua, a stone's throw from the Escambray Mountains. La Cruzada Teatral (The Theater Crusade) make an annual month-long trek through the rural mountain regions of Guantánamo. And El Laboratorio de Teatro Comunitario (Communitarian Theater Laboratory) focused on an isolated *caserío* called Dos Brazos, also in rural Guantánamo. I examined the interaction of state control, artistic representation, and the real lives of Cuban residents (non-theater people), set primarily in the island's most remote mountain regions of Escambray (Cienfuegos and Villa Clara Provinces; see maps 1 and 2) and the Nipe-Sagura-Baracoa (Guantánamo Province; see maps 1 and 3). I looked specifically at the artists and audiences who engaged in a genre of political theater that used ethnographic techniques for play creation. These groups focused on rural communities and often performed outside in a no-frills setting. They were concerned more with artistic process and education than aesthetics or the artistic product, especially since live performances of any single play were often presented just a few times, were unwritten, unrecorded, and most often unseen by professional critics' eyes.

This mode of theater making had originally been called *Teatro Nuevo* (New Theater) in the 1960s—a name echoing Che Guevara's Hombre Nuevo and the Cuban Revolution's drive to build a new society. Teatro Nuevo was conceived as a form of social and political education during the early years of the Revolution and was reminiscent of other types of people's theater, workers' theater, or consciousness-raising theater around the world—promising to articulate otherwise marginalized, silent voices and to unify and mobilize a collective community (see Boal 1979; Boudet 1983; Leal 1964). The creative process that produced Teatro Nuevo required that actors themselves engage in social investigation or ethnography (living with their focus community, conducting interviews, participant observation) to collect material for conceptualizing and writing of plays. The first Teatro Nuevo group was formed in 1968 and consisted of successful Havana theater artists who left their urban Havana homes to venture out into the countryside, eventually deciding to focus on the campesinos of the Escambray Mountain region. There, they encountered a rural population neglected by the prerevolutionary Cuban state: extremely poor, without electricity, running water, passable roads, schools, or access to medical care. The performers named their new group Teatro Escambray (Escambray Theater) and built an artistic commune in an area called Manicaragua. Living with and interviewing the local residents, the theater group collected ethnographic data and collectively wrote plays based on the information (see Leal 1978; Séjourné 1977; Villegas 1995; Weiss 1993). They ultimately brought their artistic products back to their informants for reflection, discussion, and debate. The group's goal in the 1960s was to bring rural voices into the national dialogue for the first time in Cuban history, but it also sought to "educate" campesinos about the modern world outside of their mountainous frontiers. Many other theater groups followed in Teatro Escambray's footsteps both within Cuba and throughout Latin America.

Theater as a political phenomenon in revolutionary Cuba followed a distinct historical path directly connected to performance trends in 1960s Latin America; in particular, those developed by Augusto Boal in Brazil ("Theater of the Oppressed") and to a lesser degree, Enrique Buenaventura ("Committed Theater") in Colombia. Russian theater was also a prevalent artistic influence in Cuba, especially after 1961. The "system" or acting "method" of the ubiquitous Constantin Stanislavsky (1936) was popular from the 1960s, but most of its influence entered the Cuban repertory later in the 1970s and 1980s. Russian plays were produced in Cuban theaters (Anton Chekov, Alexander Guelman, Vladimir Mayakovsky, and Sergey Obraztsov) and after 1976, Russian theater professors went increasingly to Havana to teach at the ISA (Instituto Superior del Arte, National Arts University). Despite this, socialist realism never took a firm hold in Cuba and was, in fact, criticized by artists for its propagandistic nature. Bertolt Brecht was also a significant influence through his Marxist political philosophy and his desire to "refunction" the theater as a forum for political ideas and as a force that worked to shape society.

Cuban theater ensembles were adopted as an important feature of the socialist revolution and were used as didactic vehicles. Revolutionaries believed that the education (literacy and politicization) of the campesinos would be the key to uniting the island's population into one cooperative *pueblo*, or national "community," and Teatro Nuevo became one of the hallmarks of revolutionary and socialist theater. Its goal was not to reflect the mere entertainment of previous years, but to be "efficacious" (Schechner 1988, 1993): socially useful, informative, instructive, or even transformative as in ritual, a "transformance" (ibid.; see also Turner 1988 and 2001 for the difference and relationship between efficacy and entertainment). This new national community became the overarching symbol of revolutionary Cuban unity, and this new theater one of its artistic messengers. Revolutionary ideology promoted the idea that community in Cuba was to signify "the nation" in order to evoke a broad sense of solidarity and cooperation. Unlike Benedict Anderson's theory of an "imagined community," however, the Cuban people were directly *told* what the new Cuban nation was to be and what role they would play within it. The idea of national community was not to be imagined, but consciously planned by a central political core; the "deep horizontal comradery" (Anderson 1994) *forcibly* implanted into the society through education, cultural programming, art, and coercion (cf. Lomnitz's critique of Anderson 2001:6–13). National identity and political consciousness were to be dictated and controlled by the state. Socialist ideology was not an abstract collective imagining informed by amassing social commentary and public critique through print and over time, but an official requirement and integral to a perception of national loyalty. socialism, revolution, and the struggle against corruption, inequality, and imperialism went hand in hand.

Thirty years after the emergence of the first Teatro Nuevo group, I set out to investigate how ethnography could be performed as well as how the nation was imagined, challenged, and transformed through the interpretive and political process of creating performance. I sought to find data to illustrate a heightened version of what Bakhtin calls dialogism and heteroglossia (Bakhtin 1981) in theatrical performance—the dialogue and multivoicing occurring during the creative process, performance, and post-performance discourse. I also wanted to prove that theater was not just "reflective" of national politics as commonly asserted, but that its role was essential and powerful and that the agents themselves (actors, playwrights, directors, theater people in general) were the most important elements. The product was the result of a dynamic and heteroglossic process, not of one single geographically or ethnically defined group or political perspective, even though the group consisted of all Cuban citizens, all participating in "revolutionary theater." The artists—the sum of the various groups of individuals participating in the artistic/theater world—were the ones to watch, much more than the plays they produced. Cultural and national identity, patriotism, political consciousness, and even state authority were affected by artistic elites, who were in turn informed by different realms of society.

Over the course of my research, this project became an ethnography of ethnography making, a study of performed ethnography, or perhaps better described, a "metaethnography" of how identity was defined, manipulated, theatrically represented, and received back by its own members.[6] I studied the actors who studied their rural subjects as cultural "others" and then performed their ethnographies back to their informants. The actors were not trained ethnographers or professional academics. They did not attempt to abide by what anthropologists would consider appropriate methodological standards, for example, often talking only to the men, not randomly selecting individuals from which to collect data, and not transcribing interviews for documentary proof and accuracy of analysis. But they were self-conscious of the ethnographic endeavor, recognizing the importance of doing participant observation and trying to understand the worldview of their informants. I found the justifications for their chosen research processes just as fascinating as other interpretive phases, though I did find myself biting my tongue when they made decisions a university professor might *tsk tsk* in my own institutional world. I was not concerned with analyzing the efficacy or appropriateness of the theater groups' ethnographic methods in the same way I would the monographs in the graduate seminar I teach on Ethnography and Performance. And certainly, none of the Cuban artists had read or were concerned with critiques by the likes of James Clifford and George Marcus (1986), Marcus and Michael Fisher (1999), or James Faubion and George Marcus (2009). These Cuban teatristas unabashedly sought a unique and poetic representation of the material, proud that it was historically and culturally accurate and that the "emotional truth" (as some contemporary American storytellers would say) was maintained. An artist's ethnography—whether actor, dancer, musician, storyteller, or poet—will always be distinct from that of the social scientist.

Although I generally examined modern Cuban politics and national identity through the theater, the focus of analysis was not the performance itself, but rather, the context that informed the process of creative cultural and artistic production, as well as how the artistic pieces were in turn used by the agents in a national dialogue. Richard Schechner defines performance as "the whole constellation of events [. . .] that takes place in/among performers and audience from the time the first spectator enters the field of performance—the precinct where the theatre takes place—to the time the last spectator leaves" (1988:39). I was concerned with the community formed by the goal of performance, but operated under the assumption that research does not stop at the space marking the "field of performance" (see also Bourdieu 1993) or the time when the "last spectator leaves." I looked more broadly at the concentric waves created by the "ideological transaction" between the company of actors and the community (Kershaw 1992:16) including, but by no means confined to, the actual audience participating in or viewing the creative process or its subsequent performance.

Theater's use as a political tool has been recognized for centuries, as has the function of theater as a site of critical expression. Analyses routinely describe the form and content of a given play in terms of its social and political relevance. All theater is political to some extent and is linked to the social, political, and economic context of the space where it is performed. In Cuba, theater was more directly political in a formal sense, fed and maintained by the socialist state and the many levels of cultural institutions and officials who embodied its power (Martin 1994; Medin 1990; Weiss 1977, 1993). Many analyses of theater have stressed its relationship to politics or the state as abstract entities. They have often focused on one particular site of discourse, discussing the interaction as either conflictive or complementary but neglecting the grassroots processes through which the defined relationships developed and were transformed over time and in space.

For anyone working with artists and intellectuals in a socialist country, Katherine Verdery is an essential source of theoretical historicization and comparison (1991, 1996), and her insights inform my reflections throughout this book. Her work, however, is based on text rather than action and centers on literary intellectuals instead of performing artists. My research considers her analyses of intellectual politics and ideology in light of the living, breathing enactments of contemporary Cuban socialist artists on stage, in the rehearsal room, mingling in their communities, with friends, and in their own private dwellings with family. Richard Schechner and Victor Turner emphasize the importance of rehearsals, collaborative workshops, and the ritual "becoming" of a production (Schechner 1993; Turner 1987), but do not analyze the national repercussions, discursive or symbolic, of the textual or behavioral content of such rehearsal spaces; nor are they concerned with how the resulting rhetoric becomes a part of political consciousness. Theater has been recognized as a trenchant form of political and ideological control (Gramsci 1971; Haraszti 1987; Kruger 1992, 1995; Mosse 1975), but those individuals actually affected by these manipulations have remained largely invisible. To fully understand how a sociopolitical consciousness is formed, the process, participating "actors" (individuals, community, state representatives), and their "scripts" must be included in the analysis (see Comaroff and Comaroff 1991, 1992). I take the agent-centered approach proposed by Richard Bauman and Charles

Briggs (1990) and use performance-based creative language and action to study how national identity is understood by its citizens in a time of rapid social and ideological transformation.

Revolutionary Cuban theater was based on the philosophy that theater should not be an elitist art form, but should break down conformity and acceptance of bourgeois domination (Boal 1979; Brecht [in Willett] 1957). Cuban theater after 1959 was to be popular and communitarian (Boudet 1983; Leal 1980; Muguercia 1981, 1988; Weiss 1977, 1993). The Cuban state desired that theater be used as an ideological weapon; a political or anti-imperialist tool and radical cultural intervention in campaigns such as the original Teatro Nuevo and the more recent "Mass-ification of Culture" and "Battle of Ideas." But Cuban artists have also used the theater as a platform for critical dialogue and subversive com-munication in a society otherwise highly censored—where creative and political expression have been rigidly controlled. Members of Cuban society in both urban and rural areas understood these trends in theater, and although they did not always attend the actual performances, con-versations about the latest plays were often heard repeated in nonartistic spaces and had an effect on the ways Cubans saw themselves as either empowered or oppressed in their society.

There have been historical studies of campesinos in the Escambray Mountain region (Swanger 1999) and of Teatro Escambray (Villegas 1994), and I will summarize those histories, but my study focuses on cultural production and nationalism since the beginning of the Special Period. Joining a small multidisciplinary group of self-classified *Orien-tistas* (those studying in Oriente, or the eastern region of Cuba[7]), my analysis reveals modern Cuban identity from a different perspective— from that of artists and local citizens in the most isolated "zones of silence" on the island—and it spotlights a large peripheral domain of Cuban reality which is often disregarded as a "dark corner" of the coun-try. I consider the distinction of folk versus folklore as it has developed in twenty-first-century Cuba, not only in terms of the racialized categories of white peasant versus Afro-Cuban traditions, but also in terms of the conflicted and contradictory relationship between national socialist pro-paganda and the international commercial market.

Methodology

This book is based on ethnographic data collected mainly between 1997 and 2005. I lived in Cuba as a full-time resident for just over two years, from early December 1998 to late January 2001, the majority of the time spent in the mountain villages near Cumanayagua and Guantánamo City. In March of 2001, I also accompanied one of my focus theater groups to Belgium and France on a European tour, traveled with them, observing their performances and listening to their comments during their first international experience. I have since returned to Cuba every year to revisit members of the theater groups and keep up with the changes in Cuban society generally. In my research, I looked beyond the theater in Havana that took place on proscenium stages, using pre-established dramatic texts that were routinely monitored.[8] In contrast to more conventional forms of theater, the target audiences of Teatro Nuevo (its 1990s revival called Teatro Comunitario) played a crucial role long before the play was staged for formal public viewing. I was most interested in the creative process of play making. In these cases, functional and educational value displaced both the usual aesthetic measures of "good" and "bad" theater and the question of the performance's ultimate marketability to a ticket-buying audience. This was only possible because of the socialist economic system and full state support for all artistic groups. Theater groups gathered ethnographic information about the "other" (in this case, rural campesinos), collectively wrote plays based on that information, and relayed this ethnography back to its actual subjects through the medium of performance, generating discussion and debate. To examine the relationship between center and periphery in Cuban artistic circles, I first had to distinguish the subworlds within the systemic whole. I focused on the farthest reaches of these subworlds, and then analyzed them in light of geographic, cultural, and artistic hierarchies.

Initiating fieldwork in Cuba during the 1990s was a challenge since the infrastructure for visiting students and other temporary residents had not yet been developed. After 1993, the door opened a crack to researchers, allowing a handful of the most determined to squeeze inside, but procuring both a Cuban visa and a U.S. license were not easy tasks. Faced not only with bureaucratic obstacles, but also with an inherent suspicion of Americans in Cuba and an inconsistent and as yet unformed system, researchers were forced to confront the path to legal residence as their first rite of passage into Cuban society. Acquiring letters of formal invitation and support from state cultural institutions as well as coveted signatures from their elusive directors were tasks that required three preliminary trips between 1997 and 1998 totaling six months on the island before initiating formal fieldwork. When I arrived in Havana in December of 1998 to begin my long-term research, I was grounded in the city for an additional month so that I could secure permission to work in the rural areas, procure the necessary letters, establish residence, and receive my Cuban *Carné de Identidad* (Cuban identity card required of all Cubans and residents). After a rather humorous (in retrospect) game of almost daily visits to the Ministry of Culture ("Ven mañana compañera, Fulano no está hoy" [Come tomorrow, my friend, So-and-So isn't here today]), I was finally granted the special authorization I needed to work in the countryside. This was only the first of many times I experienced Cuba's socialist bureaucracy firsthand, and I later learned that it was an important step in more fully understanding Cuba and the society in which Cubans lived.

Preliminary research was undertaken in urban Havana, Santa Clara, Cienfuegos, Matanzas, Pinar del Río, and Santiago de Cuba by conducting interviews; attending performances, festivals, and conferences; meeting artists and intellectuals (actors, playwrights, directors, musicians, dancers, critics, writers, poets, painters); and doing archival research. This initial survey of the different cultural centers enabled me to visualize the network of artists and intellectuals around the island and the extent to which they communicated with each other. Cuba is a small island nation, so I was able to identify the general structure and layout of cultural production and socialist institutionalization by analyzing the movement of performance groups and their plays (including spoken and textual discourse about the groups and plays) and by learning where and why artistic alliances and rivalries existed.

As a performing artist and amateur "theater person" myself, I participated in classes, workshops, and festivals during my first trips to Cuba, making friends and contacts with many of the island's theatrical, dance, and musical groups, both in the large urban centers of Havana and Santiago de Cuba and in the smaller cities. I enrolled in dance classes at the Instituto Superior del Arte (National Arts University, or ISA), took acting and production workshops during International Theater Festivals, and attended conferences on community art and culture. All of these activities allowed me to return later to Cuba with knowledge of how the art world functioned, and more importantly, how the socialist system shaped that world. It also gave me experiences in common with other Cuban artists, with whom I could then empathize about the successes or shortcomings of particular events. Perhaps most importantly, I became a familiar face, a foreigner they grew to know. This inclusion in the group as a fellow artist allowed me a certain acceptance and cultural capital I would not have had as just a social researcher, especially in a place like Cuba, where it was often suspected that American researchers had ulterior and counterrevolutionary motives. Joking that I was a potential CIA spy went on throughout the first several months of my full-time residence, and the inference, jokingly but with raised eyebrow, was dropped periodically by new friends and contacts throughout the duration of my stay.

Although I incorporated myself in Cuban groups as fellow artist, members of the Teatro Comunitario groups I worked with were also quite interested in having me present as an anthropologist in order to observe and comment upon (and publish articles and books about) their ethnographic methods of social investigation and play making. The idea of anthropological theater had not been prevalent in Cuba. Teatro Escambray was described as sociological theater by the French sociologist Laurette Séjourné (1977), due to its methods of research (mostly interviews) and social analysis combined with theater making. Few Cubans I encountered knew anthropology as a scholarly discipline, although everyone was in some way familiar with the term and had their own ideas about what it meant. Sociology was the nearest social science at the University of Havana. There was a small Centro de Antropología located in a suburb of Havana, where it was understood as the study of indigenous Cubans and archaeology of the precolonial era. The Center housed a mini-museum of artifacts and a few historians. There was also a Centro de Antropología in Camaguey, although it was so often closed for restorations that I was never able to visit or gather information about it. Another institution that did anthropological-like work was the Fundación Fernando Ortiz (Fernando Ortiz Foundation, founded 1995), headed by Miguel Barnet, a writer who had originally studied sociology under the well-known scholar and ethnographer of Afro-Cuban culture, Fernando Ortiz. In

2004 the foundation began to offer a *diplomado* (diploma) in cultural anthropology, a short course that included an American anthropologist and Cuba specialist, Ruth Behar, on its faculty list.

One of the theater groups I worked with, Teatro de los Elementos, connected its name directly to "man and nature," the elemental roots of culture and human life, and its members were also very interested in intercultural or transcultural theater. After reading the works of theater practitioners and theorists, Eugenio Barba and Nicola Savarese, they began to use the term *anthropological theater* in their group's description. Although the "anthropology" of Barba and Savarese differed from academic anthropology, the underlying emphasis of cross-cultural understanding and participation in "what appeared to be foreign" were comparable, at least as far as my relationship with the group.[9] My presence, public presentations, and local publications helped validate Los Elementos' idea of and claim to be anthropological theater, even when I explained that Barba's idea was different (Frederik 2001). The term worked for them. Like any trained ethnographer I tried to blend in and not affect the trajectory of their work, but my presence in a region where foreigners were infrequent inevitably affected the course of events, just as my self-identification as an anthropologist interested in ethnographically based play making was destined to have an effect.

Teatristas, or theater people, have a particular community, one that is more cohesive than many other artists and intellectuals (with the exception of musical groups and some dance ensembles), largely due to their frequent need to work collectively. While writers, poets, painters, sculptors, and other solo artists often practice and create their art alone, theater people must collaborate, utilizing their distinct, individual talents to constitute a whole—an assembly enacting a live play for an audience. The term *teatrista* (theater specialist and practitioner or both) in Cuba included the entire theatrical creative team: playwright, director, actor, critic, light technician, producer, and stage manager. It also included professional critics and *funcionarios* (functionaries, or representatives of the state) of Cuban theater who were granted authority to judge the quality and value of works presented and to censor or ban if necessary. Ultimately, the artistic team must share its work with *el público* (the public, or an audience) to be fully realized. Although there are some experimental artists and theorists who disagree on this point (e.g., Grotowski 1968), it is, on the whole, an accepted principle of performance: in order to participate in theater, a spectator or audience must be present to witness the event. In Spanish, the term *público* also suggests the necessity of a community that supports the theatrical performance. I agree that *el público* plays an important role in the creative process, but in Cuban "people's theater," audiences were not simply spectators—passive recipients and consumers of the performance. They were active agents in the actual construction of that performance, akin to Augusto Boal's "spect-actors" (spectator-actors, Boal 1979). I examined the community—local, regional, and national—as it interacted with the actors, and the concepts developed during the process of artistic production in its ongoing relationship with the teatristas. Although I did conduct various studies of audience reception in Cumanayagua, Cienfuegos, and Havana and had interesting results, these side studies were limited in comparison to my in-depth ethnography of the theater groups and their communities. Moreover, in the Cuban theater groups I studied, the audience and teatristas were sometimes analytically inseparable.

Opportunities presented themselves, like most ethnographic fieldwork, with a little bit of luck and a lot of persistence. I first met the director of Teatro de los Elementos, José Oriol González, in Havana in 1997. Standing in line to attend a play during Havana's International Theater Festival, I recognized José Oriol from a photo in a newspaper article and introduced myself. After several more meetings, some planned and some fortuitous, he invited me to Cumanayagua to observe his theater group. I began formal fieldwork in Cuba with Teatro de los Elementos in February of 1999, and lived in an apartment with two of the group's actors in the small town of Cumanayagua until January of 2000. I became the group's shadow —living with them, eating with them, attending meetings and excursions —and was given a formal role in the group and listed in their playbills, initially called *asesor* (consultant) and later *antropóloga* (anthropologist). I was present for the entire creative process of a play under construction which came to be called *Ten mi nombre como un sueño* (Remember my name as if it were a dream), which opened in the fall of 1999. I was allowed access to the group's archives, discussion notes, correspondence, and recordings of all productions dating back to its inception in 1990. I traveled with the group up into the Escambray Mountains, stayed with them in the campesinos' bohíos, and listened to the interviews they conducted with the rural residents. My video recordings became tools for Los Elementos during the process of play making, as the campesino interviews and improvisations were watched and discussed, and later incorporated into the ultimate production. As the resident anthropologist in a self-defined anthropological theater group, I was included in discussions of campesino culture, cubanía, and Cuba's place in the world. My participation was usually in the form of informal questions posed to the actors during conversation, but they, in turn, often asked me about farmers and rural areas in the United States in order to compare and contrast with their own.

In February of 2000, I was invited to join a "cultural crusade" to the far eastern end of the island, traveling with La Cruzada Teatral (The Theater Crusade) from Guantánamo City through the mountain regions to Baracoa and back. Taking a similar approach to my investigative methods in Cumanayagua, I became a participant observer, traveling, living, and occasionally performing with the theater group. La Cruzada traveled by foot, mule-back, oxcart, rowboat, and an old Russian flatbed truck for thirty days through some of the roughest and most isolated terrain in Cuba, stopping at secondary schools and small rural communities of campesinos throughout Guantánamo Province. I studied La Cruzada not as a creative process, but as a crusade, a movement, and an example of what I call *Option Zero Theater*—a type of Cuban theater performed without resources, without any extras, at the point of total scarcity during the worst years of the Special Period. I delved into the use of the campesino as part of a changing national imaginary, and compared the work of the professional artists in Guantánamo to those in the central Escambray Mountain region of Cuba.

Upon completion of the crusade, I remained in Guantánamo for the remainder of the year, spending half of my time in Guantánamo City and half in the rural caseríos of surrounding areas. I lived with one of La Cruzada's actors, and participated in the debut of a new theater project called Laboratorio de Teatro Comunitario (Communitarian Theater Laboratory), which was conceived and directed by Ury Rodríguez. With El Laboratorio, I did research that was similar to what I had done with Los Elementos: I focused on the creative process of a play ultimately called *Guajiros a los cuatro vientos* (Guajiros of the Four Winds, or Guajiro from Every Direction). I studied the ways in which the artists interpreted the information they had gathered through ethnography and how the narrative and experiential exchange between campesinos and artists fed back into Cuban cultural institutions and contributed to cultural production and "massification" during the late 1990s and early 2000s. While in Guantánamo, I also conducted short-term research with the oldest amateur theater group in Cuba, Grupo Lino Álvarez de Realengo 18 (Lino Álvarez Theater Group of Realengo 18), a group that Havana teatristas told me was "missing" and had not been seen for years. I soon learned, however, that the perception of "lostness" existed only because Havana teatristas rarely, if ever, traveled to eastern Cuba. The enduring mystique of "the East" was maintained by a lack of familiarity and access.

I returned to Havana approximately every three months for a week or two to type up field notes and relish in an almost hot shower (albeit supplied by what were precariously exposed wires heating up an otherwise cold water flow). While in Havana, I stayed in a small converted one-car garage behind the house of a family living in the neighborhood of Vedado. The household consisted of a retired doctor; his wife, who spent long hours in a small garden dug out of the driveway; their daughter and granddaughter; and a feisty Pomeranian puppy. In my little garage, I stored my laptop computer, extra clothing, books, accumulated data and handwritten notes, cassette tapes of interviews, rolls of film (in the fridge), and anything else I could not carry on my back while in the mountains. I accessed the archives at José Martí National Library and the library at the National Theater. I gathered journals, magazines, and newspapers with cultural announcements and critiques, and attended dozens of staged performances of all sorts. I also continued to participate in dance and theater classes, academic and artistic conferences. I attended performances and cabarets for tourists in open spaces and hotels, some free and some that charged in dollars, and conversed widely with Cubans in the farmer's markets, craft markets, bookstores, and the street. I spoke to people waiting in lines for bread and buses, or sitting in parks, at parties, or in their homes. I watched cultural and educational shows on television as well as news documentaries and popular *telenovelas* (Latin American version of soap operas). My goal was to understand as much as I could about the balance and connection (or lack thereof) between rural and urban living, and to assess the level of communication and "cultural coherence" (cf. Lomnitz 1992) between and through the different regions over time.

The chapter themes in this book build up and then break down Cuba's national characters. The whole scenario, in both fiction and real life, oscillates between what is desired and idealized and what is possible for a group of social agents—from theater group to state apparatus to citizens —to actualize. Chapter 1, "Revolution and Revolutionary Performance," describes how the Cuban Revolution gave rise to revolutionary consciousness; how that consciousness was assimilated by state artists and intellectuals; and how it was communicated to the Cuban public in the theater. Attempting to erase divisions by race and class, as represented on prerevolutionary stages such as Teatro Bufo (a blackface comic theater), a new form of theater joined the Latin American movement for a Teatro Nuevo, or theater for the people. Teatro Nuevo became the model of the new society, of socialist equality—a performed symbol of the idealized utopian collective and the liberation and enlightenment of the marginalized. The original national characters of *el negrito* (black man), *el gallego* (white Spanish colonist), and *la mulata* (female mulatto) were taken offstage, making way for socialist modernity, progress, and the Hombre Nuevo.

Chapter 2, "Artists in the Special Period," jumps to 1990 and the economic crisis of the Special Period in Time of Peace. It introduces Fidel Castro's concept for a last resort contingency plan called Opción Cero (Option Zero) and the theater of scarcity that developed and continued to grow throughout the decade, which was called Teatro Comunitario. Loyal to revolutionary ideals, Teatro Comunitario was in some ways a revival of Teatro Nuevo. When the U.S. dollar was legalized in 1993 and foreign tourists and investors began arriving on the island, state artists had another battle on their hands. Not only were they faced with the struggle for physical survival; now they had to fight for the ideological survival of socialism and Cuba's revolutionary mythology. This chapter introduces the resurgence of the noble campesino as one of Cuba's central iconic heroes and analyzes how the supposedly humble rural man became a popular but contradictory figure in artistic and intellectual culture.

Chapter 3, "Creative Process and Play Making in Cumanayagua," narrates the interpretive steps in the creative process of Teatro de los Elementos, relating it to similar processes in any kind of "devised" or collaborative theater projects. The steps include (1) preparation, (2) incubation, (3) illumination, (3b) adaptation, interpretation, censorship and (4) verification. By detailing the process of play making in socialist Cuba, the chapter reveals how an idea is taken, developed, and collectively translated into an act of performance—one that is experienced by actors, local community members, and state officials. It also shows how such ideas grow and are built into national projects and state rhetoric and how they become incorporated into popular belief. The capitalist (or foreigner) returns as the evil symbol of the imperialist enemy, and the romanticism of the countryside is advanced in official cultural circles. Chapter 4, "The Inundation of Siguanea and Cuba," picks up the story at the moment of "Adaptation, Interpretation, and Censorship" (phase 3b) and explains how the artists utilized ethnographic methods to complete the creative process. The national metaphors of water and waiting in Cuban society and in artist representations are analyzed alongside the famous Samuel Beckett play *Waiting for Godot*.

Chapter 5 focuses on Cuba's eastern region and investigates the "Cultural Crusades" of the "Unsung Artists of Guantánamo." It explores the idea of the *más allá* (farther out, beyond) from the perspective of professional artists in the province of Guantánamo, a concept that refers to the physical and spiritual location of the *campesino de verdad* (real, authentic campesino) as well as to Havana. These artists felt marginalized from and neglected by Cuba's cultural core in Havana and strove to associate themselves with a nationally recognized theater, a crusade (La Cruzada Teatral) to spread art and culture into the most isolated regions of Cuba. This chapter explains how the ideas of " pseudo-culture" and the "Massification of Culture" campaign affected the cultural politics of this region and the relationship between the periphery and the center. It also considers the extent to which "moral contamination" of urban domains and the dollarization of the Cuban psyche reached the seemingly unassailable zonas de silencio—areas considered the heart of Cuba's pura cepa and national cultural soul.

Chapter 6, "Storytellers and the Story Told," remains in Guantánamo and focuses on the construction of the campesino imaginary; on how campesinos tell their own stories to the professional actors, who relay these stories back to the campesinos in professional theatrical productions. Here I discuss how contemporary Cuba is perceived to be in a phase of virtuality, of desires, utopias, fantasies, and illusions. I also explore further why the campesino has been such a popular archetype in Latin American nationalist movements. Cultural authority and authorship are discussed, and the role of the intellectual and artist in the construction of cultural coherence is revisited. One final case study is introduced: El Laboratorio de Teatro Comunitario, which attempts to give voice and authority to the campesinos themselves. The chapter questions why artistic mediation is often inevitable, even in a socialist society where the peasantry is educated and nationally empowered.

To conclude, the "Dramatic Irony and Janus-Faced Nationalism" of Cuba's situation are summarized and presented in light of the growing tourist industry that supports this small island nation, even as the economic blockade by the United States continues its fifty-year-long cold war against Cuban communism. Both cultural and popular discourses lament the contamination of traditional cubanía and the corruption of memory—even though such Cubanness began only after 1959. Some loyal teatristas who once celebrated the idea of Opción Zero and fought to rescue the noble campesino take advantage of their newfound fame and defect to capitalist countries, leaving theater groups without actors. Cuba's internal campaign for rescuing so-called real folk culture from pseudo forms of it is confronted with the state's simultaneous commercial campaign to sell the previously condemned folklore (Santería and other forms of Afro-Cuban religion and performance). Recognition of the black African (now Afro-Cuban) negrito returns to the stage, along with the white gallego (now *extranjeros*, or foreigners, not only from Spain), and the struggle to define Cuban identity is once more in contention and crisis. Who will take over the national spotlight is once again up for grabs; more precisely, the question is what cast of characters will share it.

Trumpets in the Mountains traces the storytellers and the story told about Cuba and its citizens from its first hearty cries of "¡Viva Cuba!" to the muddled and ambivalent voices of the Special Period, and finally to the post-Fidel era and the first several years of Raúl Castro's presidency. I look at relationships of political power and cultural authority in communist Cuba, and examine how both active "spect-actors" and passive audiences respond to *cubanía revolucionaria* after 1990. Utilizing a classic subject (theater) in a nonclassic setting (rural Cuban mountain regions of Escambray and Guantánamo) yields new insights about how the articulation of ideas can be manipulated and negotiated, and how ideology is produced and maintained both politically and poetically. While politics is inherent to any study of Cuban society, this subject allowed me to transcend the political and to reach into the creativity and imagination of the people themselves, providing a glimpse at the raw materials of a shared consciousness. I examine the shifts in social values, historical narratives, national imagery and symbolism, and investigate the poetics of everyday struggle under an oppressive regime. This book shows how a socialist identity is structured, the forms in which it surfaces, how it adapts during times of crisis, and also how a newly forming *para*-socialist reality (not "post" or "late") was being written into history through performance, artistic expression, and popular culture.

A Note on (Inter) Disciplinary Positioning

Before sending the reader off to read the rest of this ethnography, I must disclose that I was, much like the Cuban actors I describe, taken in by the beauty, mythology, and poetics of the countryside and the campesinos living there. This subjective entanglement had nothing to do with the thrill of an anthropologist finding the lost tribe in the wilderness (though I admit, it was quite thrilling to go into places called "zones of silence"). It has everything to do with the fact that I love the mountains—the lack of concrete, buildings, noise, traffic, and densely packed people. There is a reason for an almost universal romanticism of rural areas, for there is a certain magic that comes with stillness and quiet, the rising mist at sunrise, and the murmuring hum of water flowing over rocks. I also believe it is virtually impossible to talk of art and performance without wanting to insert a little bit of one's own artistry, as *inculto* (uncultivated) as it may seem in the world of social science.

The researching and writing of this book was enlightening for me as a scholar who (as of 2007) had to straddle two disciplines: anthropology and theater. As a graduate student in the Anthropology Department and in social science at the University of Chicago, I learned to focus my analysis on people and social behavior, even when looking at art and cultural production. Often times, the complexity and artistry of the product and its reception were analytically neglected in the quest for understanding local and national ideologies. In contrast, my current institutional home of theater and performance studies, in the humanities tends to base its analyses on the text or the artistic artifact (script, performed play), often forgoing an investigation into the social context, political economy, individual agency, and the creative process. Raymond Williams and Dwight Conquergood criticize the "textocentrism" or "scriptocentrism" of most analyses, but not because the text is bad, they assure us, just that the text is not the only thing (Conquergood 2002; Williams [1953] 1983). Diana Taylor calls attention to academia's emphasis on the archive and forms of archival memory such as "documents, maps, literary texts, letters, archaeological remains, bones, videos, films, CDs, all those items supposedly resistant to change" (2003:19). In contrast, the "repertoire" "enacts embodied memory: performances, gestures, orality, movement, dance, singing—in short, all those acts usually thought of as ephemeral, nonreproducible knowledge" (ibid.:20). This binary is flawed, as are most, in that the interpretation of the archive is not consistent. Taylor explains that "what changes over time is the value, relevance, or meaning of the archive, how the items it contains get interpreted, even embodied. Bones might remain the same even though their story may change, depending on the paleontologist or forensic anthropologist who examines them" (ibid.:19). For this research, I gathered archival bones and looked at the ways Cuban artists and intellectuals told and enacted stories about them, both onstage and off. I took these stories (products, texts) seriously, but I was not concerned with finding the correct version, a futile task for sure. Instead, I looked at how the confluence and contradiction of such stories worked in Cuban society and on its citizens. Taylor might say I was looking for embedded "scenarios" reproduced by the archive, which is true, but I also wanted to know what was being created anew in the twenty-first-century economic and political context (ibid.:28–32). While I was interested in the "once againness" (ibid.), I was more interested in the sentiments of "oh, not againness" and how Cubans, especially Cuban artists, chose to deal with it. Discovery, conquest, and colonization had long been frequent and conspicuous characters on the Cuban stage for sure, but what or who else had the power to edit the national memory and master narratives so firmly set in place? And how could it be done?

In my current job as a professor of performance studies I have had to come to terms with the marriage of anthropology and theater and am challenged to find the disciplinary nexus on a daily basis, especially as I teach new groups of students every year in my cross-listed courses and am pressed to provide definitions and lineages. For me, the interdisciplinary field of performance studies blends the ethnographic and agent-based research methodology of anthropology with the performance paradigm from theater. Social theory is the glue that binds data and frame. The goals of investigation are essentially the same—to understand some new element of the performance of cultural and political life in a selected human group and then compare with other groups around the world.

Artistic performance is not just "expressive culture" or "cultural performance" as it is so often referred to in anthropology. Artistic performance is part and parcel of what shapes the quotidian in a complex and often conflicted dialectic. I look at a culture through the eyes of artists and use the analytical frame of performance to understand historical and contemporary social, political, and economic relationships. The forefathers of the field—Victor Turner and Richard Schechner (and later Dwight Conquergood)—nurtured the dialogue between anthropology and theater, but after the premature death of Turner in 1983, its development turned decidedly in the direction of Schechner—a professional theater director and theater professor. I often wonder how performance studies would have advanced had Turner continued to have a say in its growing number of definitions and its institutionalization. Turner's and Schechner's brief but productive dialogue produced concepts that are emblematic of the field: (1) an evolutionary tree from animal ritual to human ritual to sport, language, and theater, (2) the entertainment and efficacy braid, (3) a theory superimposing social drama with aesthetic drama, and (4) a focus on process, rehearsal, and liminal or liminoid space-time (Schechner 1988, 1993; Turner 1982, 1987). Conquergood proposes the scholar-artist-activist ideal of performance studies and its potential for "explaining-showing-doing" (2002). He also demonstrates how ethnography and theater can be utilized as both academic and community activism (Conquergood 1988).

But what is the state of performance studies today, and are these theories relevant more than twenty years later? I present this book in the attempt to show one of the ways that performance studies can continue to bridge, or better yet, *break down* the conventional disciplinary divides, not necessarily to build on a field that is already difficult to define, leaving its tracks in the sand "like a side-winding snake" (Schechner 1998), but rather, to shed light on the myriad ways a performance studies project can be realized and the intellectual freedom it has the potential to provide. Since I am at the anthropological end of the continuum from anthropology to theater, my work is inescapably and unapologetically Turneresque. It is anthropology *and* theater *and* performance studies—all embraced in an ever-expanding braid, or perhaps more accurately imagined "rope" of theories and observations about the performance of culture, nation, and identity. I hope that theater and performance studies scholars will enjoy learning about Cuba and its performing artists from my perspective, in the same way I am learning to see the world through theirs.

1

REVOLUTION AND
REVOLUTIONARY PERFORMANCE

or, what happens when el negrito, la mulata,
and el gallego meet el Hombre Nuevo

The modern *ancien régime* is the comedian of a world order whose real heroes
are dead. History is thorough, and it goes through many stages when it conducts
an ancient formation to its grave. The last stage of a world-historical formation
is comedy [. . .]. Why should history proceed in this way? So that mankind shall
separate itself *gladly* from its past.—KARL MARX (1844; in Tucker 1978:57)

Distinctions of *cubanía* began, as in many nationalist movements, during the long fight for independence from colonial domination in the
1800s and focused largely on ideas of inclusion based on race and bloodlines, though it also related to economic class and one's perceived level of
education and civility. In the late 1800s, the Spanish sought to maintain
control over the island, while *criollos* struggled to free themselves from
this dominance and liberate the emerging Cuban nation. Public expressions of the desire for national independence were prevalent, but the
separation of pro-Cuba and anti-Cuba was not as clear cut as in many
other colonial situations that evolved around white European versus
indigenous. Various analyses of Latin America and the Caribbean have
asserted that the genetic and cultural roots of the Cuban people were
Indian, Spanish, and African (Dávila 2001; Weiss 1993). The situation in
Cuba was distinct from other Latin American nationalist movements in
that most of its true indigenous inhabitants (Taíno, Siboney, and Arawak
Indians) were extinguished through European disease, maltreatment,
and slaughter. Thus, "indigenous" or "native" ceased to be a political
player in Cuba, and as a result Cuban national consciousness was to be

negotiated along different lines. Although there were arguably still descendants of the original Caribbean Indians in the rural mountainous areas of the Guantánamo during my time there, their images were more often found in the marketing of Cuban beer. After the conquest, what remained on the island were black slaves from Africa, white settlers from Spain, and brown-skinned mulattos. During the nineteenth century, there was also a growing population of Chinese immigrants, brought over by the Spanish between 1848 and 1878 to work as indentured laborers (see Yun 2009). While the Chinese were included as part of the national *ajiaco* (Fernando Ortiz's stew metaphor for cultural and racial mixing, see Ortiz 1906, 1940) and seen on stage, they were not documented in the archives as politically active in the nationalist movement.

A century before Fidel Castro's Revolution for social democracy and equality for all classes and races, Cuba was a society facing very different struggles. By 1868, Cuba had been under Spanish colonial control for 354 years and its population torn by racial and economic inequalities. The Ten Years' War for Cuban independence from Spain began in 1867, but Cuba was not independent until 1898. In the late 1800s, Cuba had a marked class structure, plagued with racial discrimination against former African slaves, mulattos, Chinese, and other nonwhites, as well as scorn for the *blanco sucios*—poor and often so-called uncivilized classes of whites. Economic and political power belonged to the elites, while the lower classes struggled to survive as laborers on tobacco or sugar farms and worked as domestic servants to the affluent urbanites (Horowitz 1971; Mintz 1985; Ortiz [1947] 1995; Pérez 1995). The last years of colonial Cuba were difficult for all of the island's residents, but especially for those living in poverty. While plantation owners, successful merchants, and government officials lived in relative comfort, the poor urban and rural masses were plagued by labor exploitation, unemployment, illiteracy, and sickness. Black slaves lived in even worse conditions, often struggling just to stay alive. The freeing of slaves in 1886 did not help to alleviate their hardships. And although nationalist cries for an independent Cuba were increasing and unifying those who were pro-Cuba, not all segments of society were included in this conception of "nation" in the nineteenth century. The end of the colonial era was a time of struggle by the groups who wished to be included in the process of national self-definition and identity building, particularly blacks and mulattos.

In order to understand Cuban national identity in the twenty-first century, it is important to take into consideration the history of its interpretation. This chapter describes the first declarations and definitions of Cuban national identity and examines the evolution of its cast of national characters as they developed on theatrical stages. Pre-revolutionary archetypes popularized in the nineteenth century were introduced—only to be forcibly erased in 1959 to make way for the Revolution's *Hombre Nuevo*. Subsequent chapters illustrate how twenty-first-century perceptions of the Cuban character looked back, however unconsciously (or grudgingly), to images of prerevolutionary society, subverting more than fifty years of ideological education intended to eradicate racial and class-based social divisions.

Teatro Bufo and a Cuban Commedia dell'Arte

A type of theater called *Teatro Bufo* (Theater of the Buffoon) emerged during the busiest period of the Cuban slave trade in the mid-nineteenth century, when the island contained the highest percentage of black inhabitants: roughly 55 percent black versus 45 percent white (mulattos were included in the statistics for "black" in this data; de la Fuente 1995:135). Teatro Bufo (also known as *teatro vernáculo*, or comic theater) was a blackface theater in which white actors blackened their faces with burnt cork and painted their lips white. While similar to the American minstrels in style, the Bufo scripts, especially those in the early twentieth century, had more fully developed storylines and their content reacted to Cuban historicity and social issues of the time. The three main characters—*el negrito* (negro male), *la mulata* (female mulatto), and *el gallego* (white male Spaniard)—ultimately came to be seen as the three distinct social and ethnic groups of the new Cuban nation.[1] The full history and analysis of Teatro Bufo are beyond the scope of my project here and have already been expertly investigated by the theater scholar Jill Lane (1998, 2005); the Cuban *teatrista* and sociologist, Esther Suárez Durán (1995, 2006, 2008); and ethnomusicologist Robin Moore (1997), but it is significant to my analysis of contemporary Cuban theater for its turbulent relationship with revolutionary ideology as well as its distinctive stage characters—a trio making up a genre that Cuban theater historian, Rine Leal, called "*nuestra Commedia dell'Arte*" (our own Commedia dell'Arte) (Leal 1975a:17, 20).[2] The stage versions of the trio disappeared when Bufo was ultimately banned, but they reappeared during the crisis of the Special Period.

Like most theater, Teatro Bufo was a genre that had to be experienced live in a public venue, not read in private, for without the interplay of accents (*negrito, mulata, gallego*), music (*son, danzón, rumba, tambores*), facial expressions, the timing of the dialogue, and the reactions of the audience (laughter, shocked gasps), much of its effect was lost. Indeed, I myself understood a great deal more about the genre and the relationship between the characters after I finally saw a live Bufo performance (sans blackface) in 1998, and again in 2000 when I knew more about Cuban culture.[3] It was an artistic venue to share humor, voice complaints, collectively justify social mores, and publicly debate Cuban social types and their roles. Teatro Bufo had a dual role in colonial society: it derided the black and mulatto image, but at the same time popularized and bolstered members of these groups as having an identity, including it, for the first time, in a notion of Cuban nationality. It not only provided a new form of comic relief to Cubans weary of political struggles and economic hardships, but also began to provide an image of what the up-and-coming Cuba might look like. It created an understanding of who was part of the national picture, both powerful and powerless.

This theater form provided an important example of how social critique and public opinion were embodied in popular performance in the early Cuban Republic, and many historians believe it was the first time a distinctly "Cuban" character was represented on stage and written into dramatic texts (Leal 1975a, 1980; Suárez Durán 2006). This new Cuban was not the ideal citizen, not the imagined image of the future, or the celebrated national hero, as will be seen in later chapters. This citizen of the early Cuban Republic was powerful simply in the recognition of his distinction from colonial and Spanish culture. Although Bufo productions were originally intended to denigrate and ridicule the appearance and behavior of the black and mulatto, the inadvertent result was to put them into the national spotlight. The plays were comedic and entertaining, comedy being a crucial element in its increasing popularity. Audience members enjoyed going to them, demand increased, and the number of professional Bufo groups proliferated. Black music and dance became increasingly known and popular by their inclusion on public stages, and Cuba's seemingly marginal black culture was slowly becoming associated with the national struggle for self-expression (Lane 1998, 2005; Leal 1975a, 1975b, 1980; R. Moore 1997. See also E. Robreño 1961 and Ayala 1994).[4]

Another relevant component of Teatro Bufo was the extent to which rural guajiro music and dance came to play an increasingly important role in its content. Robin Moore describes how the vogue of a growing *afrocubanismo*, as well as alternative whiter-hued nationalisms of *indigenismo* (pertaining to native Indians) and *guajirismo* (pertaining to rural peasants), were evidenced by musical styles presented on Bufo stages and in popular culture (R. Moore 1997:122–32). But while images of the guajiro and rural music and dance were also portrayed on Bufo stages throughout their duration, it seems they did not have the same celebrity stage presence as the negrito and mulata. After all, most guajiros were white, and thus a reminder of what elite Cubans might have been or could still become (see Leal 1980:44–50 for a very brief discussion of the *bufo-campesino*).

The immediate goal of these early comedies was to entertain, and by going to them audiences were able to escape the drudgery of colonial administration and work on the sugar plantations and to socialize with acquaintances. With the instant popularity and growth of Teatro Bufo in the nineteenth century, called *bufomania*, the press attested that "no hay ciudad de alguna importancia en el interior que no tenga su compañía" (there is no city of any importance in the interior that does not yet have its own company. *El País*, November 8, 1868). Teatro Bufo's surge in popularity was due to several factors. Consider Marx's aforementioned theory about the relationship between history and comedy. Cuban Bufos show that an inherent social tension between Spanish colonialists and Cuban nationals was coming to a head. Bufos of the late 1880s and early 1900s not only degraded blacks; they also covertly targeted the colonial regime, confronting and challenging dominant Spanish and European traditions. Although the negrito character still appeared to be the primary comedic target on stage, it was his relationship to gallegos, mulatas, and the occasional *norteamericano* (North American) that stole the show. In fact, the negrito, however vulgar and ignorant he was portrayed, also appeared as the most cunning of the cast, making fun of the others in a kind of inversion à la Molière. While relationships appeared equivocal, it must be remembered that *all* negrito actors were in fact white beneath their stage make-up (although increasingly, mulatas were "real" mulatas). Therefore, despite their black faces and prescribed character, there remained a significant distance between the actor and the reality of the black. The theater provided a powerful point of contact between

mainstream and marginalized. In prerevolutionary Cuba, Cuban identity appeared to be up for grabs. Its resolution depended on who had the
power to decide what characteristics constituted a Cuban citizen.

The gallego had an especially poignant role, for with the increasing
antagonism toward his character in both real and theatrical life, the
image of "Cuban" began to take on a tanner hue. This *bronceando* (tan-
ning) of the national image is discussed by Robin Moore, who writes
about the "nationalization of blackness" and the point at which the Afro-
Cuban element appears in public negotiations of nationality (R. Moore
1997). Following an essay by Argeliers León (1991), Moore describes two
stages of "artistic nationalism." The first stage, he argues, began in the
mid-nineteenth century among the Creole planter elite. This was a pre-
dominantly white nationalist phase in which blacks were only grudgingly accepted into society and were excluded from cultural expression
such as painting, literature, and music. The second period began in the
1920s and has continued into the present day, "characterized by the
rapidly increasing centrality of Afro-Cuban music to national culture, at
least as a somewhat abstract source of inspiration" (R. Moore 1997:22).
Moore calls the period from about 1923 to 1933 "Leon's axis," because it
was the "socio-historical moment linking distinct epochs of white and
black nationalism." The "sudden vogue of afrocubanismo" brought the
discussion of race and nation to a level of new immediacy (ibid.:115–16).

Despite its popularity, Teatro Bufo was highly controversial for its
provocative political content and was too much of a loose cannon for the
colonial government. It was banned in 1869 and was not seen on Cuban
stages for another ten years, until after the Wars for Independence. In the
meantime, its ensembles were forced to perform in Mexico, Europe, and
the United States.[5] When the Bufos returned to Cuban stages, the degra-
dation of the black had a smaller role. After 1895 the ambiguity of what
constituted a "Cuban" continued, as did discrimination against the
blacks, but Spanish colonization was no longer the political hot-topic.
Rather, post-independence Bufos focused on the new star enemy—the
North American (Mr. Smith and Mr. Johnson)—and the three national
Cuban types acted more as a collectivity (albeit an equivocal one) than as
opposed characters. The themes and political targets changed with the
times, but the central character types remained the same—the Cuban
commedia dell'arte holding on to its archetypes.

The popularity of theatergoing in Cuba waned both during and after the War for Independence. Dozens of plays were being written in Havana and in other urban centers, but the lack of available venues and dwindling audiences were sizable obstacles. In the political turbulence of the early 1900s, theater was at a standstill, and the integrity of the genre as high art was regulated by those who could still afford to attend or sponsor the companies. Cuba's most influential political poet and original nationalist, José Martí, had lauded the role of theater in the nation's history and had stressed the importance of participation by Cuban artists instead of foreign ones (Martí 1891), but the continuance of war and political strife between Cuba and Spain, and also between Cuba and the United States, remained priorities. Despite the debates that surrounded the potential critical power of Teatro Bufo, theater was still considered just a form of entertainment.

Theater and Politics, 1952–1959

Under the second Batista regime (1952–59), theater productions, as well as other forms of art and literature, were being watched more closely by state authorities than ever before, since the heart of political resistance in Cuba, as in many politically unstable countries, was in the universities among the students and intellectuals as well as within leftist artistic circles. In the 1950s, some of the most influential individuals of both of these groups (intellectuals and artists) began working in the University Theater in Havana, and have been described as the "cauldron" of leftist writers who were to later emerge as prominent figures under Fidel Castro's revolutionary regime (Martin 1994).[6] Batista had seen the danger of this growing nucleus of subversive artists and responded by creating the National Institute of Culture in 1954, intended to create a mechanism of government control over the arts through the control of essential subsidies. When ensembles began to go astray, he was then equipped with an official arm that had the power to either "persuade" the theatrical ensembles to redirect their energies, or cut off their ability to perform altogether—the latter being precisely what Batista did in 1956 when the critical murmurs of the University Theater became too audible. Ironically, after Batista's fall, the revolutionary government used the same kind of regulatory hold and repressive tactics to control the theater. When Fidel Castro came to power in 1959, the political and economic systems changed drastically, but the structural mechanisms of control over cultural production and the forced development of the social and political consciousness of Cuban society remained remarkably intact.

The ideology developed with the Cuban Revolution after 1959 attempted to unify the racial triad of Teatro Bufo and to transform distinctions between el negrito, la mulata, and el gallego into a singular and homogeneous Hombre Nuevo. Art for entertainment, including comedic theater such as Teatro Bufo, was sacrificed for "useful" art (educational, political, for development) and "accessible" art (free or cheap, performed in marginal neighborhoods and rural or semi-rural communities) for the masses. Although the first characters of cubanía were radically transformed with the Revolution, an officially supported resurgence of the original imagery resurfaced during the crisis of the Special Period in the 1990s. The endurance of cultural stereotypes in spite of rigid ideological education and repeated attempts to reeducate a population was striking. After the Special Period, the original Bufo characters reemerged from a long silencing. Yet while the negrito had upstaged the guajiro in the early 1900s, the guajiro was fighting for the spotlight in the 2000s; or if not the guajiros themselves, at least the actors playing the guajiro on stage.

Enter Fidel Castro and Ernesto Che Guevara

Tradition belongs to those who cultivate it. It is the task of our zealous intellectual apparatus to recommend a tradition, and that is the easiest thing in the world: one simply defines the central core—MIKLÓS HARASZTI (1987), *The Velvet Prison*

On January 1, 1959, Fidel Castro rolled victorious into Havana, and his arrival marked the beginning of the Cuban Revolution. Although "revolution" in history is often accompanied by a date, and is depicted as a temporally bounded event or a particular turning point, revolution in Cuba must be understood as a continual ideological process and motivating principle of transformation that continues into the twentieth century and beyond the reign of the symbolic originator, Fidel Castro. As long as the adjective *revolutionary* remains in the conceptual system and language ideology of the Cuban people, the system of meanings attached to it will remain embodied in their cultural practices. By "language ideology" I refer to the general definition offered by linguists who envision "ties of language to identity, to aesthetics, to morality, and to epistemology" (Woolard 1998:3) and "the cultural system of ideas about social and linguistic relationships, together with their loading of moral and political interests" (Irvine 1989:255; see also Gal and Irvine 2000; Bauman and Briggs 2000; Gal 2005). In Cuba, it is not the Spanish language that is the key association for national identity, but the ideology of Revolution, defined in large part by the millions of words spoken and published in over fifty years of Fidel Castro's many long speeches.

The word *revolutionary* has a distinct meaning in Cuba, for it refers to a particular political consciousness that grew out of the 1959 Cuban Revolution. Teatro Nuevo, along with Che Guevara's Hombre Nuevo ("New Socialist Man," Guevara 1965) were models of new revolutionary theater and the new Cuban citizen. As an adjective, *revolutionary* signified sacrifice, hard work, national loyalty, and the proper moral attitude toward the continued development of Cuban socialism. Revolutionary art was art for the masses, socially useful and educational and produced for the good of the nation, while "counter-revolutionary" art was considered to be in protest against the state and the goals of the Cuban Revolution. It alluded to selfish individualism, materialism, and imperialism. The "loading of moral and political interests" (Irvine 1989: 255) in Cuba was premised upon the ongoing process of revolution and the faith of revolutionary individuals in the process.

The transition from colonial Cuba and the Republic's independence to Fidel Castro's Revolution and socialist society was reflected in methods of artistic and cultural production. New revolutionary theater became an active model of utopia for the socialist system itself—a productive and indisputably positive movement to bring theater and art to the most marginalized rural populations in the country—all while a struggle for artistic and intellectual freedom was raging in the capital city. There were two distinct artistic reactions to the crisis of revolutionary change and two juxtaposing trends in cultural production between 1968 and 1990— los Años Dorados (Golden Years) and los Años Gris (Gray Years)—from the burst of creativity inspired by the Revolution to a vacuum of creativity when persecuted artists left the island in exile, or were imprisoned or silenced in other ways. Prerevolutionary images were weeded out, the "bourgeois" condemned and banished, and racial discrimination criminalized. Legends, heroes, and memories of the Revolution were creatively written and performed, inserted into history and language, and transformed into an enduring sociopolitical consciousness—a moral imagination that was fed artistically through the cultural reiteration of revolutionary metaphors and master narratives (see Lakoff and Johnson 1980 and James Fernandez 1986 on metaphor, master narratives, and the moral imagination).

The Hombre Nuevo replaced the trio of Bufo characters in official discourse and was situated in the consciousness of the masses linguistically (spoken and written) and in the performance of artistic culture. Teatro Escambray became one of the essential cultural catalysts in the construction of the new national identity. The group was especially important, for its legacy endured into the twenty-first century and the ideological ambivalence of the Special Period. The newly developing revolutionary consciousness and collective morality embodied by Teatro Escambray could be contrasted with the values of what was perceived to be the counter-revolutionary segment of society, specifically artists who, simultaneously and with equal passion, opposed the Revolution's new social models and restrictions on free expression and were punished in reeducation camps or prisons. The corrupt northern imperial was an adequate external enemy to justify national unity: internally, Cuba's own *gusanos* (traitors, literally "worms") also became important symbolic adversaries against which to define the parameters of loyalty and patriotism. Many of the most conspicuous gusanos were identified as being part of the artistic and intellectual sphere (Reed 1991). "Within the Revolution, everything, against it, nothing," Fidel Castro famously declared in 1961 in his speech "Palabras a los intelectuales" (Words to the Intellectuals) (Castro [1961] 1980). During the first ten years of the Revolution, the definition of this statement was most fiercely disputed. For the subsequent fifty years, it has continued to be discussed and debated, and much has been written concerning its meaning (see especially Roberto Fernández Retamar 2001 and Par Kumaraswami 2009). Interpretations of the role of the artists and intellectuals in revolutionary society have been ever-changing, along with the elusive definition of "freedom" (see chapter 2 for more on this historical era and the "Palabras" speech).

Analysis of this period of Cuban history will be familiar to those researching and writing about culture, ideology, and discourse in other socialist societies, for this chapter and those to follow reveal that the complex and expansive system of what seems at first glance to be "mutually exclusive" social contradictions are, in fact, "mutually constitutive" (Yurchak 2005). What appear to be paradoxical, ironic, and conflicting relationships or social processes in Cuban society are ultimately found to be complementary—one element necessary for the existence of the other. I worked with artists who professed to be revolutionary and loyal to the Revolution, contrasted with those labeled counter-revolutionary. However, in the end, it was evident that the two ends of the ideological spectrum fueled each other, each providing the necessary basis upon which the other made its claim. All artists had to struggle with the newly imposed restrictions even while they were in general agreement with the basic principles of the Revolution: equality, justice, solidarity, and cooperation. Similarly, most condemned the lack of totally free expression while still supporting the idea of art and theater for all the people and the sacrifice and dedication needed to make Teatro Nuevo a reality. Ultimately, both sides were driven to extremes by accusations often having nothing to do with the content of their artistic creation or individual allegiances. Instead, state manipulation of the tensions between them, professional jealousies, social stereotypes, and fears of accusation by the witch hunt for counter-revolutionaries all helped produce the increasing polarization.

More than *Negrito*, *Gallego*, or *Mulata*

The racial triad of the national characters put forth by Teatro Bufo was erased (at least hypothetically) after 1959 and reformed into the image of the liberated masses—the raceless and classless Hombre Nuevo representing the whole. The newly forming national character and the new socialist cubanía consciously and forcefully departed from the negrito, mulata, and gallego figures. One of the Revolution's many social reforms was the attempted abolition of *el problema negro* ("the negro problem"). Teatro Bufo's popularity had diminished decades before the 1959 Revolution and any similar comedic styles or character types were heavily criticized since they were seen as bourgeois forms that divided the Cuban population with their derogatory representation of blacks, mulattos, blancos sucios, and other marginalized segments of society. And legal measures were put in place to ensure that blacks in Cuba were not denied education, employment opportunities (including theater jobs), or access to public places (R. Moore 1997; Robaina 1994). Race and class discrimination were judged to be capitalist problems that the socialist revolution had allegedly wiped out (Castro [1961] 1989). The erasure of class divisions was to be accompanied by the concurrent eradication of racism— the socialist government's reasoning on these issues corresponding with the economic and Marxist interpretations of the problem. After just six years of the Revolution, Fidel Castro claimed, "with the disappearance of the exploitation of man by man, racial discrimination [has] disappeared once and for all" (Castro 1968:10). Citizens were told by the new government that all of them were now to be part of one *pueblo*, or one communal utopian nation (see Castro 1968, 1969, 1976). The alleged extinction of racism had become "official" and was thus, to be a part of every Cuban's personal philosophy. Martí's famous statement about the meaning of Cuban (more than white, more than mulatto, more than black) was invoked repeatedly by Fidel Castro, revolutionary intellectuals, and administrators. Now, for the first time, all Cubans were to be included in a public sphere that was no longer seen as exclusively part of dominant white elite society. The "masses" were also to be part of this new public because state and society were no longer separate. Every Cuban citizen— regardless of race, rich or poor, urban or rural, male or female—was to become a member of the collective, imagined as a potential Hombre Nuevo.

Despite the official philosophy, however, prejudice was not erased with economic and educational transformation and cultural stereotypes remained strong and intact. Almost overnight blacks were told that races no longer existed and that everyone was simply Cuban. After the Revolution they were legally included in public activities, yet still treated as inferior; since the end of open discrimination did not abolish prejudice. For decades, black solidarity had come from their underdog status, but it now seemed as if the new Cuban ideology was trying to erase their existence instead of integrating them. An African American traveling in Cuba was unsettled by this change, commenting that "All I had to do was to forget the rest of the world, forget that the Communists in Cuba were trying to erase the racial problem by erasing the black race, and most of all forget that blacks must stop identifying with black while whites didn't stop identifying with white" (Clytus 1970:44, 126). Another foreigner observed, "The problem is that there is a taboo on talking about racism because officially it doesn't exist anymore" (Sutherland 1969:168).[7] There was no open discussion about prejudice, nor any artistic representation on television or in the theater. Since el problema negro had officially ceased to exist after 1959, there was no reason to study or publicly deliberate it. This enforced silence turned discussion of race and discrimination into a counter-revolutionary activity that was punishable by imprisonment (R. Moore 1997; Robaina 1994). The virtual erasure of its public discussion (at least by Cubans within Cuba) continued until the early 1990s.[8] "El problema negro" as a social issue was supposedly to be resolved by the socialist Revolution's campaign to create a homogeneous and collective Hombre Nuevo.[9] This new man was to transcend racial and class divisions and to invite alienated groups into Cuba's public sphere and active national participation. Revolutionary nationalism was to be based on an ideology of unity, equality, and loyalty, and abide by an underlying social morality of selflessness, volunteerism, sacrifice, and anti-imperialism. Cubanía post-1959 did not depend on ancestral bloodlines, skin color, or bank account, but rather on the way one acted to support a new and better Cuba. The people had to be educated to learn how to do this, according to Ernesto Che Guevara:

> It is still necessary to accentuate his conscious, individual and collective, participation in all the mechanisms of direction and production and associate it with the idea of the need for technical and ideological education, so that the individual will realize that these processes are closely interdependent and their advances are parallel. He will thus achieve total awareness of his social being, which is equivalent to his full realization as a human being, having broken the chains of alienation. This will be translated concretely into the reappropriation of his nature through freed work, and the expression of his own human condition in culture and art. (Guevara 1965, full text in Lemus 1980:41, translated in Gerassi 1968:393)

The new revolutionary government was quick to make changes in what it considered to be an unfair and unequal social system, dominated by corrupt government officials, selfish bourgeois classes, and foreign (mainly U.S.) investors and residents. Fidel Castro, Raúl Castro, Camilo Cienfuegos, Che Guevara, and others in the administration were determined to end the exploitation of urban and rural workers and peasants. The Revolution was not declared officially socialist until 1961 in one of

Castro's speeches (Castro [1961] 1980), but proposed and implemented social programs showed the signs of such a move from the start. Changes were often rash, and the elites were not often happy with the techniques used to level the classes and erase the dividing concept of racial superiority or inferiority. Along with the restructuring of housing, employment, education, and agriculture came an aggressive campaign to reeducate the people.[10]

Contemporary cultural crusades into the Cuban countryside, like that of Teatro Escambray, trace their history back to the 1961 Literacy Campaign, which was a movement to rescue the campesinos from what others perceived to be their "uncultivated" traditions. The newly inaugurated socialist government launched a massive campaign intended not only to abolish the high percentage of illiteracy in Cuba, but also to inject the new revolutionary consciousness into the population, especially those living in isolated mountain pueblos. The intent was to end rural isolation and "backwardness." Young students, teachers, and other recruits were sent into previously unknown territory with a lantern and knapsack, "armed" with books and determined to educate the previously neglected peasants, the downtrodden masses of the new Cuba. Urban literacy workers lived, played, and worked alongside the country folk, women were taught on equal terms along with men, and "people who only a few years earlier had sedulously avoided political involvement found themselves tied by family and friendship to a massive governmental campaign" (Fagen 1969:61).

The literacy crusade taught campesinos to read with textbook chapters entitled "The Cooperatives," "The Revolution Wins All Battles," "The People Work," "The Revolution," "Fidel is Our Leader," "Friends and Enemies," "Imperialism," and "The People, United and Alert" (ibid.:24–53). The methods used during the literacy campaign demonstrated the importance of language and the construction of national narratives in the development of revolutionary consciousness. According to Richard Fagen (1969), illiterate campesinos experienced their first empowering moments of reading and writing through the words of the Revolution and revolutionary ideology. He explained that the final assignment of their course was to write a letter to Fidel Castro, thanking him for sending the literacy brigades and thus demonstrating the success of the campaign—their first steps toward assimilation of nationalist rhetoric embodied in the act. In return, the crusade taught the urban *brigadistas* (brigade members) about peasant culture: farming, caring for chickens, pigs, horses, and *buey* (oxen). They were taught about the centrality of rural life to Cuban identity, learning to be sympathetic to the campesinos' hard work, and to recognize different kinds of knowledge and expertise. Urban Cubans became more "culturally literate" from the campesino's perspective.

After only one year, the illiteracy rate, most pronounced in the rural regions, had dropped from 23.6 percent to 3.9 percent (Fagen 1969) (numerous other reports have claimed the rate dropped to 2–3 percent). In the process of learning the alphabet, the campesinos also learned the symbols, myths, and heroes of the Revolution. With this, the Cuban campesino was reborn—at least among those who became supporters—advancing the evolutionary march toward the Revolution's Hombre Nuevo.

The Art of Revolutionary Consciousness

Since 1959, the Cuban Socialist state has viewed the arts as a powerful agent of reeducation and has actively utilized the medium in order to shape revolutionary consciousness.[11] The fact that the state, inclusive of its commissioned playwright and actors, is often able to effectively attach its rhetoric to the symbolic and metaphorical qualities so characteristic of theatrical text and performance makes theater a favored venue for communicating its values. Although theater with political intentions does not always try to mask its messages, such messages are often strategically embedded in cultural forms, for people will more often pay attention to an artistic performance than to a political speech. Educating or politically steering the masses without their full awareness so that the political impact of their evening at the theater is akin to that of a lecture by the local Communist Party leader often proves to be a highly effective strategy (Haraszti 1987; Reed 1991; Taylor 1991). Bourdieu discusses the power of such methods, remarking that "The whole trick of pedagogic reason lies precisely in the way it extorts the essential while seeming to demand the insignificant" (1977:94–5). Other times, propaganda is overt, intended as a loud and explicit message to its audiences. Fidel Castro has used both of these strategies simultaneously, directly informing Cuban society of his plan to instill the socialist ideology through the arts and culture, but also recognizing the value of circuitous persuasion.

The newly decreed cultural revolution to accompany the political revolution was considered by Castro and his officials to be crucial to the restructuring of the Cuban state and to the reeducation (or repoliticization) of the Cuban people. Although some critics have equated this period of Cuba's cultural restructuring with Mao's violent and repressive Cultural Revolution in China (Reed 1991), others disagree (Boudet 1983; Muguercia 1981, 1988) and use the term in a more positive sense. While not condoning (or even mentioning) the abuses, they consider the aggressive transition from capitalist culture to socialist culture a necessary endeavor. In September of 1959, Castro informed his new public that it would be important to "transform the mind," in order to go "marching down the road we have to take" (Castro [1959] 1987:4). And in November of that same year, he explained that "what interests us more than anything else is the consciousness of the people [. . .] our duty is to *create* consciousness," this new consciousness being one that accommodated and supported revolutionary ideology and the new socialist ideology (ibid.:5). One of the most important ways Castro set out to accomplish this goal was through the arts. In contrast to the idea of art as a reflection of the autonomous, creative individual, art in Cuba—as in other socialist regimes—was to fill another role: one which served the collectivity. "For me," said Castro, "art is not an end in itself. Man is its end" (Lockwood 1967:111). Or, more specifically, the creation of Cuba's New Man.

Soon after 1959, new cultural organizations and government ministries were constituted, effectively centralizing artistic decision making and production and providing special privileges to those who cooperated. First called the National Council of Culture, it was later reorganized into the Ministry of Culture in 1976 and headed by Armando Hart Dávalos. Salaries were paid through the Ministry of Culture and the cultural institution with which the artist was affiliated (film, theater, dance, music, material arts). Individual artists and groups had to be authorized; they rehearsed and performed in government-owned spaces and with government resources (make-up, lights, costuming, transport, publicity, etc.). They were socialized on how to be "people's artists" and how to make art for the masses, for the pueblo. They learned to self-censor their productions to stay "within the Revolution," lest they lose their support. They were not allowed to copyright their work or to receive royalties, since copyrighting produced private property. In 1967 Castro announced that copyright would no longer be recognized and royalties were abolished (see Reed 1991:141–42; Smorkaloff 1987). All products of these "culture workers" were collectively owned by the people and by the state.[12]

Theater for the Cuban People

After 1959 the centralization of the government, industry, resource distribution, and cultural organizations exposed private domains to state intervention. Forms of "high culture," such as theater, were increasingly moved from elite theater houses to more modest *salitas* (small performance halls or spaces), community centers, and rural schoolrooms. The big colonial theaters remained in use, such as the Teatro García Lorca (Havana 1838, also known as the Gran Teatro), and Teatro Tomás Terry (Cienfuegos 1888), but were made accessible to groups, both big and small, and new theaters of less ornate grandeur were constructed in Soviet-style architecture, named for some of the ideological champions of the Revolution, such as Teatro Karl Marx and Teatro Mella. The National Theater building, located on the Plaza de Revolución, across from the José Martí memorial and the famous Che Guevara mural, was completed in 1959 and opened up small and large rehearsal and performance spaces to young artists. Theater was highly promoted, and there was a renewed interest in Havana. By 1965, attendance in Cuban theaters surpassed one million annually, an increase of 1,000 percent from 1958 (Martin 1994). The goal was that theater would no longer be perceived as mere bourgeois entertainment, but instead, an efficacious and important appendage of the Revolution—"efficacious" in its potential to educate, reeducate, politicize, and raise consciousness among everyday people, to have a social function. Revolutionary theater was to have a "dialectic interaction" with the public, giving its members a sense of individual agency instead of passivity and powerlessness (Boudet 1983:10–15). According to Rine Leal:

> El escenario no era ya el antiguo espejo de costumbres, sino que se transformaba en un instrumento de utilidad pública. El teatrista dejaba de ser un miembro individual y pasivo de la colectividad, para convertirse en un elemento transformador de la realidad. [. . .]. Como propósito de una sociedad socialista, los teatristas acogieron el principio de que el arte llamado minoritario por la burguesía, esté al alcance del pueblo, pero no a través de lo populachero o el paternalismo. El nacimiento de un teatro popular (realmente del público) se ligó al surgimiento de públicos masivos, y muy especialmente a la formación integral del hombre nuevo. (Leal 1980:152)

The theater was no longer an ancient mirror of customs, but was transformed into an instrument of public utility. The theater worker stopped being an individual and passive member of the collective, and was converted into a transformative element of society. [. . .] As a goal of socialist society, theatre workers welcomed the principle that which what was called high art by the bourgeois be made available to the masses, but not in a paternalistic way or by dumbing it down to make it popular. The birth of a popular theatre (*really* of the people) was linked to a surge of massive audiences and especially linked to the integral formation of the new man.

All ensembles were funded and strongly promoted by the state. As a result of such support, new genres began to emerge with great frequency, and many of those Cuban playwrights and actors who had been suppressed in previous regimes were given prestigious positions and responsibilities in the cultural infrastructure being built. Fidel Castro knew the success and survival of the Revolution proper depended not only on his personal ability to hold onto party power, but also on the utilization of Cuba's cultural expression and, thus, social ideologies. To create popular ideas, it was first necessary to identify the popular mediums and employ their managers. For Fidel Castro's administration to succeed, he needed the journalists, artists, writers, and actors to carry the socialist message to the public.

Fidel Castro's Revolution ushered in a new type of theater never before seen or experienced in Cuba, one that was responsive to the social conditions of the local people themselves. Rather than adhering to formalist dictates of "art for art's sake," Castro's Cuba began to actively employ the power of theater as a "useful" feature of the Revolution. Along with economic, agricultural, and other systemic transformations, theater was to be developed as a vehicle that would function on behalf of the masses, not the individual. Theater, like the new Cuban society, was to be cooperative, collective, and socialist. The new understanding was that theater was to serve Cuba by articulating, and more importantly, propagating its nascent national identity.

> *El teatro sirve a las necesidades de la Revolución sin normativas rígidas. [. . .]*
> *Porque solo desde dentro, cuando un equipo artístico se familiariza profundamente con los conflictos y no sólo con sus manifestaciones aparenciales, es posible crear un teatro crítico, que contribuya a una visión integral de los fenómenos. Estas experiencias han mostrado en escena los problemas de la transición del capitalismo al socialismo, han asumido el auténtico reflejo de la construcción de la nueva sociedad.* (Boudet 1983:32)[13]

The theater serves the needs of the Revolution without rigid regulations. [...] It is only from within, when a artistic group becomes profoundly familiar with the conflicts and not only the surface issues, that it can contribute a comprehensive vision of the phenomena. These experiences have shown the problems of the transition from capitalism to socialism on stage; they have taken on the task to authentically reflect the construction of the new society.

Teatro Estudio (Studio Theater) was the first of these revolutionary ensembles (1958), calling its new genre "flexible theater." By listening to the actual voices of Cuban people and incorporating an accompanying social analysis into the dramatic content, Teatro Estudio described and acted out the difficulties of the transition to socialism, while also attempting to provide educated "guidance" about the importance of a unified revolutionary ideology. Many of its productions centered on a family drama thematic and addressed the ways in which quotidian crises were interpreted and resolved. The crises represented, however, invariably pointed to another level that dealt with issues of revolutionary social transformation and the renegotiation of everyday life under socialism.

In 1967 Teatro Estudio divided into splinter ensembles, one of which, Teatro Escambray, took theatrical social analysis a step further. Teatro Escambray was formed in 1968, just after (and some claim in reaction to) the death of Cuban revolutionary Che Guevara (Petit 1977; Reed 1991). Theater was still in crisis at this time, for although attendance had been on the rise due to a drop in prices and an increase in accessibility, productions continued to cater to only a small group of people; those who were highly educated and located in Havana (Leal 1967; Matas 1971:434–35). They did not address pressing national issues; nor did they reach Cuban peasants (campesinos) in the rural provinces who were faced with the most extensive social transformations. Teatro Escambray's founder, Sergio Corrieri,[14] decided that what was required was a fundamental change in theater-making method and dramatic substance. As a result, the theater would not only advocate participation by the entire country, but would also ally itself with the revolutionary movement. Just as Fidel's idea of the Hombre Nuevo was cultivated, Teatro Escambray's example was highlighted as Cuba's Teatro Nuevo, which would represent a new socialist sense of inclusion and solidarity (Boudet 1983; Muguercia 1981). Teatro Nuevo was to become Cuba's new national theater of the twentieth century, just as Teatro Bufo had been (albeit informally and ambivalently) in the nineteenth. Teatro Nuevo was to represent the progressive move into a modern, educated, equal, and enlightened society.

Class Struggle and the New Theater Movement

The capacity of art, literature, and more specifically, theater to mobilize a collective consciousness, to incite and reeducate, and to do so by using symbolic aesthetics, was not only recognized by Fidel Castro. Cuban teatristas were inspired by a worldwide movement in the 1960s for more socially conscious, activist, and communitarian art and performance. Whether the style is referred to as people's theater, popular theater, political theater, worker's theater, or theater of the oppressed, the motivation for effecting some kind of consciousness raising and social change through critical aesthetics, representation, and reflexive dialogue were part of the artistic recipe. There is an extensive literature of popular and people's theater, and its long-standing tradition can be traced back before the political awakening of workers, marginalized ethnic groups, blacks, and women in the 1950s and 1960s.[15] The movements that most strongly influenced Cuban theater—and those which, in turn, were also inspired *by* it— were from this later era, especially the work of the Brazilian Augusto Boal, the Argentinian Osvaldo Dragún, and the Colombian Santiago García. The advent of Marxist artists and intellectuals also played an important role in building upon this tradition in Cuba by giving it a theoretical structure that directly fit into communist philosophy. As mentioned previously, Bertolt Brecht was one such prominent intellectual, and a key point of reference for a newly emerging political theater in Cuba. One of the first theater groups to emerge after the Revolution was named in his honor (Bertolt Brecht Political Theater), as well as an actual theater space that is still used in Havana today (Teatro Brecht).

Brecht's views on the importance of popular theater and theater for the "folk" (*Volk* or *Volkstümlich*) were familiar to Cuban teatristas and theater scholars. Following Marx and a long line of Marxists intellectuals, Brecht believed that theater should be instructional as well as entertaining. It should have social impact. On narrowing the gap between the writer (intellectual) and the people, Brecht said: "Certainly a special effort is needed today in order to write in a popular way. But at the same time it has become easier: easier and more urgent. The people have clearly separated from its top layer; its oppressors and exploiters have parted company with it and become involved in a bloody war against it, which can no longer be overlooked. It has become easier to take sides. Open warfare has, as it were, broken out among the 'audience'" (Brecht, in Willett 1957:107). And on the masses and the importance of the popular: "Our conception of the 'popular' refers to the people who are not only fully involved in the process of development but are actually taking it over, forcing it, deciding it. We have in mind a people that is making history and altering the world and itself. We have in mind a fighting people and also a fighting conception of 'popularity'" (ibid.:108). Brecht defined popular as the "means intelligible to the broad masses, taking over their own forms of expression and enriching them; adopting and consolidating their standpoint; representing the most progressive section of the people in such a way that it can take over the leadership" (ibid.:108).

In Latin America, theater has been a site of activism and consciousness-raising, and Teatro Nuevo was described as a distinctly Latin American movement that emerged in the 1950s to break away from what was perceived as bourgeois forms and traditions. Teatro Nuevo groups began with an emphasis on forging a "new polemic relationship" with new audiences. Beatriz Risk (1987) comments on Teatro Nuevo in Cuba:

> *Esta relación polémica, aunque no polémica en forma antagónica sino en forma dialéctica, es decir, una polémica que supone la unidad de intereses y de objetivos pero que discute sobre un objeto que no está resuelto y que no sé resuelve con esquemas fijos ni con dogmas: las relaciones sociales; se efectúa precisamente al hallarse convertida en expresión artística una nueva realidad concretizada.* (ibid.:14–15)

This polemic relationship was not polemic in an antagonistic form, but rather a dialectic form. That is to say, a polemic that assumed the unity of interests and objectives but which discussed a subject that was not settled and could not be worked out with fixed schemes or dogmas. "Social relations" came into effect precisely when it was converted by artistic expression into a new concrete reality.

Cuba was distinct in that its version of Teatro Nuevo carried the historical context of the 1959 Revolution and the idea of the revolutionary. Unlike most other theaters of social revolution around the world, Cuba's particular use of the word *revolutionary* had been redefined to mean socialist and loyal to the nation, not rebellion or protest. The Revolution in Cuba had been successful. Revolutionary theater in Cuba was fully supported by the state, not in opposition to it. The master narrative and metaphoric frame of Cuba's political and social ideology were revolution, struggle, and critique of the elite upper classes and domination, which remained solid components of the word's significance. But that struggle did not include revolting against Fidel Castro's government. Cuban revolutionary theater revered the local folk and the masses (the once proletariat) in an attempt to fortify national culture against potential foreign invaders, counter-revolutionary gusanos and their moral contamination.

To the Mountains of Escambray

Conjunto Campesino:
(punto libre)

Campesino Musical Group
(free form décima)

Fueron años sin descanso
y de lentas agonías;
ya no importaban los días
sólo importaba el fracaso.
Se fue acercando el ocaso
de otra familia sufrida
que sólo tuvo en la vida
un signo de fatalsimo,
un marcado escepticismo
y una angustia desmedida.

They were years without rest
and of slow agonies;
the days did not matter anymore
all that mattered was failure.
The sun stopped setting
over another long-suffering family
who only had in their lives
a fatalist symbol,
a marked skepticism
and an immeasurable anguish.

Una mañana temprano
llegó un rumor de otra sierra;
algo pasa con la tierra,
ahora va a cambiar de mano;
ay no será un don Fulano
el dueño de otro sudor.

One early morning
a rumor spread from another mountain;
something was happening with the land
now it was changing hands;
ah, it will not be just another Master
as the owner of our sweat.

Todo toma otro color;
viene un ley necesaria,
viene la Reforma Agraria,
viene a arrancar el dolor.

Everything took on another color;
a necessary law is coming,
the Agrarian Reform is coming,
coming to take away the suffering.[16]

La vitrina, script by Albio Paz, Teatro Escambray

In 1968 Cuban artists took on a privileged role in national politics when a group of highly reputable actors and playwrights in Havana ventured out into the Escambray Mountains to form a new type of theater; one which utilized anthropological research methods to gather information about the local culture and to give voice to a previously unrepresented population, the *guajiro* (peasant, hillbilly), or in more acceptable post-Revolution terminology, the *campesino* (farmer). The method privileged the audience and was more concerned with dialogue than a finished, dramatic product and text. This vanguard group, called Teatro Escambray, intended to "cultivate" the campesinos, to teach them about theater, music, and the arts. The belief that the rural populations need "cultivating" by being exposed to "culture" is, of course, problematic, and may remind some readers of the Cuban short documentary *Por primera vez* (For the First Time), where a film crew traveled through mountain communities near Baracoa and a Charlie Chaplin film was shown to those who had never seen cinema.[17] But the principal goal of this theater group and those to follow was to give the campesinos a way to express themselves in public discourse for the first time in their lives, as well as to present a different image of an oft-neglected part of the Cuban reality and the rural Cuban citizen.

> *Hasta ahora en nuestro teatro, lamentablemente, se enseñoreaba la humillante imagen del campesino como un tonto, ignorante y en ocasiones gracioso. El realismo que le impone la profunda investigación inicial y la propia experiencia de su origen, le permite al autor desafiar la imagen paternalista y peyorativa que hasta aquí se había elaborado de nuestros guajiros, proponiendo otra más auténtica.* (Cano 1992:4)[18]

> Until now, unfortunately, our theater has portrayed the humble image of the *campesino* as a half-wit, ignorant, and on occasion, laughable. The in-depth investigation and experience of their reality allow the author to challenge this paternalistic and deprecatory image that up to this point had represented our *guajiros*, and to propose another, more authentic one.

The Escambray Mountain region, located 160 miles southeast of Havana, was populated by campesinos who were being subjected to socialist land redistribution called *arrendamiento* (renting or leasing). Arrendamiento was a process by which small landowners were to voluntarily relinquish their lands for integration into a newly established communal district. Many of these campesinos were hesitant to give up their land, however modest in size and quality, and party officials were seeking new forms of encouragement. It was believed that the socialist message and the revolutionary ideal had not fully permeated this area, due to lack of education and cultural resources. Therefore, it was here that members of Teatro Escambray thought they would be most effective. Commissioned by local officials, the ensemble lived with and interviewed local residents for periods of one to three months before moving on to the next chosen village. Gathered ethnographic information was incorporated into the scripts written by ensemble members and performed both locally and in neighboring regions.[19] Part of this new socialist theater's method was to strategically choose particular rural locations and audiences. The latter included those campesinos who had not yet joined the arrendamiento; students; local communist leaders; cooperative presidents; and relatives of campesinos who had already been taken under the plan. Discussions with the audience occurred before, during, and after the performances, allowing the campesinos to voice their concerns and to ask ensemble members questions. Instead of just performing for an audience, Teatro Escambray was in dialogue with audience members. The official goal of this ensemble was "to show the peasant a contradictory image of himself with regard to his social conduct in a revolutionary context that places new demands on him" (Petit 1977).

The play that resulted from this first investigation also became its most famous. *La vitrina* (The Showcase, 1971) discussed the pros and cons of the Agrarian Reform and the incorporation of *arrendamiento*. It was the story of a campesino couple named Ana and Pancho, who initially welcome the reforms and join the collective farm. They are happy at first, until Pancho dies and a conflict arises about where to bury his body—on the land, as had always been the tradition (but which was prohibited after arrendamiento) or in the pueblo's cemetery, which his wife Ana vehemently opposes. The play demonstrated the inevitable clashes that arose when long-standing traditions and prerevolutionary practices collided with the momentous social changes that occurred after 1959. Ana and her family must work through the different sides of the issue and decide whether or not to comply with the new social rules. After the first performance of *La vitrina*, audience and actors gathered to debate the play's content, and changes were made to the script to reflect corrections and suggestions from the area's campesinos. The play was groundbreaking in its method, and illustrated how theater could be used to educate and empower. Teatro Escambray wrote the campesino into national scripts and subsequently, into the national dialogue. And by calling its new method, Teatro Nuevo, the group, as well as the artistic model it created, aligned itself with the Hombre Nuevo and the newly developing national ideology. Other notable plays by Teatro Escambray that were created in a similar fashion included *La rentista* (The Financier), *Ramona* (Ramona), *El juicio* (The Judgment), *El paraíso recobrao* (Paradise Recovered), and *Las provisiones* (The Provisions) (scripts published in Leal 1978b).

This mode of people's theater became hugely popular and successful in Cuba, both in terms of attendance and in the discussions provoked by the performances. One reason this method was so effective was the feeling of dialogic empowerment it gave to the peasant (guajiro, campesino). Through their repeated participation in interviews, personal and group discussions, and as a result of new cultural programming in the rural school systems, campesinos felt their voices were being heard and respected. Such reports came from written accounts from artists and foreign observers in the 1960s and 1970s, but I heard much of the same in 2000 from the many campesinos I met. Whether or not these repeated comments were generated more by years of propaganda and popular discourse about revolutionary art than direct personal experience was not fully determined. In any event, forty years later, the campesinos believed it to be true, which was just as powerful in the end. Ensemble members also felt their efforts were promoting compromise between the state and society and that they were creating a new cultural sensitivity. They wanted to "discover the rhythm of this life, its problems, its hopes, its personalities, and how the abrupt changes introduced by the revolution affected the people's lives" (Petit 1977). The resultant text was alive— the play, along with the creative process was a "live document." Similar to the Literacy Crusade, the development of revolutionary consciousness and of a socialist moral imagination was experienced and documented through the creation of Teatro Nuevo.

Flora Lauten, an actor and director, was the first to branch out from Teatro Escambray. Lauten, one of the founding members, created her own theater group in the early 1970s, called Teatro La Yaya.[20] Instead of using professional actors to perform for and teach the campesinos, she decided to use the campesinos themselves as actors. Another Escambray alumnus, Albio Paz, created Teatro Acero (Theater of Steel), a group formed within a Havana steel factory, and in Santiago de Cuba, the Cabildo Teatral (Cabildo Theater) produced plays about Afro-Cuban culture and the distinctive problems the Afro-Cuban populations faced in Cuba. The term *cabildo* referred to town councils in traditional African communities, and Santiago's Cabildo Theater was modeled after this idea of community cooperation and collective decision making (see Herrero 1983). In Santiago de Cuba, this kind of theater was also called *Teatro de Relaciones* (Theater of Relationships). Such Teatro Nuevo groups became models for revolutionary theater, as well as blueprints for how previously illiterate campesinos and other marginalized populations could be brought into the public sphere as conscious political subjects. At the same time, campesinos were sent to school in the cities to become teachers, engineers, professional artists, and others were sent to industrial areas to become *obreros*: the mass of workers crucial to any Marxist movement. Thanks in large part to the groundbreaking work of Teatro Escambray and its offshoots, theater became an officially respected aspect of the society, its educational value recognized by the highest officials of the newly formed state as well as the general population. Fidel Castro himself visited Teatro Escambray in its Manicaragua location to watch Albio Paz's famous production of *La vitrina*. A photograph of his visit was still proudly displayed in one of the group's rehearsal rooms when I went to visit the group and interview the director Rafael González in 2000. In an egalitarian society, art and culture would be both produced and consumed by the masses. Schools for art instructors were constructed all over the country to ensure nationwide and widely accessible cultural instruction, and *Casas de Cultura* (Houses of Culture, like community centers) were built to nurture amateur artistic groups (see Hernández Menéndez 1986; Sánchez León 2001). Cultivating the once-illiterate and unworldly population and transforming them into the new Cuban socialist subject dominated the motivations of many cultural producers.

For the next twenty years, Cuban theater prospered. Urban theater was very different from Teatro Nuevo and other communitarian theater projects, but all theater remained an important aspect of socialist education and communication. With ticket prices set at a mere 1 peso (10 cents or less), anyone could attend a performance, not just the wealthy elite. International arts and theater festivals, workshops, and scientific conferences grew in number and attendance, and in 1976, a former country club just outside Havana was converted into the first arts university, the Instituto Superior del Arte (ISA; the National Arts Institute). This segment of the artistic world was flying high during the early years of the

Revolution, and to look solely at official descriptions of artistic production during this period would create a rosy picture indeed, as literature on these Teatro Nuevo groups is very optimistic and inspirational, pointing to the ideal elements of the movement that any socialist or left-leaning liberal wanted to believe to be true (Boudet 1983; Leal 1980; Muguercia 1981). Rural populations, like other poor residents in urban areas, were, on the whole, benefiting most from the revolutionary reforms, but in spite of economic improvements, the deliberations surrounding artistic and intellectual freedom were intensifying.

Velvet and Not-So-Velvet Prisons

Los poetas cubanos ya no sueñan	Cuban poets dream no more
(ni siquiera en la noche).	(not even at night).
Van a cerrar la puerta para escribir a solas	They close their doors to write alone
cuando cruje, de pronto, la madera;	when, suddenly, the wood creaks;
el viento los empuja al garete;	the wind pushes them adrift,
unas manos los cogen por los hombros,	hands seize them by their shoulders
los voltean,	turn them,
los ponen frente a frente a otras caras	put them face to face with other faces
(hundidas en pantanos, ardiendo en	(sunken in swamps, burning in napalm)
el napalm)	
y el mundo encima de sus bocas fluye	and the world flows above their mouths
y está obligado el ojo a ver, a ver, a ver.	And the eye is made to see, to see, to see.

—HEBERTO PADILLA, *Fuera del juego*, 1968

Rumor has it that freedom is an essential condition of art: that anything which severs art from its anti-authoritarian essence will kill it; that the true artist is an individual who is independent, at least in his own creative process, that art is false unless it is autonomous.—MIKLÓS HARASZTI (1987), *The Velvet Prison*

Teatro Escambray flourished in the countryside and was given awards for its revolutionary cultural work. Meanwhile, other artists, mainly in Havana, protested against the growing restrictions on their art and what seemed to be the building of a Velvet Prison—an ideological prison, perhaps, but one lined in soft velvet (Haraszti 1987; see also Reed 1991; Ripoll 1985, 1985; cf. Barmé 1999). The Hungarian Miklós Haraszti, writing on the production of art under socialism, distinguishes "hard" or militant censorship from a type of "soft" censorship, or "censorship without victims," where censorship is not the skin of the culture, but its skeleton (1987:5–9). He explains that artists working for the socialist state (Eastern European countries in particular) were taught to cooperate with official culture and to become part of the system—that the artist and the censor became the two faces of official culture, "diligently and cheerfully cultivat[ing] the gardens of art together." Continuing, he says: "Censorship professes itself to be freedom because it acts, like morality, as the common spirit of both the rulers and the ruled" (ibid.:7–8). Fidel Castro's "Palabras a los intelectuales" speech showed that the new Cuban state had similar plans for their own version of censorship without victims, even though many artists and intellectuals ultimately did become victims of this system.

In its theoretical form, socialist morality was difficult to critique: co-operation and equality were ideals few would reject, even the most vehement of individualists. In "Palabras" Fidel Castro (1961 [1980]:14–15) rationalized that " por cuanto la Revolución comprende los intereses del pueblo, por cuanto la Revolución significa los intereses del la Nación entera, nadie puede alegar con razón un derecho contra ella" (since the Revolution understands the interests of the people, and since the Revolution stands for the interests of the whole Nation, no one can rightfully argue against it). Here lay the ambivalence of many of the accused dissident artists and counter-revolutionary citizens. The Velvet Prison, or state control of total artistic freedom, was instilled, it was said, for the good of the society. In 1961, Fidel Castro assured artists and intellectuals that the Revolution "defended liberty," and that they should not fear that the Revolution would smother their creative spirit (11). He also admitted that learning to become a "true revolutionary" was a process and that artists and intellectuals had to find the balance between critique and loyalty. In his speech, he recognized that it would take time to dispel doubt and ambivalence: "el campo de la duda queda para los escritores y artistas que sin ser contrarrevolucionarios no se sienten tampoco revolucionarios (aplausos)" (doubt remains for those writers and artists that, although not counter-revolutionaries, might not feel they are revolutionary either [applause]; ibid.). But what was most important, Castro believed, was "un espíritu revolucionario" and "una actitud revolucionaria" (revolutionary spirit and revolutionary attitude). Castro said that those who tried to adapt to the new reality and who were honest should feel at ease. "El pueblo es la meta principal. En el pueblo hay que pensar en nosotros mismos y ésa es la única actitud que puede definirse como una actitud verdaderamente revolucionaria" (13). (The pueblo [people, nation] is the principal goal. In the pueblo one must think about us, ourselves, and that is the only attitude that can be defined as the true revolutionary attitude). Those artists who complied with the creative boundaries were left alone, even rewarded. But those who proved to be "mercenaries" or dishonest, or worse, who lacked the desire to adapt and acquire the requisite revolutionary spirit, were harassed and persecuted. Many were imprisoned. Some deemed most dangerous to the security of the state were even executed (Reed 1991; Ripoll 1985). These extremes have led Western observers to wonder why artists in these countries tolerated such treatment. Haraszti, however, explains that while these artists were forced to accept constant censorship of their work and were expected to communicate a certain revolutionary or socialist message, they enjoyed the special luxuries and economic security of state support. The trade-off was perceived as fair, for although artists were held to rigid restrictions (metaphorical prison bars), their lives became easier when economic stresses were lifted. No longer slaves to a market system, an audience and a paycheck were guaranteed. Some artists considered this security liberating, while others thought that the distinction between art and propaganda was being erroneously denied and have been frustrated by state regulation and the redefinition of creativity and free expression.

To win over as many of the intellectuals and artists as possible (those influential enough to have an effect on society in some way), Fidel Castro offered them access to foreign travel, cars, prestigious jobs, and the opportunity to publish and produce selected plays. Once he made such promises (and had delivered on them), he was then able to manipulate and exploit the artists by threatening withdrawal of those same privileges. This game of Fidel Castro's became an effective mode of control, for those who accepted the offers were exalted and valued in official Cuban society and were economically secure, while those who were perceived to have trespassed upon his generosity were punished. Cultural capital was also highly valued in Cuba, and although they were not able to earn royalties or large quantities of money, they were given other intangible incentives. While capitalist artists competed for fame and fortune, socialist artists competed for influence on politics and within the national writer's unions (or other organizations that mediate artistic production). They also competed for certificates of recognition, national and regional prizes, and the ability to decide the future direction of the national culture in the form of curricula, literary canons, and so on (cf. Verdery 1991:189 on similar processes in Eastern Europe). Through these rewards, artists earned cultural capital and cultural authority and the power to judge instead of having to be judged. The artist/intellectual had the potential to become a national model. Legitimacy, in this case, was not measured in dollar amounts, but in public recognition and intellectual validation. The perpetuation of particular ideals through artistic and intellectual narrative and imagery, the educational system, mass media, and popular discourse (and rumor)—along with strict punishment for those crossing the line—ensured self-censorship and increasing compliance from the general population.

From about 1968 to 1976 (some would argue until 1990), there was a McCarthy-type witch hunt for enemies of the Revolution, which focused on artists, intellectuals, and other potentially dangerous ideological deviants. During the so-called Dark Age or Gray Years, the socialist government displayed the extreme measures it would take in order to maintain authority and power. Suspected dissidents were sent to special camps to "deepen" their consciousness or "rehabilitate" their attitudes. There were different camps for different types of counter-revolutionaries. Individuals sent to camps for the *profundización de conciencia* (deepening of consciousness) were seen as those with the most potential for ideological transformation and *mejoramiento* (reform, improvement) (José Oriol González, interview, 1998). Although they were not yet sufficiently conforming to party line, they were not thought to be dangerous to national security. Similar, yet much more rigid (and controversial) camps were originally labeled UMAP camps, or *Unidades Miltares de Ayuda a la Producción* (Military Units to Help Production). From 1965 to 1968 they were known as concentration camps, which functioned to sequester those opposed to the Marxist-Leninist ideology established by the Revolution. Along with dissident artists and intellectuals, this persecuted group included homosexuals and devout religious believers.[21] Thousands (some estimates reach 25,000) were transported on buses to several stadiums in the province of Camagüey, separated into groups, and transferred to mills to work. At night they were watched under guard.

After several years of international protest, the UMAP camps were disbanded in 1968, but throughout the subsequent decades, other camps continued to function under different names: "Battalions of Decisive Effort," "Young People's Column of the Centennial," and the "Young People's Work Army." If not sent to one of the UMAP camps, dissident artists were blacklisted or fired from their jobs at cultural institutions, and they found themselves unable to perform or publish within Cuba. Many writers managed to smuggle texts to Europe and Latin America. They became famous internationally for their artistic talent and nationally for their subversion.

A theater director from Cumanayagua, José Oriol González (Teatro de los Elementos), described his experience in one of these camps in an unpublished autobiographical narrative (a six-page typed document stored in the group's only file cabinet), and in one of my interviews with him. José Oriol, who was born in Cumanayagua in 1954, proudly told me that his parents were revolutionary campesinos who participated in the *arrendamiento* (agricultural reform) and the *lucha contra bandidos* (fight against counter-revolutionary bandits).[22] José Oriol's unpublished memoir emphasizes this fact, listing the political involvement and accomplishments of his parents and sadly telling how his uncle had died at the hands of the *bandidos* in the Escambray Mountains. He then describes his own involvement in politics while studying at the ISA as vice president of the *Federación Estudiantil Universitaria* (FEU; University Students Federation) and as the secretary of culture at the University's Communist Party Base. He explains how he was "temporarily separated," that is, taken out of school and sent away in 1980 to a camp in Moa for profundización de conciencia after writing a suspicious letter to a friend in Miami. When I spoke with José Oriol in 1999 about the material in his autobiography, he was hesitant to elaborate on his experiences in Moa and tried to make it appear that it had been a more flexible and open system than the original UMAP camps of the 1960s. I do not know whether this softer representation of the UMAP camps was just for me, the visiting American, or was, indeed, what he experienced, but I did not want to press him further on the matter, amazed that he was telling me the story at all, especially since it was early in my residence with the group. He quickly pointed out that he should not have been sent there— that it had been a misunderstanding, that he had always been a loyal revolutionary. He said that he was evaluated as having an excellent attitude by the *Unión de Jóvenes Comunistas* (UJC; Union of Young Communists), the FEU, and years later by the same cultural office at ISA that had originally sent him to the camp.

The camp was in Moa, located in Holguín Province on the eastern shore of the island. For seven years, José Oriol was sent to work in the sugarcane fields, pick coffee beans, and work in a nickel factory. His "separation" included an official ban from working in the arts or culture, and letters were sent out to every cultural branch and agency in the country, saying that he was not to work in culture ever again. In spite of this ban, however, Oriol created an amateur theater group in the nickel factory that he named Tierra Roja (Red Earth) after the red-clay-like dirt of Moa and its surrounds, and later, another group named Teatro del Este (Theater of the East). The groups were made up of workers in the community, some from the nickel factory, along with engineers, construction workers, teachers, office workers, and art instructors. Plays addressed local issues, often including problems in the workplace, and public debates followed each performance.

These groups were so successful that the officials could not object, said José Oriol. Certainly this type of theater was "for the Revolution," he explained, very Teatro Escambray in essence and therefore any action to discontinue it might have also been construed, ironically, as counterrevolutionary. A critic for the national theater journal, *Tablas*, reflected upon the social utility and the powerful effect Tierra Roja had had on its participants, and how "this seemingly simple fondness for theater by a group of young people has, in fact, been converted into a political act," political in the sense that culture had been used in the development of the community, that it was true to the campesinos' reality and socially pertinent.[23] In 1986, José Oriol was allowed to graduate and return to the professional theater world, and it was during this time that he became a professor of theater at the Escuela Nacional del Arte (ENA; National School of Art) in Havana.

This story demonstrated Fidel Castro's belief that the revolutionary attitude was most important for the success of his "rehabilitation." Certainly, José Oriol and his group, like Teatro Escambray, became pillars of revolutionary theater and models of theater for the people and the Revolution. But their success also demonstrated the power of the Velvet Prison, for José Oriol's loyalties as a professional artist and revolutionary citizen often proved to be directly at odds with those of other individuals faced with similar obstacles, discriminations, and frustrations associated with socialism.

Rules of the Game

The distinction between what was within or against the Revolution was decided by state officials and censors, and interpretive freedom was taken from the hands of the artists themselves. Heberto Padilla, a Cuban poet, became famous for his book of poems, *Fuera del Juego* (Out of the Game), which he submitted in 1968 to the UNEAC. The book won a national prize by the unanimous vote of a five-member international panel, but it became very controversial in Cuba for its poetic content.

¡Al poeta, despídanlo!	The poet! Kick him out!
Ese no tiene aquí nada que hacer.	He has no business here.
No entra en el juego.	He doesn't play the game.
No se entusiasma.	He never gets excited.
No pone en claro su mensaje.	His message is never clear.
No repara siquiera en los milagros.	He never sees the miracles.
Se pasa el día entero cavilando.	He meditates all day.
Encuentra siempre algo	He always finds something
que objetar [. . .]	to complain about [. . .]
Pero no hay quien	but there is no one who
lo haga abrir la boca,	can open his mouth,
pero no hay quien	but there is no one who
lo haga sonreír	can make him smile
cada vez que comienza el espectáculo	every time the spectacle begins
y brincan los payasos en la escena;	and the clowns play on stage;
cuando los cacatúas	when the parrots
confunden el amor con el terror	confuse love with terror
y está crujiendo el escenario	and the scenario creaks
y truenan los metales	and metals thunder
y los cueros	along with the drums
y todo el mundo salta	and everyone jumps,
se inclina,	bends forward,
retrocede,	retreats,
sonríe,	smiles,
abre la boca	opens his mouth
"pues sí,	"well yes,
claro que sí,	of course,
por supuesto que sí . . ."	certainly . . ."

y bailan todos bien,	and everyone dances well,
bailan bonito,	beautifully,
como les que sea el baile.	as they should dance.
¡A ese tipo, despídanlo!	Kick that guy out!
Ese no tiene aquí nada que hacer.	He has no business here.

—HEBERTO PADILLA (1974:68–71).

Subsequently, plans for its promised publication were dropped, and Padilla was arrested. An international outcry from artists and intellectuals around the world freed him from an actual cement prison, but not from the almost equally perceptible Velvet Prison that still existed in Cuban society. Padilla was forced to write and publicly recite a thirty-page apology or "self-criticism" to UNEAC, which was positioned at the beginning of his book *Fuera del Juego* when it was finally published in 1974 in the United States. Padilla writes:

> *Yo he difamado, he injuriado constantemente a la revolución, con cubanos y extranjeros. Y he llegado sumamente lejos en mis errores y en mis actividades contrarrevolucionarias. No se le puede andar con rodeos a las palabras. [. . .] Es decir, contrarrevolucionario es el hombre que actúa contra la revolución, que la daña. Y yo actuaba y dañaba a la revolución. A mí me preocupaba mucho más mi importancia intelectual y literaria que la importancia de la revolución. [. . .] La poesía de comienzos de la revolución, la misma que yo en etapas breves, era una poesía de entusiasmo revolucionario, una poesía ejemplar, una poesía como corresponde al proceso joven de nuestra revolución. Y yo inauguré el resentimiento, la amargura, el pesimismo, elementos todos que no son más que sinónimos de contrarrevolución en la literatura.* (Padilla 1974:106–9)

> I defamed, I constantly insulted the Revolution, both with Cubans and with foreigners. I went extremely far in my errors and in my counter-revolutionary activities. One cannot mince words. [. . .] A counter-revolutionary is one who works against the Revolution, one who does harm to it. And I was acting in such a way as to harm the Revolution. I was more interested in my intellectual and literary importance than in the importance of the Revolution. [. . .] Cuban poetry at the beginning of the revolution was exemplary poetry, such as corresponded to the youthful stage of our revolution. And it was I who started—and this was a sad initiative—I who started the resentment, the bitterness, the pessimism—all those elements that are all synonymous with counter-revolution in literature. (Padilla 1974:122–25)

"The Padilla Case," as it came to be known, marked the beginning of Los Años Gris and "The Great Purge" in artistic and intellectual circles, for it publicly demonstrated what would happen to those who dared to venture outside of Fidel Castro's stated boundaries, and publicly marked the extent to which state censors would go to control artistic expression. It was also an important tipping point for leftist artists and scholars abroad who had initially celebrated the Revolution and believed in the creative freedom promised, but later became more suspicious of Fidel Castro's plans for the country (Reed 1991; Weiss 1993). Other well-known writers and artists who were persecuted during this time included Lezama Lima, Virgilio Piñera, Reinaldo Arenas, and Guillermo Cabrera Infante, among others.[24]

So were these early years of the Revolution golden or gray? The answer to this question depended largely on who was being asked. Among artists and intellectuals, these years were seen as golden, as long as they were content to live within the boundaries set for revolutionaries. Certainly they were gray if one chose to be outwardly dissident and to display discontent with the authorities. This is not to say that there was a ban on social critique in Cuba. On the contrary, artists and intellectuals were highly critical and were allowed to be so up to a certain threshold: a threshold that, while invisible, was socialized into every Cuban citizen attending Cuban schools (Blum 2011; Fagen 1969), watching Cuban television and film (Chanan 2004), listening to Cuban radio (Hernandez-Reguant 2002), looking at Cuban art (Camnitzer 1994), and reading Cuban newspapers and literature (Álvarez 2002; Smorkaloff 1999; Whitfield 2001). What was interesting was that the most extreme examples of artistic production reflecting Fidel Castro's "within" and "against" burst forth at the same time—all at once, a creative explosion of socialist utopias and a vacuum created by socialist persecution. By the 1980s, the struggle was further divided by ninety miles of ocean, after many dissidents emigrated to Miami or New York, or had moved even farther away to countries such as France and Spain. Many dissidents within Cuba went underground, and those who attempted to speak out were given no news coverage. Thus protest actions went largely unnoticed and were unknown on a national scale. The dialectic struggle of within or against synthesized and led to a self-censoring equilibrium, at least until 1990.

2

ARTISTS IN THE SPECIAL PERIOD, OPTION ZERO, AND THE HOMBRE NOVÍSIMO
or, the heroic rescue of Liborio and Elpidio Valdés

Voz en la radio:

> *Información a la población: el gobierno revolucionario de nuestro país hace saber que, debido al período especial en tiempo de paz por el que atraviesa la nación, consecuencia directa de la reciente desaparición del campos socialista, los recursos disponibles para el desarrollo del país disminuirán considerablemente, por lo que se pide a nuestro pueblo la comprensión y el espíritu de sacrificio que siempre lo han caracterizado.*

> *(Pausa. Algunos dejan de comer.)*

> *Asimismo, se comunica que las reservas de combustible se han visto reducidas en un 50%, con las consecuentes afectaciones en el fluido eléctrico y el transporte nacional. También habrá recortes drásticos en la canasta familiar, la cual se reducirá considerablemente. Nuestro pueblo debe estar consciente del momento histórico por el que atraviesa el país, y debe estar preparado para afrontar, si fuera necesario, la Opción Cero para salvaguardar las conquistas.*

> *(Los actores han dejado de comer; están conmocionados por las noticias. Se levantan y lentamente caminan hacia atrás. Apagón.)*

Voice on the radio:

> Information to the population: the revolutionary government of our country announces that, due to the Special Period in Time of Peace that our nation is presently facing, which is a consequence of the recent disappearance of the socialist camp, the available resources for the development of the country have diminished considerably. For this reason, the people are asked to understand the situation and to continue with the spirit of sacrifice that has always characterized it.

(Pause. Some stop eating to listen.)

Additionally, we are informed that fuel reserves have been reduced by 50%, which has consequently affected the flow of electricity and national transportation. Also, there will be drastic cuts in family foodstuff rations. These cuts will be substantial. Our country must be conscious of this historic moment and it must prepare itself to undertake, if necessary, "Option Zero" to safeguard what has been gained.

(Actors have now all stopped eating. They are shocked by the news. They stand up and begin to slowly walk backwards. Blackout.) [1]

These lines, from a play called *Opción Cero*, were performed by Teatro de los Elementos in 2001. Back for a visit the autumn after my long-term fieldwork had ended, I was updated by Isnoel, one of the actors, on the groups' new artistic work. He handed me the script to read, brushing it off as "just a short historical piece," as nothing significant in their repertoire. I was immediately struck by the term, *Opción Cero*, for it had never been uttered in the previous four years of my research in Cuba. Though literally translated as "Zero Option" (no options left), the idea was discussed like a covert spy plan, in low whispers, as if *Option Zero* was the code phrase to signal the entire population to wordlessly spring into action. I began to ask around in both the rural and urban areas and discovered that everyone knew about Option Zero—from artists, campesinos, and rural street vendors to hairdressers, office workers, and neighborhood doctors in Havana—and all would flash their eyes upward, put a hand to their chest, and thank God (or Chango or Yemeya) it had not come to pass. They told me that Option Zero was the worst of what the Cuban Special Period crisis might have become. Unlike the Hombre Novísimo, there was absolutely no nostalgia for this, traditional or preemptive. That it had never been mentioned before surprised me, but when I saw the fear and dread in people's eyes, I began to understand why it was a best-forgotten part of the collective national memory.

With the fall of the socialist bloc and the loss of billions of dollars in aid from the Soviet Union in 1989, Cubans fell into a severe economic crisis and the onset of the "Special Period in Time of Peace." In 1990, Fidel Castro's speeches warned of the difficulties to come, his words haunting the thoughts of Cubans and making them fear for their future more than ever before. [2] Even more frightening than the predicted scarcity and hardship was the regime's plan for the potential occurrence of a total blockade and aggressive attack; a last resort strategy. Option Zero called for urban evacuation and retreat to the countryside in the center of the island. Without fuel, there would be no electricity, transportation, or communication, and the population would be forced to live entirely off the land and its natural resources. Food would be rationed, and Cubans I spoke with had conjured up visions of large soup vats placed in the town center; people waiting in long lines with bowls and spoons (interview, Miguel Sánchez León, Havana, 2003). It would be truly revolutionary, the people were told, just like the original guerrilla fighters from the Revolution. Once again, they were called upon to sacrifice everything and fight for the Patria. Although the idea was never published in state newspapers or in Fidel Castro's speeches, rumor and gossip worked their magic throughout the country and Option Zero became a mythological "what if?" Ten years later, the rural theater group Teatro de los Elementos produced a theatrical version of this "what if." The play begins with a radio announcement (above), and in slow motion the actors position themselves into statues "of triumph"—into compositions "typical of the aesthetics of Socialist Realism" (*Opción Cero* script). Once frozen in place, the actors sing a "well-known Russian song" (unspecified). After a few minutes, the song becomes distorted, more and more so until the human statues crumble and the actors fall to the ground. Actors begin to speak one by one.

Coro:

—*1989. El planeta se estremece: cayó el Muro de Berlín.*

—*Fin de la Historia, dicen algunos en el norte del mundo.*

—*Comienzo de la agonía, dicen otros un poco más al sur. Fin de la guerra fría y del socialismo real, dicen casi todos.*

—*El estremecimiento del derrumbe llega hasta el Caribe.*

—*Desaparece la vaca bolchevique, y con ella las tetas de las que mamaba el ternero caribeño, que de pronto se ve solo, y hambriento.*

—*No sabe como sobrevivirá: son los peores días de su vida.*

—*Es un ternero aislado. Aislado en una isla.*

—*Ahora tendrá que arreglárselas solo para sobrevivir.*

—*O entrar en la misma fila que los otros.*

—*O morir.*

Chorus:

—1989. The planet shakes: The Berlin Wall falls.

—In the North they say it is the End of History

—In the South they say the agony now begins. Everyone says it is the end of the Cold War and of Socialism.

—The quaking of the collapse is felt as far as the Caribbean.

—The Bolshevik cow disappears, and with her the teats of those that nursed the Caribbean calf: a calf that is suddenly alone and hungry.

—No one knows how it will survive: these are the worst days of its life.

—It is an isolated calf. Isolated on an island.

—Now it must adapt to being alone in order to survive.

—Or get into the same line as the others.

—Or die.[3]

When the play begins, it appears to be a critique of Option Zero and of the crisis of the Special Period, but it very quickly transforms into a play about how this particular theater group (Teatro de los Elementos) decided to continue their artistic work and *luchar* (to fight) for socialism in spite of the hardships. They profess to do this by "saving the spirit" of the people. Two actors walk to center stage, "acting out characteristics of the Afro-Cuban culture and religion":

Isnoel: *(mientras pasa unas ramas sobre el cuerpo de Fredy). Salvar el espíritu es lo más necesario. Hay que salvar el espíritu.*

Coro: *No pierdan la fe . . . no pierdan la fe . . . ¡No pierdan la fe!*

Fredy: *(Corte de la luz eléctrica. Penumbras) ¡Otra vez! Ya son tres veces que se va la jodida luz . . .*

Héctor: *Así no se puede.*

Danilo: *Yo tengo hambre. Y un bufón con hambre no hace reír a nadie.*

Isnoel: *No pierdan las esperanzas, compañeros.*

Isnoel: *(while passing branches over the body of Freddy, "cleansing" him as in Afro-Cuban rituals).* To save the spirit is most necessary. The spirit must be saved.

Chorus: Don't lose faith . . . don't lose faith . . . Don't lose faith!

Freddy: *(The electricity goes out. Semidarkness)* Again! Now it's been three times that the damn lights have gone out . . .

Hector: We can't go on like this.

Danilo: I'm hungry. And a hungry clown cannot make anyone laugh.

Isnoel: Don't lose hope, comrades.[4]

Maintaining hope and restoring a lost cultural spirituality in the population became the mission of groups like Teatro de los Elementos and other

Teatro Comunitario groups, who adopted official discourse of luchar—using art as an ideological weapon to save the Revolution and mobilize the mass of people necessary to support it: a method championed by Fidel Castro.

Luckily, Cuba never had to resort to Option Zero, although it did slip into an intense economic crisis and a distinctly "Special Period," where scenes such as the one above were frequent and familiar. Due to the extreme scarcity of resources (basic foodstuffs, soap, oil, fuel, clothing, paper, building material, specialty items, etc.), many cultural traditions and artistic endeavors were set aside, considered peripheral to daily survival. In urban areas, long *apagones* (blackouts) slowed the usually busy pace of city life, and residents waited long hours in the sun for buses that never arrived. Factories and businesses shut down, and stores that remained open displayed only empty shelves. Cubans, both rural and urban, told stories of how they were forced to *inventar* (invent) and *resolver* (resolve) problems in creative ways in order to survive—sugar and potatoes often their only nourishment. Photos were brought out which showed themselves and their families twenty to fifty pounds lighter.

Many professional artistic endeavors were put on hold, especially when the last remaining spotlight burned out, the last canvas and paints were used up, and strings for musical instruments had deteriorated and snapped. In mountain pueblos, many campesino traditions were abandoned, such as the *corrida de cinta* (similar to ring jousting on horseback), *palo de grasa* (greased pole-climbing), *peleas de gallo* (cockfights), *altares de cruz* (altar of the cross rituals), and inter-pueblo baseball games. Amateur musical and theater group activities were also suspended, since campesinos had too much to do just to survive. Their days began before dawn, working fields with ox-driven plows; caring for farm animals and protecting them from increasing incidences of theft; washing clothes in the river; and collecting wood for cooking. A hurricane in the early 1990s destroyed the meager crops that had initially made the countryside a potentially better place to live during the crisis. The survival of rural cultural traditions was further threatened when many rural youth fled to the cities, or fled the island altogether. With the flight of the young people went the promise of *el campo's* legacy. The continuation of rural traditions and ways of life was threatened.

Raymond Williams uses poetry to analyze the dialectic of change in the historical relationship between country and city—between the perceptions of pure nature and contaminated capitalism. To discuss the different perspectives of country and city, and to describe "nature's threads" and "green language," he quotes Oliver Goldsmith's *Deserted Village* (1769): "E'en now, methinks, as pondering here I stand, I see the rural virtues leave the land" and also William Wordsworth's 1798 verse: "In nature and the language of the sense, / The anchor of my purest thoughts, the nurse, / The guide, the guardian of my heart, and soul / Of all my moral being" (Williams 1973:10, 68, 132). Williams traces the historical associations with the "country"—nostalgic, utopian, liberating, wild and unspoiled, but also isolated, impoverished, and rejected as old. He also traces what is classified as "city"—money, wealth, luxury, capitalism, bureaucracy, and centralized power (ibid.:287–92). These perceptions are developed in the particular socioeconomic context of the era in question, but a particular relationship between city and country remains distinct in many parts of the world: nostalgia for "the land" and the idea of purity withstanding the threat of urban contamination.

During the Special Period, and especially after the legalization of the U.S. dollar and increasing "materialistic opportunities" in the cities, similar types of associations and ambivalences were increasing in Cuba, and on Cuban stages. Cubans joked about the rural migrants who flocked to Havana; police from Oriente were teased for their ignorance of city ways and disrespected behind their backs, perceived as uneducated hillbillies who could be easily fooled and eluded. *Que guajiro* (what a hillbilly) was a common pejorative, and although these displaced guajiros were romantic and noble when imagined in their own territory (el campo), they became backward and brutish when in physical proximity with city people. Conversely, in the countryside, visitors from the city, especially returning relatives, were seen as shallow, superficial, and greedy, the painted nails and flashy clothes bought in "shopping" regarded as a sign of *jineterismo* (hustling or prostitute-like behavior). Resident campesinos shook their heads knowingly and clucked their tongues at those who came back out to the *bohío* smelling of foreign perfume and wearing knock-off Tommy Hilfiger jeans. In the city, they were hip and cosmopolitan, but in the countryside, their ways were considered impractical and their morals contaminated. Physical and geographical exodus from country to city marked the withdrawal of campesino identity and empathy—of their common *alma de guajiro* (guajiro soul, or soul of the land). Rural communities dwindled in number, and once socially and musically active, the mountains retreated into a more profound silence than ever before.[5]

Yet, just as some traditions appeared to be dying out, a new one was rising up from within the crisis. In 1990 a new type of theater emerged with a method and philosophy that were directly shaped by the economic predicament. This new theater rekindled the model of Teatro Escambray; its mission was to bring theater to the community and utilize local people in its creation. However, instead of seeking a radical transformation of political consciousness and a shift to socialist practicality, this theater of the Special Period and its *teatristas* sought to preserve the old, to rescue dying traditions, and to reinsert a sense of beauty and spirituality into the lives of the Cuban people. They searched for the *pura cepa* of cubanía, for the noble inner core of the Cuban soul—the artists still optimistic about the future of their struggling society. The emerging new theater looked very much like the Teatro Nuevo of the 1960s and 1970s, but like the aging Hombre Nuevo, this reference was dated.

Randy Martin describes Teatro Nuevo in Cuba as primarily "conjunctual," noting that there were six official Teatro Nuevo groups in Havana's Theater Festival in 1980, two in 1982, and none in 1984. Teatro Escambray was still producing theater in 1984, although less frequently in official artistic circles, and the group was not traveling as often to national theater festivals where it would have been officially counted as "active." By 1985, the original director, Sergio Corrieri, had left Manicaragua to return to work in Havana, and the group had changed its investigatory and creative methods. According to Martin, Teatro Nuevo groups in their original form had completely died out by 1984 (Martin 1994:132; see also Swanger 1999; Villegas 1994). Although Teatro Escambray never disbanded, there were fallow periods that may account for this statement (interview with director, Rafael González, Manicaragua, 2000). The 1990s revival of this rural, grassroots people's theater was called *Teatro Comunitario*.

The term *Teatro Comunitario* (Communitarian Theater) was only loosely and unofficially used at first. But by the late 1990s it had become the catchphrase to mark a new kind of theater, one that appealed to cultural officials and artists alike (interview with Isnoel Yanes, Cumanayagua, 1999). "Theater in the community, for the community, and by the community" was the mantra of Teatro Comunitario, echoing similar cries in the popular theater of other Latin American societies. Losing faith in state officials' ability to resolve Cuba's problems and feeling helpless in the face of the national crisis, the population was turning its attention to its own local communities and issues. Teatro Comunitario was celebrated as a moral contribution to the Revolution, touting the values of cooperation and artistic experience for both actor and audience. More importantly, its style fit in with the logistical restrictions of the economic crisis. Like Teatro Nuevo, Teatro Comunitario groups often took their theater on the road, out to marginal areas with little access to formal cultural performance. Ethnographic methods of investigation supplied information and inspiration for their productions, and local residents were utilized either as actors or creative consultants in their productions. Unlike Teatro Nuevo groups, these groups were subject to the scarcity, pessimism, and desperation of the Special Period, yet their artistic zeal seemed to originate from these very hardships. Teatro Nuevo groups were born with the enthusiasm and momentum of the Revolution, coddled with resources, and internationally recognized. Teatro Comunitario groups of the early 1990s were appreciated, but there was no momentum or resources, rather inertia and shortage. The sacrifice necessary to withstand the difficulties of producing theater or any kind of artistic performance during the 1990s was part and parcel of the form's success in the eyes of the actors, their audiences, and the Ministry of Culture. The return to nature, to the land, to the fundamental elements of human survival, became the alternative in these artists' eyes to politics, progress, and modernization. Rural Cuba and its campesino residents were thus sacred ground for rescuing Cuba's cultural pura cepa. Teatro Comunitario was born of the crisis of the Special Period, thrived on it to a certain degree, and was a key coping mechanism for the hardest-hit areas.

The remainder of this chapter looks at how and why the emphasis on el campo and the campesinos grew and developed, and the ways in which contemporary versions of Teatro Nuevo (the heirs of Teatro Escambray) reinterpreted the image of the campesino in national narratives after 1990. Artists responded to the economic crisis in distinctive ways; some became frustrated and quit altogether, while others persevered and used the misery of the Special Period to their advantage, promoting a new type of theater to buttress the dying "revolutionary spirit" of the people.

Special Period Artists Return to Nature

When nostalgia turns political, romance is connected to nation-building and
native songs are purified. The official memory of the nation-state does not
tolerate useless nostalgia for its own sake.—SVETLANA BOYM (2001),
The Future of Nostalgia

After the Special Period began, artistic production reflected the confusion of how to represent the Revolution, revolution-*ary* ideology and
morality, and thus national identity, during its bumpy and unpredictable
process of transformation. Urban artists looked abroad for answers,
bemoaning opportunities lost, condemning the contradictions in Cuban
society, and calling for social change. Some urban artists turned away
from politics and reality altogether, focusing on more experimental and
corporeal forms of performance art. In contrast, rural artists who defined their groups as Teatro Comunitario often focused nostalgically on
what was fading away, celebrating the humble and uncontaminated elements of Cuban culture, and privileging their role in the rebuilding of
the Cuban spirit. The primary character in such representations was the
campesino in his natural territory, *el campo* (rural countryside), as yet
untouched by the contaminants of the urban "areas of consumption"
(places selling products in foreign currency or in *pesos convertibles*) and
the growing obsession with profit and accumulation of goods.

Interestingly, depictions of the campesino before the Special Period
differed markedly from those that emerged after its onset. Sergio Corrieri's Teatro Nuevo or Teatro Escambray (and Flora Lauten's spinoff,
Teatro de la Comunidad in La Yaya) had sought to showcase the campesino's transformation and progression into the Hombre Nuevo:

> *Cuando los pobladores se mudaron al pueblo nuevo, recibieron junto a la casa, el*
> *agua, la electricidad, los equipos electrodomésticos y los servicios sociales, algo*
> *mucho más importante. Abandonaron bohíos de yaguas y piso de tierra, dejaron*
> *atrás su miseria y sus vidas aisladas y sin esperanzas para encontrar un marco*
> *social y cultural; la posibilidad de rescatar una vida más digna y más plena.*
> (Boudet, introduction to *Teatro La Yaya*, in Lauten, 1981)

> When the population moved to the new pueblo, they received, along with the
> house, water, electricity, domestic appliances, and social services: something
> much more important. They abandoned huts made of palm, with dirt floors;

they left behind misery and isolated lives that were without hope of making a social and cultural impression. They were given the possibility of rescuing a more dignified and fuller life.

A more "dignified" life in this case means a more "modern" life and enculturation from Cuban peasant to Cuban citizen. In contrast, the Teatro Comunitario that emerged during the Special Period aspired to safeguard and preserve the old, the traditional, and the unchanging. Like the groups of Teatro Nuevo, those of the new Special Period aspired to "rescue" the campesinos, but not from their primitive lives in the countryside; instead, they were now to be rescued from the modern contaminants that threatened to change them. Producers of Teatro Comunitario did not want to showcase the modernization of the campesinos; they wanted to defend their distinct identity and protect their long-standing traditions—not traditions that were considered part of their prerevolutionary impoverishment, but the select best of nature and culture.

After living with rural theater groups and seeing countless performances by both professional groups and amateur campesinos artists, I distinguished two broad but distinct ways the teatristas tended to represent the noble campesino in the 1990s. *Poetic Fantasy* presented the past and present in dreamlike, romantic, and fantastical visions, with cooing crickets, soft flickering kerosene lamps, and old men in straw hats singing *décimas*. Characters types were exaggerated, sometimes mythical. Nostalgia took a more traditional form here—of longing for a lost or displaced time or place, and as a "romance with one's own fantasy" (Boym 2001:xiii). Stories were based on fables or well-known Cuban stories with a new interpretive twist. To place it into more conventional theater terms, Poetic Fantasy incorporated aspects of allegory, or fairy tale. In contrast, *Folk Rusticity* took the campesinos at face value, focusing on their rawness, rugged demeanor, and bloody cockfights, celebrating these elements while also infusing them with unabashed humor and sarcasm. This nostalgia was not romantic, but rather self-mocking and satirical, tragic, and comical. The performances were entertaining, but also powerful, displaying the strength of the rural population and the ability to survive under the harshest circumstances. City people were displayed as petty, selfish, and weak. Folk Rusticity could best be compared in theatrical lingo to comedy of manners, domestic comedy, burlesque, or folk drama. Poetic Fantasy was usually structured like a full-length play—multiple scenes in two acts—since it was more often being performed by visiting professional actors for campesinos. In contrast, Folk Rusticity appeared in long vignettes or sketches, not unlike the presentational form of the *actos* (acts, both theatrical and political) of Luis Valdez's Teatro Campesino (Farmworkers' Theater, founded in 1965 in rural California), although Cuban farmworkers were certainly not using their theater for agitprop or activism.[6] As should be evident, pinning down these genres into conventional terms was not a simple categorical task. Different professional Teatro Comunitario groups adopted one or the other of these artistic approaches, often depending on where the play was to be performed and for whom, but both styles intended to revive the essence of culture through representation and reception. Artists hoped that "reflection" would bring about reinvigoration of the ideals connected to the campesino—that they would not fall into "retrospect" (Williams 1973:72).

The growth of Teatro Comunitario was facilitated by the institution of newly formed *proyectos* (projects) developed by the Ministry of Culture in 1989, which permitted the creation of smaller theater collectives. During the spring of that year, the Ministry of Culture was reorganized for reasons other than the impending economic crisis: the overcentralization of artistic resources was considered detrimental to the continued growth of Cuban theater. "The model of the grand production did not encounter adequate sustenance in the existing infrastructure. Converted into grand companies, the theater collectives did not know space of experimentation; they had a slow rhythm of premieres and did not succeed in systematizing the formation of their public" (Cuban theater scholar and critic, Graziella Pogolotti, quoted in Martin 1994:164). The five artistic divisions within the Ministry of Culture—including literature, cinema, music, *artes plásticas* (painting, sculpture), and theater—were reestablished as separate national councils or boards (*consejos*), made up of the some of the highest-esteemed figures in their respective artistic category. The newly formed theater board began accepting proposals for one to five year projects. By June 1989, there were over seventy submissions in Havana alone, many of which were by new artists who had never worked in professional theater (ibid.:165). This restructuring of theater project approval and funding was undoubtedly what saved the theater from ruin and almost total closure during the crisis, for at the time, large companies were centered mainly in Havana (to a lesser extent in Santiago de Cuba), and during the frequent blackouts and transportation shortages of the Special Period, theaters were more often "dark" (closed) than open for business (interview with Haydee Sala Santos, Havana, 1999). However, even the proyectos did not solve all the problems, at least not in the big cities. Spectators were often unable to actually get to the theater houses or smaller *salas* (halls), for although there were more of them after 1989; spaces were still mainly located in the neighborhoods of Vedado and Old Havana. The situation even tried the patience of avid theatergoers. To attend a play, someone living outside the area often had to leave at least two hours before curtain, to wait in long lines for infrequent and overloaded buses coming into town from distant neighborhoods, and then sit for the long duration of the trip itself. When the determined spectator finally arrived, she or he discovered a dark theater, the play canceled due to an *apagón*, a missing actor (also waiting for a bus or otherwise held up), or some other catastrophe blamed on the Special Period. *Me complique* ("I was hindered") was a common excuse for many Cubans, artists or otherwise, and I never once heard anyone ask for explanatory details when this phrase was uttered. Unnamed "complications" were accepted parts of the Special Period, thus impeding people's abilities to be on time or to arrive at all. Whenever I was in Havana, I tried to see as much city theater as possible. I always began early, traveling on my bicycle or in *máquinas*[7] (collective taxis) from theater to theater to find an actual performance. I would frequently have to go to more than two theaters before finding one with working lights and with a play actually scheduled to happen. More often I would return home, unsuccessful. A normal Cuban, however zealous and devoted a fan, did not have the time, patience, money, or incentive to do this. While I was at first frustrated that these failed attempts were valuable time wasted, I soon realized that they were an important part of my ethnographic experience and cultural education in Cuba. As a researcher, I could not give up, but I certainly would have eventually thrown in the towel and stayed home had I been in my own country.

The advantage of the proyectos was that actors were no longer dependent on finding work with already established companies housed in particular theaters. Instead, small groups of two or three individuals could develop from scratch. This restructuring enabled new ensembles to perform in whichever theater or sala was available, as well as to go out into the communities, both urban and rural, and to perform in more informal venues, even if ill equipped. The revolutionary government was undoubtedly pleased with this outburst of artistic initiative, and support for the arts was channeled into such groups. Although Teatro Nuevo had effectively died out by the early 1980s in spite of the Ministry of Culture's attempt to nurture it, its method and philosophy was revived as Teatro Comunitario in the 1990s, and its distinctive concentration on nonurban, simple, no-frills presentation fit conveniently into the country's predicament. As the popular *salas de video* (video salons) and cinemas began to close down, live theater survived. For the theatre, the lack of electricity simply meant that performances had to be held before sundown or designed and blocked for a spotlight powered by a gas-fueled generator. Performances were still hit or miss ("me complique"), but at least there was never a lack of bodies with which to act and make music. It was here that the advantage of live theater showed its muscles over the usual bullying of video, television, and film (cf. Auslander 1999).

From Zones of Silence to Intellectual Zones

After the first groups began to emerge and gain official approval, Teatro Comunitario became all the rage in intellectual circles, and theater groups used the term to define a myriad of different projects. A conference, called Congreso Iberoamericano y Caribeño de Agentes del Desarrollo Sociocultural Comunitario (Ibero-American and Caribbean Congress of Agents for Socio-Cultural Community Development), or simply *Comunidad* (Community), began in 1994 and focused on the development of community culture, including music, dance, visual arts, and theater. The concept of Teatro Comunitario soon became a popular and central topic of intellectual discussion and a theme for various panels and presentations.

Teatro Comunitario groups were professional, and worked in both urban and rural areas, although critics and intellectuals agreed that the most respected groups resided in what were called "areas of difficult access," also referred to as "zones of silence." These groups were characterized by a dedication to bring theater to the farthest reaches of the island, to those isolated places where campesinos still lived off the land, and had no reliable electricity or transportation: in short, where an implementation of Option Zero would not have required much change from their daily lives, and where the theater project itself embodied the return to the supposed simplicity and primacy of nature and living off the land. Rural Teatro Comunitario groups searched actively for "virgin" audiences: their definition of virgin being audiences that had never seen professional or conventional forms of theater (proscenium stage, curtain, spotlight, actors, script, two acts) and would experience it for the first time with their performances. The use of "virgin" as an adjective to describe rural communities in regard to the Revolution was also used by Fidel Castro in 1961:

> *El campesino posee una mentalidad virgen, libre de una serie de influencias con que en la ciudad envenenaban las inteligencias de los ciudadanos. La Revolución trabaja sobre esas inteligencias fértiles, como trabaja sobre la tierra. Y se incorporarán al país esas inteligencias que antes se frustraban.* (Castro, March 8, 1961)

> The peasant has a virgin mind, free of a whole series of influences which have poisoned the thinking of the citizens in the cities. The revolution is working with these fertile minds, as it is working with the land. And the country will incorporate these minds, which were previously disregarded.

The actors also hoped for an audience with an "organic" appreciation of the cultural spirituality and enlightenment they had to offer—free from so-called civilization and development—potentially evoking an audience reception quite unlike the critical and elitist intellectuals in the cities who would belabor their lack of material polish. It was also unlike that of ordinary urban and semi-urban theatergoers, who were burdened and embittered by the increasing hardships, and who, without reliable transport, were often unable to reach the theater at all, even if they wanted to attend, and often times (as previously described), even if they tried. These teatristas did not wait for the people to come to them in official theatre spaces; they went to the people or performed in central plazas that were within walking distance of the bohíos of the campesinos.

Approximately six of the most so-called authentic groups emerged in 1991. Just what constituted an authentic group varied in my investigation, depending on who was judging the level of authenticity and how officially authoritative their voice was, for example, my garage-apartment landlord in Havana, who never went to see theater versus a worker in the Ministry of Culture or a professional actor. The Consejo Nacional de Artes Escénicas (National Theater Board) officially listed six professional Teatro Comunitario groups in 2000. The word *authentic* was used repeatedly in an interview with a consejo official, Alexis Abreu, to qualify which groups deserved support and which did not (interview with Alexis Abreu, Havana,

2000). These Comunitario groups embodied the spirit of the Special Period and, to a great extent, of Option Zero as well, since their projects were fueled and inspired by the very scarcity that waylaid so many others. Sacrifice and selflessness defined their artistic mission, and the harsh conditions defined the reason for their existence. From the broader category of Teatro Comunitario, this smaller cohort is what I call "Option Zero Theater." After several years of research and fieldwork, I developed my own threefold criterion for an Option Zero Theater group (within the Teatro Comunitario circle). First, as part of their working philosophy or principle, the group retreated to or resided in rural zones of silence. Second, they embraced the scarcity and hardship, and joined together to spread theater, storytelling, and music to isolated communities that were otherwise without access to artistic endeavors. Third, the group had to follow the Teatro Escambray play-making model—utilizing some form of social investigation (interviews, living with campesinos, participant observation, research into particular idiosyncrasies of area, debate, rewriting), and communicating, in some way, the "voice" of the people themselves. The groups were both officially and self-defined as "significant" sociocultural and collective projects. During my fieldwork, I worked closely with one group in Cienfuegos Province (Teatro de los Elementos) and two groups in Guantánamo Province (La Cruzada Teatral, El Laboratorio de Teatro Comunitario). To a lesser extent, I also investigated an amateur theater group called Grupo Lino Álvarez de Realengo 18.

Revolutionary Theater—Not What It Used to Be

When I first arrived in Cuba, in January of 1997, I asked about existing Teatro Comunitario groups and where I might find them. I was always first referred to Teatro Escambray, usually followed by the comment: "But they're not what they used to be." By 1997, campesinos of the Escambray Mountains were well versed in the proper etiquette of theater behavior after having the benefit of Teatro Escambray's proximity for thirty years. The director, Rafael González, told me it became more and more difficult to get the campesinos to engage in debate once they learned that quietly listening and watching were more polite and "civilized" than yelling out at the actors in performance (to agree or disagree with the lines being spoken) or critiquing the artists after the show. The campesinos had become shy and afraid of being wrong. As their "civilizing" and "cultivating" ultimately stifled their previously spontaneous behavior, performances became less "efficacious" and more for entertainment—educative entertainment perhaps, but not socially or ideologically transformative (cf. Schechner 1988; Turner 1982, 1987). Further, a new generation of campesinos had grown up under socialism, and thus, their conflicts and concerns were distinct from those of their parents and grandparents. What was relevant in 1968 was not in 1988. Teatro Escambray, like any cultural institution, was forced to shift its focus to other social issues and populations, such as youth and schooling, alcoholism, disputes in the workplace, and so forth (interview with Rafael Gonzalez, Manicaragua, 2000). The erstwhile champion of the campesino had to adapt as the communities of the Escambray Mountain region changed with the times.

The comment "not what they used to be" was accompanied by a nostalgic sigh and a shake of the head. Eventually, the conversation led to other suggestions. There were professional Teatro Comunitario groups scattered across the country, which included Korimacao in Playa Girón, a group that routinely received awards, but was sarcastically labeled by some other artists as "political cabaret" and full of "dancing and singing Che Guevaras." Grupo Andante (Traveling Theater) in Granma Province was a well-known group, but its productions were largely street theater (as "street" as one can be in the Sierra Maestra mountains), with music, actors on stilts, and clown work, with little text. La Cruzada Teatral (The Theater Crusade) traveled to the most remote pueblos of Guantánamo Province, but the group worked together for only a few months annually, from November to late February (see chapter 5). La Guerilla de Teatreros (Theater Guerrillas) also worked in the Oriente, in Granma Province. Like La Cruzada, whom they sometimes joined in collaboration, Los Teatreros planned an annual month-long trip up into the mountains.

I was also told to look up José Oriol González, the director of Teatro de los Elementos, located in a small town called Cumanayagua in the Escambray Mountain region. According to the cultural specialists at the National Theater Board, this group was the most "authentic" of the professional Teatro Comunitario groups since it was most like the legendary Teatro Escambray and was located just an hour from Escambray's artistic commune in Manicaragua. Los Elementos had a respected national reputation, and José Oriol frequently rubbed elbows with the higher-ups in Havana's intellectual circles, providing a link with Cuba's central artistic core (cf. Verdery 1991). Such connections also granted the political power to host and take responsibility for a visiting American for a year.

The self-proclaimed *hijo* (son) of Teatro Escambray—José Oriol Gonzalez's Teatro de los Elementos—was a well-known group in its own right, although those in Havana rarely, if ever, saw it perform, given its rural location, and contacting the group in 1998 turned out to be exceedingly difficult. I first tried to call the phone numbers listed for Los Elementos by the Theater Board. The numbers did not work, no one was able to tell me what they had been changed to, and email accounts were not yet commonplace in Cuba.[8] Nor had anyone in the Havana theater office actually seen José Oriol or the group since the last international theater festival two years before. Thus, even though it was on the list of well-known and authentic Teatro Comunitario groups, the quality of Los Elementos' work was only collectively imagined among urban intellectuals, but was not usually experienced directly by them. It seemed that the only way I was going to make initial contact with Los Elementos or any other rural Teatro Comunitario group was to travel into the mountains myself.

Buses, Colas, and Waiting Lists

Much of the Cuban theater I saw between 1997 and 2009 contained themes of waiting, of scenarios centered on bus stops or transportation problems. I did not realize the seriousness of this theme until I began to work in the rural areas and had to rely on something other than my trusty bicycle or my tolerance for long walks in the heat. Performances routinely depicted waiting and the lack of transport in humorous ways, but the problem was not funny at all when one was in the midst of the experience. The first trip to Cumanayagua was, thus, part of my introduction to the sources of artistic imagination in Cuba, as much as its hard-core reality. The first challenge was to find out how to reach Cumanayagua. I had a Cuban *Carné de Identidad* and had temporary resident status in Cuba. Therefore, I was officially able to pay for everything in pesos (the exchange rate of the time was twenty pesos to the dollar). But it also meant that I should not take the foreigner shortcut and simply walk to a separate line and pay in *divisas* (in 1999, the word *divisa* meant U.S. dollar, though literally it referred to hard currency). I had to do it as the Cubans did—part of good fieldwork to be sure. Carné in hand, I was ready to go, or so I thought. Cubans were not able to simply go to the bus station to buy a ticket for their desired destination, but had to reserve a ticket exactly two weeks before their departure date. For instance, someone planning to leave on June 1 had to go to the bus station to buy a ticket on May 15. On this same day, the person could purchase a return ticket for one week after arrival, or June 8. If passengers wished to return on a different day, they would have to return to the bus station to buy their tickets three weeks before the chosen alternative date. There were a limited number of seats reserved for any one bus on a particular day: sometimes fifteen, ten, six, four, or even just two. Therefore, hopeful passengers arrived as early as possible to ensure their strategic place in the *cola* (line). This often meant 2:00 AM or 3:00 AM, or even earlier depending on the popularity of the destination.

The cola was actually quite a remarkable phenomenon in Cuba. Unlike American lines, where one would normally lose their place if they left the line, Cubans had a well-developed system that had undoubtedly been created over the previous four decades to retain peace and the sanity of those having to wait in multiple lines every day, often for hours on end. When you arrived at an established cola you asked for *el último* (the last one in line). El último raised his/her hand and nodded, making eye contact, thereby designating you as the new último. This person also pointed to the person ahead of him or her, so that you could recognize the two people in line immediately before you. This step was necessary in case one of them left the line (to take a taxi out of frustration and desperation or to give up and go home). Once you had an established place in the cola, you could sit or walk around or look for shade wherever you liked. You did not have to maintain your space in a physical line. The cola cohered through a string of últimos who knew who was before them and after them. When the ticket vendor arrived, the cola mysteriously reformed itself and people usually waited with discipline, although still with anxiety and a fidgeting impatience.

Once established in the cola for a long-distance bus ticket, some individuals actually went home (if they lived close enough) to sleep until later in the morning, to go to drink coffee, to eat breakfast, or to visit a friend. When they returned at 7:00 AM, their place in the cola was still safe and sound. Fully socialized in the United States, I never fully trusted this system and thus would arrive at 3:00 AM and stay physically "in line," going so far as to sit closely to those before and after me until the ticket office opened, afraid to lose my spot, yet all the time envying those Cubans who had gone home for a little more sleep and marveling at the Cuban cola. An alternative to waiting in the cola yourself was to send someone in your place, and that substitute was paid in money or reciprocal favors. Any individual was able to buy up to four tickets. For Cubans who had dollars, a transaction could also be made on the day of departure with the ticket seller, depending, of course, on the particular ticket seller, their devotion to the Revolution, and whether or not their *jefe* was standing nearby. For $3.00 to $5.00, a peso ticket could be ensured by secretly placing one's name at the top of the waiting list. Since the bus was never sold out two weeks before (a block of seats were saved until the day of departure and the names of the lucky individuals taken off the waiting list), there were always several seats sold to those at the top of the waiting list. I was never brave enough to try this strategic act of bribery, nor did I feel it my place as a temporary resident (with more *divisas*) to displace those Cubans with the finesse to work the system. I sat with the majority of the crowd, waited, and fidgeted nervously.

The waiting list was yet another distinctly Cuban phenomenon (comically reflected in the film *Lista de Espera* by Juan Carlos Tabío). If a trip had to be made but one did not yet have a ticket (or was unsuccessful in the cola two weeks previous), they were *notado* (noted, written down) on the waiting list. Requirements changed depending on the city or town, but generally this had to be done between twenty-four and two hours before the bus's departure time. In Havana, buses left from a terminal in New Vedado, near the Plaza of the Revolution, but the station for the waiting list was Old Havana. Passengers with tickets boarded in New Vedado, then the bus stopped in Old Havana to fill the remaining seats. Cubans sat for hours, sometimes for days, to secure a place on a bus, especially if the trip had an urgent purpose. There was a large open lobby filled with people—sitting on benches, lying on the floor, walking back and forth, venders selling food, clothing, music, newspapers, babies crying, and students reading. It was a desperate and stressful place, but also a calm place; calm at least until the arrival of a bus, at which point a mass of waiting passengers rushed toward the ticket office to await the calling of their name. Safely behind a glass window, the ticket seller yelled out names as fast as he or she could pronounce them. The crowd pushed forward, money in outstretched hands, anxious and determined to acquire the golden bus ticket. They pushed inward toward the booth, crushing anyone less determined or crazed. If the teller yelled your name and you did not respond immediately, you lost your place in line and had to start anew. Once a ticket was in hand, you quickly rushed outside to the awaiting bus, lest it leave without you. I can only thank a kind Cuban woman for grabbing me by the hand when the gun went off and dragging me onto the bus. Without her I may have remained in the crowd, bumped from side to side until the successful dispersed, the unsuccessful slumped away, and me, the clueless *extranjera* (foreign woman) standing shocked and wide eyed in the aftermath, wondering what had just happened.

Of course, one bypassed this entire ordeal if willing to pay twenty U.S. dollars instead of twenty Cuban pesos. In Cuban banks, airports, and hotels, one peso was officially listed as equal to one dollar, so they argued that foreigners could pay the same price in their own currency. But one peso was actually equivalent to about twenty dollars according to international rates in 1999–2000. Foreigners paying twenty U.S. dollars were thus paying four hundred pesos for a bus ticket, the state earning a hefty profit. On each bus there were between two and four seats (depending on the desirability of the destination) reserved for foreign tourists or Cubans willing to pay fully in dollars. The latter was infrequent and usually impossible for most Cubans as it far exceeded their monthly salary. This more expensive ticket could be bought up to one hour before the bus's departure. There were also private collective taxis that waited outside the *venta en divisa* (dollar sales) office recruiting dollar-paying travelers before they bought their bus tickets. Sometimes official state vehicles— other times illegal individuals with cars—they filled the car with four people and charged roughly the same amount to the more popular locations. These "popular" locations were directly aligned with popular tourist attractions, such as Cienfuegos, Trinidad, Varadero Beach, Santa Clara, and Pinar del Río.

Confused, but determined, I somehow survived my first bus-ticket-buying experience (but not my last) with a lot of advice from Cuban friends, and after a six-hour bus ride from Havana, I arrived in Cienfuegos—still over an hour's drive from Cumanayagua, my ordeal not yet over. To get to Cumanayagua from Cienfuegos, I had been advised to wait on the corner outside the bus station and to look for a máquina, one of the old 1950s American cars which worked as collective taxis between the two locations. Ten pesos (fifty U.S. cents) was the going price. Unfortunately, I had arrived at 12:30 PM, long after the usual flow of taxis had ceased for the day. I went outside to the corner, as instructed, and began to ask around for transport. There were three other people waiting for taxis, one to Havana, one to Trinidad, and the last to Cumanayagua, like myself. We talked, and teamed our efforts. Finally, a chauffeur with a faded blue, 1957 Chevy agreed to take us. He wanted twenty pesos each (one U.S. dollar), since there were only two of us and the normal fare depended on a full car of four to six passengers. My companion balked, but I quickly agreed, desperate to reach my destination. Upon hearing my foreign accent, the chauffeur looked up at me and asked if I was a foreigner. Well, yes, I said, but I am a Cuban resident and have a Cuban Carné de Identidad. Still nervous at the prospect of having a foreigner in his car, he refused, began to walk away, hesitated, and then told me he would drive me there for six dollars. The haggling continued for fifteen more minutes, including repeated demonstrations of the Carné and my promises that it was, in fact, legal for him to drive foreigners if they were Cuban residents. My companion also continued to argue on my behalf, wishing to get home and having nothing to lose. After establishing mutual acquaintances in Cumanayagua, and desperate for the work during the midday slump, our chauffeur finally relented, provided I pay three dollars and my Cuban companion twenty pesos (one dollar). Although feeling slightly peeved that I hadn't passed muster as a Cuban resident, I let it go. The deal was done, and we were finally off to Cumanayagua.

Cumanayagua is a small rural town in the foothills of the Escambray Mountain region, an hour northeast of Cienfuegos on a thin, winding road. In 1999 (and still, in 2009), the bus from Cienfuegos was sporadic and unreliable, often not coming at all, so most Cubans waited on the side of the road and hitchhiked (*en botella*), not willing or able to pay the expensive fare for a máquina. Leaving the bustle of Cienfuegos, the road quieted and soon the only passers-by were on foot, horse, or tractor. Houses became sparse, the route narrowed and curved, and was soon lined with only coffee trees, orange trees, and green open countryside. The mountains of Escambray loomed serenely in the distance. Although Cumanayagua referred to a relatively large county, the main pueblo itself was small. Most of the population lived in the surrounding farmland and mountains and the place had a sleepy feel—people living life at their own sauntering pace. There was one main street, lined with open cafés selling mostly coffee and rum, the public library (closed down for renovations five years previous), a small farmers' market selling vegetables and grain for pesos, several *shopping* stores offering goods in divisas, a small Cubans-only hotel,[9] private houses whose owners peddled lighter fluid and fried pork sandwiches on front porches, and a cultural center called the Casita de Prado (Little House on the Boardwalk), where the local theater group, poets, and musicians held *peñas*. Peñas were open artistic gatherings where anyone could bring their poetry, stories, songs, instruments, and perform in turn for each other. Often a bottle of rum was passed around, and the gathering lasted well into the night. Máquinas and buses arrived at a small terminal at the north end of the pueblo and then returned to Cienfuegos or continued north to Trinidad or Santa Clara, only passing through Cumanayagua if the driver decided to seek out a meal or *un trago* (shot of rum) with a local friend. The only public transport within Cumanayagua itself was a horse cart that trotted up and down the short length of the main street, called Calle Principal, and charged one peso per passenger. Another horse cart periodically picked up passengers from Coppelia, the local ice cream parlor, and dropped them off at the hospital three kilometers outside of town.

Cumanayagua is located in the southeast portion of the province of Cienfuegos, comprising 1098.98 square kilometers. Eighty-five percent of the area is mountainous, its highest point reaching 1,139 meters above sea level at Pico San Juan, in the Macizo Guamuaya zone of the Escambray Mountains. In 2003, Cumanayagua's population was approximately 50,365, of which 31,982 lived in or within an hour's walk or ride to town and 18,383 lived in the outlying rural zones. Of the latter, 6,257 were part of a rural "reinvigoration" project called Plan Turquino Manatí—a rural development program that coincided with the national Massification of Culture Campaign. Mount Turquino is the highest point in Cuba, part of the Sierra Maestra Mountains. It is politically sacred for it was in this area that Fidel Castro, Che Guevara, and the revolutionary guerrilla rebels fought in the late 1950s. Plan Turquino's goal was to raise the standard of living in the rural areas so that campesinos would not have such a desire or need to move into urban areas, and thus, not leave the agricultural areas short of workers. Initially the plan focused on food supplies, electricity, running water, and better housing. After 2000, the "development of culture" in these areas also became a concern. For this reason, increased state support was reaching Cumanayagua. Town residents worked in various sectors, including state administration, public health (1 doctor per 637 people), culture (dance, theater, fine arts, literature, music, etc.), in the local museum, as scientific investigators, and in the industrial cooperatives—largely dairy production. Ironically, it was very difficult to find milk or cheese in Cumanayagua, and Coppelia, the local branch of the country's foremost ice cream parlor, was often closed with a small sign hung outside reading "No hay helado hoy" (There is no ice cream today).

Cumanayagua's claim to national fame was its local theater group, Teatro de los Elementos, which, after its initial years of traveling, settled in the hometown of its director, José Oriol González, just an hour down the road from Teatro Escambray's base in Manicaragua. Like Teatro Escambray, members of Los Elementos constructed their own artistic and agricultural commune on a farm about five kilometers outside of town called El Jovero. The land had been owned by José Oriol's grandfather before the Revolution. Afterward, belonging to the state (and also to "the people," José Oriol reminded me), the land was eventually reassigned to Teatro de los Elementos. Here, the group planned to truly return to the natural elements—cultivating vegetables and beans, raising chickens and pigs, building small houses for the actors to live in, and clearing outdoor rehearsal and performance spaces. José Oriol and the actors told me that the farm was to be an ecological demonstration of their commitment to the true *elementos* of nature.

Cumanayagua was unique for a small mountain town in that it had such a highly recognized professional theater group in residence. While there were ten professional Teatro Comunitario groups in Cuba in 2003, few were well known on the national level, or even outside of their own municipality, since the thematic materials in their plays were based on local issues, and they were not exportable or attractive to those tourists who did not understand Spanish (in fact, very few Spanish-speaking tourists attended the theater, unless an Afro-Cuban dance and music show was playing). Teatro de los Elementos was a small group, composed of one actress, Kirenia; four actors, Isnoel, Lolo, Héctor, and Joel; one producer who also worked as an actor, Freddy; one actor who doubled as an artistic consultant, Lexis; and the artistic director, José Oriol. From January 1998 until March 2001, they included me in their group number and in their playbills as "anthropologist and investigator." Six of the eight group members were originally from Cumanayagua and lived in their family homes.

The other two, Isnoel and Lexis, were from Havana and Trinidad respectively, and lived together in a small apartment provided by the state. During my year-long residence in Cumanayagua, I also shared this apartment with Isnoel and Lexis. Finding one's own apartment or house was virtually impossible in Cuba, and newly married couples (or the newly divorced) were put on a long waiting list for available housing. This was largely due to the economic crisis and a lack of building resources, but Cubans told me it had been a problem before the onset of the Special Period as well. In the mountain regions, campesinos simply built their own bohíos from natural resources found in the forest, but in urban or semi-urban areas, people had to live with their families, friends, or ex-spouses. That there was an apartment given to Los Elementos for its actors was incredibly lucky, despite the lack of a kitchen, and despite the bare cement floors, unfinished bathroom, and cracking walls that leaked during rainstorms. When a well-respected novelist and playwright came to work with the group (see chapter 4), three cans of paint were allotted to Isnoel and Lexis to gussy up the space. The only available color in the store at the time was lavender, which, however inappropriate, was an improvement. The group's luck ran out after I left Cumanayagua and they had to leave their cozy purple apartment. In February 2000, the state turned it over to a pregnant woman and her husband, and Isnoel and Lexis were forced into a series of temporary housing situations. By 2003, Lexis had left both the group and the country to live in Belgium, and Isnoel had no option but to move into a small room, previously used for storage, behind the Casa de Cultura theater stage. Unfortunately, being a Level 1 actor (the highest category) in a prominent theater group after 1990 did not ensure adequate housing. As of 2011, Isnoel was still living in the theater storage room.

The Politics of Revolutionary Aesthetics

Although similar in method, José Oriol's work with Los Elementos differed from Teatro Escambray and other Teatro Nuevo groups in its fundamental premise. Teatro Escambray began in 1968 with a social agenda in line with the times. Its original intentions were to investigate and represent the new problems and changes facing the campesinos in the mountains of Escambray just after the Revolution. Providing a public platform to previously voiceless peasants, Teatro Escambray worked to unite the country, to reach out to the humble and marginalized, to make art and culture accessible to all, to educate and *cultivar* (cultivate, make cultured). Cooperation with and adherence to a growing socialist philosophy was a necessary and commendable endeavor for many artists after 1959. In the early years of the Revolution, the idea of "serving the state"— more often referred to as "serving the Revolution"—was not thought to be a shameful act, but rather, admirable, since serving the state at this moment meant serving the nation, the masses, the Cuban population, "the people," and those who had been neglected pre-1959. Dedication to the new government defined the new revolutionary artist.

After 1990, however, many artists attempted to transcend the political realm, even though their existence was dependent upon socialist cultural institutions. Some veered off into the abstract physicality of experimental theater, avoiding the censorship and rigidity of textually based scripting. Another route was to turn to Poetic Fantasy—fantastical and mythical productions, based on traditional fable or legend and focusing on universal moralities (do not kill, do not steal, respect your elders, etc.). Teatro de los Elementos, by its very name, celebrated the primacy of the earth and its natural elements—land, fire, water, and air—attempting to circumvent any political implication with this symbolic move.[10] None of the group believed they were evading politics, but rather, digging underneath it, pushing in front of it, flying over it, or perhaps more precisely, forging ahead in spite of it.

In the twenty-first century, few artists admitted to be directly working in collusion with the state, though many still admitted to being "sympathetic" to its philosophy of the collective and art as socially functional. Teatro Escambray's difficulties in the late 1990s were based on this essential conflict: the group's self-definition in relation to its history. Teatro Escambray's reputation was built on the devotion toward building a new socialist social structure and developing cultural competency in the rural areas. Its focus changed with the times, but theater intellectuals' primary critique in the early 2000s was that Teatro Escambray was no longer committed to the same methods and motives that made it famous. The inherent contradiction in the continuing fame of Teatro Escambray was that it committed to these motives at all. Members of the group were made famous by their dedication to the Revolution and their unique participation in forwarding a national goal to educate campesinos and make their voices heard. Thirty years later Teatro Escambray was criticized for no longer being what it once was, yet at the same time it was indirectly criticized for *being* what it had been—for the very revolutionary commitment that won it national renown. When I asked about this incongruity, Rafael González shook his head and sighed, explaining that Teatro Escambray's critics simply did not understand that any theater group had to grow and change with its environment (interview, Manicaragua, 2000).

In May 2000, the journal *Conjunto* launched issue number 117 at an open event at the Casa de las Américas (House of the Americas) building, located in Havana. This prestigious organization was founded in 1959 by Haydee Santamaría and has been host to many international cultural events. One of its journals, *Conjunto*, was published quarterly (depending on paper availability and funds) and focused on theater and performance in Latin America. The May 2000 issue was dedicated to Teatro Comunitario and included an article I had written about Los Elementos and its interpretive process entitled "Una mirada dentro del trabajo colectivo de Teatro de los Elementos" (A Look at the Collective Work of Theater of the Elements). One of the opening paragraphs of the article discusses the fundamental contrast with Teatro Escambray: "*Aun cuando proveían de un plataforma pública a los anteriormente silenciados campesinos, el Teatro Escambray también representaba directamente los intereses del nuevo Estado cubano al llevar la "cultura" (teatro y otras artes) al interior del país y enseñarle al campesino los valores de la sociedad socialista*" (Frederik 2000: 60–61). (Although providing a public platform to previously voiceless peasants, Teatro Escambray also directly represented the interests of the new Cuban State, bringing culture [theater and other arts] to the countryside and teaching the campesinos the value of a socialist society.) In this article, I explain that all Cuban theater was necessarily political to a certain extent due to the country's centralized system of artistic support, but in the 1990s, José Oriol and his actors claimed to depart from many Cuban theater groups in their focus upon *el hombre* and *la naturaleza* (man and nature) and the profound relationship between the two, asserting that the natural elements of nature preceded, underlay, transcended, and also subsumed any society, cultural identity, and political system. The remaining fourteen pages describe the creative process of the play *Ten mi nombre como un sueño* (Remember my name as if it were a dream), its social investigation, improvisations, play-writing, rehearsals, final product, and audience reception.

Commentary on the issue was given at the Casa de las Américas in May by one of the original founders and continuing members of Teatro Escambray, Carlos Pérez Peña. Starting with the first article of the journal, he began to summarize the content and give brief opinions on each. When he reached my article about Los Elementos he read the title, abruptly looked up at the audience, and then said simply, "I am tired of criticisms about Teatro Escambray and I will say, for the last time, that Teatro Escambray is not, never was, and never will be an official arm of the State." Although the reference to Teatro Escambray is in a single paragraph of a fourteen-page text, it was enough to put Carlos Pérez Peña on the defensive. Accustomed to increasing attacks on the group's current changes, he had interpreted my innocent attempt to contrast early Teatro Nuevo and Teatro Escambray with newer, politically transcendent groups as an attack on the group's historical integrity. I was shocked and dismayed, to say the least, feeling very much like I had put my *extranjera* foot firmly in my mouth and offended an important teatrista. But I was also frustrated that he had interpreted the entire article so dismissively and aggressively. In one of the most-cited books about Cuban theater, Cuban historian Rine Leal begins a chapter on Revolutionary theater and Teatro Escambray by proudly stating, "El Arte es un arma de la Revolucion" (art is a weapon of the Revolution) and explaining that theater is a communicative and dialectic form, important to the transition to a new society (1980:151–52). Many other writings of the time use similar terminology to describe the group in laudatory tones.

After the journal launch event, I confronted Pérez Peña, apologizing and explaining that my intention was never to attack Teatro Escambray, a group I admired and which had inspired my research in Cuba. "I did not mean to imply that it was an official arm, I said, "rather that its artistic goals were in accordance with those originally outlined by the Revolution—goals that were and continue to be commendable." Pérez Peña listened, nodded, and said, "But this journal has been attacking us for years," thereby aligning me with the institution (either the Casa de las Américas itself or the "institution" of writers and critics) and with the apparently antagonistic opinions put forth in its publications. According to Judith Weiss (1977), who wrote on the history of Casa de las Américas and its national politics during the first twenty years of revolutionary society, Pérez-Pena was probably right in assuming the institution's ongoing underlying critique of Teatro Escambray, for she describes this tendency in some detail. Looking back on the writings of Rine Leal, I wondered if my faux pas would have been avoided by using the word Revolution instead of State, or if Revolution was equally imbued and negatively associated with officialdom by the late 1990s.[11]

Those who truly have criticized Teatro Escambray have tended not to consider the changes in political ideology over the past forty years, especially in the last ten. In 1968, participation in revolutionary activities and nation building through cultural education was admired and exalted. Even disenfranchised bourgeois could not hinder, in good conscience, efforts to bring literacy and art to the destitute peasants in the mountains. Although commissioned by Fidel Castro and the revolutionary government to send a particular message, propaganda was not a conscious goal; the stated goal was including otherwise forgotten Cubans in the new egalitarian socialist mix. The actors of Teatro Escambray were not attempting to brainwash or coerce rural peasants, rather to share with them and to learn about their traditions and concerns. It truly was a revolutionary effort and their accomplishments were justly rewarded by the distributor of gifts and resources: the state. However, by the 2000s, following ten years in a "special period," it was no longer admirable to support a crumbling political philosophy, and for an artist to be supportive of the state regime—especially through artistic representation—was a source of embarrassment. Theater critics nostalgically longed for the original Teatro Escambray, just as they longed for a Revolution that had never really achieved its utopian goals; one that was still chanting "hasta la victoria."

Although my *Conjunto* article contrasts the work of Los Elementos as an artistic quest toward la naturaleza and nostalgic remembering of a long lost morality, it quickly became evident that politics was never a separate entity for Los Elementos either, and that socialist education and socialization had infiltrated even the most earnest professions of "nature" and "spirituality." "Man cannot live by bread alone," director José Oriol said and wrote (in interviews and the group's mission statement), in context suggesting that man also needed cultural and spiritual nurturing (through the theater, for example). Meanwhile, actors joked that it was the *Cuban* man who could not live by bread alone, especially during the Special Period, since there was no bread to eat anyway.

Teatro de los Elementos

Teatro de los Elementos worked with the local campesinos, collectively wrote original plays or "devised" them (collaborative created through a variety of techniques), and then brought the finished product to stages in larger cities, such as Cienfuegos, Santa Clara, and Havana. Actors also produced shorter monologues and children's plays, which were performed locally. Their method of social investigation and contact with the community was not novel, as discussed above. But in 1990, José Oriol aspired to reinvigorate Teatro Escambray's model and to refurbish it according to Special Period conditions. The particular socioeconomic context allowed him to stake a claim as one of the originators of a new kind of community theater, one whose intentions were more revolutionary than any artistic movement since 1968. José Oriol proudly told the history of Los Elementos—to reporters, to theater critics, to foreign investigators, to potential contributors—describing it as a tradition that was born with the Special Period—one created in hardship, without resources, when Cuban theater emerged in its purest forms (no frills, actor focused), and with purest intentions (to perform for the people, to share art).

In the economic crisis that began in 1990, Cuban teatristas tried to ideologically distance themselves even further from the supposedly "evil" and "misdirected" capitalist stages—adjectives I heard often during both informal conversations and public intellectual roundtables. Broadway productions toted budgets in the millions of dollars, Cuban directors exclaimed, priding themselves on the fact that they could produce their art for only a few thousand pesos (a few hundred U.S. dollars). Theater directors cut their own, already meager budgets in half, thanks to the *voluntarismo* (extra voluntary work, donating space, resources) of actors and spectators. Once again, theater was to be created for education, community building, and socialist solidarity during one of the most difficult *luchas* of the Revolution.

> *Casi por accidente venimos proponiendo desde principios del decenio, una modalidad de trabajo que es consecuencia inmediata del período especial; pero siempre nos hemos negado a que por ello sea de factura pobre, para "entretener," sino que defendemos el principio de que sea una imagen rica, desbordante de humor y sabiduría, representativa de la mixtura y diversidad de la Nación Cubana y de su*

profundo acervo cultural. [. . .] [Queríamos crear un teatro] por personas que no tienen arraigo ni sentido de pertenencia con la cultura de la región o donde sus principales dirigentes y estrategas no tienen plena conciencia de que no solo de pan vive el hombre. (Mission statement, private files, Teatro de los Elementos)

Almost by accident, from the beginning of the decade we have been proposing a mode of work that was an immediate outgrowth of the Special Period. We always refused to settle for a cheap product, something only to "entertain." Instead, we defend the principle that it must be a rich image, overflowing with humor and wisdom, representative of the mixture and diversity of the Cuban Nation and its profound cultural wealth. [. . .] [We wanted to create a theater] for people who did not have roots or who did not feel like they belonged to the culture of the region, or for people whose principal leaders and strategists did not have a full understanding that man cannot live by bread alone.

José Oriol began by taking several of his students at the ENA (National Art School), looking for a class project, to a marginal neighborhood of Havana, called Romerillo. The actors paraded through the *barrio* (neighborhood) on stilts, dancing, singing, using the patios and houses of the people themselves in the performance. Their unsuspecting and surprised audience quickly warmed and soon began to dance and sing along, thereby deeming the experience successful. Taken away from the daily drudgery of finding food, washing their clothes by hand, cooking long hours over kerosene stoves, waiting for buses in the blistering Caribbean sun, they were transformed, and according to José Oriol, their spiritual sides revivified during a time when personal spirituality was dying out with the stress of the crisis. "Habíamos triunfado" (We had triumphed), he said, we converted this method of street theater into "an artistic event, worthy of consideration and worthy of a name in the archives as a 'new experience' that enriched the history of Cuban theater" (typed history of the Romerillo project, in the private files of Los Elementos). The group continued to work in Romerillo for four months, slowly gaining the trust of community members, working with local children, and getting to know the problems and particular concerns of the locale. They performed for Romerillo musically, acrobatically, in short skits and monologues, always incorporating the particular flavor of the neighborhood, its legends and its personalities, which they accomplished with masks, costuming, and fantastical imagery and metaphor. In January 1992, then minister of culture, Armando Hart Dávalos, attended one of the performances.[12] With his subsequent support, José Oriol and his actors were finally considered "serious" and encouraged to apply to be an official *proyecto* (project), funded by the state and recognized as a professional theater group. Now they were trusted not only by the community, but also by the authority which had the power to either promote or destroy their efforts.

The Ministry of Culture officially approved the new proyecto in 1992, and the group traveled to Isla de la Juventud (Island of Youth), a small island off the southwest coast of Cuba, categorized as a "Special Province." Using the Romerillo model, they stayed in the small coastal town of Jacksonville for four months. The inhabitants of this area, also known as "Cocodrilo," were originally immigrants from the Cayman Islands and Jamaica. English, albeit broken, was still spoken by the older generation. Jacksonville was founded sometime between 1903 and 1910. Initially, the community did not trust the group of actors and kept their distance, but with time, and with the actors' participation in daily activities (fishing, working the land, children's workshops, performances), they were accepted and incorporated into the quiet rhythm of the pueblo. Social issues—such as alcoholism, marital infidelity, poverty, lack of respect for elders and local history, lack of motivation, and general discontent—all made their way into the group's monologues and skits. Foremost in the minds of the actors was the need to "save the history and identity" of the people in Jacksonville, who were, according to members of the group, forgetting who they were, who they had been (interview with Isnoel, Cumanayagua, December 1999). Another cultural rescue mission was carried out in a region called Barrancas in Santiago de Cuba Province. Haitian immigrants lived in high numbers in this area, speaking both Creole and Spanish. It was a very poor community, and often misunderstood by other area residents, due to the difference in ethnic, cultural, and linguistic identity. Los Elementos arrived, and after a period of local interviews and research, re-created the mythical story of the resurrection of a Haitian god (Mackandal), using the entire Haitian-Cuban community to help enact the play. François Mackandal was a voodoo priest from Guinea who became a famous runaway slave in Haiti. At night, he would burn plantations and kill their owners, and historical accounts claim that he and his followers poisoned and killed close to 6,000 whites. In 1758, the French captured him and intended to publicly execute him. However, Mackandal's followers believed that he had special powers and was invulnerable, and the myth was that he escaped from the flames. According to actors in Los Elementos, the story was empowering for the Haitian community, since it inspired them to be strong in the face of discrimination and prejudice.

After several months had passed and the initial experience had come to an end, two Barrancas residents decided to permanently join the group. Juan Bautista Castillo ("Nego") joined to become a professional actor, and a young Cuban-Haitian boy, Adoney, was adopted as a son by the director, José Oriol. Both returned with Los Elementos to Cumanayagua. In many of the group's memoirs and statements, this assimilation of two members of communities the group had focused on became a point of pride, high-lighted in public relations, and proof of its social efficacy and community commitment. When I last visited Cuba in 2009, Nego had his own house on the El Jovero farm and still performed with the group, and Adoney was a full-grown man, still living with José Oriol in Cumanayagua.

During the 1990s, Teatro de los Elementos prided itself on its ability to make theater in a time of extreme scarcity. The group was proud to infuse a new "spirituality" (beauty and poetics) and a new sense of cultural identity into a tired nation. The members discussed the disposi-tion of the group as collective, one in which members worked together, without hierarchy, each with equal power and voice, just like Teatro Escambray had claimed to do at its inception. Yes, José Oriol was the director, they explained to me when I first arrived in Cumanayagua, but he was only a figurehead, a public face. Their return to *la naturaleza* was adopted out of necessity. In the absence of the technology that theater groups typically depend upon, they developed a working philosophy based on a nostalgic yearning for living off the earth, and of the noble savage (or noble campesino in this case). They performed in outside spaces, in forest clearings, on the rocky ocean banks, on grassy hills, and on front porches of the bohíos of the campesinos. They spoke of the purity of the Cuban soul as uncontaminated by the outside world, by its urbanity and banality. Like Wordsworth above (1798, in Williams 1973), Los Elementos considered nature and the Cuban countryside as "the anchor of [its] purest thoughts, the nurse, the guide, the guardian of [its] heart and soul, of all [its] moral being." The performed aesthetic of Los Elementos was dreamlike, falling squarely into the representational cate-gory of Poetic Fantasy. Productions were fantastical, beautiful, highly poetic, and intellectual. Its vision of history and nostalgia for the campe-sino was manifested in something relatively *un*-real on the ground, but very real in the Cuban imagination.

Reviving the Noble Campesino

Teatro de los Elementos was one of the first artistic groups to take the image of the noble campesino back to intellectual roundtable discussions in Havana. Although the campesino as national symbol was certainly nothing new in Cuba, the reasons for its revival, and the way in which that was accomplished were distinctive—symbolic of the *pura cepa* of Cuba and of the purity of the proper socialist morality. In other words, the revival of the campesino's image served to combat the contamination of capitalism, materialism, and individualism, and to serve as a rallying point around which twenty-first century Cuban identity could be focused. The group's initial introduction of the image was relatively innocent: when a group works in the countryside and calls itself "communitarian theater," the local subjects are, in fact, campesinos. Thus, there was nothing mysterious or unusual, or particularly revolutionary about the group's subject matter. As part of the creative process, the questioning of national identity and the role of these rural subjects came to the fore, and were decidedly "theatrical"—a necessary part of play-making. The first community Los Elementos worked with in Jacksonville had a discernible "lack of community identity" according to José Oriol and the actors. They felt that the high levels of unemployment, alcoholism, and despondency were indicators. Once this issue was identified and characterized in a single region, the disposition of ideological confusion and lack of social solidarity seemed to exist all over the country. But neither marginalized urbanites nor Haitian descendants won the hearts of Havana intellectuals. It was the campesino who was victorious.

Images of the guajiro cartoons of poor and humble Liborio, and the ever-intrepid revolutionary fighter, Elpidio Valdés were retrieved and latched onto with enthusiasm and sentiment. Liborio the guajiro was a popular cartoon character of the early 1900s, created by Ricardo de la Torriente for a newspaper called *La Discusión*. Liborio was a symbol of the *pueblo* (the nation, the people), who has most recently appeared in Cuban political cartoons outside of Cuba by anti-Castro artists (see figures 1 and 2). Elpidio Valdés was and continues to be a well-known cartoon—a mambí fighter for independence against Spain, created by Juan Padrón in 1974. Both figures were rural campesinos; although Liborio was often used as the weak, barefoot guajiro, the hapless but innocent victim, while Elpidio Valdés symbolized unselfish heroism, strength, patriotism, and noble morality.

1. Liborio the guajiro, classic drawn image by Ricardo de la Torriente, 1920s

(below) 2. Liborio cartoon with Fidel Castro, by the cartoonist Alfredo Pong, 1991 (Fidel Castro: "Listen, Liborio, remember that . . . the future belongs to socialism!" Liborio: "No!" or "Shit!" The "ño" and the "enye" accent over the "n" is a shortened and slang version of the Spanish curse word, "coño.")

Because of professional and personal links to the capital's newspapers and cultural roundtables, Los Elementos' work was increasingly discussed and became an important point of artistic and intellectual contact between the rural and urban imaginaries of the 1990s (which explains why so many people recommended Los Elementos to me as the most authentic). In 1999, José Oriol and the actor Lexis Pérez Hernández cowrote a theoretical essay on the work of Los Elementos, which was intended, in part, to attract the monetary support of an international ecological organization. The essay was presented at a large conference called Cultura y Desarrollo (Culture and Development)—an important occasion, during which Fidel Castro appeared at the close and gave one of his trademark eight-hour speeches. In the course of composing this presentation—a process they took very seriously and that lasted over a month—Teatro de Los Elementos as a group was transformed from rural artist to urban "intellectual" as it gained the ability to reflect on and be reflexive about its place within national cultural politics. They were conscious of this shift, and proud of it, and Cultural y Desarrollo became the start of many other appearances in the capital in which they were given an official stage to represent the rural viewpoint. Rescuing the image of the noble campesino, of Liborio and Elpidio, became the rallying cry of many of the rural artists, one topic about which they had more authoritative voice than their urban colleagues.

This chapter has outlined the situation of artists, specifically theater people in the countryside during the Special Period and the difficulties they were facing in the 1990s and early 2000s. The next chapter will narrate the process of the rediscovery of the noble campesino and his (not her) place in cubanía—how the synthesis of political context, social history, socialist ideology, and creative imagining happens over time and in stages.

3

CREATIVE PROCESS AND
PLAY MAKING IN CUMANAYAGUA
or, waiting for Atilio on the side of a country road

So you see, imagination needs moodling—
long, inefficient, happy idling, dawdling and puttering.
—BRENDA UELAND, *If You Want to Write* (1938)

Estragon: *(giving up again)*. Nothing to be done.
Vladimir: I'm beginning to come round to that opinion. All my life I've tried to
    put it from me, saying, Vladimir, be reasonable, you haven't tried everything.
    And I resumed the struggle. *(He broods, musing on the struggle.)*
—SAMUEL BECKETT, *Waiting for Godot* (1956)

Anyone who has attempted to paint, compose, choreograph, or write has experienced long frustrating moments of "moodling," "dawdling and puttering." And if such moodling goes on long enough, as happens to Beckett's character Estragon, we feel like giving up, blocked. Artists in Cuba have the luxury of being paid while they moodle, but the frustration is felt just as deeply as an artist who must survive on her own dime. What is it about the creative process that inspires us to continue, even when it seems the creative spark and ultimate actualization will never arrive? I first began to analyze this process in Cumanayagua with Teatro de los Elementos, this time as an ethnographic participant observer instead of moodling artist. But as I accompanied them in their quest to develop a new play, I became entrenched in the same angst that permeated the individuals in the group. Although not beholden to produce or perish (as much) in a socialist system, there was an inherent sense in every artist that a work of art should ultimately be created, lest the lack of productive success threaten their identity as "artist."

Integral to an analysis of theater creation and contemporary political consciousness is a discussion of creativity and the creative process. The skills required in the creative process of art making, or play making in this case, are developed toward a distinct goal, which is to form an aesthetic or intellectually stimulating artistic and cultural product; one which will be viewed and interpreted by other people, one which will inevitably be assessed or judged by a cultural authority, and one which may determine the livelihood, reputation, and social status of its maker. The ultimate product will also reflect, it is believed, a measurable talent and artistic ability. Such processes have been theorized by some social scientists in terms of liminal and liminoid (Turner 1969, 1974, 1982), emergence and generation (Barber 2000; Bauman 1984 [1975]; Wagner 1981), the movement of metaphor (Fernandez 1972, 1974), and virtuosity (Royce Peterson 2004). Karen Barber's fascinating 500-page book, *The Generation of Plays: Yoruba Popular Life in Theater*, set in Nigeria, is the closest I have found to a comparable academic description of the fully detailed play-making experience observed in Cuba, though it is far from the only comparison in practice. To comprehensively document such intricate processes requires long texts, yet theater (especially devised theater), is best experienced live, in the moment and in three-dimensional space—for both actors and audience. Theater people and other artists strive for creativity and reflect upon the creative process for a living: their memoirs are usually accompanied by adjectives such as new, experimental, alternative, cutting-edge, avant-garde, radical, nontraditional, unconventional, and postmodern.

There has also been no shortage of popular theories on the mechanisms leading to creativity. Psychologists, motivational speakers, educators, business people, and even athletes have all tried to find the definitive key to increased innovation and production and better performance. While all of these theories are intriguing and helpful in understanding the process, I often missed the human element in the explanation. Perhaps it is because an actual creative process is often so long, complicated, and personal that the case studies are not representational. Yet due to the very nature of its existence—the mysterious impetus that seems to spontaneously appear in a single burst of insight to create that something extra or extraordinary—it may be futile to attempt to ever explain it definitively. One Cuban actor told me that the very act of scientifically pinning down the creativity and improvisation leading to artistic innovation would, in fact, destroy the "magic." Perhaps, like a unicorn, the magic is contained in the mystery and rarity, its power deadened when the horn is cut off for dissection. While there may be too many variables in every instance of creativity to devise a model that works for each distinct situation, the more general the steps, the more exceptions and variations can be inserted into the framework.

I was intrigued by the creative mechanisms through which a group of Cuban artists was able to collectively summon ideas, images, and characters and create a meaningful and theatrically presentable story in spite of months of logistical setbacks and uncertainty, and months of waiting for ideal creative conditions. The meaning that the artists hoped the performance would deliver and the general understanding of Los Elementos' motivations differed from the individual stories of each member. My time with Los Elementos provided a grassroots look at the process of creation and the inherent obstacles associated with collective work in Special Period and socialist Cuba, as well as audience reactions to the final play presented in both rural and urban settings—flash interpretations of the performed play by those who had not experienced the process of its making. Questionnaires queried how theatergoers felt the play related to their own lives, to Cuba, and to their sense of national identity, providing a glimpse at the gap between creator and receptor, and an analysis of the space—by no means empty—underlying the artistic phenomenon.

The creative process I witnessed and participated in while living in Cumanayagua with Teatro de los Elementos (February 1999 to February 2000) was lengthy and reflexive, clearly illustrating the steps through which creative production passed, the internal tensions of the members of a Cuban theater collective as well as the political games which were played with state officialdom along the way. It was an example of how a story was conceived, written, and then told back to the original storytellers (*campesinos*) and the broader, theatergoing Cuban public (urban and rural intellectuals and regular folk). Real-life events were interpreted and made "theatrical" during the creative process. Facts were poeticized. Emergent metaphors and symbols entered the political dialogue and were fed back into the national narrative.

A Model of Creativity and How It Fits

In 1926 Graham Wallis devised a cognitive model of creativity, a set of four general phases that was later built upon by a long line of psychologists and other scholars: preparation, incubation, illumination, and verification (sometimes an additional phase is included after incubation called "intimation": making personal and familiar). This model was helpful to me in organizing the process of creative production as it happened in Cumanayagua since it was so general, and thus exceptions and particular Cuban elements could be easily inserted into the flow.

In Wallis's first phase, "Preparation," the problem, need, or desire is defined; information is gathered; and criteria are set up. Cuban theater groups "needed" and "desired" to create new performances to remain viable professional cultural workers. Information was gathered through investigation. Whether such investigation was literary or social depended on the basic theme to be addressed and the theater group's style. Criteria in Cuba were defined by lines of self-censorship drawn after years of experience by professional artists in the socialist system. Lines were also drawn by direct censorship of the supervising cultural officials in the National Theater Board, by professional theater critics, and by the operative artistic and political philosophy of the group. Since Teatro de los Elementos was a rural theater group that aspired to contribute to its local community, "preparation" included taking into account the concerns of the area residents, as well as building upon an artistic repertoire that emphasized the "elements" of nature and the human being, ideally transcendent of politics.

Phase 2 for Wallis is "Incubation," where the mind is left to contemplate (merge, mix, and reinvent), and where "moodling" and "puttering" are necessary parts of the process. To create a play, an artist must think up a new idea or theme. A broad theme must be condensed and clarified; made specific; assigned a particular imaginary, a general storyline, and an underlying conflict or polemic. This phase may take minutes, weeks, or even years. Conditions may change during the Incubation period, thus causing an idea to fluctuate, turn back on itself, or even be canceled out. In socialist Cuba, artists rarely had iron-clad performance deadlines, and therefore this period was open ended and flexible, contrasting with capitalist countries where artists were often forced to adhere to demands of sponsors, producers, or fulfill contracts with particular stages or spaces. The length of the Incubation phase in Cuba seemed to be affected only by an upcoming festival in which the group wished to present a play, or an invitation to perform in another province (exceptionally motivating if the invitation was from Havana), or if the group had not reported any creative output for six months to a year and was under official pressure to increase its annual number of *funciones*, including plays, shorter theatrical performances, or *unipersonales* (one-actor shows or monologues).

None of the professional actors or Consejo members I talked to were able to tell me the official number of expected *funciones* in a specified period of time, although there was definite pressure to produce new *obras* (works) on a consistent basis. Theater groups were required to send monthly updates of their work to their local Consejo, to explain what stage they were at in the creative process, and if there were any special circumstances hindering their progress. Alexis Abreu, program director of the National Theater Board in 1999, admitted that the reputation and status of the group and director made a difference in expectations and that more prominent groups were given more slack when obstacles arose. Teatro de los Elementos had little production from approximately September 1997 to May 1998, due in part to the death of José Oriol's mother, an illness of his own, and several of his actors taking leave from the group to do individual projects or collaborations with other companies. When the group finally attempted to begin a new play in spring of 1998, the assigned playwright, Atilio Caballero, was also delayed by illness and a family death. State support for Los Elementos did not waver during this time, though by February of 1998, José Oriol was openly concerned about the length of the group's creative hiatus.

The third phase in Wallis's framework is "Illumination," wherein ideas suddenly arise in the mind. This phase provides the basis of a "creative" response and subsequent acceleration of the development process. Such ideas may emerge in pieces, or as an entire concept. The Illumination phase is often very brief, and is designated by a "rush of insights" within just a few minutes or hours. At this point, the designated conflict or polemic for a play and its characters come together, with the artist able to envision exactly how the performance will appear when completed. There is acceleration in the creative process, and the "product" is quickly produced during and immediately following this phase. This moment of illumination for Los Elementos was, indeed, swift and lasted only a single moment, a moment I was present for, although the incubation had been building up to that moment for many months previous. The story of Los Elementos' illumination—one of my favorite parts of the process—is told later in the chapter.

Wallis names the last phase "Verification," which is when one must demonstrate whether or not what emerged in Illumination has filled the need and criteria designated in Preparation. This phase was important in Cuba, where individual and group need and desire had to be coordinated with state criteria. Without official approval, the play could not be shown and months of hard work would be lost. The Verification phase was easier for older, established groups that had years of experience in the system—their bursts of creative illumination already controlled by a deeply embedded political consciousness and system of self-censorship. Critique by the theater world, and the artistic and intellectual sphere in general was also very important, even when actors appeared to brush it off as a marginal concern. In a small country such as Cuba, a centralized core of artists and intellectuals in Havana held a great deal of national power; therefore, rural groups in outlying provinces were under pressure to "live up" to the standards of those in the cities, especially the capital. Favorable receptions suggested potential regional and national awards, which in turn provided the much-sought-after cultural authority and bureaucratic leverage (see Verdery 1991, 1996). Artists under socialism did not require mass audiences for survival. What they needed was the positive attention of cultural officials to fund and promote their projects (ibid.:94). Or more aptly put: "In socialism, the point was not the profit but the relationship between thirsty persons and the one with the lemonade" (Verdery 1996:25). Verification came when the artistic work was judged to be useful and concerned with the good of the nation (cf. Castro [1961] 1980; Haraszti 1987; Verdery 1991).

To be functional in real life, Wallis's model must be mapped onto a more social scientific analysis of creativity. Certainly motivation and Preparation are affected by the social upbringing and sociopolitical situation of the thinker and artist. What is experienced in the minutes, weeks, or years of Incubation also influences the outcome. In the 1990s, the majority of living and working artists in Cuba had grown up and been trained within a socialist system and under the political philosophy of Fidel Castro. Their creative vision had been developed largely within

Miklós Haraszti's Velvet Prison, a vision that may have "incubated" for many months on the state's nickel, but also one where creativity was directed by the knowledge that crossing certain lines could cost them personal freedom and jobs.

James Fernandez (1986) refers to the movement of creative imagery through metaphor: metaphors performed as strategies, as organizing principles of social classification, as models, linking domains of experience and operating upon a continuum. He shows how the creation of metaphors has "performative consequence" and converts ideas to action (e.g., in Cuba, guerrilla fighting and revolution metaphors moving into everyday life struggles). Creativity in this sense acts in the building of new associations, new metaphoric references, which then act in society in real ways (Fernandez 1986:20–25). For example, symbols and metaphors of the Cuban Revolution are distinct and thus shape creativity. Cuba's metaphors are based on both the "shape" of experience—which James Fernandez calls "structural metaphors"—and the "feelings" of experience—resulting in "textual metaphors" (Fernandez 1974:120). The younger generation, born post-1959, who never had direct experience with fighting, is more likely to be guided by (whether complying with or attempting to break free of) structural metaphors. The older generation, born pre-1959, who remember the revolutionary context or who actually fought alongside the rebels, had personal experience with the sign-images on which the metaphors were first predicated. When they think with or use these textual metaphors, they are guided by real feelings from lived histories.[1] Performative consequences are evident in both Cuban cultural ideology and in artistic creation.

Creative thought requires convergences and divergences, elaboration, syncretic and analytic thinking, practical ability, awareness, and also persistence. It also necessarily involves remaining within a state of the incomplete, the unknown, and the unpredictable for an undetermined period of time. In short, it requires *waiting* along with an ability to be comfortable in a state of relative chaos—a condition that most Cubans were very familiar with and accustomed to in their daily lives, whether creative and quotidian. Creative process is movement and flux, transition and instability, liminality (or in the theatrical case, Victor Turner would say *liminoid*), which in turn causes uncertainty and stress, but also *comunitas* (Turner 1969, 1974, 1982; see also Schechner 1985, 1988 on the rehearsal process). The challenges inherent in such a state of being were evident during play making in Cumanayagua, and this situation of be-twixt and between emerged as a central metaphor for the entirety of Cuba's then social reality.

Victor Turner discusses "process" in terms of ritual action and social drama, and it is here that social context and cultural specificity become determining factors in the uniqueness of any creative endeavor. Society, says Turner, is dictated by a community's social rules and traditions, and is represented through metaphors and ritual symbols; therefore, any consequent action will be based on such. As residents of a small island in the Caribbean organized under a socialist philosophy for over fifty years, and as overwhelmingly Spanish speakers, they had a distinct history and set of cultural and religious traditions, hence a distinct set of popularly understood metaphors and symbols. Artists were subject to censorship, as well as salaried by the state. When these factors combined with a constant pressure to be talented and creative (as good artists are) and with the need to work collectively (as theatrical artists do), new layers of creative process must be acknowledged.

Being creative in Cuba was a simpler process when only one individual was involved. Independent generation of an idea could be more chal-lenging at first, but the artistic product followed the desires of a single mind—the only definitive guideline looming over the individual being Fidel Castro's famous words to the intellectuals: "Within the Revolution, everything. Against it, nothing." A Cuban artist had to be creative and "revolutionary," never directly uttering "down with Fidel and the social-ist government," but beyond that, the artist was relatively free to make art as desired. In a group situation, however, various artistic minds worked together and come to an agreement on how their chosen images, sym-bols, and metaphors were to be arranged and what they would mean in combination. This was especially true for groups such as Teatro de los Elementos that "devised" or collectively collaborated to create original plays instead of using an already written script.[2] Each of the seven artists in Los Elementos was distinct in demeanor, personal history, political belief, and creative specialty.

Isnoel, an Elementos actor, was a member of the Communist Party and served as the secretary for the *Unión de Jóvenes Comunistas* (UJC, Union of Young Communists) in Cumanayagua. He was quiet, gentle, and intro-spective, with thick eyeglasses and wavy long black hair held back in a ponytail. He wrote poetry, loved to read and play the guitar, and worshiped the beauty of the surrounding mountains. Isnoel became an important informant and good friend during my entire stay in Cuba, despite our unlikely national affinities and political ideologies. While loyal to Fidel and the Revolution and a Communist Party member, he enjoyed good intellectual debates, which were frequent events both in private and amongst the entire theater group, usually with a bottle of street vendor rum passed around the circle in a gesture of collective goodwill (and usually the goodwill was preserved, even when debates became political and heated). On the other hand, my second apartment-mate, Lexis, was outgoing, talkative and quick witted, eager to be the center of attention and to make his audiences laugh. Tall, lean, and clean-cut handsome, his imitations of Fidel Castro were hauntingly accurate and never failed to send the group into belly-holding hysterics (but to my dismay, I was always asked to please turn off my video camera during these performances). Lexis had graduated from the University of Havana with a degree in art history and was often called upon by José Oriol to help with press statements, conference papers, and theorizing the mission statements of the group. Another actor, Héctor, was also a poet, a shorter, catlike man with shoulder-length curly hair. He was the shaman of the group, the mystic, the percussionist. He lived in an old wooden house with his family on the central *prado* (public walk, main strip) of Cumanayagua. Kirenia was the only woman in the group and the youngest at age eighteen. Beautiful and willful, a trained dancer, she smiled wherever she went, but was often resentful of the treatment she received from the male-dominated core of actors in the group. She was a talented actress and had one of the most charismatic stage presences. Freddy was the oldest actor, at age forty, married (but separated) with two children. Tall and bulky, Freddy originally joined the group as a producer and then was recruited into acting when the play required more characters. Freddy repeatedly told me he saw himself more as a working man than as an artist (he was also a Communist Party member), but Freddy grew and changed throughout the year I lived in Cumanayagua, slowly finding his creative rhythm and self-confidence on stage. Lolo, like the other actors, was in his late twenties, but acted as if he were many years older and was the official curmudgeon of the group. Often grumpy, he only grudgingly smiled and grunted when one of the actors was periodically able to break through his pessimism. He was an observer, sitting, brooding, and I often found him sitting beside me. Without comment, he occasionally nudged me with eyebrows raised to see if I had understood the rapid Spanish conversation shooting in every direction around me, ensuring that I had heard the most interesting or most polemic parts. Finally Joel—tall, lanky, and unpredictable—was a trained clown and juggler, and continually begged me to give him tap-dancing lessons. He seemed impatient with the rigors of working in a group but was unable to branch out on his own. Longing to make connections abroad and not at all interested in producing a play about local campesinos, Joel left the process halfway through and went to Havana to try his luck. Another official member, Nego, the actor adopted into the group along with little Adoney, boasted Haitian roots and was a mostly silent yet powerful force in the group. Dark skinned with dreadlocks, he was a talented drummer and was becoming increasingly invited to perform in Havana and abroad. During my stay in Cumanayagua, Nego floated in and out of the artistic circle, his participation frequently interrupted by trips to the city and elsewhere.

In the end, this group of artists succeeded in creating one collective work of art, but the individual understandings of its significance differed. José Oriol's personal history, those of the actors who joined his theater collective, and their aggregate experiences in the first several years as an officially recognized theater group in Cuba's Special Period were to provide a unique backdrop upon which a new play would be produced, a play which demonstrated incredible complexity of interpretation on every level—the actors, their characters, the story, what it represented, what it communicated, and the variation in audience reception.

The Structure of Play Making

ACT I
A country road. A tree.
Evening.
—SAMUEL BECKETT (1956), *Waiting for Godot*

In February 1999, Teatro de los Elementos decided to produce a new play. The planned process of creation was to be unlike the conventional Western theater formula. Normally, a theater company or director will decide on a written text by an independent writer who works outside of the group. Even if the text has been written by the group's director or an inside playwright, the work is still presented at the onset as a finished narrative, to be learned, memorized, and performed. From the beginning, all participants know the characters, what the central conflict and storyline are, and how the play ends. After roles are auditioned or assigned, the chosen cast begins directly by rehearsing lines and staging. If the play is a musical, performers will receive a score and learn the music simultaneously. As rehearsals progress, performers may discuss what a particular line might mean, and the director will announce how it could or should be projected. New adaptations of a play may reinterpret it extensively, but they are still based on a preexisting script. The Preparation, Incubation, Illumination, and to a certain extent, even Verification phases have been completed before the introduction of actors and director to the new theatrical project. "Interpretation" and "Adaptation" phases might also be added to the creative process, inserted either before or instead of Illumination (in conventional theater) or before Verification (potentially in all theater), but only if the group decides to change the preestablished play in some way, to experiment with it, or to modify it to suit their own particular historical and social reality. And in places like Cuba, a separate "Censorship" phase may also precede Verification, regardless of conventional or experimental style. As actors continue to learn their lines, the director begins to "block" or spatially design movement sequences in the scene.[3] The play takes shape rapidly, since its content and structure are already known. Therefore, in this type of production scheme, a play can be rehearsed, perfected, and presented in less than a month. There is always a timeline, deadline, and set performance dates. The theater space must be reserved, promotional posters tacked to walls, and tickets sold.

Obviously, many productions are exceptions to this process, but when the company has a set script, the variations will be taken from this fundamental structure. This description of the process of theatrical creation refers to professional groups in general. Amateur productions usually take longer, around three months, since cast members work or go to school during the day and rehearse for only several hours in the evenings. For them, theater is just a hobby. In Cuba, the amateur process was also elongated because there was no real pressure to finish the work quickly. Plays were usually of a smaller scale and performances held in schools or Casas de Cultura. There was no amateur community theater movement as existed in the United States (see Cohen-Cruz 2005, 2006). Teatro Comunitario in Cuba referred to professional and full-time "communitarian" theater that worked specifically for local, marginal, or rural populations.

The creative work of Teatro de los Elementos differed from most conventional groups in Cuba because its plays (at least up until 2003) were often produced collectively through a process of social investigation, improvisation, interpretation, and experimentation, and with the input and energy of the actors, director, and *asesores* (consultants). This collective and investigative approach to play making was used by Teatro Escambray and has been used around the world, especially since the 1960s with socially conscious communitarian or activist groups (see de Costa 1992). Teatro de los Elementos used ideas, themes, and conflicts, selected through a series of discussions. Physical images and music were inspired and developed through group improvisations, often including live musicians, and portions of the text were initially introduced by individual actors—from their own personal repertoires. Teatro de los Elementos utilized a combination of different textual sources—including classic dramatic literature, poetry, fiction, mythology, and original writing— each participant adding different segments from various sources in order to construct a whole. Creating a play using this technique required more than a single month. Depending on the proposed content of the play, its complexity, and the tangibility of the initial ideas, collective original productions sometimes required six months or more, creative "emergence" an often slow and undetectable occurrence until looking back at the steps retrospectively (cf. Barber 2000; Bauman 1984; Hallam and Ingold 2008).

This process was complicated to an even greater extent in the group's most recent play *Ten mi nombre como un sueño* (Remember my name, as if it were a dream), for several reasons. The first reason was that the investigation required several trips farther up into the mountains. *Ten mi nombre como un sueño* represented the culture of Cuban campesinos. In order to effectively understand this type of lifestyle, the group decided it was important to carry out interviews and to experience firsthand *la tierra* (the earth, land) in which the *campesinos de verdad* (true campesinos) lived. In Cuba, transport was a significant hindrance to any project, a hundred times more difficult in the countryside. Thus, going *más allá* (farther out) to interview real campesinos made the group's Preparation and Incubation phases dependent on luck and opportunity—in other words, on how many open-bed trucks with space for ten artists to ride aboard *en botella* (hitchhiking) would happen to pass by on the days we planned to travel.

Another challenge in this process was its method of playwriting. The dramatic structure—its beginning, climax, and conclusion—was *unknown* at the start of the process and was only envisioned as the scenes were put together, the unifying of parts slowly revealing the shape of the whole. Included in this challenge was the fact that the entire group (actors, director, *asesor*, anthropologist, and invited author) was to participate in this investigation and was to collectively assemble the play's pieces. Although this kind of collective approach inevitably contributed to differences of opinion and thus potential setbacks in the process, it also ensured an incredible artistic richness and personal commitment to the play being created. The cover of the finished script announced that the author of the play was Atilio Caballero, which was true in a formal sense, since he physically put words and ideas to paper. But when one thinks of an author, one typically summons the image of a solitary man or woman, locked up in a room behind a typewriter (nowadays computer), writing a play that emanates from the depths of his or her own imagination and experience. Atilio was certainly the collector and organizer of the text and the creator of the scene structure—filling in the gaps and adding a bit of his own poetic and narrative style. However, it was the entire group and "the process" which, in fact, "wrote" the play: it emanated from the synthesis of the diverse experiences of the group. I arrived in Cumanayagua at the very beginning of this process of creation, when the group was just beginning to conceptualize its new play, before there was a script, sets, characters, or even a designated idea or conflict. And the author was not to arrive for two more months.

Searching for Real Campesinos: Phase 1. Preparation

The process began with the discussion of three possible themes. Each theme revolved around the campesinos of Cuba and their way of life, as well as the importance of memory and history to one's cultural identity. Members of the Los Elementos talked about what kind of play they wanted and how to go about doing it. I joined this meeting, excited to formally begin the play-making process, which in my mind, also ritually marked the beginning of my formal fieldwork. We sat on white plastic chairs, arranged in a circle at the Casa de Cultura in Cumanayagua. This was the only room in the building with an air conditioner, and the group arrived off the street one by one with a relieved sigh upon entering. I was new to the group, so I sat next to my new apartment mates, Isnoel and Lexis. Before addressing thematic options, José Oriol asked the group to respond to three questions: "What do you want?" "What do you need?" and "What do you expect?" Although these were very general questions, the first nascent roots of the play emerged with the answers. They wanted something aesthetically beautiful, the use of myths or legends, and social polemics to drive the storyline. Isnoel, the group's most devoted *militante* (militant, Communist Party member), specifically wanted polemics with "an underlying revolutionary position." Most in the group agreed that they wanted to represent a conflict involving the relationship of the pre-revolutionary countryside and its present situation, and also, "something discussing our existence." What the actors and director needed was to "feel" and experience *el campo* and la tierra and to create a play with meaning for both the group and for the local campesinos. They also said they needed to develop a solid text. Finally, what they expected was a play that showed campesino culture, one that shed light on the "errors of the past," and one with a serious social theme concerning Cuban culture at the end of the twentieth century (group meeting, February 1999).

For the next several months, the group held ongoing theoretical discussions about campesino identity and the implications of the word *campesino*. They debated whether the word should be politically or culturally defined and how campesino identity differed from that of a *guajiro*. After listening to these discussions, I concluded that the Cuban *guajiro* could be translated into English and U.S. culture as "hillbilly." It denoted a campesino that was more isolated and more "primitive" than others. The guajiro was poorer and spoke with a stronger accent of el campo. Neither *guajiro* nor *campesino* could be accurately translated as "peasant" in Cuba (by Cubans) after 1959, since agricultural workers were no longer subsistence farmers and were not employed by large landowners (cf. Wolf 1966, 1969). And of course, official rhetoric claimed that peasantry had been eradicated with the Revolution and with socialist reform. The actors backed this up, explaining to me that rural people were now all campesinos, and that the word *guajiro* was no longer a true descriptive, just used occasionally out of habit. Héctor felt that *campesino* could be described as a philosophy of life and something that came from within. This quality was not part of a social class per se, but existed as an inherent attitude. The modern identity of the campesino was compared with modern-day *jovenes* (young people, teenager to thirty) in Cuba, the "good" and "noble" values of campesino tradition contrasted with the "contamination" of the youth—their use of and desire for U.S. dollars, relationships with foreigners, materialism, and resistance to what they considered old-fashioned socialist ideology.

Several members of the group felt that there were no more real campesinos; no more "noble" and iconic rural folk who existed in the past, and that their existence as a social class had disappeared as well. They also deliberated the existence of the *memoria campesina* (national memory of campesino life). José Oriol argued that it had been lost, while others insisted that it still abided within the consciousness of all Cubans. Lexis believed that *campesino* was more of an idea than an actual type of person, for the real campesino always lived más allá or *más profundo* (deeper) in el campo. Lexis claimed that there would always be a model of the campesino that differed from reality. Héctor disagreed and reasoned that many Cubans, including his uncle, still called themselves campesinos and, therefore, the campesino still existed—identity claimed and proven though the power of the self-identifying statement "I am." Questions concerning the definition of this term included: "Did campesinos have to work the land or could they just live on it?" "Did they have to have animals?" "Were people who went to *shopping* stores still campesinos?" "Could real campesinos have *cafeteras* (metal percolating-style coffee makers)?" Cafeteras were set over gas or fire. No electricity was necessarily required to use a cafetera, just a small focused flame, but the heat had to be even and consistent for it to be successful. A cafetera would not balance on a typical campesino stove, which consisted of two slabs of cement or stone with a lengthwise gap in the middle to burn wood for cooking. In this context, cafeteras were seen as a sign of higher technology. Campesinos living in very isolated areas traditionally made coffee by running hot water through a homemade cloth filter, having first harvested the coffee beans from their fields, broken open the coffee beans by hand, roasted them over fire, and then ground them in a hand mill. Usually, such grounds were not fine enough for use in a metal cafetera bought in a store. Just watching this laborious process awed and exhausted me, and drinking the resultant coffee became a much more sacred ritual (see figure 3). I participated in the conversations about why a skill set that allowed campesinos to reap and fully process coffee from the land actually meant they were more primitive. What on earth would urban Cubans (or North Americans) do without a metal cafetera and store-bought (or rationed) ready-to-brew coffee grounds?

In the midst of these discussions, three potential themes emerged. The first theme addressed the social conflicts of the *nuevo campesino* (new farmer, and interestingly the artists said *nuevo campesino* instead of the usual and more grammatically correct, *campesino nuevo*). Lifelong resident campesinos told us that the nuevo campesino identity was confused, that it did not reflect that of the *campesino de verdad*. After the Revolution, many of the campesinos in the Escambray Mountain region were relocated and sent to work in the pueblos surrounding the mountains, soon becoming *obreros* (workers) instead of campesinos. Years later, when the state began repopulating the rural areas with descendants of these *campesino-obrero* mixes, a new type of culture began to develop. The earlier, "real" campesinos had been inherently linked to la tierra; they were born on it, and their lives centered and depended upon the land. However, the nuevo campesino had lived in cities for most of his life, only later moving to the countryside as an adult. These individuals aroused

3. Campesino crushing coffee beans, Escambray Mountains (photo by Laurie Frederik, 1999)

suspicion, for rural residents believed that they could not be trusted, that they were only after money, that they had brought corrupt city ways into the countryside. A play following this thematic would have portrayed a "pure" campesino in contrast with a new or "contaminated" campesino, and represented the social conflict through the relationship of these two characters. Although this theme was not ultimately chosen, the character made its way into the play as a "rogue" guajiro, not even politically upgraded to the more revolutionary terminology of "campesino":

> Guajiro Pícaro: *¿Ya usted cobró, señora? ¿No? Pues apúrese, que se acaba el dinero. ¡Dinero!*[4]

> Rogue Hillbilly: Have you cashed in on your property yet ma'am? No? Well, hurry up, because the money is going to be gone. Money!

The second potential theme was the *Alumbrado* fiesta. Alumbrado literally meant "lit up," probably since the ritual was held at night by candlelight. Known in Guantánamo as *Altares de Cruz* (Altars of the Cross), Alumbrados were celebrations once held by campesinos in many rural regions of Cuba, although by 2000 they had all but disappeared from the countryside. They celebrated various occasions, such as the coming of a new baby or a good harvest, giving thanks to a particular Afro-Cuban saint (always in addition to the Virgin Mary) determined by the *padrino* or *madrina* (male or female host) of the event. They were also held to ask the saint for better rains, health, or the healing of a sick relative. The image of the Virgin Mary and the chosen saint topped the five-tiered altar, which was covered with candles, sweets, rum, and other offerings. Los Elementos initially favored this theme since its representation would be very theatrical, but while it might have been a beautiful image on stage, they decided that a more profound social conflict might have been difficult to pinpoint had it been pursued. The group watched several videos that showed Alumbrados (Altares de Cruz) celebrated in rural Guantánamo, and they discussed the possibility of incorporating the ritual into one of the other themes. Like the nuevo campesino, the Alumbrado made an appearance in the play, *Ten mi nombre como un sueño*. The stage directions opened the scene with:

> (*Entran la Señorita y el Bobo. La Señorita comienza a armar una especie de altar al fondo. Lo alumbra con farol y velas, y adorna con varias ofrendas que selecciona al azar entre los objectos que la rodean.*)

(Enter the Young Lady and the Town Fool. The Young Lady starts to build a sort of altar in the background. She lights it up with a lantern and candles, and decorates it with various kinds of offerings that are selected simply by chance from the objects that surround her.)

Bobo: *Esta noche hay alumbrao en casa de casa de . . . de . . . ¡de las Macías!*

Town Fool: Tonight there is an Alumbrado in the house of, the house of . . . of . . . of . . . the Macías family!

(Entra el Predicador. Mira el "altar." Saca un libro y lee el Sermón de la Montaña. Bienaventurados los pobres, porque de ellos será el reino de los cielos, bienaventurados los que lloran, . . . etc.)

(Enter the preacher. He looks at the altar and reads from the Sermon on the Mount: Blessed be the poor, because they will prevail in heaven, blessed be those who cry, etc.)

Pepillo: *(A la Señorita) ¿Y qué se celebra hoy?*
Señorita: *El final de la cosecha.*
Pepillo: *Eso ya lo sé. Pero para eso están las fiestas, no los Alumbraos.*

Pepillo: *(To the Young Lady)* And what is being celebrated today?
Young Lady: The end of the harvest.
Pepillo: That, I already know. But there are parties for that, not Alumbrados.[5]

The third and final thematic option was to center the new play on the history of a small pueblo called Siguanea, once a thriving country town, located along the shore of the Río Negro in the Escambray Mountain region, but now gone: buried by a large man-made lake. The lives of these campesinos had not changed with the Revolution as the lives of so many other communities had been, but had been wiped out completely one year before Fidel's victory. In late 1956 a North American company, (sometimes written in Cuban documents as Dallas-Telcom, and at other times as Telcom-Dallas), was contracted in Cuba to build a new hydroelectric plant along the Río Negro and the waterfall of Hanabanilla. In order to provide the water necessary to run the plant, the company planned to flood the region and to create a large lake directly over Siguanea and its surroundings. The local campesinos were compensated in pesos for their lost land and belongings, but no amount of money, said the journalists of the time and interviewed ex-residents of Siguanea, could replace the loss of their home and community. A play based on this theme would address tradition, identity, nostalgia, and the loss and recovery of memory.

Poeta Loco: *Esta es la tierra de nadie. El aire de nadie, la pasión de muchos que se quedaron sin nada. Miles de hectáreas que no se pagaron y ahora se desvanecen entre los dedos. El sueño de varias generaciones se vuelve polvo al simple contacto, la memoria se volatiliza de solo rozaría. Yo no quiero vivir así. ¡Yo quiero saber!*

Guajiro Enamorado: *Ya no es más siempre. Ya no sirve para eso. Y aquí se acaba la tradición.*

Crazy Poet: This is no one's land. No one's air, the passion of many that were left with nothing. Thousands of hectares that were not paid for and which now fall through one's fingers. The dream of various generations turns into dust at first touch, and memory wipes away just by rubbing it. I don't want to live this way. I want to know!

Guajiro in Love: There is no longer such a thing as "always." It doesn't work that way anymore. Here, tradition is gone.[6]

The line "There is no longer such a thing as 'always'" subtly reflects the feeling of the population after the 1990s, here stated in the words of a fictional prerevolutionary peasant, talking to the town intellectual (cf. Yurchak 2005).

Greeting the Sun, Kissing the Land: Phase 2. Incubation

ACT II
Next day. Same time.
Same place.

Estragon: What do we do now?
Vladimir: While waiting.
Estragon: While waiting.

Silence

Vladimir: We could do our exercises.
Estragon: Our movements.
Vladimir: Our elongations.
Estragon: Our relaxations.
Vladimir: To warm us up.
Estragon: To calm us down.

—SAMUEL BECKETT (1956:61, 86), *Waiting for Godot*

The three potential play options (nuevo campesino, Alumbrado, Siguanea) were only discussed once in the first two months of meetings, but were not pursued more actively until later in the summer. This happened for several reasons. First, a much broader conflict developed foremost in the minds of the director and actors—that of *hombre y naturaleza* (man and nature)—and this relationship became the focal point of group discussions and improvisations. This very broad issue did, of course, include the existence of the campesino, whether a "real" one or a "new" one, but its very breadth made it nearly impossible to discern any single representable theme within it. The power of theater often lies in its capacity to take a very small and specific idea, conflict, or event, and to unfold its inner complexity outward in many directions (much like the analytic work of an anthropologist). Plays might be inspired by a particular event that lasts no more than a few moments, but to truly explain and effectively portray its full meaning always takes more than an hour and a half. Thus, taking a huge idea such as "man and nature" and trying to designate a *smaller* theme within it would, therefore, be tackling the challenge from the opposite extreme, making it an almost impossible endeavor.

Another reason for not considering seriously the three possible themes was the prolonged delay of the playwright invited to collaborate: Atilio Caballero. Atilio, who had been designated to put the fruits of the investigation into dramatic text, did not arrive in early April as planned. Nor did he arrive in May. Or early June. Without Atilio, the actors were frustrated by having to decide whether to formally start the play in his absence or to wait until he was present. As will be evident in the description of the creative process, the actors' talents lay mainly in the formulation of images, personalities, relationships, and social conflict, while the writer was responsible for the storyline, historic context, and word sequence. Yet what will also be evident is that although Atilio's talent as a writer was incontestable and his presence indispensable, it was his ultimate *arrival* that turned out to be the most important happening of all.

After many hours of meetings, discussions, debates, and after over a month of "waiting for Atilio" (the group's initiated "Godot"), the group decided to begin without him. I was excited that the creative process would finally "start"—only much later realizing it had never actually stalled, that it had started months before. I was, after all, an American, ever impatient for movement, action, and results. I prepared my running shoes and small notebook for the "training" that was to begin the following morning. On May 27, at 6:30 A.M., we ran out into the countryside. Past the grazing cows and the horse-driven carts, past the campesinos calling out "hooooaa," "yeeeaaaas," and "hitooouw" to their oxen, past the eggplants and the mango trees and through the cornfields we ran. Upon reaching a large pasture, we climbed the fence and situated ourselves on a patch of grass that faced the rising sun. Silent now, we each found our own individual space and our own inner peace; some actors closed their eyes as if in prayer; others stared out into the countryside and over the horizon; some still and meditative and others slowly stretching, swaying. Here we *saludamos el sol* (greeted the sun) in the hopes of truly experiencing la tierra and la naturaleza (see figure 4). Away from noisy *vecinos* (neighbors), old Chevys with blown out mufflers, salsa music, telephones, El Rápido hamburger stands,[7] and the constant murmur of Cumanayagua, we sought out the namesake of the group, *los elementos*— the natural elements of life: fire, water, earth, and air. Every morning was to begin in this way from that day forward, said José Oriol, followed by "integration" exercises and improvisations in the theater. The integration

4. Teatro de los Elementos in "training" and "saludando el sol" (greeting the sun) in the countryside, Cumanayagua (photo by Laurie Frederik, 1999)

exercises were initially included because the group had admitted two new actors, Lexis and Freddy (not to mention the new *antropóloga*, "Laura"), and therefore warm-ups included exercises to better synchronize the rhythm of the whole. To work in collective effort, José Oriol believed that the ritualistic assimilation of new individuals and the development of group harmony were necessary. As new initiates, we were asked to lead the exercises on some days, to decide which path to take on others, and to "sing to the morning sun." On several mornings, Lolo insistently requested, "Laura, sing that song 'Morning Has Broken' [Scottish hymn popularized by Cat Stevens]. I like that song. And sing it in English." I complied the best I could, tapping into my own creative facilities and making up verses after singing the only two I knew, hoping the actors would be unable to detect a lack of rhyming in a foreign language or deem it unworthy of group membership.

Improvisations were first done in smaller groups of twos and threes, only later incorporating all six actors. José Oriol instructed the actors to concentrate on one particular natural element in these improvisations, be it dirt, leaves, feathers, tobacco, fruit, or the like. Each morning the actors would find something to use in the day's improvisation. The actors also inserted bits of text from poems, plays, or other literature when it was appropriate, then responded to each other either with action, text, or their own invented dialogue. Sometimes they would use recorded music in the background—Afro-Cuban, Hindu, Guajira (décimas, punto, son, and danzón), instrumentals, or New Age—and other times they would sing and play drums, guitar, harmonica, or flute. These early improvisations normally lasted from forty-five to sixty minutes, José Oriol periodically calling out instructions or inserting his own textual fragments to turn the improvisation in a different direction. Each of these improvisations was without set characters or themes, although the personalities of the actors and their natural performative tendencies began to surface very quickly. José Oriol sometimes let these improvisations last for over an hour, allowing the action to develop upon itself and to transform when an actor or two made a choice that shifted the theme of the action. Although never referenced directly, established improvisational methods such as "saying yes and," "discovery," "developing an action," and "giving and receiving" were utilized in their actions.[8]

After several days of improvisation, each actor had adopted particular preferred "elements." Héctor, for example, often used feathers and drums, while Isnoel claimed a conch shell and basket. Freddy had found a large cow skull and often used it during the course of an improvisation, and Lolo had discovered that tobacco ashes floated in the air when blown in a certain way. Kirenia, the only female in the group, usually became the center of romantic or sexual attention in the improvisations, taking turns as *la novia* (the girlfriend) with the male actors, and she often utilized a handful of seeds, which had been given to her by one of the *campesinas* during our first trip to the mountains. Cigars were also smoked by the actors during many of the improvisations, utilizing their shapes, their smoke, their ashes, and creating the first direct link between la naturaleza and la tierra with Cuban culture. These first improvisations were much more animal-like and ritualized than those which later followed, and the actors more often used each other's bodies and actions to create group images, each acting out a different part of the resultant whole. However, with the eventual development of theatrical personalities, improvisations changed markedly. The collective animal which had once been changing its form in every improvisation, soon turned into individual characters which were repeated and who demanded their own personal space: characters given names and titles, and characters with histories and particular political beliefs.

Political Ritual and the Artists' Obligation

The creation of a play about campesinos, in whichever form the group ultimately decided upon, required investigations and interviews. Although the majority of the group was from Cumanayagua, the pueblo's residents could not be described as campesinos (in spite of what residents in the capital city of Havana believed). The definition of campesino had yet to be agreed upon among the actors, but the fact that campesinos actively lived on the land (versus in concrete apartment structures), cultivated the land for sustenance, and often bred animals was generally accepted. On our morning runs we had come across the local campesinos working in the fields, but we had not had conversations more than several minutes long. The actors thus felt it necessary to go farther into the mountains to encounter campesinos de verdad: those without access to the resources available in Cumanayagua or Cienfuegos and those forced to depend upon the fruits of their own labor.

On June 1, 1999, we went up to a mountain pueblo called Cuatro Vientos, still within the municipality of Cumanayagua, but higher up in the Escambray Mountains. Teatro de los Elementos had been asked ("obliged," according to José Oriol and the actors) to perform at a "political act" planned to celebrate a national *premio* (award) given to the campesinos and workers in the area. Political acts in Cuba were official rituals recognizing the power of the socialist state, the Revolution, and revolutionary loyalty. Cubans were usually required to attend and were bussed in to the event. If they gave an excuse or did not show up, eyebrows were raised in suspicion and judgment. The group groaned at the news of a mandatory political act, as it would mean a two-to-three-hour hour trip in a one of the small mountain buses. These small buses were actually half bus and half truck; the power of the latter necessary to motor the vehicle up the steep hills. They did not pass through town, but from Jovero over five kilometers away, which meant that the group would have to first get to Jovero (hitchhiking on the back of a cargo truck or walking), then wait on the side of the road for the bus, which sometimes simply never arrived. José Oriol tried to mollify them and said that it would be an easy performance to prepare. "All we have to do," he said, is to "show a campesino saying how he had nothing before the Revolution and has everything now," which elicited an appreciative laugh. José Oriol also told them that the president of the local cultural board wanted only the highest-quality artists in the area to participate, meaning "it could be a very important moment for the group." By this, José Oriol explained, the cultural official implied that new resources might "become available" if Los Elementos cooperated politically. The party official promised that there would be "absolutely no problems with transport" and that "a lot of other things would be facilitated" if they worked on behalf of the party. "Vamos a conversar," he had said to José Oriol. "Yo pongo mi parte. Tú pones tuyo" (Let's talk. I'll do my part. You do yours.) This kind of political game was played at every level of the cultural bureaucracy, from Cumanayagua up to the national levels, and José Oriol and the actors similarly utilized the system when it suited their own needs.

The premio being awarded in Cuatro Vientos was to recognize the development of the area overall—in agriculture, industrial production, culture, and education—and it was rumored that Raúl Castro, or possibly even Fidel, *El Comandante* himself, would show up to commemorate the occasion. This rumor was sufficient to ensure a full-scale production, complete with newly constructed stage and bamboo scenery, music, dancers in white with waving Cuban flags, political speeches by area officials in each of the recognized sectors, and actors to read poetry by José Martí and famed Cumanaguense poet and *decimista*, Luis Gómez. Isnoel, chosen to read José Martí, proudly dressed in white pants, a white *guayabera* (Latin American dress shirt), and straw campesino hat. Area campesinos filled the fold-up chairs in front of the stage as well as the low hills behind it to watch the spectacle (see figures 5 and 6).

While up in the mountains, José Oriol decided to take advantage of downtime during the day's preparations to talk to *campesinos de verdad*. He gave me the okay to tag along with the actors, but advised me not to ask questions, since "some campesinos in this area do not like capitalists, especially Americans," he warned. I offered to take notes and photos and promised to stay quiet. Since these were to be initial investigatory interviews and the particular theme of the new play was yet to be determined, the actors had no set questions. José Oriol hoped the trip would inspire the group and provide a physical experience from which to create images. We were told to look, listen, smell, taste, and feel la tierra and to experience the world of the campesinos who lived in these mountains. The group planned to use natural materials on stage; so one of our errands was to collect various seeds, trees, and plants found only in the mountain regions, such as Ojo de Buey, Peonias, Flamboyan, Santa Juana, Yagruma, pojas, and guidas. We split into two groups and walked in opposite directions down the only road running through Cuatro Vientos. Doors opened and we were welcomed into house after house, the hosts offering us small cups of sweet, dark coffee. The afternoon was filled with general questions about life in el campo, their backgrounds and life experiences, their farms and families. They told stories about how they were affected during the Revolution and in the *lucha contra bandidos* (fight against bandits) later in the 1970s.[9] Despite José Oriol's warning, the residents of Cuatro Vientos were friendly and curious about my background. They greeted me warmly and invited me into conversation, even when I tried to remain on the sidelines.

The older campesinos were proud and resolute in their opinions, recounting their experiences—how they had helped revolutionary soldiers during the Revolution and fought off the bandidos and *americanos* during and after the Bay of Pigs. They showed off old photographs and letters, telling us proudly about the importance of the countryside and its culture. The speakers were usually male, between the ages of fifty and

5. Rural theater audience in Cuatro Vientos, Escambray Mountains (photo by Laurie Frederik, 1999)

(below) 6. Rural theater audience in Dos Brazos, Guantánamo Province
(photo by Laurie Frederik, 2000)

eighty. Women were never consulted and rarely contributed to the conversation, other than for verification of a date or a fact their husbands and brothers happened to neglect, and only with hesitation at interrupting the conversation. The women hovered in the background, flitting around like silent butterflies, preparing and serving coffee and, just as unobtrusively, collecting empty cups. But that they listened was evident. They would smile or nod in response to a particular story, shaking their heads at others. The actors themselves considered *los viejos* (the old men) the ones to seek out, the givers of historical knowledge. When I asked them why they did not talk to the mothers, grandmothers, and sisters, they shrugged and said, "Pues, los viejos saben de todo" (well, the old men know about everything), as if it were obvious, and of course, this was the logical explanation in a country with strong cultural *machismo*. The men were the ones who had experienced the history, who had had a role in the making of the nation. Female equality and political inclusion, touted in revolutionary rhetoric of the 1960s, appeared to be a primarily urban movement. But when Kirenia finally did sit down with one of the women to talk, I began to wonder if it were also, in part, because of shyness or a sense of cultural inappropriateness that the male actors had not ventured to do the same.

Younger campesinos were asked about the lives of jovenes in the countryside and about their campesino identity, and it was with this group that I was finally able to relax and participate in the conversation—invited especially by the jovenes who were amazed that an *extranjera* was interested in their rural culture, even more so when they found out I was a "real American." The actors were interested in how these jovenes adapted to rural life in contemporary times and were quite visibly relieved to have a break from the well-worn stories of the Revolution told by the older residents—stories similar to those heard countless times over from their first day of formal schooling. The actors asked: Did they plan to stay in these isolated zones forever? Had they been to the city? What did they do when they weren't working in the fields? How did they meet members of the opposite sex? There were no young girls at the gathering, as unmarried girls usually stayed home with their family, so how did they date? The actors were surprised to hear how content these jovenes were, and that many of them did, in fact, plan to remain campesinos, that they did not like the noise and congestion of the city. However, this desire to remain in the countryside was not a nationwide trend.[10] The state knew that most young people wished to leave their rural homes to live in the cities. It was primarily for this reason that Plan Turquino had been augmented, that incentives (fertile land, better housing) were given to those who wished to move to the countryside from the cities, and that the nuevo campesino phenomenon developed as a result.

When it was time for the older folks to go to sleep, members of Los Elementos followed a younger campesino named Macho into the woods for a short walk down the hill to his own bohío. At the announcement of visitors, his wife, Zoila, began to pluck and prepare a pheasant for stewing and Macho brought out a bottle of rum. We stayed with them until 4:30 the next morning, eating, drinking, and telling stories. The group returned from this trip excited and motivated from what they had experienced, and the encounters in Cuatro Vientos were talked about for a long time afterward, although when it was time for character naming, no one could quite remember the names of the wives.

Idle Puttering

The creative momentum from the Cuatro Vientos visit was enough to inspire the group for several weeks, and it was a time of dynamic incubation, ideas swirling and memories of the events in the mountains, all fresh and exciting. But in June, while the group was still waiting for Atilio to arrive, the initial improvisations had reached their final potential. As the weeks went by, the delay in Atilio's arrival put a damper on the momentum of the process, and the initial energy and excitement began to subside. By the first week of June, the vigor of the morning run had slackened off, many of the ritual exercises had been abandoned, we were no longer asked to sing, and it seemed the magical experience of la naturaleza was no longer enough.

The group was frustrated, full of ideas and images, sounds and smells, but without the focus to put them into a cohesive structure of words and thus into a play which could be presented on stage. This frustration was psychologically instilled by the anticipated arrival of Atilio. To deal with their anxiety they made jokes. Each morning an actor would ask how Atilio was doing or wonder aloud why he had not yet arrived at the theater. Since Atilio was to move into the group's (newly lavender-painted) apartment with Isnoel, Lexis, and me on his arrival, the questions were usually directed toward one of us. The appropriate response was that Atilio, poor thing, had been up all night writing and that he was simply too tired to come that day. Or that he had awakened early with such a great idea for the play that he had decided to stay home and write. Others half-jokingly concluded that Atilio did not really exist at all and that he had been fabricated by the director, José Oriol, as a motivational ploy, or that Atilio was actually *una fantasma* (a ghost), and was hovering over the group, teasing and taunting them. "Waiting for Atilio" became the condition around which decisions were made, and plans were either postponed (in order for Atilio to participate) or carried out anyway (without Atilio).

Although the particular reference to Beckett's Godot character was never directly made by the actors themselves, in my participant-observer (and Beckett-loving) eyes, the parallel was unmistakable, just as waiting for Godot (or Godot's death) was analogous to all of Cuba. The idea was perhaps, as Michel Foucault might say, "transdiscursive"—an idea created by an author that becomes a familiar narrative or discourse beyond just the book on which it was first presented: "a theory, tradition, or discipline in which other books and authors will in turn find a place" (Foucault 1984:113). Cuba's "waiting" discourse was nothing new, nor was the idea of rescuing an element of nature that was in peril. But Los Elementos needed an author to proceed with their play, for the ideas had to be written down and transformed into theatrical vernacular. However, not just any author would suffice. They wanted Atilio Caballero, a nationally recognized Cuban novelist. Through his authorship, they would, by extension, be accorded authenticity and originality (ibid.:119–210), not to mention aesthetic quality and distinction. In their opinion, it did matter who was speaking, and evidently, it could not just be the campesino, whether farmer or professional artist.

Restoring El Rumbo: Phase 3. Illumination

Estragon: I can't go on like this.
Vladimir: That's what you think.
Estragon: If we parted? That might be better for us.
Vladimir: We'll hang ourselves to-morrow. (*Pause*).

Unless Godot comes.

Estragon: And if he comes?
Vladimir: We'll be saved.
—SAMUEL BECKETT, *Waiting for Godot* (1956)

On June 16 Teatro de los Elementos began its morning meeting with the most negative energy I had seen of the group thus far. José Oriol began by telling the actors that he was unhappy with the cooperation of the collective. He expressed concern that the group's collective "community" was not functioning, for each individual was not taking responsibility for his or her part. "Your actions are not revolutionary," he exclaimed. This statement was a strong one in Cuba, even in a room full of *jovenes* who claimed to be beyond the use of the communist watchword, *compañero* (comrade) and who considered Fidel Castro old fashioned and "out of date." José Oriol also told them, in tired exasperation, that he had concluded that Atilio was simply not coming and therefore they would have to come to a concrete decision about what to do. There was a thick cloud of disappointment in the room. What had begun months before as an exciting new process had been reduced to a string of obstacles and setbacks. José Oriol complained that the improvisations "no tuvieron rumbo" (had no set path or direction) and that they should not just be doing movements without some sort of scheme. The fact that the improvisations *no tuvieron rumbo* also referred to the group's creative energies and to the process of creating the new play.

As for me, I was stressed and anxious about the fact that my first research year had sent me spinning into a new direction, but that now I would not be able to study the creative process of a play. What would I have to show after six months of fieldwork? José Oriol berated the tired and dispirited actors for a solid hour, until he sighed and said simply, "Go home." Silence filled the room. There was a sullen pause; nobody moved for a moment. As we began to pack up our belongings, mumbling to each other in gloomy tones about dinner plans and errands to run, the door suddenly opened and in walked our Godot. The silence returned as we all stared in shock, unable to believe the extraordinarily timing of his entrance. Atilio stood, tired and ruffled from the trip, suitcase still in hand, smiling at us. The energy of the room changed immediately. Amazement, wonder, and intense relief filled the faces of the group, accompanied by incredulous laughter and applause. José Oriol asked that the group's producer, Rafael, bring a thermos of coffee, and without asking Atilio if he wanted to rest, eat, or unpack, he excitedly commenced telling him of all we had done in the previous months to begin the new play.

This surprising and remarkable appearance by Atilio was the catalyst needed to reignite the imagination and motivation of the group. After bombarding Atilio with all that the group had done since April, José Oriol suddenly reintroduced the three themes that had been discussed months before. Since the themes had not been addressed in so long, I thought they had been abandoned in order to pursue the more universal conflict of man and nature. Yet in the company of the playwright, they were immediately recovered. It was as if José Oriol felt the need to present Atilio with something more concrete than la naturaleza and that possible storylines and particulars were now necessary, especially in light of the time restrictions. There would be no more time to discuss the unanswerable, no more time to contemplate the beauty of la tierra and our place on it. No more time to define the campesino in light of modern-day social theory. And perhaps we would never understand the magnitude of memory and nostalgia, nor identify the value of history to national identity. These important issues did, of course, resurface as the process continued, thereby reassuring the group that in spite of the apparent uncertainty of the first three months, they had accomplished a great deal toward the making of the play. But it was Atilio's arrival that restored their faith in the process. Godot did exist and had arrived. Their rumbo had been restored.

4

THE INUNDATION OF SIGUANEA AND CUBA
or, the near drowning and rescue of Cuba's Godot

Field notes, June 24, 1999, 11:30 P.M.
The house is completely dark except for the soft glowing of a small kerosene lamp placed in the middle of the table, the small light flickering with the evening breezes coming off the mountain hills. The only other light tonight is the occasional flash of green from the eyes of the Kikuyu bugs dancing in between the nearby trees. It is chilly in the mountains in spite of the sweltering Cuban summer in the lower valleys, and we are all dressed in long pants and jackets, listening to an old *campesino* named Macías tell his stories. The interview is taking place on the porch of Macías's small wooden house in the hills of Hanabanilla, located in the Escambray Mountain range. We sit here enraptured by his stories of a lost pueblo that was inundated by a man-made lake in 1958. The same lake lies just below us down the hill, shimmering in the soft moonlight. We try to imagine the pueblos' cemetery, its dead still buried below the water, as well as the *danzón* music that we might have heard on a Saturday evening 42 years ago. So beautiful is this place that the lake seems to dare us to believe that it doesn't have a right to be there. Macías also sings us *décimas*. Décimas of his childhood in the mountains. Of love and loss. Of Siguanea.

To what extent my presence had an effect on the process of investigation, I do not know, but my inclusion in the *Ten mi nombre* playbill as *antropóloga* (anthropologist) showed that they recognized me as a validating presence of their method. Teatro de los Elementos had used the term "anthropological" before, but their understanding of the term stemmed from Eugenio Barba's notion of "theatre anthropology," which focuses on multicultural techniques of acting (Barba 1995; Barba and Savarese 1991), not anthropological research as defined in university academics. Yet the research methods used in Los Elementos' play-making process were ethnographic and were consistent with the discipline, even if they did not do near as extensive (long term, in-depth) fieldwork, were not analytically critical in the same way, and had different end goals. Los Elementos considered the campesinos a cultural "other" and realized the need for living and talking with them to ever begin to understand and theatrically enact their perspectives on life. They used ethnographic methods such as participant observation, formal, and informal interviews. They understood the importance of spending extended periods of time with their informants, with "deep hanging out" and "thick description" (Geertz 1973). Unfamiliar with Gayatri Chakravorty Spivak's famous essay on the subaltern voice (1988) or the intense polemics of the task, they claimed to let the campesinos speak for themselves, at least to the extent it did not hamper in the successful execution of their theatrical story. As in most artistic rendering, true stories intended for performance were subject to editing, condensing, exaggerations, omissions, and subtle changes. They aimed to provide the "emotional truth," "honoring" the actual history if not perfectly representing. Their final product, the play, was a performed, theatrical, and ethnographic rendition of campesino life—not quite a performed ethnography, but certainly ethnographic art. I then interpreted this product through my own analytical frameworks. In contrast with many analyses of art, however, I was with the artists every step of the way and thus witnessed and experienced the investigation as it happened. Seeing how they interpreted the material differently than I would have was a fascinating demonstration of the power of perspective, whether social-scientific, cultural, or artistic.

The Story of Siguanea: Phase 3B.
Interpretation, Adaptation, Censorship

Although not part of Graham's original four phases of the creative process, Interpretation, Adaptation, Censorship are, I believe, crucial, especially when artistic creation is occurring in a group context and when attempting to transform someone else's words into a collective artistic representation. They are essential parts of a working phase: the slow building of a piece during workshops ("workshopping" a raw idea), rehearsals, design, and production. Just as ethnographic analysis and writing are acts of interpretation, so is the movement of "real life" to art. Three-dimensional experiences in time and space must be reduced to two-dimensional words organized on a page. In theater, that text, the script, must then be brought *back* to three-dimensional life in a theatrical way, usually with a proscenium visual frame, even if not performed on a proscenium stage. In Cuba, state censorship and self-censorship also played a part in just how real experiences could be safely performed, and although not often mentioned, this factor was an important part of the process of self-preservation. I insert this phase into the creative flow of Los Elementos as "3B."

After the fateful arrival of Atilio, the play-making process forged full steam ahead. It was quickly decided that the play would be premised upon the history of the lost pueblo of Siguanea, and our next plan was to go up to the valley in which Siguanea had once been and to talk with the *campesinos* living in this region. After the pueblo's inundation by a man-made lake, many of its residents had relocated to other cities, such as Santa Clara, Cumanayagua, Cienfuegos, and Sancti Spíritus, while others had moved higher into the hills. Interviews were first held with local Cumanayagua residents who had once lived in Siguanea. On a routine visit to the local winemaker, Sabina, we discovered that his wife, Milagros, had lived in Siguanea as a child. She told us over and over again that the pueblo had *tenía de todo* (had everything), including a pharmacy, barber, bakery, and doctor. It even had a bus that traveled between Siguanea and Cienfuegos daily. The actors of Los Elementos found it incredible that there was a daily bus between a town so isolated as Siguanea and the city of Cienfuegos in 1958, since the bus between Cumanayagua and Cienfuegos—a distance much shorter on a better road—barely functioned over forty years later. Milagros had an old photo of this first bus along with an article from a 1958 edition of a well-known Cuban journal, *Carteles*, describing the inundation and the trauma suffered by the resident campesinos.

Our second interview was with another Cumanayagua resident named Wansa Ramos (see figure 7). Although he was ninety-four years old and no longer able to walk very well, Ramos had an incredible memory and told us many details about the pueblo's music, its danzón, its traditional fiestas, and its people. He even remembered the actual names of the pueblo's stores and storeowners. Like Milagros in our earlier interview, he told us that Siguanea had "tenía de todo: farmacia, barbaría, panadería, medico." He said that he thought about Siguanea every day and would miss it until the day he died. His daughter, Inés, stood in the doorway behind him, embellishing his story from time to time, filling in parts. Wansa then sang the décima he had written about the loss of Siguanea.

Claramente digo así	Openly, I tell it this way
sin que a mí me quede magua	unless it has all been a joke
que hoy se encuentre bajo el agua	that today you find under the water
tierra donde yo nací	the land where I was born
porque me puse fatal	because for me, it was catastrophic
de manera criminal	and of a criminal nature
quien que me lo crea	he who will believe me
porque perdía Siguanea	because Siguanea was lost
que era mi tierra natal	which was my land of birth.

On June 23 we finally received an invitation to travel up to Siguanea itself or, rather, where Siguanea had been forty-two years before. Once again the group hitchhiked out to Jovero to catch the mountain bus, up winding hills so steep we were amazed the little bus ("that-could") continued forward without slowing to a reluctant stop and plunging backward into the valley. The narrow paved road then became a dirt path, winding through the trees. Like any bus full of artists, guitars were played, songs sung, impromptu poetry and stories recited, and predic-

7. Atilio Caballero interviewing Wansa Ramos, Cumanayagua
(photo by Laurie Frederik, 1999)

tions made about what we would find in a ghost town covered in water. After what seemed like days, the bus sputtered to a stop, and we discovered that we had arrived at the edge of a lake. We gratefully got down from the bus, stretched, and took in the scene around us. There was no town center and no stores. Local residents told us they had to travel to a neighboring pueblo to collect items apportioned by their *libreta* (ration book or "supplies booklet") and find any other items only available in the *bodega* (state store) such as matches, soap, cooking oil, sugar, and rice. The result of this considerable inconvenience is that they rarely took the day-long trip, relying on whatever they could make due with, *inventar* (invent), or *resolver* (resolve, find the solution for) in the mountains. Some campesinos made their living by going back and forth to the pueblo on horseback, fetching necessary items for the community at an extra fee. Apart from Hotel Hanabanilla, there were no visible houses or trails from where we stood, just an expanse of water and a precarious-looking dirt hill leading down to a crumbling boat dock.

Older generations of Cubans remembered a large waterfall in a pueblo called Hanabanilla, which was called El Salto de Hanabanilla (Hanabanilla's Waterfall) or in moments of awe, referred to as the "Niagara of Cuba." We were led to this area by one of the hotel workers and saw where the river and the waterfall had once been, but which had since been replaced by a hydroelectric plant, a dam, and a large lake, now called Lake Hanabanilla. The story of the waterfall and the building of the dam were to hold a central place in the play:

Poeta Loco:	Crazy Poet:
Sólo la insensatez	Only foolishness is
es capaz de adornar	capable of adorning
la cabeza destinada a sufrir,	a mind destined to suffer,
la que aún no es	that which is not yet,
y ya padece	but which must already endure
por lo que encontrará.	that which it will encounter.
Es estruendo y la furia,	The uproar and the fury,
el caos, la confusión,	the chaos, the confusion,
sólo ellos pueden desencadenar	only they are able to unleash
cascadas en Ontario . . .	the waterfalls in Ontario . . .
Bendita sea la locura	Blessed be the madness
si hace germinar nuestras cabezas.[1]	if it allows our minds to bloom.

The Hotel Hanabanilla had been built beside the lake and catered to Cuban tourists. We were to stay at this hotel for the night before continuing on to Siguanea. As was usual in these rural areas, my status as a foreigner created some confusion among the hotel staff. Hotel Hanabanilla was designated a "Cuban" (versus "tourist") hotel, therefore, one of the few hotels in Cuba reserved especially for Cubans paying in pesos (also the only hotels Cubans were even allowed to enter at that time). José Oriol explained to the manager that I had temporary resident status in the country and had a Cuban *Carné de Identidad*, which officially authorized me to pay in pesos as well. There was a flurry of discussion. I was asked for my passport and ID card before I was even allowed to leave the lobby to use the restroom. My name and personal information were meticulously recorded on several sheets of paper, and we were finally allowed to settle into our rooms for the night.[2]

The next morning we walked down the path from the hotel to look for food and wait for the ferry. Unsuccessful in finding any country bodega or *casa particular* (private house) with snacks for sale, we suddenly felt Cumanayagua to be very urban in comparison and the actors commented on as much. Groggy and grumpy from the lack of a morning *cafecito* (even more serious for Cubans than Americans, perhaps) we sat on the dock in the morning heat. After an hour, the stillness was disrupted by a coughing motor. A small ferry had arrived. We boarded and anxiously prepared to float over the sunken town itself, caffeine withdrawals partially forgotten in our collective excitement. Periodically stopping at random places along the shores and letting off campesinos into what was seemingly undeveloped forest, we finally arrived at our stop. The boat stops were curious things in that nothing was visible from the water's shore. Only later would we learn that hidden behind the trees and up in the hills lay *bohíos*, most made of cut wood and palm, without electricity or running water. We walked up the path until we reached the house of eighty-year-old Luis Macías (who went by simply, Macías or *abuelo*) (see figure 8), who lived with his son, Alexis. The house was small, with two bedrooms and a kitchen. There was no outhouse—one simply went into the woods and found a private place. Bathing was done behind a panel with a bucket full of cold water from a nearby pump. Two large oxen were hitched to a tall pole near the back, and chickens roamed freely both in and outside of the dwelling. Daylight seeped through the cracks, giving the inside of the house a soft glow, rays shooting over the bare walls and dirt floors.

The location was serene and beautiful, the kind of place I expected to see fishermen and cabins lining the shore, children jumping off docks.

8. Macías with his oxen in Siguanea, Escambray Mountains
(photo by Laurie Frederik, 1999)

But as we looked out over the water, we saw only gentle ripples and reflections of the trees that surrounded it. There were no people in sight, as if they were hiding from another possible displacement. For the next week we stayed with Macías, listening to hours of his stories and asking questions. Descriptions were often accompanied by the appropriate décima. During our time with residents of Siguanea, the only music played (or sung a capella) were décimas—retelling the history of the place and revealing more emotion and personal feeling than the hours of conversation preceding and following the musical sessions. Macías himself was not able to get through an entire story without singing at least one décima, and for him, it seemed, the musical performance was more essential to communication than straight spoken words. In *el campo*, décimas were often performed impromptu, with a guitar when available, but more often without accompaniment of any kind, as though it were the most natural thing in the world to suddenly break into song. Everyone was present for these stories: director, author, actors, and anthropologist (and I was now invited to fully participate), but each asked distinct questions and were interested in different details. José Oriol and the actors wanted to know what things had *looked like* in Siguanea—the clothes, the stores, if there existed particular types of people, such as a town drunk, homosexual, artist, storeowner, or *santero* (priest of Santería).They also wanted to know about the kinds of music played and food eaten. In short, they wanted to vicariously experience the *images* and other sensory elements of the place and to begin to combine these pictures in their minds for later theatrical representation. In contrast, Atilio asked questions about the history and general story of the pueblo. He wanted to know the people's actual names and about their particular personality traits. He wanted to know if there had been any scandals or interesting events in the pueblo. Images are also important to an author, Atilio explained, but to begin a storyline one must have a sequence of events suitable for narration. Once Macías began telling the actors about the town fool, the prostitutes, the landowner, and the barber, it was Atilio who asked what their relationships were to each other and how they fit into the history of the pueblo. In this combination of image and story formation, tangible ideas for a new play were finally beginning to take shape. The play would begin with the actors performing themselves in the act of investigation:

Los Jóvenes:
—*Debe ser por aquí . . .*
—*Mete la cabeza y mira al fondo con tus ojos de tilapia.*
—*Macías decía que sí . . .*
—*La brújula no marca nada. Se ha vuelto loca.*
—*Loco estoy yo por dejarme arrastrar hasta aquí . . .*
—*Al pasar por la Loma de los Caballos el viento dejó de soplar. Los pájaros enmudecieron, y el agua se hizo más espesa. Ahora siento que algo tira de mí hacia abajo.*
—*Yo tengo miedo.*
—*¿De qué?*
—*No sé.*
—*Debe ser por aquí . . . Pero no veo nada.*
—*¿A quién se le ocurió apagar un pueblo, ahogarlo para producir luz?*
—*Vamos a mirar. Todos a la vez. No respiren.*

Young Men and Women:
—It should be around here somewhere.
—Put your head down there at the bottom with your fish eyes.

—Macías said so . . .

—The compass isn't showing anything. It has gone crazy.

—I'm the crazy one for letting you all drag me here . . .

—Passing through the Hills of the Horses, the wind stopped blowing. The birds are left speechless, and the water has thickened. Now I feel like something is pulling me down below.

—I'm scared.

—Of what?

—I don't know.

—It should be around here . . . but I don't see anything.

—Who thought of it—to switch off a town, to drown it in order to produce light?

—Let's take a look. Everyone at the same time. Don't breathe.

(As if all praying together, the group begins to move forward. Sound of water bubbles.)[3]

The following day we got back on the ferry and after a brief ride we were dropped off, seemingly in the middle of nowhere, once again walking up a dirt trail to a house we could not yet see. We followed our tireless guide, Macías, hiking for six hours that day, stopping in various bohíos, talking to the campesinos living there, learning about how they lived and who they were. We saw different levels of comfort. One bohío actually had a periodically working television thanks to a very (very) long generator cable line and its relative proximity to Hotel Hanabanilla. We soon learned that any electric appliance (television, refrigerator, tape player) was a sign of wealth in the countryside, more so than in the cities, even if they never worked and were used instead as tables (televisions) or closets (refrigerators). The residents laughingly told us that all of the neighbors within walking distance—up to two hours on foot or horseback—came by once a week to watch the *telenovela* (soap opera). The generator worked about half the time, he said, and when it didn't turn on, they just passed around a bottle of rum and visited, catching up on the local gossip. Another household proudly showed us a refrigerator powered by gasoline, even though gas was not usually available in these mountains (or anywhere else in Special Period Cuba). The important thing, I sensed, was that it *would* work if they had the fuel. We also saw a house with a single light bulb hanging from the ceiling, but were told that the current rarely came and it was seldom that they were able to see any light from the bulb. Nevertheless, it was always very exciting when the light did appear. The vast majority of the houses visited had nothing in terms of technology—only small kerosene lamps to be lit at night, homemade from old tin cans and ripped-up strips of discarded clothing. But the *promise* of technology, whether it eventually came from the hydroelectric plant or the Revolution, was tangible.

The theater group discussed the living conditions of these campesinos and found it ironic that this area higher up in the hills had been so isolated by the production of the lake and the electric plant (no tourists wanted to see a man-made lake or electric plant), yet lacked the benefits of the generated electricity itself. The campesinos told us that unfortunately, the electricity from the hydroelectric plant flowed in the opposite direction. They said this without cynicism, without sarcasm or recognition of the irony, or without any emotion at all. It was a matter of fact. In later discussion, the actors voiced their frustration with this resignation, shocked that the campesinos did not display outrage or resentment. Why didn't they fight for what was owed them? The Revolution would never stand for this. Why did they remain passive and unresponsive? "¿Qué pudimos hacer?" (What could we do?) the campesinos answered. The revolutionary sentiment of *lucha* and *victoria* were so ingrained in the consciousness of Los Elementos' generation—Fidel's oft-quoted refrains echoing in their ears—that the actors could not conceive of having no reaction to such a blatant injustice. Whether or not the protests would ever change anything was not the issue; it was failure to react that was significant. And usually there was an expectation that the Revolution (or the state) would provide. Such expectations were common in Cuba, both in country and city, and they came to light every time there was a long period of waiting for a necessary resource, service, or mode of transportation. Most of the campesinos of Siguanea had been born before the Revolution and had been in their twenties and thirties when Fidel Castro took over in 1959. Their upbringing had differed greatly from that of later generations. Schools in rural areas were rare, many residents not bothering to go to class even if there was one since there was too much work to do on the farm. The Hanabanilla Hydroelectric Plant did not supply electricity, but neither had the Revolution. They had always been distanced, in contrast to their urban counterparts, from the television and charismatic speeches on revolutionary glory and justice. In 1999, the only difference in their lives was that they now lived higher up in the hills, there was a big lake where their hometown had been, and they had to travel much farther to reach a town for basic resources (Cumanayagua instead of Siguanea). The frequently repeated joke among campesinos in these zones of silence was that they were so far away from "civilization" in these zones of silence that "even Revolution had not yet arrived."

This response differed markedly from the more urban areas of Cuba where *la lucha* was ever present in daily consciousness, from buying bread, to finding milk for the children, surviving the summer heat, or warding off the evil capitalists who flooded to "areas of consumption." Revolutionary ideology was ubiquitous, even among those who claimed they were not interested in politics and attempted to wave off political discussions. It has often been said that the very act of defining one's actions and intent as nonpolitical is itself political, and this was as true in Cuba as anywhere. The difference was that these supposedly nonpolitical Cubans used political rhetoric without being conscious of its original source. The hegemonic control of revolutionary language was overpowering (cf. Friedrich 1989; Gal 1989; Yurchak 2005).

Bit by bit, the actors and Atilio were able to reconstruct the history of Siguanea and its inhabitants—not from the facts that had been published in the newspapers, which were scarce, but from the contradictory stories told to us by the people themselves and their selective memory: romantic or bitter, nostalgic or indifferent. The actors pieced together that there had been no police or system of law outside of the valley's primary landowner, Pepillo Hernández, and that Pepillo was a well-respected and admired figure in the pueblo, even though Pepillo's national status placed him in the social (and politically corrupt) circles of then–Cuban president, Fulgencio Batista.[4] Upon hearing that they were going to lose their homes, the campesinos of Siguanea had not protested, as one might expect. These prerevolutionary campesinos had been poor and humble, never asked their opinion or given power to make decisions. Feeling that there was no way to make any difference, they had simply accepted the situation and had left the valley. At least this was the story told in 1999. It was possible, of course, that there *had* been resistance; if so, there were no archives, and its occurrence was lost in the memories of those no longer able to tell us their stories. The sadness of its loss was written into *Ten mi nombre*:

Poeta Loca:	Crazy Poet:
Sonido de trompetas en las montañas.	Sounds of trumpets in the mountains.
Tocan a nacimiento.	Marking a birth.
Siguanea como el Tibet, el universo,	Siguanea, like Tibet, the universe,

como un reloj de bolsillo	like a pocket watch,
y mi alma como un jarrón	and my soul like a vase
donde florece el mundo	where the earth blossoms,
que mañana no será más.[5]	but that will not exist tomorrow.

Traditions of *El Campo*

Along with the information collected on Siguanea, we observed the customs and daily habits of our hosts and listened to the singsongy shouts that campesinos made while plowing or calling their animals in from grazing in the field ("hooooaa," "yeeeaaaas," "hitooouw"). One campesino named Pepe told us that he had left the countryside for a short period after the Revolution to study law. Many campesinos were, during this time, being sent to study in the cities. He soon decided, however, that he did not need books, realizing that they would not help him do anything on the farm. His wife validated this decision when she said that the current economic changes in Cuba had not affected them very much since "a peso or even a dollar will not do much good out in the mountains anyway." Indeed, the actors joked, a peso didn't get you much in the cities these days either. Peso stores held nothing on the shelves and "dollar stores" (*shopping*) had nothing for under a dollar.

I joined the group in horseback riding, hiking, swimming, and rowing in a small boat on the lake. There were only one horse and one rowboat, so we took turns during the long quiet afternoons when the campesinos were too busy working with their crops and animals to answer questions. The actors asked to help with the farm work, but the campesinos would not allow it, insisting that it would slow them down too much and might agitate the oxen. Although this disappointed me, never having farmed or gardened even in my own country (let alone gotten that close to an ox), I could tell that José Oriol, Atilio, and the actors were relieved. We visited neighbors in the evening, drinking rum and coffee by the kerosene light, listening to stories, *guajiro* music, singing, and dancing. It was not just the history of Siguanea and its descendants we were learning about; we were also learning about campesinos *de verdad* still living in the hills of Hanabanilla. Although the actors were working on a contemporary sketch of the culture in the countryside for their play, they were hypnotized by the romance and idyllic beauty of the place, frequently remarking on how they had gone back in time and were connecting to their

9. Macías and José
Oriol by the lake in
Siguanea, Escambray
Mountains (photo by
Laurie Frederik, 1999)

campesino ancestors. As guests, we were not expected (or allowed) to
herd the oxen, plow the fields, gather and crack the raw coffee beans, or
wash the family's clothes in the river, therefore exempting us from the
harsher realities of this natural paradise. The myth of the noble campesino was maintained, and those actors who had previously questioned
his existence during the earlier group discussions were proven wrong.
After just a few days in Siguanea, the questions changed from "are there
still *campesinos de verdad*?" to "how do these campesinos de verdad shed
light on Cuban culture?"

Macías showed us where the cemetery would have been if not covered
by a lake (see figure 9). Some campesinos repeated rumors that when the
lake was low, one could see the tips of the headstones and a stone cross
protruding from the water. The group was more interested in this phenomenon than in the actual existence of the cemetery, for it was the

imagined lost pueblo underneath which was more provocative. The thought that the ill-fated Siguanea could still be located and especially that real vestige of its *dead* could still be seen—something lost but yet still existing—was a powerful image, and it would return many times in the improvisations to follow, as well as in the final play. It was, in fact, this idea of what was under or buried by the water that became the play's central metaphor in tú both its physical and conceptual representations.

The Capitalist, Pepillo Hernández

After returning to Cumanayagua and continuing interviews with local descendants of Siguanea residents, we were shown many of the original legal documents that assessed the properties and belongings of each *finca* (farm, plantation) and listed the amounts in pesos that were to be paid in compensation to the displaced campesinos. A legal document dated November 30, 1956, claimed the Dallas-Telcom company's right to all the buildings in Siguanea, their materials, trees, fruits, and everything else existing on each lot. Other documents listed the possessions of each family and their worth in pesos. One farm listed its *casas de viviendas* (dwellings), houses for workers, factory buildings and workshops, and a tobacco-curing house, all valued at 21,500 pesos (US$1,075). Tractors, ovens, tools, and other equipment were also listed, with values of between 300 and 1,000 pesos. Some farms were valued up to 56,000 pesos (US$2,800). I calculated these equivalencies with an exchange rate of 20 to 1. The payments were undoubtedly worth much more to a prerevolutionary campesino in 1956 and would have been very enticing if it weren't also for the forced capitulation of one's home and entire community. The sales, as imagined by Atilio and Los Elementos, were ultimately performed in various scenes:

> Guajiro Pícaro: *Dos caballos con sus monturas, una vaca, dos terneros, tres puercos gordos, un molinillo de café, un par de botas nuevas, ocho gallinas . . . ¡ciento veinte pesos! Esto es lo que yo llamo un buen negocio.*
>
> Mesero: *Solo en medio del desastre puede el buitre hacer su festín. Las hecatombes y los apocalipsis, las guerras y las epidemias llenan el buche a las aves de rapiña. Este mundo es para las auras tiñosas, ya no queda lugar en él para un alma sensible y borracha como yo.*
>
> Guajiro Pícaro: *¿Y tú? ¿Quieres vender algo?*

Rogue Hillbilly: Two horses with harnesses, one cow, two calves, three fat pigs, one coffee mill, one pair of new boots, eight hens . . . 120 pesos! That's what I call good business.

Barman: Only in the middle of a disaster can the vulture make its feast. Catastrophes and apocalypses, wars and epidemics fill the stomachs of birds of prey. This world is repulsive. It is no longer the place for a sensitive soul and a drunk like me.

Rogue Hillbilly: *(to the barman)* And you? Do you want to sell anything?[6]

As the anthropologist looked through these documents in order to understand the legal process of the man-made inundation in Cuba, the actors sorted through a large pile of old photos the family had saved. Examining photos had been important throughout the artistic process in order to get an idea of what the people had looked like in this era, but this particular pile of photos was even more pertinent in that it contained images of Siguanea itself, before its watery burial, and the actors studied the photos over and over again. The highlight was when a photo of Pepillo Hernández himself was discovered, almost exactly as he had been imagined: tall and thin; dressed in an immaculate white suit, hat, and cane; elegant from head to toe; handsome and regal (see figure 10).

Pepillo had been the richest man in the region, a *latifundista* (large landowner), normally despised, especially within Cuba's revolutionary ideology. Yet every description of Pepillo we heard over those months was of admiration and respect. Pepillo had, it was said, been a successful capitalist and one of Batista's personal friends, and he had sold the valley and pueblo of Siguanea at Batista's urging. Atilio later referred to the Pepillo character as "The Capitalist" or "The Power," and it was in this contentious image that he was theatrically re-created.

Poeta Loco: *He ahí al hombre más poderoso de este pueblo. El único, también, que conoce el gran mundo, tanto, que ahora le ha dado por bautizar estos barrios con los nombres de las grandes ciudades donde ha estado. Mírelo, sin embargo . . . ¿no ve su rostro sereno, sus manos en calma, su regocijo? Ahora nieva en su imaginación, y nosotros aquí sentimos su frescor. Mientras sonría, nada malo podrá suceder.*

Barbero: *Está bien, pero yo lo siento en el óxido que endurece mis tijeras. En el moho sobre el cuero de afilar la navaja. No es frescor, sino humedad que reblandece corroe y pudre.*

Crazy Poet: Here is the most powerful man in this town. As well as the only one who has seen the world and to such an extent that now he has gotten

10. Scene from *Ten mi nombre como un sueño*: the Poeta Loco (Isnoel) cutting through the words of the capitalist, Pepillo Hernández (Lexis), Cumanayagua (photo by Laurie Frederik, 1999)

into the habit of naming these neighborhoods with the names of some of those big cities he has visited. Look at him, though . . . Don't you see his serene face, his calm hands, his delight? Now it is snowing in his imagination and we are feeling the freshness. As long as he is smiling, nothing bad can happen.

Barber: Well, okay, but I feel the rust that is thickening on my scissors, and the mold on the leather that sharpens my knife. It is not freshness, but rather humidity that pacifies, corrodes and rots.[7]

Pepillo's character became very important in the investigations, improvisations, and writing to follow, as if this actual historical figure was the beacon for the creation of the other figures yet to be conceptualized. The play was not to be a re-creation of the actual events of Siguanea, especially since those events were buried forever under the lake and in the now quieted memories of its dead, but Pepillo became a set character in the improvisations to follow. While *el poeta loco, el guajiro enamorado, la señorita, el mesero,* and *el bobo* took several months to become fully established—changing and slowly developing with improvisation, trial and error—Pepillo's character held constant. A clear model for his personal motivation was displayed by the daily news stories in the Cuban newspapers of profiteering, economic blockades, and violence by the United States. It was easy for Cubans to imagine the theatrical figure of "the capitalist," since their government was painting that picture for them on a daily basis—Pepillo was an Uncle Sam in white, sans red, white, and blue hat, holding a cigar.

Romance or Reality: The Weight of Water

Improvisations and theoretical discussion were to be utilized to inspire and direct the writing of the text and scene structure. Atilio had been shown the taped improvisations from before his arrival and was therefore able to begin with both the images that actors had created earlier in the summer (*hombre y naturaleza*) and the Siguanea experience fresh in his mind. At our first meeting upon arriving back in Cumanayagua, members of Los Elementos discussed how Siguanea was to be used in the process and in the final play. José Oriol said that he did not want to use Siguanea as a place or a focus, but rather as a motivation. The group agreed that it would start with the reality of the place—the experience we had all just had on the lake and the history of the lost pueblo—and then *dar una vuelta* (change direction) and incorporate *el sueño* (the dream).

The first step was to gather the impressions of each actor resulting from the trip to the mountains. José Oriol asked that they present their ideas for consolidating the different issues that had been discussed over the previous months, including memory, identity, history, man and nature, land, the campesino, and Siguanea. They could use images in the form of artwork, video, text, or any other element necessary to communicate the idea. When we met the following day, the actors had prepared short presentations. Héctor brought in a poetic passage that he had written about el campo. The text contained images of animals and farming, décimas of love and memory. It reflected on the legacy left by one's ancestors: their discoveries and their secrets. Héctor said that this poem had been written from the strong impressions he had gotten from Siguanea—the water and mud and the feel of it beneath his shoes; the grinding of maize with a hand-cranked mill; the way campesinos called out to distant, unseen neighbors in the mountains; the total blackness of the night pierced by the light of a single flashlight; a late-night fiesta and the singing of off-tune décimas, while outside crooned another orchestra of crickets and roosters. José Oriol also found the fiesta to be a strong image, calling attention to the interesting synchronicity between the guajiros and the actors, and the strange juxtaposition of primitive conditions of the campesino's bohío with my modern video camera recording the evening—entangling the supposed lines between past and present. Kirenia also talked about the past and present and how several of the campesinos interviewed had chosen to remember certain details and not others, how memory was often very selective in what it retained.

Lolo then reminded the group of its earlier discussions about man, nature, and lost identity and how these themes related to its more recent experiences. His presentation was also centered on our trip to the mountains, but he focused more on how to utilize these images on stage. He listed important objects, situations, and actions and the metaphors with which they could be associated, such as coffee and grinding; animals and plowing; and playing dominos on the old wooden table of Macías's house. He suggested how these objects could be used as symbols of the local culture and life, and he also talked about how the beauty of the place was used to hide other realities, such as hardship, suffering, and loss. Isnoel agreed with Lolo and said that particular photos and texts could be used to enhance the symbolic meaning of physical images. He discussed the possibility of portraying the lake as the "spirit of the mother" or a god. The entire group talked about the strong sensations they had received from the lake. Water thus became a potent symbol in the making of the play, along with light (or rather the lack of light): as metaphors of modernity and development, and of life and death. The use of water as metaphor was prevalent on the island generally, the water acting as walls within which Cubans were caged but also as the barrier that protected them from the outside. Virgilio Piñera's poem "La isla en peso" (The Weight of the Island, 1943) was often used in plays and in literature to express either one or both of these conditions:

La maldita circunstancia del agua por todas partes
me obliga a sentarme en la mesa del café.
Si no pensara que el agua me rodea como un cáncer
hubiera podido dormir a pierna suelta.

The dammed predicament of water on every side
obliges me to sit at the coffee table.
If I did not think about the water surrounding me like a cancer
I would have been able to sleep more soundly.

In conversation among artists and writers, Piñera's lines were recited to accentuate a particular frustration of being Cuban, when talking about surviving the contradictions and uncertainties of the Special Period, or to accompany one of the many small cups of strong dark coffee Cubans drank throughout the day, especially if the only coffee available in the *bodega* was mostly chicory.

Just after the lunch break one day, Héctor ran excitedly back into the rehearsal room to show us a recently published edition of Piñera's poems. As part of the Special Period's "flexibilization of culture" and the "Massification of Culture" campaign to save and disseminate classic *cubanía*, Piñera's dramatic texts, prose and poetry had somehow passed through the hoops of censorship and been added to the Cuban repertoire of those things considered *culto* (cultured, cultivated). Although persecuted in the 1960s and 1970s (during the Gray Years) for his homosexuality and counter-revolutionary writings, Piñera was increasingly being celebrated in the 1990s as one of Cuba's finest cultural producers. Piñera's poetic words were subsequently added to Los Elementos' script. Héctor's *espiritista* (shaman or sorcerer) character reverently quoted lines from "The Weight of an Island" as he burned incense and attempted to divine the future of Cuba by reading cowry shells scattered on the floor of the stage—predicting ghastly consequences from being surrounded by so much water:

Curandero: *La maldita circunstancia del agua por todas partes me obliga a sentarme en la mesa del café. Si no pensara que el agua me rodea como un cáncer hubiera podido dormir a pierna suelta. Mientras los muchachos se despojaban su ropa para nadar doce personas morían en un cuarto por compresión.*

Predicador: *¡Vade retro, Satanás!*

Curandero: *Ya lo dije de tanto invocarla, se arrepentirán. Peces y no palabras saldrán de sus bocas, branquias en lugar de narices, algas y no begonias crecerán en vuestros jardines.*

Bobo: *(Al Curandero) ¿Por qué no me das un poco de eso que tú tomas?*

Sorcerer: The damned predicament of water in every direction obliges me to sit down at the coffee table. If I did not think that the water surrounded me like a cancer, I would have been able to sleep soundly. While the boys strip their clothes off to go swimming, twelve people die in a room from compression.

Preacher: Away! Get back, Satan!

Sorcerer: I've already told you, after much conjuring, you will all be sorry. Not words, but fish will leave their mouths; gills instead of noses, seaweed and not begonias will grow from your gardens.

Town Fool: *(to the Sorcerer)* Why don't you give me a little of what you're drinking?[8]

Once the actors had shared their impressions and given suggestions about how the play might take *visual* form, it was the playwright's turn. Atilio's ideas were much more defined than the others and were in potential *story* form. While the actors had been collecting the necessary images and loosely associated symbolic meanings, Atilio had been assembling the same stimuli into sequences of events and motivated actions. While the actors had been asking about shapes and colors, Atilio had been trying to understand the living rhythm of the town itself. Did the people gather on a *prado* or central walkway? Or in a park or plaza? What kinds of things did they do in these places? How did the young people meet and fall in love? Where did they dance, read, and hold the circuses that came to town? Atilio was also very interested in using Pepillo Hernández, since in the stories told by the campesinos, Pepillo appeared as a cacique figure. Atilio suggested that the Pepillo character could be used as "the capitalist," contrasting capitalism with the Revolution, and suggested that his history and personality could shape the play; organizing its ideas, relationships, and conflicts. Atilio proposed two different organizational themes: (1) the loss of place and a group of people in conflict in this place, and (2) the loss of memory and how a group of modern *jovenes* attempts to recover it. It was becoming evident that the key images and ideas around which the play would be written were coalescing. What happened in the months to follow was an exchange of the actors' images with the author's storylines and character relationships. Instead of the open improvisations with sparse instruction they had had at first, they were now given daily topics based on what Atilio needed to see or what he had written the night before for testing and development.

This second stage of improvisations was based on simple relationships between two designated characters, such as Pepillo and the town fool or the crazy poet and the young woman. The characters had been developing throughout all of the improvisations, including those from before Atilio's arrival and our trip to Siguanea, but with the injected storyline, they became more defined, and their relationships to each other took on a historical significance. Actors told me that once their particular character was assigned to them, they also imagined their own histories to better embody and enact the made-up individual. For example, Insoel chose the name "Feliciano Rivero" for his "poeta loco." According to Isnoel, Feliciano had been born near Cienfuegos, but had later gone to a school for monks in Trinidad to study science and letters. After he returned from school, he moved with his family to Siguanea for the opportunities it offered. He and his father both worked on a farm owned by José Barista, but Feliciano preferred to read. Feliciano loved the young woman (who Atilio had named "Almerik") from afar and wrote poems about her. There was some antagonism between him and Pepillo Hernandez because Pepillo was also interested in her. Feliciano took care of the town fool, defending him from the jokes and jeering of the others. He liked playing cards and games with the town barber. Kirenia told me that her character was leery of Pepillo since he used to be her mother's lover. As a washerwoman, her mother once worked in Pepillo's big house. "Almerik" did not just want to go through life as a *guajira* and the wife of someone, and she was frustrated in Siguanea. She flirted with the guajiro enamorado, the poeta loco, and other men in town, but she was not a prostitute (and Kirenia said this twice with great emphasis). She decided to get pregnant by the town drunk because he would not remember it, and the baby would be hers and no one else's. She planned to leave Siguanea as soon as she could. In an extended circus scene, the comic relief in an otherwise serious play, Lexis named his clown character "Kryptonita" although Isnoel called him "Liti." Isnoel's circus clown character was named "Matasiete," but Lexis called him "Witi." Each actor had set up their own histories and motivations for relationships with the others. Not surprisingly, each actor's Siguanea character also closely resembled those from the earlier "man and nature" improvisations. Atilio's responsibility was to take these initially raw and ambiguous identities and to give them historical meaning in terms of a mythical Siguanea and the storyline being created. It was in this evolution that one could see the uniqueness of collective writing and play making.

Ten mi nombre como un sueño (que al despertar es incierto)

On June 29, Atilio presented the first sketch of his ideas to the group, dividing it into ten *cuadros*, or scenes: (1) *el descubrimiento* (the discovery), (2) *la fiesta* (the party), (3) *el parto* (the birth), (4) *el alumbrado* (the Alumbrado), (5) *el bautizo* (the baptism), 6) *el circo* (the circus), (7) *el vuelo* (the flight), (8) *el velorio* (the wake), (9) *la partida* (the exodus), and (10) *la inundación* (the flood). He had also preliminarily designated the characters as El Poder (the Power, or Pepillo Hernández), El Predicador (Preacher), El Bobo del Pueblo (Town Fool), Lavandera or Señorita (Young Washing Woman), Curandero/Espiritista (Shaman), El Poeta Loco (Crazy Poet), El Mesero de la Fonda (Bartender), El Barbero Confidente (Confident Barber), and El Guajiro Enamorado (Young Guajiro in Love). Each character stemmed from a story or décima or experience in Cuatro Vientos, Cumanayagua, or Siguanea. These characters were further developed by interaction with the stereotypes of Cuban campesinos and their traditions, and by the actors' improvisations.

It was far from a finished script, but the fact that it was a written document with set ideas in a particular order was a crucial step in the process. José Oriol excitedly read the four-page outline to the group, and after three months the group was now finally able to visualize how its many discussions and ideas had materialized into a theatrical story. The seemingly simple act of putting names to circumstances and assigning particular actions to motivations catapulted the imagination of the group's future play to a new level. Everything was familiar—having stemmed from the actors' own ideas, debates, and improvisations as well as from our shared experiences in the mountains—yet everything was new at the same time. It was as if the thousands of words and images floating in the air had been reorganized into a form none of us could have predicted. The real was mixed with the imagined, physical experiences with intangible spirituality. This simple list of premises and cuadros slowly worked its way into complete situations over the weeks, and was filled in with sequences of text, blocking, and music.

> Pepillo: *Hubo una vez un fértil valle*
>   *en él un pueblo feliz*
>   *que alguien, como un desliz*
>   *inundó con sus casas y calles,*

> *sepultó tiendas al detalle*
> *barberías, bares, cafetales*
> *con aire más bien indiferente*
> *pues lo importante era la corriente:*
> *las personas, el lugar, la memoria*
> *serían olvidados por la historia.*
> Señorita: *¡Terrible! ¡Terrible!*
> *Nunca vi un fiesta tan extraña.*

> Pepillo: Once upon a time
> there was once a fertile valley,
> and in it, a happy town,
> where someone, as if just by mistake,
> flooded its houses and streets,
> buried its stores and everything inside,
> barber shops, bars, coffee fields,
> with a rather indifferent air,
> but what was most important was the electric current:
> the people, the place, the memory,
> will be forgotten in history.
> Young Lady: Terrible! Terrible!
> I have never seen such a strange party![9]

The finished play presented the story of Siguanea in a dream sequence. It was a story that might have happened, but a story in which the details were not as important as the ideas it portrayed. The play superimposed past and present, ancestors and jovenes; it displayed the tragedy of *desarraigo* (being forcefully ripped from one's home or, more generally, uprooting, exterminating, and ripping away) and relayed the importance of history and the recovery of memory. The play also attempted to illustrate the importance of knowing one's heritage and of respecting those traditions and values of the past that had been lost in the chaos of the modern world.

Ten mi nombre como un sueño begins with a group of jovenes, a symbol of Cuba's young, up-and-coming generation. The six actors appear in regular clothing, performing as themselves, as their own actual identities (Héctor, Lolo, Freddy, Isnoel, Léxis, Kirenia) and not yet as characters, perched on a suspended landing over what subsequent dialogue indicate is a lake. The jovenes speculate upon what might be below the water's surface; if their history is buried there, if what Macías said was true. One by one they overcome their fear and jump down into the lake. There is a blackout with cacophonous music. When the lights go up, the scene has been transformed, as have the actors. Lexis is now costumed as Pepillo the Capitalist, dressed in a white suit and smoking a cigar. Isnoel is the pensive yet Crazy Poet (later to become the Rogue Hillbilly, trying to make a profit once the inundation begins). Héctor is the Guajiro in Love (later to become the Barber and Shaman/Spiritist who predicts the forced exodus), who attempts to seduce Kirenia, the Señorita. Freddy is a Preacher (later to become the Circus Magician and the Barman). Lolo is the Town Fool, barefoot and ragged, remaining so throughout the play, with just a brief transformation into the circus magician's assistant. In fact, all characters are transformed for the circus scene, during which José Oriol also makes a cameo appearance as the Ringmaster, along with his real life dog, Sucia.

Their interactions demonstrate the general serenity of the community, as well as the conflicts and competitions inevitably underlying any composed surface. They are suspicious of Pepillo but also in awe of him. There is an Alumbrado party that begins as festive but soon becomes awkward and absurd, especially when the Shaman arrives, shakes his cowry shells, and envisages the ominous future of Siguanea. The circus is festive and raucous and opens Act 2, but the acts are eerily flawed and sad, the clowns are scary instead of funny, the lion is scrawny and disheveled, and the accompanying music is screechy and piercing, as if the music box were rusted and slightly bent out of shape. The play darkens, and the action on stage swells to depict the chaotic and terrifying danger of an oncoming flood. Sounds of water become audibly louder and louder and the characters begin to flee, stage right, stage left, and down the aisles of the audience seating area, taking what they can and also taking advantage of whomever they can. The final scene is again in blackout, as the deluge seems to fill the theater (see figures 11 and 12).

Ten mi nombre was the product of six months of theatrical work, as well as an illumination of the personalities of José Oriol, Atilio, and the six actors—their particular perceptions, histories, and identities. Elements of all of the initial meetings and improvisations were visible, as well as elements from the many theoretical debates concerning campesino identity, hombre y naturaleza, memory, and cultural values. Each line of the play had a history of its own and could be traced back to its

11. Scene from *Ten mi nombre como un sueño*: the Guajiro in Love (Hector) and the Señorita (Kirenia), Cumanayagua (photo by Laurie Frederik, 1999)

(below) 12. Scene from *Ten mi nombre como un sueño* with full cast, Cumanayagua (photo by Laurie Frederik, 1999)

original conception, including the play's name, which was the culminating verse of one of the décimas Macías had sung in Siguanea about a lost love. The play also reflected the artistic and philosophical development of the group as a whole: contemporary jovenes looking for meaning, for history, for their roots, and finding them buried, drowned out, by technology and capitalism. Looking back, they found poetry, beauty, and honor in what was—in the pure souls of their campesino ancestors, and in the natural elements used and celebrated in their daily lives. In the rediscovery and public reenactment of this history for an audience, they believed that they had "rescued" its memory and ensured that it would not be forgotten. Those who saw the play discussed its content, articles were written about it, critics accessed it, its performance was repeated in different locations around Cuba, and it gained a permanent place in the group's repertoire of works, although it was never published (as of 2011) or distributed.

At the debut of *Ten mi nombre como un sueño* on September 12, 1999, the front row of the theater in Cumanayagua was reserved for special guests. Present were Juan and Macho, Milagros and Sabina, Wansa's daughter Inés (Wansa had been too weak to walk to the theater), Alexis, and Macías. As the curtain closed, Macías stood clapping, quiet tears running down his cheeks.

Asking the Audience: Phase 4. Verification

Like many creative endeavors, the theater genre is not one which often reveals the process of its making. Audience members lead busy lives and are interested in seeing something that is finished, rehearsed, well conceived, interesting, entertaining, and less than two hours, please. But when analyzing the levels of interpretation in such a communicative medium, it is impossible to look simply at the finished project, because "communication" implies that there are two parties participating in the exchange; in this case, actors and audience. Attempting to tap into this communicative act, I distributed questionnaires to audiences in Cumanayagua, Cienfuegos, and Havana. I handed them out to individuals before the play began with small pencils, and asked them to complete part I before the play began and part II after it ended. I then waited outside the theater to collect them after the play ended. After six performances in three different locations, I collected just over 200 completed questionnaires. Those collected in Cumanayagua revealed that many local residents understood the fundamental points of the play as discussed by Teatro de los Elementos and were also roughly familiar with the historical context, but this was an audience that had grown up around the Escambray region and included people who were already familiar with Siguanea's actual history (some were actually former Siguanea residents themselves). Although this type of knowledge was helpful in understanding the play, the audience's interpretations seldom went beyond that which had been physically or verbally presented on stage. When asked what the play meant or how they identified with it as individuals and as Cubans, their answers were largely limited to "amor de la tierra" (love of the land), "cultura campesina" (*campesino* culture), and "el pasado del pueblo de Siguanea" (the history of Siguanea).

In contrast, most of the questionnaires collected in Havana (which included respondents from eight different provinces of Cuba and six different foreign countries) had a completely different perspective on the play's meaning, often departing markedly from the simple history of Siguanea and campesino culture. These audiences tended to interpret the play's meaning in more personal, philosophical, or abstract ways, identifying those elements which spoke to their own lives in some way, their experiences as Cubans, their experience of the Socialist Revolution, of living on an island surrounded by water ("la maldita circunstancia del agua por todos partes"), and of living with *incertidumbre* (uncertainty) about their futures. The play was also interpreted in more spiritual ways, one individual commenting that its "message" was that "hay que buscar la luz en las tinieblas" (one must look for the light in the darkness), while others identified with its representation of "la pérdida, el absurdo, y lo maravilloso" (loss, the absurd, the marvelous), the ambiguity of life, and the need to pursue one's own ideals and dreams. Not knowing the exact historical context of Siguanea and the actors' investigations, Havana audiences were free to interpret the play in their own way. Although some audience members expressed their frustration at not knowing the historical basis of the play beforehand, these results showed that not knowing the background of a play also had its advantages, for in its factual ignorance the public was able to seek out broader meanings and was not limited by the story presented on stage. In Susan Bennett's words, their "horizons of expectations" differed markedly and were revealed in their interpretations (Bennett 1997).

Whether or not *Ten mi nombre como un sueño* actually had any lasting impact on the actors or the residents of Cumanayagua, Santa Clara, Cienfuegos, Havana, or even on audiences in Spain (where the play was also performed) was questionable. The second, unpublished part of the play's title, "que para despertar es incierto" (since waking up is uncertain) went unstated for various reasons. The first and most important reason was simply that a play's title should not be so long that potential audiences could not remember it. A second reason was that this phrase had a despondent tone, one that does not place trust in future recovery—whether for Siguanea or Cuba—and which may have raised a red flag for the *consejo*, even if the censors never made the trip down to Cumanayagua to see the first performances. Audience surveys as well as interviews with the actors showed that "uncertainty" was the overriding sentiment represented by the play, as well as desarraigo. Some were able to articulate a personal connection with these feelings, connecting them to the relocation of their families from Escambray to Pinar de Río during the *lucha contra bandidos* or the ripping apart of family members to the United States or other locations abroad. Others took the more existential perspective of "where am I going?" or "where is this country going?"—interpreting the play as an analogy for Cuba itself. This, in itself, was not a counter-revolutionary question, but whether or not one would ever wake up from the dream or from the hell of the Special Period was, perhaps, too suggestive for a well-respected theatre group to address during a national crisis.

Whether or not José Oriol and the actors ever really intended this play to be an analogy was not important once the play had been produced and performed, since by then the artistic product was in the hands of its spectators and would be interpreted and utilized in new ways—its meaning taken in individually, sometimes never disclosed in public. The big question remained, however, in Cuba and around the world: What would happen to Cuba and what would be its future? Would old morals be brought back from the dead? Would the campesino become the cultural model for the new Cuba, or perhaps better said, *how* would it be incorporated? What role did the intellectual community actually play in these social and ideological processes? The actors and the theater people in Cumanayagua were waiting for direction and for authorship, just as the Cuban population was waiting for a resolution to the crisis of the Special Period and of the inadequacies of modern socialism. Many decided with resignation to wait and see what [Godot/Atilio/Fidel] would say about their fate. There was "no use wriggling" for there was "nothing to be done" and "the essential doesn't change" (Beckett 1956: 17). Cuba's Godot might have referred to social change in general, Fidel, the state, or perhaps more abstractly "la victoria" and the socialist utopia that Che Guevara had been immortalized as waiting for. The play ultimately depicted the watery inundation of a rural mountain community called Siguanea. It symbolized the drowning of Cuban culture by globalization and a younger generation alienated from revolutionary mythology and the values of socialism. By the end of the play, the town was covered by water and its inhabitants had fled. But the meaning of *Ten mi nombre* was ambiguous; it could have been considered a warning of impending danger, a preemptively nostalgic look at Cuba's future, or a gesture of surrender to an unavoidable future. When I asked each member of Los Elementos what the play meant to them, answers varied as much as their audiences.

Ten mi nombre como un sueño was Poetic Fantasy without a doubt. Any raw folk rusticity that was collected from the campesinos in Siguanea, or which remained during improvisations and early rehearsals, was edited out before the play's debut. Audience questionnaires and interviews revealed that campesinos and local community members did not fully understand it, although they recognized the beauty of the imagery and verses, as well as the rural characters and culture upon which it was based. Havana intellectuals found it esoteric, slow, and not politically provocative (critical) enough, although, unlike rural audiences, they were often able to draw out broader meanings and comment upon the "authorship" by Atilio Caballero (who was already known as an award-winning novelist in Havana). Clearly it was the process that was most useful for artistic participants and rural subjects. The performance satisfied the actors' desire to perfect an artistic work and perform it in front of an audience, as well as their need to show the state that they were producing quality work "within the Revolution." And campesino informants and audiences felt that their voices were being taken seriously enough for professionals to spend time with them, listen to them, and represent their history and culture on town and city stages in a beautiful way.

At the end of this story, I continued to question whether or not the "real" campesinos of the *más allá* were actually spoken for and accurately represented. Teatro de los Elementos traveled out to what it believed to be the heart and soul of el campo to uncover and rescue the campesino:

the essential root of pure Cuban identity. The group used ethnographic methods to investigate rural traditions and quotidian life and to define the identity of the communities studied in text and imagery. But instead of letting the campesinos speak for themselves by utilizing their actual spoken words, Los Elementos waited and waited for the cultural authority, for Godot, for the poet, for Atilio to arrive and provide them with the necessary script. Certainly, the script was how Havana would be judging them. The script had to be written out and typed, legible for an editor at the national publishing house, Editorial José Martí, to polish and distribute (even if it never happened). The resulting words were not the product of "the folk" at all, but of the artists and intellectuals, and bore the shadow of the authorities' promises to "do their part" if Los Elementos did theirs.

The Near Drowning and Rescue of Cuba's Godot

After spending an extended period of time in turn of the millennium Cuba, one could sense a general resignation in the consciousness of many Cubans, both urban and rural. Sometimes it was layered with resentment and anger, but more often, it was accompanied by a heavy sigh or a shake of the head. The population seemed to wait for the definitive end of the Special Period and for the "damned circumstance of water on every side" to somehow recede with the tide of economic change. At the same time, people seemed to be waiting for a new savior to arrive on their shores in spite of the island's watery barrier. Yet just who or what that savior was had yet to be defined. In Cuba, the act of waiting in line for bread, the bus, other scarce goods and services, or for the electricity to come back on, was one of the common characteristics of lived experience under state socialism, an experience aggravated during the economic crisis of the 1990s. Cuban citizens were also waiting for the definitive "victory" and social utopia promised by revolutionary leaders almost fifty years ago—Che Guevara's "hasta la victoria siempre" (ever onward until victory) suggesting, perhaps, that the word *until* would assure the arrival of Cuba's long-awaited Godot and a cathartic moment of true nationalist realization. The character Godot, in Samuel Beckett's original play, was never seen on stage and never arrived, but he symbolized the particular entity, event, or divinity one waits for, hopes for, and has faith in—whoever or whatever would save the day. In social-ist Cuba before 1990, Godot represented revolutionary victory, utopia, and the realization of the Hombre Nuevo, but in Cuba's modern para-socialist society, Godot was transformed. Blind faith no longer guaran-teed the survival of his imagining or the obligation to wait. In 1953, Beckett's play inspired a new performative genre: the Theater of the Absurd. What dramatists meant by absurd was the "metaphysical an-guish at the absurdity of the human condition," or the futility of human existence (Esslin 1991:23–24). And Albert Camus writes in *The Myth of Sisyphus* that "This divorce between man and his life, the actor and his setting, is properly the feeling of absurdity" (Camus 1975:13). Certainly, this was the Cuban anguish caused by the seemingly hopeless act of waiting, of hoping for someone or something that may never arrive.

So who was Godot in early twenty-first-century Cuba? What did Cu-bans continue to wait for if not socialist victory? What was it exactly that the artists were attempting to rescue from inundation, from the "water closing in on every side"? By 2011, Cubans still lived in a socialist society. Although Marx and Lenin were no longer popular ideological referents and José Martí was considered a bit old-fashioned (although still re-vered), the image of the socialist revolutionary continued to frame the national narrative in very real ways. Yet these socialist ideals changed in the 1990s and early 2000s. The evolution of Cuban socialism was in a state of dislocation, of pause—or shall we say, in intermission—while it changed its costume, refreshed its make-up, and got ready for the next act of this fifty-year-long (and counting) play. Did Godot exist in this newly scripted version of Cuba's parasocialist world? Was he getting ready to make his entrance in Act 2, in the post-Soviet or post–Cold War era of Cuban socialism?

In order to speculate about what Godot was, I should first say what Godot was not. Godot was not God, since gods in various forms had officially and publicly returned to Cuba since 1990—Catholic, Protestant, Jewish, Afro-Cuban, and those speaking through the *espiritistas* or *cruza-dos* of eastern Cuba. Godot was not capitalism, for although Cubans desired consumer goods, they were critical of what they believed went hand in hand with capitalism: moral contamination, individualism, and materialism. Capitalism was evil and imperialist. In artistic circles, cre-ative production for dollars and foreign tourists was considered a form of "selling out"—it was not true art. It was pseudo, banal, frivolous, and without integrity. Godot was also not the noble campesino. Although artistic enactments romantically and nostalgically displayed the campesino de verdad and discussed the necessity of rescuing rural traditions before it was too late, campesinos were also considered *inculto*: uncultivated, uneducated, and backward. And certainly the urban population had no desire to move out to the countryside, work long hours on the farm, drink bad homemade rum, or sing off-key décimas in the moonlight. Godot could have been the biblical David, come to save the cultural and moral *pura cepa* from the big bad North American Goliath, but David was no longer envisioned as the communist *militante* yelling "Socialism or Death!"—he had become a hybrid of the ideologically "unlocked" Davíd character in the film *Strawberry and Chocolate*; the publicly liberated homosexual; the Afro-Cuban Santero; the humble (but sometimes illiterate) campesino; and the sexy salsa-dancing *muchacha* in Old Havana's tourist areas.

Godot was partially unmasked, at least symbolically, when the theater group in Cumanayagua used the penetrating words of Virgilio Piñera in a public performance about the romanticism of rural Cuban culture, but at the end of the play, the audience left the theater without really understanding the actors' intentions. Cuba's twenty-first-century Godot transcended the Hombre Nuevo. I believe the Cuban Godot was the elusive (and perhaps absurd) *Hombre Novísimo* (Even Newer Man) and all that yet another (Even) New(er) Man might represent. The Hombre Novísimo was a campesino in essence—in his humility, work ethic, and loyalty to revolutionary value. But he was also educated, progressive, and *culto*. In the end, he was not really a noble campesino anymore; nor was he an urban Habanero. By definition, Godot could never be a real entity that actually existed or ever arrived. Godot was an ideal to be anticipated: a utopia that drove the struggle and sacrifice necessary to build a new society or transform the old. The notion of *hasta* (until) was vital. Héctor, Lexis, Kirenia and Freddy all left Cuba soon after 2000, rejected this ideal, and stopped waiting for Godot. Or rather, they took the initiative to go and search for him despite the "damned circumstance of water on every side." The choice *not* to wait in Cuba was more difficult and more complex (I would argue, though Beckett might disagree) than what Beckett's characters, Estragon and Vladimir, had to face. Cubans had psychological, political, and logistical barriers to overcome. They were waiting in time and also weighted in space. According to Fernando Ortiz,

Cubans were historically weightless to a certain extent, "aves de paso sobre el país" (birds of passage over the country, Ortiz 1991:23 [1940]). However, in 2011, they were still tied down by revolutionary mythology and the political authority of Fidel Castro's reign. They were also tied down by love for and pride in their nation and the unity that sprang from collective struggle.

In his poem "La Isla en Peso" (1943), Piñera lamented that "¡Nadie puede salir, nadie puede salir!" (No one can leave! No one can leave!), and ultimately concluded by modulating the metaphors of water and weight. While *peso* was translated as weight or a burden, it was also used to refer to the significance or importance of a particular element. Piñera wrote that as the nation sank into the watery depths, its weight or importance was felt more keenly:

> un pueblo desciende resuelto en enormes postas de abono,
> sintiendo cómo el agua lo rodea por todas partes,
> más abajo, más abajo, y el mar picando en sus espaldas;
> un pueblo permanece junto a su bestia en la hora de partir,
> aullando en el mar, devorando frutas, sacrificando animales,
> siempre más abajo, hasta saber el peso de su isla;
> el peso de una isla en el amor de un pueblo.

> a nation of people descends into an enormous pool of dung,
> feeling that water surrounds them on every side,
> lower, lower, the sea stinging their backs;
> a nation of people stays next to their beast at the hour of departure,
> howling at the sea, devouring fruit, sacrificing animals,
> always lower, until they know the weight of their island;
> the weight of an island in the people's love.

Ten mi nombre como un sueño's dramatic conclusion was similarly melancholic and ambivalent about waiting and the weight of water. Although the actors' characters (the townspeople of Siguanea) ultimately abandoned the town and gave up hope that "el rey del pueblo" (the king of the pueblo, or Pepillo) would come to save them, the message was that they had to continue la lucha toward "Illumination." Meanwhile, in 1999 Cumanayagua, as well as in Cuba, the question remained: Did Godot, or, rather, the Hombre Novísimo, really exist?

5

CULTURAL CRUSADES AND
THE UNSUNG ARTISTS OF GUANTÁNAMO

*or, how Don Quixote saves humble
Harriero from the devil*

Yo vengo de todas partes,	I come from many places,
Y hacia todas partes voy:	And toward these places I go:
Arte soy entre las artes,	I am art among the arts,
En los montes, monte soy.	In the mountains, I am a mountain.
Yo sé los nombres extraños	I know the strange names
De las yerbas y las flores,	Of the herbs and flowers,
Y de mortales engaños,	And of moral deception,
Y de sublimes dolores.	And of sublime pain.

—JOSÉ MARTÍ, *Versos sencillos* (Simple Verses) (1891)

El arte por el arte es ridículo. Es artista tiene que reír junto a su pueblo. Dejar el ramo de azucenas y meterse en el fango hasta la cintura.

Art for art's sake is ridiculous. The artist has to laugh together with his community. He has to leave the bouquet of lilies behind and get into mud up to his waist.
—Certificate of appreciation, La Cruzada Teatral, Punta de Maisí, 2000

Although I spent a full year in the foothills of the Escambray Mountains with Teatro de los Elementos, my experience with *campesinos de verdad* had been limited to assorted trips up into the more isolated areas *buscando campesinos* (searching for *campesinos*) for brief investigations of one or two weeks.[1] I was repeatedly told that the real campesino was always *más allá*—more isolated, deeper into the mountains, farther away from wherever you were, and by definition, in places that were difficult to access. Since the province of Guantánamo was the farthest eastern region of Cuba, it was surely as *más allá* as one could get before hitting the ocean. In Guantánamo City, even urban dwellers often referred to themselves as campesinos, because either they or their parents had been born in rural areas before migrating to the city. Moreover, relative to Havana, Cienfuegos, or Santiago de Cuba, Guantánamo City really *was* part of *el campo*; in contrast to the ways of campesino-hood in Cumanayagua, my acquaintances in Guantánamo City retained their campesino identity when traveling out into the mountains.

Getting ready to wrap up my research at the end of 1999, I was surprised to win a Fulbright-Hays fellowship that granted me a second year in Cuba. It was the first year the application did not restrict Cuba completely as a red-flagged country with "no diplomatic relations" (a short-lived opportunity during Bill Clinton's presidency), and it was not yet considered a potential "terrorist nation" (later designated under George W. Bush), which significantly slowed my customs inspections on research trips after 2001. With an extra twelve months of support in hand, I decided to venture más allá to find those elusive campesinos de verdad and the artists who worked among them, and I was excited to receive an invitation to go on La Cruzada Teatral's annual trip through the mountains of rural Guantánamo. In January of 2000, I splurged on an airplane ticket and settled in for the quick two-hour flight from Havana to Guantánamo City. This chapter describes the artistic world in the region farthest from the Havana core and follows a traveling theater group on a crusade to bring "culture" to the most isolated mountain regions of Cuba. The relationship of the center to the periphery is analyzed and the eastern, or "Oriente," perspective on the Special Period crisis is examined through a *Teatro Comunitario* group called La Cruzada Teatral Guantánamo-Baracoa (The Theater Crusade Guantánamo to Baracoa). The position of these artists within the national cultural bureaucracy was revealed by their attempts to procure necessary resources from a distant central power, as well as their personal efforts to establish cultural authority and recognition in a region that was often looked down upon or overlooked altogether.

One of my most distinct and memorable impressions of Guantánamo was arriving at the city's airport for the first time. Located roughly five miles outside the city center, it received only one plane per day from Havana. The building was big enough for a small ticket office and for luggage to be brought back from the plane, sitting just fifty feet away, and then placed inside on a cement platform for passengers to collect. Outside, bag in tow, approximately fifteen other passengers were greeted by friends and family and taken away in cars. There I stood, staring out into a field of nothingness, with one empty road leading out of the airport. No one had come to meet me, and unlike the José Martí International Airport in Havana, there were no taxis lurking to pick up confused foreigners. I soon learned I was not alone. A writer and a photographer from a Cuban journal called *Bohemia* introduced themselves to me and said, "You must be the American." Tomás Barceló and Jorge Ignacio Pérez had also been invited to participate in La Cruzada in 2000 and had heard an *extranjera* would be joining them on the plane. Together, we looked out over the dry yellow land and wondered what in the world we were about to experience. Like the American, these two city boys had never been to Guantánamo, but were interested to see how Cubans from Oriente lived, as was their editor who had sent them to write a story about it. We waited for an hour and were about to get to the city in the usual Cuban way—walking or *en botella*—when our ride finally appeared, flustered and apologetically explaining "Me complique."

In 2000, Guantánamo City's population was approximately 270,000. Many Americans still did not realize that Guantánamo was actually one of Cuba's fourteen provinces and not just the U.S. naval base (see map 3). Without fail, when I told people (non-Cuban) I was doing research in Guantánamo, they would ask, "Have you been to the Base?" and an Internet search called up pages of information on the base, its locale, and, post 9–11, its growing number of Middle Eastern prisoners. The city of Guantánamo was Cuba's fifth-largest urban center, but was more akin to a large rural town. This was made clear when compared to populations in Havana (2.3 million), Santiago de Cuba (550,000), Camagüey (350,000), and Holguín (320,000) (*The World Gazetteer*, www.worldgazetteer, accessed 2005). Along with Santiago de Cuba and Granma Provinces, it was the home of part of the famous Sierra Maestra Mountain range where Fidel Castro and the rebels based their revolutionary battle. Guantánamo Province was made up of ten municipalities, all of which were mountainous and rural. Its primary industries were sugarcane growing and sugar milling, salt processing, and, most importantly, coffee production.

Foreigners were not allowed throughout most of rural Guantánamo without permission and accompaniment, largely in order to protect the area's most valuable crop: coffee. Tourists were easily spotted by the special license plates on their rental cars (black and beginning with *T*), and were routinely turned back when attempting to cross certain boundaries. Another reason for this regional protection, I was told, was for the protection of military strategy—the mountain ranges in Guantánamo had been important military points during both the Revolution and the guerrilla protests which followed and, therefore, the bases were being constantly prepared for any future attacks. In 2000, there were still periodic military checkpoints along the road. During the daily mountain treks with La Cruzada from January–March 2000, large cement tunnels were occasionally seen behind the brush or protruding out from a hill, built in case of an attack during the Cold War years. "¡No los diga!" (Don't tell them!) warned one Cuban actor, suggesting, in jest, that I might go home to the United States and tell them where the Cubans would hide when the Americans came to attack.

In 2000 (and also as of 2011), many of the peripheral residential roads were still dirt, pigs and chickens were kept in backyard enclosures or in spare storage spaces, and city transport consisted mainly of horses and carts, costing one peso a ride. The more expensive option was a "bici-taxi," which was a large tricycle with a two-seat passenger bench. These bicycles were relatively new additions to the city, modeled after the ubiquitous bici-taxis in Havana, which took tourists on leisurely jaunts along an ocean boardwalk called the Malecón. In Havana, a short ride cost between two and five U.S. dollars. In Guantánamo, passengers were not interested in seeing the sights, and most agreed there were none. They were going home from work and would splurge for the ride if they were carrying too many packages to comfortably fit on a horse cart or if they were in a hurry. The ride cost between five and ten pesos (twenty to fifty U.S. cents), which after a few months in Guantánamo (riding mainly on a horse cart or *en botella* on a tractor), seemed expensive to me as well. Although the city had electricity, blackouts occurred daily, often for hours on end, and the running water worked only every other day. Large plastic tanks were filled on water days and rationed for cooking, drinking, washing, and toilet flushing on nonwater days. Aside from a handful of old American cars that carried passengers longer distances along main roads, any travel into the countryside required flagging down a passing tractor, an empty flatbed supply truck, or a *carro*, an old Russian cargo truck. During the Special Period the carros were reserved specifically to transport people, who were then packed in as tightly as possible, standing and clinging on to the metal railings or onto each other as they passed over unpaved roads filled with potholes and rocks. These carros were certainly not my favorite mode of transportation, as a three-to-five-hour ride in the Caribbean afternoon sun left the rider utterly exhausted, sunburned, and completely covered in dust, but it was often the only way to arrive at one's destination short of walking. Several times, en route to the *zonas de silencio* (zones of silence), I waited by the side of the road with the actors for over four hours. The sight of that carro rumbling toward us was a very happy moment indeed—dust, sun, and all.

The residents of Havana and other cities in northwest Cuba saw Guantánamo, both province and city, as extremely rural and remote. The eastern region (Santiago de Cuba, Granma, Guantánamo) was popularly referred to as Oriente or sometimes *el Este* (Oriental region, or the East), while everything north of Camagüey (Havana, Santa Clara, Trinidad, Cienfuegos) was called Occidente (Occidental region). I personally, never heard it called "the West," perhaps so as not to confuse with the "imperialistic" West. Perceptions of Occidental Cuban culture toward that of the East echoed, in some ways, Edward Said's more expansive theory of the "Orientalism" (1979) between Western "civilization" and the exotic, yet primitive Far East—one difference being that most scholars from Occidente (largely located in Havana) did not bother themselves to visit or write about Oriente. The exception to this west–east prejudice was the tourist-destination city of Santiago de Cuba, against which I never heard the same sort of disparagement. In Cuba, the capital's relationship with Guantánamo was that of city–country, center–periphery, and even first world "empire" to underdeveloped "hinterland" in the minds of some artists and intellectuals (cf. Coronil 1996; Lomnitz 2001; Williams 1973). Unless they had family in Guantánamo, most Cubans had never visited either the city or the rest of the province; nor did they wish to do so. They viewed Guantánamo as a distant, backward place, filled with dangerous *negros* and criminals (if a white or mulatto was speaking) or as a poor, run-down place, and just generally "disagreeable" (if an Afro-Cuban was speaking). By American standards, a twelve-hour car drive (500 miles) may be long, but it does not constitute an impossible journey. However, since most Cubans did not own automobiles or have access to one, and they could not afford, or were not allowed, to stay in hotels, even a seemingly short distance from Havana to Cienfuegos (140 miles) was difficult and time consuming. As I have explained, the rigors of simply buying a bus or train ticket were considerable, and if traveling to Guantánamo, the traveler had to endure an uncomfortable eighteen-to-twenty hour overnight ride. Buses improved greatly in the 1990s, thanks to international donations and tourist dollars fed back into public transportation, but bus conductors overzealously pumped up the new-fangled air-conditioning units to produce frosty gusts, smoking was allowed, and if your seat was broken, it remained broken with you sitting in it for the duration. Most drivers also allowed hitchhikers (en botella), so the stopping, starting, jostling, noise, and concern for the safety of one's belongings were constant. At 2:00 A.M., 2:30 A.M., 3:30 A.M., and 4:15 A.M., the bus stopped, doors dinged loudly as they opened, and light automatically flashed on for the new passengers who finished out the ride standing in the aisles. The long-distance "express" bus thus became "local," the extra fares pocketed. The antiquated Russian trains were cheaper and tickets easier to get than a bus or plane, but they had not been renovated for decades and seemed to break down more often than they functioned, leaving passengers stranded. Travel, or general movement from place to place, whether temporary or permanent, was a complicated endeavor in Cuba—a freedom I had taken entirely for granted in the United States.

In 2008, the then-president Raúl Castro legalized the sale and private use of cell phones for those with the money, and they were becoming more frequently seen in Cuba (though by 2011, users still only numbered about one million of the eleven million population). There were very few cell phones seen on the streets of Guantánamo, but the fact that there were any at all was a significant change from my own experience. While living in Oriente during most of 2000, I had nearly no communication with my friends and family in the United States. There were not many private landline telephones in the city, and virtually none in the rural areas. And private landlines could not call outside the country. Those with professions in medicine, academia, or government were more likely to have their telephone line applications approved; the remaining population borrowed them or paid higher prices at a call center in downtown Guantánamo.[2] Even existing telephones did not often work or took several hours to connect with faraway places (anything west of Camagüey). In very isolated zonas de silencio there was no phone service at all, and residents relied instead on a daily radio broadcast that devoted thirty minutes every morning to transmit personal messages from Guantánamo City to those living in the rural areas. This lack of telephones in Oriente was due, said the Guantanameros, to the *antiguo* (antiquated) phone lines, while *allá* (up there) in Havana, in Occidente, there were *nuevas técnicas* (new technologies) that improved communication. There were also fewer televisions in Guantánamo. Although the state tried to make televisions as accessible as possible to even the poorest Cubans, a lower level of income and higher number of areas without electricity hampered its best efforts. In some rural pueblos, the community owned one television, which was kept secure in a large wooden box with a padlock during the day, mounted in a small outside park plaza with rows of viewing benches bolted to the cement platform. At 6:00 P.M., the box was unlocked and opened, the television turned on (if the generator was working that evening), and the public invited to watch the nightly news. The box was also opened for special newscasts, *tribunales* (political demonstrations), or Fidel's speeches. Residents complained that the TV box was not opened for the *telenovelas*.

Another factor that created alienation from the capital and its surroundings was that many of the cultural influences, via radio and television, came into the area from the Dominican Republic, Mexico, and Haiti, or from the English-speaking channels received from the neighboring U.S. naval base—in other words, not from Havana. Many local people could list the best Mexican pop stars more readily than the newest salsa coming out of their own country's capital, and in the rural areas, they danced only merengue, *son montuno*, and *guaracha*, rejecting salsa as "too urban" and *no-bailable* (not dance-able). Guantanameros from the city frequently led me from the street and into their houses, excitedly showing me their televisions and radios to demonstrate the clear-sounding American stations, sometimes proudly braving a translation. Young people blasted boot-legged recordings from the latest Dominican bands, and local Casas de Cultura promoted Haitian GaGá dance and musical troupes.[3] These trends suggested that another reason Guantánamo appeared so culturally remote to Habaneros was not because it was so far away, or because it was inhabited by primitive *guajiros* steeped in authentic *cubanía*, but, ironically, because the region was influenced by so many other "foreign" Latin American cultures—Caribbean and Central American in contrast to Havana's resident Canadians, Swiss, Belgians, and Italians.

Más Allá

Guantanameros saw themselves as being very far away from the center of Cuba (culturally as well as geographically), and often referred to Havana simply as *allá* (over there, way up there) using a waving hand movement to spatially indicate its extreme distance. It was often said with a certain degree of longing and admiration if the speaker had never been there, while an experienced traveler said it with raised eyebrows and a sigh, as if remembering the long and uncomfortable trip it required. Maribel López Carcassés, a theater director and puppeteer, explained that Guantanameros once had a particular pride in their home region and felt that they were special and separate from the rest of Cuba, even if part of this solidarity resulted from a common feeling of state neglect and national disrespect. However, in the early 1990s, residents had lost some of this pride because "veía sus ojos en La Habana. La meta era La Habana y los lugares donde haya buen turismo" (Their eyes were on Havana. The goal was Havana and those places where there was good tourism) (interview with Maribel López Carcassés, Guantánamo, July 2000). Although speaking in general about the people, she was referring to the artists in particular, who have had the opportunity to profit from the industry:

> *[Turismo] motiva a las personas para mejorar sus vidas, precisamente por el atraso económico que tiene Guantánamo. El artista guantanamero no es como él de la Capital, que tiene acceso al teatro, a la radio, a contratos en la televisión, de que venga el cine y te capte. El de aquí de Guantánamo simplemente tiene que conformarse con el grupo en que está. Eso es lo que hacía que la gente se fuera. Tienen condiciones, se veían con condiciones y arrancaban y se iban, porque aquí tú no descubres todas las potencialidades que puedes tener.*

> [Tourism] motivates the people to better their lives, precisely because of Guantánamo's backward economy. The artist in Guantánamo is not like the artist in the Capital who has access to the theater, the radio, television contracts, who can go to the cinema and learn from it. The artist here simply has to conform himself with the group to which he belongs. This is what made people leave. They have certain conditions. Artists have seen these conditions and have picked up and left, because here you cannot discover all of the potential you could have. (ibid.)

Allá was a reference to something better, to a place with more opportunity and freedom and, more importantly, with chances to make better salaries and improve one's standard of living, yet the word also held a shimmer of resentment and social critique. Living in Guantánamo, even in the city, was certainly much more difficult than in many other parts of the country. Interestingly, in Havana, the same *allá*, spoken loudly with more emphasis and with the characteristic hand movement, signified the United States.

Unlike the large mass of artists and intellectuals in Havana, some famous and many unknown, artists of different genres in Guantánamo knew each other personally and were highly recognizable in the community. This was especially true for the *teatristas*, since groups were few and specialized, were required to attend official meetings, and competed for limited resources allocated by the Consejo. Also adding to their familiarity, was that most of these artists collaborated in La Cruzada, the annual theatrical tour through the mountains of the province. Every year since 1991, Guantánamo's actors and directors joined together on José Martí's birthday, January 28, to set out for the mountains. La Cruzada's director was democratically elected each year, and a producer was also appointed to help with the complicated logistics of the trip. In 2000 the ensemble was made up of four local theater groups, Teatro Güiñol (Puppet Theater), Palomita (Little Dove Theater), Teatro Trianon (Trianon Theater), Teatro Rostro (Face Theater), and two independent artists, Tío Tato (Uncle Tato) the clown and El Mago (the magician).[4]

Teatro Güiñol was directed by Maribel López Carcassés, and had approximately six members. Every Cuban province had a Teatro Güiñol, which was dedicated to children's theater and puppetry, so this group's name was followed by "de Guantánamo." The groups' performances delivered universal moral messages to their audiences: stealing is bad, reciprocity is good, respect your elders, tell the truth, and so on, through fables, myths, and fantasy. Kings and queens, little girls and boys, evil witches, gypsies, fairies, dragons, wolves, and pigs—along with the Cuban farmer protecting his demure *campesina* daughter from the handsome stranger—occupied the stage, although unlike the Güiñol company in Havana, they did not put on shows based on Santería fables or myths. Having a clearly designated audience (children) and thus a set repertoire, along with national recognition as a Güiñol ensured a base of support from the Consejo, both provincial and national, and in 2000, an old, gutted-out theater was in the process of renovation for its eventual use. Although it was unlikely that the group would be able to use it in the near future (and by 2011 the renovations were no further along), the simple promise and possibility of its eventual construction caused resentment and frustration among other Guantánamo groups who had no permanent rehearsal or performance space, nor hopes of procuring one. The second children's group in Guantánamo, Palomita, had three members

13. La Cruzada Teatral puppet performance for rural school children,
Guantánamo Province (photo by Laurie Frederik, 2000)

(Pindi, Lula, and Rafael) and produced similar puppetry pieces. It joined
Güiñol from time to time when more puppeteers were needed for larger
productions, and also for the La Cruzada tour (see figure 13).

Teatro Rostro (Face Theater) was a group of two, Ury Rodríguez and
Virginia López. It had a varied repertoire, ranging from monologues and
short plays to storytelling and puppetry, and performed for both adults
and children. There was no set rehearsal space for the group, but it had
been given a small storage room by the Casa de Joven Creadores, to
which Ury belonged.[5] The storage room, measuring two by three meters,
held costumes, make-up, props, and sets from previous and ongoing
productions, and also functioned as a meeting room, with two chairs
crowded behind a small round table. The actors began their day early in
the morning to avoid the unbearable midday heat, utilizing a small,
open-air patio inside the Casa's structure. By noon, they were forced to
stop, taking refuge in the storage room to talk and plan the next day's
rehearsal.

Teatro Trianon, directed by Edilberto Juárez, was a slightly larger group with five members. A graduate from Havana's prestigious Instituto Superior del Arte in theater direction, Edilberto was more prone to experimental and postmodern theater (self-defined), resulting in, said his peers, plays that no one in Guantánamo could understand. Other Cruzada members claimed that Edilberto was "too educated" to work in Guantánamo and that the local residents did not have the theoretical basis to appreciate his work. His plays were often full of symbolic imagery, movement, poetic text, and ambiguity. Like Teatro Rostro, Trianon did not have a permanent workspace, but moved from place to place, from the rehearsal studio of Danza Libre (Free Dance, a local professional dance company) to a small patio in the UNEAC building, to the backyard of Edilberto's cousin's house.

Tío Tato (Uncle Tato) was a local clown, played by Carlos Pérez (see prologue and figure 14). His act was sanctioned by the Consejo as an official theater project, even though he was the only member. Once an actor in the well-respected Cabildo Theater of Guantánamo, he was

14. Tío Tato (Carlos) performing in Yumurí, Guantánamo Province (photo by Laurie Frederik, 2000)

allowed to maintain his *proyecto* status when the group was dismantled in 1995. Carlos admitted that he made most of his money by being hired to perform as a clown at private birthday parties and not in the formal state-supported system. Although tourism was nonexistent in Guantánamo, many retired Cubans received pensions from having worked at the Guantanamo Bay Naval Base (paid in U.S. dollars), and others received stipends from family abroad. The lavishness of children's birthday parties and *quinceañeras* (a traditional coming-out party for fifteen-year-old girls in Latin America) had become a sign of status and economic affluence in Cuba, and hiring a clown was an expectation for children of wealthier families. Carlos could earn over twenty U.S. dollars for four hours of entertainment, which was more than double his monthly salary from the state. He wistfully dreamed of working in Havana, as another clown from Guantánamo had done—one who worked independently from the state (illegally), and earned over $100 per party. In Guantánamo, however, Carlos retained his status as state artist. While ambivalent about whether to stay home with his family or go to Havana, he felt it was important to stay in Guantánamo, more for the feeling of personal security than out of a political loyalty or desire to contribute to national culture. Fidel repeatedly promised that the Special Period was destined to end, at which point American dollars would no longer be used. The *peso convertible* (convertible peso, also called a CUC or in slang, *chavito*) was to be the future currency of Cuba. The peso convertible was newly Cuban-made in 1993 and, like the Cuban peso, was initially given equivalent value to the American dollar, until 2006, after which it was pegged to the Euro in an attempt to de-dollarize the economy. Carlos, like other Cubans, feared that the moment of de-dollarization would mean a marked decline in the private market economy and the end of lucrative employment such as birthday clown hiring. This fear proved relatively unwarranted in the end, especially in Guantánamo, but the informal market did change nationally after 2004 (see Domínguez, Pérez Villanueva, and Barberia 2005).

Artists in Guantánamo routinely complained that they were neglected by the National Consejo and that they received no aid from the capital; that they were the last to be considered when allocating resources. Unlike neighboring Santiago de Cuba and nearby Baracoa (popular tourist destinations), Guantánamo was so isolated that both "outside" national and international and visiting groups were rare. Local artists were seldom given the opportunity to bring their own performances to other provinces. The only theater group invited to travel to Havana to perform was Teatro Güiñol, toward which the others harbored a sulking jealousy.

Theatrical Frontlines and the Massification of Culture

Guantánamo's provincial isolation began to lessen slightly with the onset of the "Massification of Culture" campaign. In 1999, Fidel Castro proposed the implementation of this movement, another "crusade" to expand the population's "cultural horizons," especially in the most secluded places on the island. The minister of culture, Abel Prieto, later described it as a "genuine program of development, [. . .] wholly justified and necessary," he said, "when we see what is happening with mass communication in the rest of the world—that being an avalanche of frivolity, foolishness, and fetishes in an unethical market" (talk given at UNEAC, Havana 2000). Prieto claimed that it was important to educate Cubans in order to "create a greater capacity for cultural discernment [. . .] primarily so that the public [would] not be so easily manipulated by globalization, mass culture, by what [was] popular and non-Cuban" (ibid.). At issue, he asserted, was the maintenance of "real values versus fictitious ones," and the fight against pseudo-culture—a culture that was "banal," without history or without memory.

Since the mid-1990s, tourists in Havana and Santiago de Cuba had been treated to "traditional" and folkloric performances—the most popular of which included either Afro-Cuban ritual, dance, and drumming in bright-colored costumes correlating to the various Santería *orishas* (Yoruban or Santerian gods), or sexy *muchachas* in high heels and low-cut dresses, dancing to live salsa bands—imitations of real culture, certainly, but not the desired part of real culture according to Abel Prieto and the Consejo. Such performances were labeled "pseudo-culture" or, sometimes if also Afro-Cuban in nature, "pseudo-folklore," because they were being done for commercial purposes and had changed their original forms to please foreign audiences. Katherine Hagedorn describes this phenomenon in detail in her ethnography about the Conjunto Folklórico Nacional (National Folkloric Dance and Music group) and Afro-Cuban drumming and dance in Havana (2001). Performances imitating foreign popular culture were also given this stigma. Little girls imitating the gyrating Spice Girls received an intensely critical response from La Cruzada members when the act welcomed the group in one of the small mountain *caseríos* (small scattered groupings of campesino dwellings)— the cultural contaminants having reached even the most remote places on the island.

The Massification of Culture was the state's crusade against pseudo-culture and against the effects of the dollar market in socialist Cuba. Although artists grumbled at the idea of "massifying" their individual works of art and what they considered unique and creative performance, they were glad to receive additional resources and official support. With the Massification of Culture, prominent groups from Havana and other city centers were being "encouraged" to travel to other provinces to perform, often to the farthest and the least desirable ones (although seldom were distant provincial artists invited to the center). One Havana critic explained it as "subtle coercion." The bureaucratic process of this sharing of national culture was tedious: one municipal board called another, inviting a particular group to come and perform in their town. The municipal board where the group was based then had to decide if it had the funds to send the group, since expenses were shared between traveling and host groups. Even if the invited group did not want to go, the political pressure of the Massification of Culture often forced them to comply, lest they seem anti-revolutionary and unwilling to participate in the new cultural movement. The hosting cultural board and member artists had to act graciously toward the visitors for the same reasons. Thus, since 1999, even the easternmost region of Oriente had received visiting performing groups in music, dance, and theater. This was especially exciting to the local artists themselves, who were anxious to share their art with others and to get to know their compatriots from other regions, but maybe not so exciting for the visitors, who might have preferred Barcelona, Brussels, Paris, or Caracas.

In October of 2000, it was announced that Teatro Buendía (Good Day Theater) was bringing its latest play, *Historia de un Caba-yo* (History of a Horse) to the main stage theater in Guantánamo, the Teatro Guaso (Guaso Theater House). Usually reserved for large musical concerts or formal award ceremonies, local theater groups were seldom allowed access to Teatro Guaso. Teatro Buendía was famous, in part, for its legendary director, Flora Lauten. Lauten had been a member of influential theater groups in the 1960s: Teatro Estudio (Studio Theater), Teatro Los

Doce (Theater of the Twelve), and was also one of the founding members of Teatro Escambray. In the late 1970s, she had moved on with the Teatro Nuevo movement and had directed her first group, Teatro de La Yaya.[6] In the 1980s, she returned to Havana and became an instructor for the prestigious Instituto Superior de Arte (ISA), eventually forming Teatro Buendía with her most talented students. The artistic director, Raquel Carrío, was also a powerful figure in the Cuban theater scene as a critic and as a representative of the Casa de las Américas (House of the Americas). Teatro Buendía was housed in a small converted theater space in Havana, in a neighborhood called Nuevo Vedado, several blocks from the imposing National Theater and the Plaza de Revolución (Revolutionary Plaza). Its beautiful and haunting plays were heavily symbolic and complex, often superimposing local references on universal classics, such as its 1999 version of *The Tempest*, which depicted the Caliban–Prospero relationship laced in multilayered racial and colonial politics and lost utopias, and which included, for provocative spice, a hint of Fidel Castro.[7] Teatro Buendía's actors were all ISA-trained, beautiful people, polished and disciplined, and often bare-chested (both men and women). Given Lauten's, Carrío's, and the group's reputation, they were well supported, which was apparent from their elaborate costuming and sets. Teatro Buendía was one of the top three groups in the nation and their cultural authority was matched by few others.

As the audience entered Teatro Guaso that opening night in November, anticipation was high. Approximately fifty of Guantánamo's professional artists, actors, and local government officials were invited to sit in chairs on the stage itself to simulate the intimate setting of Buendía's home theater space, while about half of the eight hundred seats in the main auditorium were filled with the general public. I sat on stage with the actors, equally excited to see a new piece by Teatro Buendía, since I was rarely in Havana and my visits did not always coincide with their performances. Soon, the assistant director, Nelda Castillo, arrived on stage to give an introduction to the group and to greet the Guantanameros, apologizing that the directors, Lauten and Carrío, had not been able to make the long trip. During this introduction, this highly respected theater group from Havana, referred to the province—on the city's main stage, in front of an audience made up of 100 percent Guantánamo residents—as an *oscuro rincón* (dark corner) of Cuba: "It took us a long time to get here [laughing and looking conspiratorially at the

Buendía actors], but we are very happy to have finally reached this dark corner of Cuba" (paraphrase of Castillo's remark, November 2001). Although not truly intended, at least not consciously, to be derogatory, it was certainly interpreted as such by an audience sensitive to such insinuations, and a disgruntled murmur quickly filled the theater, several audience members even walking out of the auditorium altogether, highly offended. Artists seated on stage looked at each other with raised eyebrows, some making comments such as "Well, she can go back home if she sees us that way." Realizing her blunder, she nervously attempted to explain, "I only meant that, uh, . . ." but the damage had been done, and the audience watched the play with a heightened sense of critique. Her comment was talked about for weeks afterward, actors and non-actors alike criticizing the snobbery of the artists from Havana and their erroneous and pretentious perception of Guantánamo as *inculto*, backward, and provincial.

After living in Guantánamo for almost a year, Nelda Castillo's remark even offended me on behalf of my friends and colleagues, although I had to admit that there was, indeed, a distinct difference between living in or near Havana, and living in the farthest eastern reaches of the island. In Cumanayagua and rural Escambray, there was some feeling of being far away, but in Guantánamo, the feeling was many times amplified. Even living in the semiurban area of Guantánamo City produced this feeling of distance. Perhaps the biggest mistake Nelda Castillo made was adding the adjective "dark" to her comment, suggesting an unwanted or dangerous element lurking. Her comment also awakened the actors' sensitivities to being professional artists in Guantánamo, and the paradox of having pride in their campesino roots while also being *culto*—on the same cultural level as the city folk, or more importantly, as Havana folk. Their perceived level of talent was at stake. If they were really talented, why were they still working in Guantánamo? Why did they stay in this *oscuro rincón*? Why hadn't they moved to Havana? Were artists in peripheral areas as "underdeveloped" as the area itself, untrained by official institutions such as ISA and thus primitive in their artistic ability? Such questions were not only asked by the artists themselves, but also the general public.

The "making it in New York City" analogy serves well here, for American artists are not conceived to have truly "made it" unless they are successful on the biggest theater circuit in the country, or at least in the major theaters of a big city. Being a professional actor or director in rural Missouri or West Virginia does not carry the same legitimacy. Moving to Havana was usually impossible for most Cubans living in other provinces, regardless of profession and artistic talent, although artists were some of the few who had a better chance. They could not just pick up and go, find a cheap apartment, find a temporary (or permanent) job as a waiter or receptionist, and give it their best shot. Moving to another province and especially to Havana required the unlikely procurement of state permission, preceded by long months of dealing with the socialist bureaucracy. Artists had to have a new job lined up with a formal invitation by the new director or employer. The state had to deem this an acceptable situation and necessary for both parties. If the artists were then lucky enough to pass these obstacles, they were faced with the daunting task of finding a place to live. Without the family house or apartment available, they had to rent a room or apartment in Havana, sometimes paying in *divisas* at double an individual's monthly salary. If they wanted to continue taking advantage of the sparsely allocated goods provided by the state, their *libretas* (ration books) had to be transferred to the new location, squeezing another individual into an already oversaturated urban system. Uprooting and moving to a new province, especially one so far away as Havana, was also rare for reasons of family. Unlike the fickle American, who moves 2,000 miles away from family and friends for a new job or change of scenery, most Cubans I met preferred to live close to their extended family and network of social support.

Therefore, since Guantánamo's artists often could not validate their talent in Havana, they looked for their own sense of value, their own unique contribution that could not be matched by urban workers. They allied themselves with the Revolution in general, and also with the socialist morality intent on spreading art and theater to the less fortunate, especially during the Special Period. One way to distinguish themselves from what they perceived to be self-serving Havana groups playing to elitist audiences was to share their art with campesinos and inhabitants of the zonas de silencio, to educate them and make them more culto, to "awaken their lost spirituality," to bring light and color to an otherwise tedious and physically strenuous life, and to take part in the creation of the seemingly intangible *Hombre Novísimo*. Artists in Guantánamo claimed that this was a task urban artists could not do as well. Urban artists, they believed, did not have specialized cultural knowledge of the countryside, and thus could not achieve the necessary degree of mutual trust with the campesinos. Nor did they have the commitment, the patience, or the endurance to adjust to an "Option Zero" lifestyle. Guantánamo artists nodded knowingly when hearing rumors of Los Elementos and other rural groups losing group members to the city or Europe on a consistent basis. And those places were not even *más allá* enough to be populated with *campesinos de verdad*. City artists were soft.

The Theater Crusade

José Martí, nuestro más alto intelectual, nos dejó en su diario de campaña "Subir lomas hermana hombres. Y hombres que se hermanan crecen cada año porque cruzamos por nuevos sitios cargados por la esperanza—de un hombre más culto. La Cruzada Teatral Guantánamo nace de las ansias de un colectivo que quiere extender su práctica profesional a todo el territorio, hasta hoy virgen, para conocer sus problemáticas comunitarias y adquirir nuevos espacios, nuevos públicos y nuevos temas para repertorio.

José Martí, our most exalted intellectual, wrote in his field diary: "To climb hills unites men." And men that unite, grow every year because we pass through new places, full of hope—for the development of a more cultivated man. The Theater Crusade of Guantánamo was born from a collective's desire to share its professional abilities with a territory that had been, until now, virgin. It wanted to learn about the social problems in these communities and to obtain new spaces, new audiences, and new themes for its repertory.
—URY RODRÍGUEZ, from an unpublished conference paper
about La Cruzada (1998)

In 1991, a small group of actors joined together to create La Cruzada Teatral Guantánamo-Baracoa, a theater crusade to seek new audiences, and to bring theater to extremely isolated rural communities which otherwise had no access to the arts or to national cultural programs. The project began in 1990, at the onset of the Special Period, when most artists were not traveling at all, let alone performing locally. Tula, an actor, explained that "nosotros creamos este evento para, precisamente, poder salir a brindar nuestro arte, sin necesidad de que nos pusieran una guagua, petróleo, dieta" (we created this event for precisely that reason;

to go out and offer our art, without anyone giving us a bus, fuel, or food) (Tula, interview, Guantánamo, 2000). From 1990 to 1995, food and basic resources were extremely scarce in Cuban society generally. The development of a new theatrical group requiring special provisions thus confronted serious challenges. To take theatrical productions into areas with no electricity, no running water, no stores, virtually no modern developments whatsoever, was an unusual and, some said, ludicrous proposal during this period. Cubans could barely find enough food to keep their families from going hungry, let alone materials for puppet and costume making. Participants also worried that it would be difficult for their campesino hosts, having nothing to offer such a large group of visitors. Actors slept on the ground in open air, in bunk beds of vacant dormitories, or on the floors of empty building spaces without complaint (at least not *too* much complaint, admitted one actor), but they still had to find food and other daily supplies.

The campesinos in rural Guantánamo Province lived very isolated from the nearest city (Guantánamo City) and even from neighboring pueblos, much more so than residents of areas of difficult access in the Escambray Mountain region. They lived in *bohíos*, thirty minutes to two hours away from each other (walking), even when from the same "town" (see figures 15 and 16). Many campesinos had never even seen a very small city, such as Guantánamo City, much less a capital city such as Havana, which lay, in their eyes (and in the Cuban reality) too far away to fully conceptualize. Cubans living in these zonas de silencio (also known as "areas of difficult access") were forced to walk everywhere, and were not fazed by a two-hour hike to visit a neighbor or return from work in the fields. Although most were familiar with buses and trains, they rarely used them, since reaching the bus stop often required hours of hiking or hitching rides on infrequent and uncomfortable tractors. Many of the wealthier campesinos had horses or mules to help with transport and cargo, and horses were especially helpful for human travel (though not the mules, which lived up to their stubborn reputation). Sometimes tractors or jeeps were able to reach these isolated areas, but only if there was a wide enough path through sometimes rocky terrain, and only in the dry seasons. Rain and mud invariably made such trips impossible. Oftentimes, the sick or injured were carried down the mountains on a cot, framed with wooden rods on the shoulders of two to four men, and locals explained, both joking and disturbingly serious, that if someone

15. Bohío and campesino family in Dos Brazos, Guantánamo Province

(below) 16. Corina, campesina in her bohío, Dos Brazos, Guantánamo Province
(Both photos by Laurie Frederik, 2000)

was sick enough to be carried away, they would probably return in a coffin. Until 1991, when La Cruzada was launched, most of these campesinos had never seen a play or any kind of artistic performance outside of their own local amateur music groups.

La Cruzada began every year on José Martí's birthday, in homage to El Maestro (The Teacher), and continued for a full month. The group passed through five municipalities of Guantánamo: Yateras, San Antonio del Sur, Imías, Maisí, and Baracoa (see map 3). It stopped in small towns along the main road, but focused on reaching the tiny caseríos located one to three hours off road (driving, riding, or hiking) on dirt paths. La Cruzada presented itself as a "sociocultural" project, more interested in the effects it had on the community than in the aesthetic of the particular production. This differed markedly from the majority of conventional theater groups in the cities, and especially those in Havana, which depended on the intellectual artistic community and professional critics to gauge their quality and worth. Yet in the farthest reaches of these small mountain pueblos, such opinions were hardly important. Gauges of success and talent were the amount of laughter and applause received from the campesinos after a performance, as well as the extent to which actors felt they were leaving behind their *huellas* (footprints, traces). Their brochure proudly stated that *La Cruzada "hizo ganar en la consciencia de lo que aquel casi imposible sueño, traspasaba las fronteras del arte para convertirse en un formidable vehículo de real transformación social."* (The Crusade was able to build a consciousness that had once been a far-out, almost impossible dream. They transcended the frontiers of art to convert it into a formidable vehicle for real social transformation.)[8]

The first Crusade was done on foot, with the help of several mules to carry necessary cargo, such as food, tents, and theater props. "We weren't able to go too far, since we were moving so slowly," said Maribel, current director of La Cruzada, "but we accomplished a lot." Most long-time members remembered the early days with nostalgia, and although they appreciated the miles covered by the truck instead of their tired legs, they lamented that the experience was more "authentic" with mules. Freddy, the group's producer and Maribel's husband, said he felt more a part of el campo on foot, that the act was more "gallant," but now, he added, "we aren't so exhausted when we arrive and can present more plays." After 1995, the group had obtained the use of a Russian flatbed truck, upon which supplies and the more than twenty participants were loaded.

17. La Cruzada Teatral members and the author on the truck at Punta de Maisí, Guantánamo Province (photo by unknown photographer, 2000)

(below) 18. La Cruzada Teatral, rowboat ride to next performance in Boma II, with two of the actors, Edilberto and Pindi, and a campesino rower, Guantánamo Province (photo by Laurie Frederik, 2000)

When the truck was not able to pass certain routes, the actors got off and walked the rest of the way or found alternative transport. "Alternative" transport during my experience in 2000 included an oxcart, a rowboat, a tractor, and a mule (see figures 17 and 18).

On entering each pueblo or caserío, we were greeted by a group of children lining the road. Warned ahead of time by local municipal officials of our arrival, they were strategically placed and instructed to sing and cheer as the truck rolled up the path. In Yumurí, we were thrown little white flowers. These receptions were remarkable experiences, and the actors were very touched by them, perhaps feeling a trace of the fame Teatro Buendía seemed to take for granted. Miles away from the overly critical eyes of urban playgoers and professional critics, they were greeted here with revolutionary songs, José Martí's poetry, and traditional rural treats, such as *galletas de leche* (milk cookies), fresh coconuts expertly opened with slashes of machetes, fresh tangerines, and freshly made *cucurucho*, sweet coconut candy wrapped in palm leaves. In 2000, we were also bombarded with songs dedicated to Elián González, and remakes of the television theme songs played whenever a national *tribunal* was aired (nightly demonstrations in protest of the "kidnapping").[9] An *Altar de Cruz* ritual (also known as an *Alumbrado*) featured Elián's photo, placed on the altar itself next to Santa Barbara and Chango, and some of the ritual songs were sung in his honor in a bizarre juxtaposition of local tradition and international politics. One children's group in Baracoa chanted " ¡Elián, amigo, te quiero estar contigo!" (Elián, my friend, I want to be with you!) as we rolled into town. With an impish grin, Edilberto questioned under his breath whether that meant the children wanted to be with him *aquí* in Cuba or *allá*, in the United States. These sorts of events during La Cruzada interrupted the imagined pristine experience of *pura cepa*, and reminded the group that the most isolated areas, however romantic and idyllic at first glance, were still part of a national and international system.

Los Incultos

During the early years, the plays selected to go on the trip were kept "simple," according to Maribel, who said that they "first had to win [the campesinos] over since they had never seen theater before" (Maribel, interview, Guantánamo, 2000). Plays by Rómulo Loredo were presented, since they were "all about *guajiros*," and the group also adapted well-known stories by the writer Onelio Jorge Cardoso, who often used popular and rural language familiar to La Cruzada audiences (Tula, interview, Guantánamo, 2000). Most of the rural audiences were fascinated upon first sight, clamoring for more when the hour-long production ended. They were excited by the new colors and melodies, by how life could be enacted, made beautiful, made fantastical, made humorous, and by how they could escape from their daily lives if only for an afternoon. Others, however, mostly children but including a fair share of adults, were suspicious of the plays, primarily the masks and puppets, which they saw as having potential religious or ritual significance which departed from their own. Maribel recounted one instance after a puppet-making workshop when the town minister forced a little girl to throw away the doll she had just made, saying that the figure was surely demonic and that the girl should not have such things. To the Cruzada artists, this was a sign of cultural primitivism—of not understanding art and representation. Although many of Cuba's churches were either closed or downsized in the first decades of the Revolution, religious *cultos* (cults, small worship groups) in the mountains did not suffer the same level of religious discrimination or persecution as those in the cities. Many of the small pueblos we visited in Guantánamo had a large population of *religiosos* (religious people), who belonged to *cultos* set up mainly by American Baptist missionaries in the 1940s and 1950s. Through informal conversations and interviews I learned that many of the religiosos disapproved of the average Cuban campesino, who they thought were uneducated, who fought and stole, committed adultery, and drank too much. Interestingly enough, these same religiosos led us to an old cockfight ring set into the side of a mountain rock and told nostalgic stories about how many generations of their families had held fights at this location. As will be seen in chapter 6, the *pelea de gallo* appeared to be an essential element of campesino identity, God-fearing or not. Religious services were held mainly in private homes in a special room with homemade pews and plastic flowers. La Cruzada actors were invited in for the opening part of the ritual in one small town near Baracoa, and they sang musical hymns led by a woman with a tambourine. Hymnals were traditional-looking Christian books, printed in Kansas, 1948, words in Spanish. We watched with fascination at a part of rural culture few knew existed or at least never acknowledged as a "traditional" part of el campo. The actors marveled at how a group of people could sing a hymn without the least bit of collective melody, never having had a piano or tuned guitar to set the key or the tone progression. It was also probable that without a piano, no one had ever learned to read music. Unfortunately, we were asked to leave when the more "serious" part commenced, this group of city people not considered members of the religioso (or mountain) community.

During the first few years, Tula and Maribel explained, there were times it seemed they were not performing for anybody, since the section of land cleared of sticks and stones for the audience was empty. However, upon closer inspection, timid eyes could be seen peeping out of windows and heads peering around corners of houses. In some pueblos, curiosity would overtake fear. Eventually, the campesinos would sit in front of their houses to watch, in full view, and finally, begin to approach the stage. The "stage" here, and in most mountain venues, consisted simply of the flattest clearing the actors could find, preferably against a small hill or bank so that the audience could sit comfortably on logs or rocks, or lean against their horses.

The other aspect of theater that was initially foreign to the campesinos was, and remains, its distinct etiquette of behavior. Even ten years after its inception, the campesinos I witnessed during the 2000 Cruzada seemed to find it difficult to remain seated quietly during a play, particularly comical scenes, longer monologues, or perhaps those that bored them. They yelled out at the characters, inciting laughter or additional commentary from fellow audience members. Children too young to be afraid, or those dared by their friends, approached the action in the performance space, looking up at the actors and trying to touch them or play with them, the naughtier ones trying to distract them until mothers eventually realized the transgression and pulled them back. Applause is also a learned tradition and pueblos already visited would clap for just five seconds, if at all, before jumping up to leave. In the so-called virgin pueblos, however, those audiences without previous experience with La Cruzada or other theater groups would sit and wait silently until an actor stood up to tell them the play had ended, inviting them to talk with the actors. Most would nervously look at each other and then slowly wander back to their homes, choosing not to engage with the visitors or to discuss the play's content, though some of the more confident men or those involved in "cultural work" would periodically stay to ask questions. For someone who had participated in the American theater for over twenty years, this was a unique thing to see, although I had read many similar accounts in other parts of Latin America and Africa. In Guantánamo, the Cuban actors seemed to be just as amazed as I was (though much more experienced) with the campesinos' reaction or non-reaction, even a decade after their first mountain trip. The actors told me that campesino reactions were not consistent or predicable, especially as they added new locations every year. New audiences often needed to be "broken in" or "theatrically educated."

At the Punta de Maisí, the farthest eastern tip of Cuba, an even more interesting phenomenon was witnessed, one that the group mused about for several days afterward. La Cruzada's performance of the play *La muerte juega el escondido: una leyenda guajira* (Death Plays Hide and Seek: A Hillbilly Legend) was scheduled for a Sunday afternoon at 3 P.M. In "Cuban time," this meant the performance began at 4:15 P.M. About three-quarters of the way through the play, over half of the audience quietly got up and left. Several individuals started the exodus, and the others took their cue and followed in small groups of two and three. We were flabbergasted. The play was funny, full of ghosts and wacky campesino characters, and usually a hit with the rural audiences. Why on earth would so many people be leaving at one time? There were no comments muttered, no sighs of impatience or harrumphs of disapproval, nor were there any apologetic glances as they left the space. They just upped and left. The actors finished their performance with a bit less enthusiasm and confidence than was usually displayed, only a handful of people left watching until the end, and we gathered together to pack up and leave. As we walked back to camp, we noticed a large group of people sitting on the beach, staring out at the water at what looked like a tiny bright light off in the distance. Approaching the group, we realized it was our lost audience and one of them explained that every Sunday at 6 P.M. they went to the beach to watch *el dominguero*. *El dominguero* was a large American cruise ship (it was rumored) that passed by the island's eastern shore every Sunday. We sat down with the group and watched the light slowly bob in the distance, as if watching a fireworks display, but without the ooohs and aaaahs. This was a quiet and melancholy show, almost meditative, like watching a sunset, and when the light disappeared, the people simply got up and walked home. The actors discussed *el dominguero* afterwards wondering if it was a way for these Cubans living at an isolated edge of the world to dream about what lay beyond, what lay *más* allá, only in the other direction, away from Havana and the United States. Perhaps they imagined the glamour of the dining rooms and women in pearls and furs, as in the movie *Titanic* (a huge hit in Cuba). Or maybe it was the awe of movement and of change represented in the passage of the ship across the horizon. Unfortunately, we never got the chance to investigate further, since at 5:00 the next morning, the truck was packed and we were en route to the next town. Ten years later I learned that the image of el dominguero had been just as compelling to others as it was to me, for when I reconnected with the *Bohemia* photographer Jorge Ignacio (but by then living in Spain) and we began to reminisce about Guantánamo, he asked "Ay Laura, ¿recuerdas el dominguero?" (do you remember el dominguero?).

As the first years of La Cruzada passed, the group began to present more "complex" types of plays such as Cervantes and other classics. This was possible, said Maribel, once the campesinos had learned how to discern "good" theater from "bad" theater. Their 2000 play, *La muerte juega el escondido: una leyenda guajira* (Death Plays Hide and Seek: A Guajiro Legend; see figure 19), had been converted from a Don Quixote story. Although this was a typical morality tale of greed and generosity, good and evil, life and death, there were clear signs that modern-day political topics had reached the countryside. In one scene, the script calls for the Devil to tempt the main guajiro character, first with prostitutes (which the actors referred to as *jineteras*[10]), and second, with a bag of gold coins. In the La Cruzada version, the Devil (played by Ury Rodríguez) first pulls out a photocopied and enlarged U.S. dollar, and when he throws the bag of "gold coins" to the ground, the audience sees two large U.S. dollar symbols printed on the side ($$)—certainly devilish in its truest form, and a symbol that all Cubans would recognize as such. Although the greedy and "contaminated" sister, Santona, wants to keep the money for herself, the noble campesino (in this legend, a guajiro) Harriero does not succumb.

Santona: *¿Qué tienes en las manos?*
Harriero: *Una bolsa.*
Santona: *¿Quién te la dio?*
Harriero: *Vino de . . . (señala con el dedo hacia arriba).*
Santona: *¿Y qué contiene?*
Harriero: *Mucho dinero. [. . .]*
Santona: *¡Guajiro, te le escapaste al diablo! Tienes ahora una bueno bolsa de*

monedas de oro. Vamos a ver cuanto es. (Trata de arrebatarle la bolsa a Harriero, este no se deja.)

Harriero: *Saca la mano que te pica el gallo. Esta bolsa es mía. ¡Me la gané yo! ¡Soy millonario! ¡Soy el hombre más rico en el mundo! ¡Y tengo tanto dinero que lo voy a repartir para solucionar todos los problemas de mis amigos y vecinos!*

Santona: *¡Cállate la boca guanajo, que la gente va a venir a sacarte hasta el último centavo! No diga más nada y esconde esa plata.*

(Los amigos y vecinos entra a escena con mucha alegría, bailan y cantan.)

Santona: What do you have in your hands?

Harriero: A bag.

Santona: Who gave it to you?

Harriero: It came from . . . *(he points a finger up into the sky)*

Santona: And what does it have in it?

Harriero: A lot of money [. . .]

19. La Cruzada Teatral, Don Quixote (Carlos), Sancho Panza (Juan Carlos), and guajiro characters (Maruha and Edilberto) in *La muerte juega el escondido*, Guantánamo Province (photo by Laurie Frederik, 2000)

Santona: Guajiro! You ran away with the Devil! You have a big bag of golden coins. Let's see how much there is. *(She tries to snatch the bag away from Harriero. He doesn't let her.)*

Harriero: Get your hand away or the rooster will bite it. This bag is mine. I won it! I am a millionaire! I am the richest man in the world! I have so much money that I'm going to give it out to solve the problems of my friends and neighbors!

Santona: Shut your mouth you simpleton! People are going to come to take it from you up to the very last cent! Don't say anything else and hide that money.

(His friends and neighbors enter the scene with much happiness, dancing and singing.) [11]

What might have appeared preconceived (but fortunately wasn't) occurred when an unlucky swipe with a machete took one of the actresses temporarily out of commission, and I was recruited to perform two of her roles: a *jinetera* and a soldier. Her heavily bleeding thumb required stitches, so the actress was rushed down from the mountain town into Baracoa for a few days. With three hours before the play's performance, Maribel, the director, approached and asked me to step in for her non-talking scenes. All I had to do, she said, was to dance and play the Devil's assistant in one scene and an armed soldier in the second. Since I had watched the play every night for several weeks, I knew the parts and was happy for the opportunity to get on stage with the group, but the role selection did make me stop and reflect. While my musical debut in Cuba had been singing John Lennon's "Imagine" in Cumanayagua during an anti-imperialism rally, my acting debut in Guantánamo was to be the seductress, promising money and sex to those who succumbed, as well as a soldier with a gun, threatening to force my will on the poor, innocent, *pura cepa* of Cuba.

The play was partly Poetic Fantasy in its phantom characters, including "Death" herself (played by Virginia López) and a group of scary dead spirits dressed in white. Don Quixote (played by Carlos Pérez, a.k.a. Tío Tato) and Sancho Panza posed as God and Saint Peter with the power to grant wishes, as saviors of humility and as the guajiro's, or perhaps Cuba's, conscience—and, ironically, the Spanish author, Cervantes, was chosen as the one to do this. But it also lay in the realm of Folk Rusticity, filled with cursing and the crudity of real rural life. Even God and Saint Peter spoke in *campesino*-isms, and Death's symbolic involvement was to play the game "hide-and-seek" with Harriero—a soul-selling scene. The play was rustic enough to have the campesino audience laughing and staying in their seats until the end (except for the day of el dominguero).

The organization of La Cruzada remained consistent through its ten-year history: children's theater and puppet shows during the day, held at the local secondary schools, plays for *jovenes* in the late afternoons, held at high schools, called *pre-universitarios*, and plays for adults and the entire community in the evenings, in outside clearings, or anywhere the actors could set up their presentations. Night performances began at 9 P.M., after everyone had eaten dinner, animals had been tended to, and the daily chores were finished. If it rained, the play was canceled. If the generator died, the play was canceled. Depending on the size of the pueblo, anywhere from ten to two hundred spectators gathered to watch the annual play, often the only professional artistic production they would see for the whole year, and campesinos living in neighboring communities that were not visited by the group walked long distances to attend the performance. La Cruzada owned one spotlight with a stand, powered by a small generator, all provided by the Ministry of Culture after the third year of the project. Compared to the dim flickering of the usual handmade beeswax candles, or small kerosene *faroles* (lanterns) made from old beer or soda cans, this single spotlight appeared to illuminate the entire town.

When La Cruzada members were asked to speak publicly, and also theoretically, about the experience, statements aligned the project with the official jargon of Teatro Comunitario:

> *Esperamos que los resultados de este informe investigativo contribuyan al conocimiento más detallado de la identidad cultural de nuestras comunidades de montaña, de manera que la continuidad de este experimento permita elaborar una estrategia de trabajo comunitario en consonancia con la política del estado cubano.*

> We hope that the results of this investigation contribute to a more detailed knowledge of the cultural identity of our mountain communities, and that the continuation of this experiment permits us to build a strategy for community work in consonance with the politics of the Cuban State.[12]

This was a very noble mission, although their public statements often differed from the informal commentary heard while bumping along on yet another arduous mountain pass, or at night, as each member took turns cooking, cleaning up, and breaking down camp. During radio, TV, or newspaper interviews, they spoke of sacrifice, of socialist comradery and revolutionary spirit, selflessness, and national pride, of bringing culture to those campesinos without access, to educate, to share with and learn from their *compañeros del campo*—again illustrating the objectification of culture and the idea that it can be lost, saved, or transported through the mountains on a crusade. La Cruzada members described the beauty of the countryside and the sincerity and hospitality of the campesinos; how remarkable they felt to be welcomed by rows of singing children, throwing flowers and embracing the actors with genuine emotion, and how proud they were to see their Cuban flag raised above the most isolated of pueblos, with the obligatory bust of Martí placed prominently in front of the school.

However, after one week of difficult traveling, camping outside on cement or dirt floors, working from 6 A.M. to 11 P.M., and sharing every moment with twenty other people who were not their families, communal living in Option Zero conditions became less noble and less romantic. Actors told me that in the early years of its formation, the group was very tightknit and there was a sincere feeling of trust and friendship within the group, created by the drive to develop the project. However, in the last several years internal politics and personal feuds had formed irreversible rifts in the group, and several said they continued to participate in the annual trip only because they felt they "should" and that they were doing it only for the campesinos they visited. Yet after several more months in Guantánamo, it became apparent that more was at stake than just dedication to their audiences. La Cruzada was, in fact, their only link to national recognition.

Mutiny

In 1993, at the height of the Special Period, La Cruzada was plagued with its worst shortages, and many of the promised supplies were not delivered for the annual trip. Then the director Ury Rodríguez was faced with the decision to either abandon the project, stopping the momentum of their noble crusade and succumbing to the national crisis, or to persevere, demonstrating the level of personal sacrifice they were willing to endure for their country. There was much discussion within the group, no one truly realizing just how problematic the shortages were going to be. One week into the trip, a meeting was held among group members, without Ury's presence and without his knowledge. They were angry, blaming the problem on Ury's inability to procure the necessary resources. The group felt helpless, frustrated, and, most of all, hungry, and they debated about whether or not to abandon La Cruzada that year, vowing to vote in a new president. Ury was bitter when he spoke about this incident, resentful that his fellow actors had blamed him, personally, for shortages brought on by a national crisis.

When I asked the current La Cruzada actors as well as Ury why they did not, in the end, abandon the project, they reminded me of the daily receptions by the children and campesinos, and how powerful and emotional this was for an actor who was used to the cool indifference of the city folk. The act of giving up and leaving was also, they said, just like the thousands of *gusanos* (worms, traitors) attempting to flee the country from Havanah in homemade rafts, or from Guantánamo, swimming miles to reach the American territorial waters around the naval base.[13] La Cruzada stood in defiance of defeatism even more than most Teatro Comunitario groups in that the actors were putting themselves in relative discomfort for a full month, and were sacrificing family, friends, and their homes in order to perform for strangers in the mountains. According to several of La Cruzada members, Teatro de los Elementos' living conditions were luxurious in comparison. Part of the romance and power of the project was found in such daily struggles, and to give up for lack of food and resources in the early 1990s would have displayed weakness and selfishness: characteristics highly criticized in revolutionary rhetoric. In 1993, Ury had been the hapless scapegoat, the only one the group had control over during this difficult crisis. Ury had stood in place of the state, in place of party officials, in place of the U.S. embargo, and in place of the gusanos who had gone in search of (and had found, according to the myths) an easier and more luxurious life. But by challenging Ury, the group had also vicariously confronted the ultimate power—the invisible Foucauldian panopticism which watched over and dictated their lives, but which was not taking care of its captives.

Providing food for the actors was no longer a problem in the 2000s. Campesinos were then some of the richest people in the country, rich in the resources necessary for subsistence and also in pesos. With the new allowance for semi-private farmer's markets, campesinos could earn a profit once they had fulfilled the production quota required for national distribution. Most of the internal discontent in La Cruzada in 2000 was due to the increase in the number of pueblos visited and the number of functions per day. Although La Cruzada's quest to reach more and more pueblos began before the official onset of the Massification of Culture, it still corresponded to the quickly growing number of Special Period theater groups and the competition for national recognition. La Cruzada directors learned that with more members, higher creative output, and increased audience attendance, state aid was more forthcoming. In 1999 they were given $1,500, with which they bought sleeping pads, cooking pots, boots, and cold-weather jackets, and the group continued to receive $1,000 for the next two years. After winning the National Award for Teatro Comunitario from the Ministry of Culture in 2000, they were given another $2,000, and an additional 200 pesos of support (about ten U.S. dollars) came from a young artists' association called La Asociación Nacional Hermanos Saíz (National Association of the Saíz Brothers). Not surprisingly, surpassing the number of pueblos visited each year on La Cruzada became one of the group's goals.

Antes de tener el camión, no estábamos tan preocupados por cuantos lugares podríamos llegar durante el mes. A pie y en mula, que se mueven muy lentamente y no es mucho que puede hacer. Pero ahora podemos llegar a más lugares. Es más como un concurso, de cómo muchos más lugares en los que puede llegar a más que el año pasado. (Tula, personal communication, Guantánamo, 2000)

Before we had the truck, we weren't so worried about how many places we could reach during the month. On foot and mule, you move very slowly and there is only so much you can do. But now we can reach more places. It's more like a contest now, of how many more places we can get to over last year.

By the mid-1990s, a chart (see table) had been drawn up to keep official track of the increase in numbers of communities visited and audiences in attendance (La Cruzada Teatral Performances, group archives, Consejo Provincial de las Artes Escénicas, Guantánamo).

As a result of the rigorous schedule that developed by 2000, the group had stopped giving workshops on puppet making and storytelling, as extra time was now spent traveling to yet another school or community instead of focusing on just one. Additional transport was also rented in participating regions, and extra trucks or jeeps were offered to help divide and bring smaller groupings of actors to different locations. Hence, three small groups could be sent to three different communities on a single afternoon, the vehicles dropping off two of the groups, the

TABLE Numbers of Communities Visited and Audiences in Attendance at La Cruzada Teatral Performances, 1991–2001

Year	Performances	Communities	Audience
1991	114	46	36,130
1992	79	49	26,650
1993	124	44	128,620
1994	120	60	19,002
1995	131	70	13,412
1996	131	92	17,500
1997	164	92	19,328
1998	176	113	25,400
1999	192	131	28,749
2000	263	159	41,746
2001	249	191	39,039

Source: La Cruzada Teatral Performances, group archives, Consejo de Artes Escénicas, Guantánamo.

third walking or riding on borrowed horses to another. In the evenings, the entire group would join together to present a collective play for the adults. The next morning, at sunrise, they would break camp, prepare the truck, and set off to the next pueblo, sometimes traveling for several hours before arriving and starting the whole daily cycle again. Such an intense work schedule made the actors tired and frustrated. Unable to rest, read, or even do their laundry, they became resentful and felt manipulated by the expectations placed upon them. "We're doing this for free, after all," they sometimes mumbled (meaning not paid extra for the additional hardships). But fulfilling their political obligation to the Revolution was the price they had to pay for salaries, resources, and for their reputation as professional artists (cf. Haraszti 1987; Verdery 1991).

Premio and Privilege

In spite of their frustrations, the actors continued to participate and agreed to go on La Cruzada's tour every year. Solidarity had become a political obligation, maintained by a growing national reputation— something otherwise unattainable for small theater groups in Guantánamo. Without some kind of *national* mission, these small groups were essentially forgotten and neglected by the country's Ministry of Culture, and were unknown in the country, even in intellectual circles. But as part of La Cruzada they gained artistic recognition and respect. They gained publicity with the delivery of papers at conferences in Havana (such as *Comunidad* and *Cultura y Desarrollo*), and articles were published about them in popular journals (*Tablas, Revolución y Cultura, La Gaceta, Bohemia*) and national newspapers (*Granma, Juventud Rebelde*). A few foreign visitors (an Italian journalist, an American anthropologist, a Columbian actress) also expressed interest, writing or talking about them in their respective countries and languages (see Frederik 2005). Thus, the incentive to remain affiliated with the project continued to build. Media coverage of La Cruzada put more pressure on its success, and increased expectations of the quality and quantity of cultural output. The Massification of Culture campaign especially influenced the project, and in the summer of 2000, artists were required to attend several official meetings with the Consejo of Guantánamo to discuss the importance of their role in the movement. Although, like artists elsewhere, they did not like the chosen name, "Massification" or idea of "massifying" their art, they did respond to the call for action since their "crusading" mission was directly in line with the campaign, much more so than projects like Los Elementos, which did not attempt to reach anywhere close to 39,039 people in a single month.

La Cruzada's success was defined in different ways. Public television announcers and newspaper and journal writers admired it for sharing its art with the humble campesinos in the mountains. These commentaries focused on the romance of the countryside, its flowing rivers, rugged peaks, and the hearty Cruzada hikers returning to nature and educating *los incultos* (the uncultured, uneducated).

> *No sería tan exagerado afirmar que el paso de los artistas subvierte los pensamientos a muchos campesinos que viven noches larguísimas, gente afincada en zonas de silencio donde la radio y la TV no existen, ni siquiera otra familia cerca para cruzar el amor y los apellidos. Sitios a los que el Diablo, por vago, no se atreve a subir, han llegado un día dos o tres actores y han trocado la puerta de la ilusión: Traemos títeres, ¿quieren verlos? (. . .) Los cruzados no son ángeles ni misioneros. Simplemente están montados en el carro de la aventura porque no pueden prescindir de su esencia de actuar.* (Pérez 2000)

It would not be an exaggeration to say that the passage of the artists alter the thoughts of many *campesinos* who live through long quiet nights: people who reside in zones of silence, where neither radio nor television exist, and where there is not even a nearby family to exchange love or last names. The actors go to places where even the Devil, being lazy, would not dare to climb, opening the door of illusion: "We brought puppets; do you want to see them?" [. . .] The crusaders are not angels or missionaries. They are simply riding on the truck of adventure because they cannot hold back their motivation to act. (Pérez 2000)

Meanwhile, scholarly journals focused on the group's contribution to the development of "national culture," identity, and the rebuilding of morale and solidarity in a time of crisis—both economically and in the theater. The effective "distribution" of their cultural product being the most important thing for the Massification of Culture:

La Cruzada se presenta desde su fundación como una alternativa a la crisis de circulación y distribución del producto artístico, en este caso, teatral. Frente al quehacer monótono en la ciudad y un cierto agotamiento del espacio conquistado allí, así como el reconocimiento de la escasez o inexistencia en varios casos de opciones culturales en la montaña, se determinó abrir esta experiencia. (Valiño 1997)

The Crusade, from its foundation, presents itself as an alternative to the crisis of circulation and distribution of the artistic product, in this case, theatrical. Facing the monotonous tasks in the city and a certain exhaustion of the available spaces there, as well as the recognition of the scarcity or even nonexistence, in some cases, of cultural options in the mountains, it was determined to create this new experience.

While the romance of campesino life and the nobility of the project had always been part of its discourse, distribution of their "product" was a new addition, and with it came a new expectation of how they should be compensated. Like Los Elementos, the experience, the process, and the relationship between actor and spectator and the Boalian notion of the participant "spect-actor" (Boal 1979) became the selling point.

Omar Valiño and wife, Maite Hernández Lorenzo, the designated La Cruzada experts in Havana, had written various articles about the experience and its significance. They were both ISA-trained theater critics and ministry of culture workers, and their efforts were welcomed by La

Cruzada, since each article increased the group's renown. In 1999, Valiño and Hernández presented a short paper at a large international conference called Cultura y Desarrollo (Culture and Development), during a session called "Integración y participación en el desarrollo comunitario" (Integration and participation in community development), touting La Cruzada as an effective mode of cultural development and identity building in rural areas. Their paper was presented after a round-table discussion, which included illustrious intellectual figures in Cuba such as Rigoberto Fabelo, Teresita Segarra, Nidia González, Nisia Agüera, Carlos Cremata, and Esther Pérez. The expertise of Valiño and Hernández on La Cruzada, and beyond that, on theater in Guantánamo (although they only wrote about La Cruzada) earned them a place in the Cuban intellectual world. As they were part of the younger generation of revolutionary scholars, their special knowledge ensured a favorable niche in both culture and intellectual politics.

I met Omar in 1997 when he was still a master's student, writing his thesis on the history of and modern changes in Teatro Escambray (Valiño 1994). Over a period of five years, he ascended from up-and-coming writer to prominent theater critic, publishing widely and becoming the editor of Cuba's top theater journal, *Tablas*. While he was distrusted and considered a *funcionario* (state functionary, official) by some members of Los Elementos in Cumanayagua (who, instead, had their own political and national connections through José Oriol), artists in Guantánamo considered Omar an important liaison. By association, his cultural authority boosted their own. In the *oscuro rincón* of the nation, this door cracked open to political power was very important to a group of artists who otherwise had no material incentives. "Moral" recognition and incentives, and the official nod toward national legitimation offered by the state only went so far for actors needing to buy cooking oil, milk, and clothing for growing children, not to mention materials for sets, costuming, make-up, and puppets.

Cultural Authority

Katherine Verdery reinterprets Pierre Bourdieu's "space of legitimation" and "intellectual territory" in cultural politics for the socialist context, excluding Bourdieu's economic element, and mapping a direct two-coordinate relationship between political status and cultural authority. The more political status one has, the more cultural authority, and vice versa (Verdery 1991:92–93). She explains that the political dimension consists of holding a particular bureaucratic office "and/or titles having some political significance." The cultural dimension consists of an artist or group whose works are well known. The cultural and political sides need each other to move forward, the goal being more political power than cultural authority, since the former is often the only way to procure scarce resources and social advantage in a socialist country. Both sides must adhere to state guidelines of ideology and national identity, and in Cuba, both must condemn the gusanos who betray *Fidelismo* and accepted revolutionary behavior. Members of La Cruzada (and Teatro de los Elementos in their way) were clearly attempting to jockey between cultural and political power. According to Verdery, the "currency" of the competition for this power works as follows: "The processes that take place within this field of positions are crucially framed by the mechanisms of bureaucratic allocation. [. . .] Many participants strive continually to justify claims to resources, and in this process ideas about the Nation and 'proper' representation of its values play a vital part. [. . . .] Because cultural and knowledge claims are intellectuals' only justification, however—that is, because they are constrained from directly exercising political power—the currency of the competition will be the defense of culture, the 'authentic' values, of standards of professionalism and knowledge" (Verdery 1991:92–93).

In fact, many of Cuba's most respected artists went on to influential political positions. Teatro Escambray's founder and director, Sergio Corrieri, became the president of the Amistad del los Pueblos (Friendship Among [Socialist] Nations). A famous *decimista* and poet, Waldo Leyva was later appointed the president of the Centro Nacional de Cultura Comunitario (National Center for Community Culture, overseeing all amateur art programs in Cuba, including programming in the *Casas de Cultura*). Carlos Martí, president of UNEAC, was once a well-known essay and literary writer. And finally, Abel Prieto, also a writer and poet, became the minister of culture. Once known as a rebellious artist with long hair and progressive ideas, Prieto's eventual placement as minister of culture was a welcome relief from the previous minister, Armando Hart Dávalos, whose rigid policies had directed los Años Gris (The Gray Years; see chapter 2), the oppressive period sometimes likened to China's Cultural Revolution (Reed 1991).[14]

Omar Valiño became powerful in Cuba's intellectual world for his place as a cultural expert and blossoming political functionary. La Cruzada aspired to cultural authority as a unique theatrical and rural community project, and the group's association with and recognition by Valiño helped them to acquire the political clout they so badly needed: "the authority of certain persons is recognized by all factors, as the competition to 'capture' these scholars confirms" (Verdery 1991:92–93). "Capturing" someone like Valiño was not as important to Los Elementos, which had other political connections and was closer to the central artistic and intellectual core of Havana, but it was crucial to La Cruzada and other artists in distant areas, such as Guantánamo, which rarely attracted visitors from Havana. Promised visits by officials from the Consejo Nacional de las Artes Escénicas to view plays and hold *pruebas* (auditions, tests) for higher actor categories (and thus, accompanying salary and status increases) were frequently canceled at the last minute, leaving the Guantánamo artists waiting for hours in the theater space, nervously ready to perform. Judges were either detained by a lack of transportation ("me complique") or, according to local actors, could not be bothered to make the long trip for "just a group of rural artists."

Cuban artists and intellectuals also gained cultural authority and cultural capital by accumulating *premios* (awards, prizes). The premio was coveted, and winners proudly listed each one on their curricula vitae. Sometimes the premio was given with a cash bonus, even sometimes in *divisas* after 1993, but more often than not it was merely a token sum, and the more important win was the title itself. The sense of honor, purpose, and heightened reputation these artists gained from premios was crucial to inspiring a certain kind of artistic production in this socialist system. There were dozens of premios awarded in Cuba, from the local to the national level, the most eminent being those awarded by UNEAC and the Ministry of Culture. With more premios came an increased probability that the artist would receive permission to travel,[15] have a car, or be given the opportunity to live in a better apartment—all extremely difficult things for Cuban residents.

Over the years, Fidel Castro repeatedly reminded these artists and intellectuals of their crucial role in the cultivation of revolutionary ideology. In speeches to them in 1961, 1985, and 1999, he reiterated his request that they assume responsibility for the education of the population. As Cubans, they were to be loyal to Fidel and the Revolution. As artists, they were responsible for the moral development of the country and the healthy maintenance of *cubanidad*. "Without culture, there is no development," Fidel has exclaimed with increasing frequency over the last several years. In regard to the responsibility for national moral development and what's at stake for the artists, Katherine Verdery explains:

> Often [values of culture and the spirit] will be wrapped around definitions of national identity and national values. The stakes are who gets to write the school manuals that present a particular version of reality, or to produce an official history, or to define the literary "canon," or to render the lineage of philosophical knowledge; whose books will be published, and in what press runs; whose projects will receive investments that will facilitate still other investments later; whose works will receive prizes—valuable not because they increase sales and therefore, incomes, as in the capitalist world, but because the mere receipt of the prize enhances one's claim to future allocations and promotes the values on which one has staked one's work. (Verdery 1995:94)

The ways the *teatristas* I encountered (both rural and urban, Oriente and Occidente) described and analyzed their own work was often at odds with the way they played the politics of the "revolutionary artist." Despite the critical discourse wafting through intellectual circles, the teatristas rarely seemed conscious of the place their art had in a circulation-distribution loop, nor did they reflect upon how effectively their cultural product was being spread around the country. Yet, at the same time they used the Massification of Culture and its national propaganda to further personal and group goals, to garner resources, and to take advantage of the opportunities to travel and perform in new places. Most artists I met in Cuba—dancers, musicians, and visual artists, but especially those working in the theater and outside of Havana—just wanted to create something beautiful, something unique and enlightening, provocative and polemical. They did not usually plan to create art for political consciousness raising, but rather to enhance the spiritual side of a population already supersaturated by politics and ideology. They did not have to worry about finding an outside job to support their art. They also did not have to worry about how many audience members were in attendance, at least not for economic reasons. This "Velvet Prison" freed them to concentrate on creativity. Every time I attempted to engage in a discussion about the connection between art and politics, I was dismissed with a shake of the head or a brush of the hand, and told that their art had nothing to do with politics, that it was art, it was transcendent, and should not be mixed with the mundane. They complained that foreigners came to Cuba and always wanted to hear about the methods teatristas used to "communicate" political sentiment to their public, whether supportive or in protest against the socialist regime. Art is different than propaganda, I was told repeatedly, and [mass] communication was only for distributing propaganda. Politics, they said, only affected art in the amount of resources they received: their paints, instruments, costume material, make-up, paper, lights, and other theater-making necessities. Politics, they claimed, only affected them economically, not ideologically.

Weary of confronting the daily propaganda that cried "Socialism or Death!" these actors, directors, and writers attempted to retreat from politics back into art, wishing simply to share it, much like the image of the old storyteller who wishes to pass on his lore. They wanted to refine and to distinguish a particular Cuban theater tradition and ensure its continuance and excellence. They wanted appreciation and recognition from their audiences and cultural institutions. They wanted to know that their creation had enhanced the "spirituality" of their audiences, not necessarily their revolutionary political vigor—that their art had allowed both spectators and "spect-actors" to escape from real life and into a dream. This desire contradicted the fact that their stories were about the evils of capitalism and that children welcomed them with chants about saving poor little Elián González from the belly of the beast. Was escape truly possible in a country relying on the "Novísimo" (even newer), on yet another cultural rebirth, or from a newness/rebirth supposedly based in the natural and poetic but still really based on socialist politics and ideology?

Certainly the peripheral placement of provincial artists, more so for those working in Guantánamo, had something to do with this desire to transcend political meaning in art. In contrast to the career options for teatristas in Havana, they were much more limited in both Cumanayagua and Guantánamo. Politically dangerous content would have been identified much faster by local officials in these outlying areas than in a large city center, where many small groups were performing every weekend in various neighborhoods. There was more to lose in the rural towns and less to gain, and thus self-censorship was an important dimension of their cultural production, even if it was often subconscious. That said, the revolutionary consciousness among rural artists and informant campesinos appeared stronger than in Havana. Although the usual grumbling and muttering sorts of criticism occurred on a daily basis (see James Scott on the grumbling and muttering of the subaltern, 1990), there was less access to alternative ideas or prospects—befriending or marrying foreign tourists or investors, access to books written and films distributed abroad, earning divisas by renting rooms or selling crafts or street food, access to products sold in *shopping* stores, and so on.

Artists are supposed to be, by nature, rebellious and provocative, but they are also popularly touted in many noncritical analyses as the "mirrors" of society. In Cuba they were celebrated as the cultural and ideological vanguard, but they were also responsible for the proper maintenance of revolutionary consciousness in the population, thus different sorts of mirrors—mirrors in which the reflection was not of the seer, but of the mirror-maker. So how were the two faces of the artist—vanguard and propaganda machine—fused into one? How were the masks taken off and put back on in a single scene? Perhaps the answer lies in the division between conscious and subconscious ideology and in the deep socialization of socialist education and culture. Socialism and nationalist politics permeated every step an individual took in Cuban society, from the first day of school to adult life. A large part of this upbringing was not interpreted as political, rather as moral and humanitarian. Rebelling against an oppressive government was one thing, while rebelling against social equality and cooperation, the request to help your neighbor, volunteering ("sacrificing") time and labor for the development of a better pueblo—these latter types of rebellion appeared selfish and irreverent. The words *revolutionary* and *vanguard* were appropriated by state and socialist discourse, their meanings resignified. The double face of the Cuban artist was also simply due to the need to adapt to and accept one's place in Cuban society where no one was fully autonomous as an individual agent.

Back to Real Life

On March 3, 2000, we rolled back into the city of Guantánamo after the month-long mountain tour. With audible relief, the group climbed down from the truck into Plaza Martí in the center of town, tired, dirty, and wind-blown. It was midday and Guantanameros were busy at their daily chores, some resting from the sun and extreme heat in the shade of the tree-lined park. Family members of Cruzada participants were waiting to help siblings, spouses, or parents carry home their small bundles of belongings and floor pads. After a brief chaotic milling around, unloading the truck, and quick kisses goodbye, the actors soon scattered to their respective houses. With a quick wave to me, they turned and left without a second glance back, the tour finished for another eleven months. They went back to their real lives, loved ones, and the nightly telenovela. The dispersion was almost surreal, as if a wind gusted through and whisked them away all at once. Once the last pack and last puppet were off the old blue Russian truck, it sped away, spinning its huge tires and grunting loudly down the road. Suddenly I was left standing alone in the park, literally left in the dust. Momentarily confused, I watched them walk off in separate directions, disappearing into alleys and around street corners, La Cruzada finished and forgotten until next year. The end of La Cruzada marked the end of an annual obligation for most Guantánamo actors, and a liberation from a project that, however noble, was indeed a sacrifice for them. I looked around, somewhat amused (and somewhat distressed), thinking what an excellent cartoon this moment would have made. Luckily, I was not left standing alone in the central plaza for too long. One of Guantánamo's actors had decided to turn the annual crusade into a longer-term project he called the Laboratorio de Teatro Comunitario (Community Theater Laboratory) and he invited me to come along, beginning with an invitation to share *un trago de ron* (a shot of rum). Ury Rodríguez of Teatro Rostro was critical of what he perceived to be too much artistic mediation in the cultural representations of rural communities, and he wanted to create a new type of Teatro Comunitario that would allow the campesinos to truly speak for and represent (perform) themselves on stage.

6

STORYTELLERS AND THE STORY TOLD:
VOICES AND VISIONS IN THE ZONES OF SILENCE

or, who wins the wager if the cockfight ends in a draw

The living utterance, having taken meaning and shape at a particular historical moment in a socially specific environment, cannot fail to brush up against thousands of living dialogic threads, woven by socio-ideological consciousness around the given object of an utterance; it cannot fail to become an active participant in social dialogue.—MIKHAIL BAKHTIN, *The Dialogic Imagination* (1981)

Now the strange thing about this silly if not desperate place between the real and the really made-up is that it appears to be where most of us spend most of our time as epistemically correct, socially created, and occasionally creative beings. We dissimulate. We act and have to act as if mischief were not afoot in the kingdom of the real and that all around the ground lay firm. That is what the public secret, the facticity of the social fact, being a social being, is all about.
—MICHAEL TAUSSIG, *Mimesis and Alterity* (1992)

Cuba's "storytellers" are individuals and institutions—the state, artists, and local people—who tell national stories. The "story told" refers to both the actual wording of Cuba's national narration (the story constructed), as well as the people to whom the story is told (those listening), for it is the dialogical relationship between storytelling, story enacting, and story reception that creates an illusion of historical continuity that is ultimately absorbed into popular discourse. This multivoiced creation is naturalized, internalized, built upon, criticized, or revolutionized. The mediation or interlocution of the local *campesino*'s stories by the artists is scrutinized in this chapter through a case study that shows how a group of artists attempted to break down the system of discursive intervention to allow the campesinos to finally speak for themselves. The experiment was a relative failure, and one can see why it was a failure and also why the "folk" (or other marginal, subaltern, "non-intellectual") populations) are often not agents of their own history making. In this chapter, I also examine why the campesino became such a key player—adventurous and heroic—in the national narrative, and look at how this figure has been directly linked to a broader "American" narrative. I discuss the campesino in the history of Latin American "folk," commenting on the campesino's relationship to the professional artist and the state.

Artistic Translations and the Dialogics of Cultural Symbol Making

The importance of the artists' role in the perpetuation of the campesino figure throughout history has been evident in the Cuban case, for one can trace how the image emerged and was represented in theatrical performance, and how the campesino figure was analyzed and guided by cultural critics and scholars. Theorization of the campesino figure was at the center of an ongoing heated debate at a Havana conference nicknamed *Comunidad* (Community), held every two years to discuss the development of local arts and culture. The conference grew in importance throughout the late 1990s, and in 2000 keynote speakers included prominent scholars such as Miguel Barnet, Waldo Leyva, Jesús Guanche, and Natalia Bolívar.[1] Discussions of rural culture intensified during the Special Period and after-hours social events included *campesino guateques* (rural-style parties), musical and folk-dance performances, and highly promoted visits by the far-off and exotic campesino theater groups themselves. A visit by the most exotic and *más allá*—the amateur theater group Grupo Lino Álvarez de Realengo 18 (Lino Álvarez Theater Group of Realengo 18)—happened at Comunidad in 2000. This was the first time members of this group had ever traveled to Havana, and they were excited and proud to have been invited.

Realengos—before the Revolution's land redistribution—were circular or irregularly shaped land areas between square farms or plantations. Legally they were not owned by anyone, and therefore, peasants squatted there and built *bohíos*, often working for nearby landowners (see Corbitt 1939). In the 1920s, these large landowners attempted to evict the squatters and rebellious violence erupted, especially in realengo # 18, led by a man named Lino Álvarez.[2] Although very isolated and virtually forgotten until recently, this small community was very important historically. The campesinos of # 18 were famous for the struggle to retain their land during a time when large landowners were attempting to sell it to foreign companies. Unwilling to leave, campesinos took up arms and fought for what they believed was rightfully theirs, including those who had built their bohíos on the realengos. Before "Patria o Muerte" (Fatherland or Death) in Cuba, there was "Tierra o Sangre" (Land or Blood), which was the slogan of Lino Álvarez and his followers.

Álvarez soon realized that local *fiestas* and cultural activities would be good camouflage for the political meetings necessary to mobilize and organize the rebellion. During the activities, the leaders of the rebellion were able to discuss their next move without bourgeois officials and Batista's police becoming suspicious. The theater group, called Cuadra de Comedias (Comedy Sketches) became an integral part of these activities and was strongly promoted by Álvarez himself. When he died in 1953, the group was renamed Grupo de Teatro Lino Álvarez, in his honor.

Many of the campesino-actors in the group had never even been to Guantánamo City from their tiny *caserío* in a remote *zona de silencio* called El Lechero, in the municipal of El Salvador. For them, Havana may have well been across the ocean. El Lechero was one of the poorest caseríos I encountered in Cuba, with crumbling houses (in part, from unrepaired hurricane damage) and little food. Tuberculosis and hepatitis were becoming more frequent, and there had been an increase in crime, such as robberies and personal attacks. The area was accessible only by hitching a ride on the back of a tractor from Guantánamo City to an unmarked encampment (reminiscent of the unmarked boat stops in Siguanea), and then hiking for hours through sugarcane fields, past a putrid-smelling sugar mill and factory, and up a long rocky mountain path that became muddy and impassable during the autumn and spring rains. This was not the Poetic Fantasy–land of Siguanea. El Lechero was not beautiful and not a nice place to be, though the residents were as warm and welcoming as every other part of Cuba I had experienced, and the campesinos living there made the best of their situation, optimistic for future improvements that were promised them. They also had fascinating stories to tell.

Grupo Lino Álvarez was the oldest-known theater group in Cuba, formed in 1934 by a farmer named Rogelio Baratute.[3] First performing in the mountains for members of Fidel Castro's guerrilla rebel army, the short plays, or *cuadros de comedia*, were passed down orally from generation to generation because, until the 1960s, rural residents of the area (and potential actors) were illiterate. Over the years, cast members were primarily chosen and theatrical roles passed down through the extended Baratute family and their spouses (see figure 20). These campesino-actors had no artistic training, and only a couple of them had seen a limited amount of professional theater performances or television. They were, by most standards I had heard, the most "authentic" Teatro Comunitario and Option Zero Theater group in Cuba; authentic, perhaps, because they lived so far away from any cities, not only in distance, but also due to the location's heightened inaccessibility. Their theatrical and musical productions were entirely their own and were performed only for, and by, a very small local community. They had no resources other than a one-room *Casa de Cultura*. Havana elites assumed they were a self-sufficient and committed group of artists, like Teatro Escambray "used to be," only more so. Some Habaneros I spoke to imagined the campesino-actors of El Lechero sacrificing comfort and higher (urban) standards of living for their art, as if they had a choice. In spite of this dubious distinction, Grupo Lino Álvarez was not included in the Consejo's official numbers because the actors were amateurs, not professionals.

When I began my investigation in 1997, Havana intellectuals referred to them as the "lost theater group" since no one had ever seen them, although many had heard rumors of their existence. Mentions of Grupo Lino Álvarez were infrequent, but over time, many in the theater world knew I was interested in rural theater and would ask if I had "found" them yet. When I finally reached El Lechero and met the actors in mid-2000, I am embarrassed to admit that I felt the thrill of the traditional anthropologist finding an unknown tribe hidden in the jungle—demonstrating the power of long-told stories of rites of passage in my own culture and profession. The rumors of the existence of Grupo Lino Álvarez had been one of my prime motivations for leaving Cumanayagua and moving to Guantánamo during my second year of fieldwork. In mid-2000 I worked with the group for several months, in and out of El Lechero, and was the first to transcribe three of their plays. Sitting around a table with four of the actors, I handwrote their spoken lines one by one. One of the group's founders, eighty-four-year-old Regino Baratute, remembered many of

20. Grupo Lino Álvarez de Realengo 18, the Baratute family, other theater company members, and the author, El Lechero, Guantánamo Province (photo by unknown photographer, 2000)

the parts he had performed in over sixty years with the group and was still able to recite most of them by heart. Each actor who had taken on a particular role in the plays had to be present for archiving the script, since no one individual knew all of the lines, only their own character's and the cue lines that preceded.

Their group had been attracting more and more interest from local culture workers in Guantánamo's Centro de Cultura Comunitaria due to the increasing national promotion of community theater in the 1990s. My own interest in the group was, I believe, the key catalyst for one particular culture worker in the local Cultural Comunitaria center to submit his own paper to the Comunidad conference about Grupo Lino Álvarez and to solicit state funds to bring them to Havana. Interestingly, once a foreigner became interested in the modest group and had actually made the tedious trek out to meet them, the Cuban scholars perked up their ears and began to take them more seriously. Grupo Lino Álvarez was a novelty at the 2000 conference in Havana, and their performance was initially sought out and watched with much curiosity. In the end, though, the group was very harshly criticized by Havana *teatristas* and other cultural intellectuals. People were generally intrigued by their history, but less impressed by what they considered crude and unsophisticated performances, the unmediated stories of the campesinos not considered good art.[4] The romance and the conjured imaginary of the lost campesino theater troupe turned out to be, in the end, more desirable than the real thing.

Both the 1998 and 2000 Comunidad conferences included papers and theater roundtables that focused on the defense of Cuban identity and rekindling of lost traditions in the countryside. A new topic in 2000 was the intervention or cultural mediation of professional artistic groups in the rural areas. Workshops on Paulo Freire and Augusto Boal's consciousness-raising and mobilization techniques generated animated discussions. Proposals were offered on how to go about using similar methods in Cuba. Although Flora Lauten's Teatro La Yaya had initiated the idea of letting amateur campesino-actors "speak" for themselves in the early 1970s (Lauten 1981), the social issues at stake were different in the 1990s–2000s, and the necessity of empowering the campesino individual and community voice in a campesino-generated fashion had intensified. The campesino was a hero in time, if not in space. His humble, nonmaterialistic image and his supposed moral ideals were to be upheld, even if physically he remained isolated in inaccessible regions of the country. Of course, Grupo Lino Álvarez was a perfect example of such a project, but without the advocacy and political connections of professional artists, this group was not seriously considered. They were also just too más allá, too far away and isolated. Nor did Julio Baratute want professional artists from the cities (especially Havana) to go up and visit El Lechero, since he realized that the group's reputation was based on this very isolation from the mainstream theater world. While walking together through one of the area's sugarcane fields on a hot, dusty afternoon, Julio explained that he wanted to maintain his own unique *línea* (line, artistic path) and claimed he was not at all interested in *fama* (fame) (interview with Julio Baratute, Lechero, 2000). The other problem was that the actors had not written new plays for many years; those passed down and performed still addressed illiteracy and the coming of revolutionary changes. The campesinos speaking were not from 2000. The voices on the stage were of ghosts—revolutionary ghosts, but ghosts nonetheless.

Although my time in El Lechero was much more limited than with the other theater groups, it quickly became evident that the Baratutes and their extended family were not artists working in zones of silence, but instead were campesinos who liked to produce art and whose grandparents had given them a legacy to maintain. But spare time in *el campo* is rare, and after several weeks living in El Lechero, I understood why the group's scripts were over thirty years old. Unlike in the cites where there was generally much more time spent *en la calle* or *paseando* (hanging out, having fun), or even just sitting down to watch the latest *telenovela* (soap opera) after dinner, campesinos were constantly working to care for their farms, animals, and children; repairing houses and equipment; or trekking many hours up and down mountain paths to trade, see the doctor, go to the *bodega*, or talk with distant neighbors ("neighbors" who never lived close by in these regions).

During my stay in 2000, there was a drought in the region, and all daily meals consisted of plantains cooked with salt and a touch of precious *manteca* (pig fat, added only, I suspect, to make the dish more palatable for the visiting American). There simply was nothing else to eat. When the sun went down, the day was over. Lamp fuel was limited and used sparingly. Walking an hour through the countryside to get to a play rehearsal was not always possible, let alone embarking along the complex and time-consuming creative process of writing and developing a new script. The fact that Grupo Lino Álvarez de Realengo 18 had persevered and continued to perform at all was a remarkable feat in itself.

The Storytellers

Around this time, in 2000, a new professional theater project in Guantánamo, El Laboratorio de Teatro Comunitario (Laboratory of Community Theater), formed with the intention, once again, of giving the campesino the opportunity to self-represent. This idea was greeted with much enthusiasm by local and regional cultural institutions, and a token amount of start-up funding was provided. This new mini-crusade was launched by the actor and director Ury Rodríguez. A long-time member of the well-known La Cruzada Teatral, Ury decided to take the project one step further. After years of traveling through the mountains with La Cruzada, he came to realize that if he were to truly influence and encourage the development of local cultural programs, he would need an extended period of contact with one particular community instead of short periods with many. He also believed that the direct participation of the local people was essential: the campesinos were to tell their own story, supposedly without the mediation of the professional artist. Ury intended to educate and *abrir las mentes* (open the minds) of the community—to *liberar* (liberate) them by encouraging them to speak out and express themselves artistically (personal communication, 2000). Together with other community theater groups during the Special Period, he wished to restore "lost identity" and cultural consciousness, a familiar refrain in Teatro Comunitario and in Cuba generally during the Special Period, but Ury felt his project would differ from the other groups in that he wanted the campesinos themselves to act and perform, instead of having their stories acted out for them. In this way, Ury believed, the campesinos would be empowered in their collective role as cultural producer. When explaining the new project to me, his artistic partner Virginia sitting with us, sipping a coffee and nodding at his words, Ury said, "Art should play an active role and invest in those spaces where a virgin public is found—one which is eager to consume, as spectator, at the same time that it participates in the making of the performance." Although there had been a huge national revival of community work oriented toward the "re-animation" and promotion of community values in the 1990s, he felt the projects were not well researched, and he critiqued them for the "superficiality of their analyses" (interview with Ury Rodríguez Urgelles, Guantánamo, June 2000).

The project was launched in a caserío called Dos Brazos, south of the pueblo of Puriales, in the municipality of San Antonio del Sur, Guantánamo Province. Ury wanted to select what he considered to be the "neediest" community, one that was among those suffering the most from the effects of the Special Period and was "losing its culture." The choice of the community was also based on its logistical capability to sustain the extended visit of a theater group. In Dos Brazos, Abel, the pueblo's local doctor, became a pivotal link. Cuban actors, like foreign anthropologists, needed access to communities in the zones of silence, often by introduction through a trusted resident. Doctors in rural areas were provided a one-bedroom cement house with nurse's quarters, and a solar-powered generator for periodic light and medicine storage. They were considered to be among the leaders of the community in which they resided, despite the brevity of their two-year alternating residency, because they were so important for the survival of the residents. Local campesinos told terrible stories of serious accidents with machetes, falling off horses, or having life-threatening sicknesses and difficult pregnancies. The closest medical facility to Dos Brazos was in Puriales, requiring an eight-kilometer hike down the rocky mountain path, with the injured or sick individual supported or carried on the back and shoulders, or in a homemade gurney carried by four people.

In April 2000, one month after returning from La Cruzada, I made the trip to Dos Brazos with members of El Laboratorio to begin a period of social investigation before playwriting and play making. There were no long theoretical discussions over the definition of campesino, for we were going to ask the campesinos to define and perform themselves in their own terms, and what's more, we were going into the most *más allá*—to the most silent of the zones of silence and to *campesinos de verdad*. Although by 2000 I had heard it all before, I hoped this trip would be the final adventure into and arrival at the ideal mythological space and time so often and so passionately described by my informants. We rode in the back of a pickup truck from Guantánamo to San Antonio del Sur and then hitched a ride in a *carro* to Puriales. From there, we hiked the eight-kilometer path up the mountain to Dos Brazos, crossing the same winding river twenty-three times. The forest was utterly quiet, save for the distant sounds of campesinos calling out to their oxen, the birds, and the running water of the river. Periodically we met a lone campesino on the path with his mule or horse or hiking to or from his fields with a machete in hand. We would stop, shake his hand in greeting, and ask him whereabouts he lived and after the well-being of his family. Women and children were seen less frequently and were less likely to stop and greet us, only nodding politely and continuing on their way, the children turning their heads back to stare curiously at the strangers. The rural bohíos were well hidden from the sight of the path, located off other small trails only the local eye could discern. Without the usual bright pink-and-yellow paint of urban Caribbean dwellings (albeit relatively faded in Cuba), they were naturally camouflaged by their surroundings.

We arrived at the doctor's house, and he showed us the small solar panel he used to keep a small refrigerator running. The generator did not always work, he admitted, and thus the limited medicines he kept inside were not always kept cold, but they were, he assured us, colder than the outside air. The house was luxurious by campesino standards, made of cement, with two bedrooms, an indoor bathroom, and a kitchen. The lower level had one bedroom for the nurse, who, like the doctor, was assigned to the rural areas every two years. There was one room for the medical clinic. The doctor's house was located in a large grassy plaza, which served as the central meeting place for the community. On the second day in Dos Brazos, Abel and his nurse, Yaíma, took us trekking through the hills to meet the area residents. Such personal introductions were crucial for the actors to later conduct interviews on their own. Unlike my first experience with Los Elementos, I was not warned to stay quiet, nor could I have a group of just two artists. In Dos Brazos, I became a much more integral member of the ensemble. Like Macías in Siguanea, Abel, Yaíma, and the area campesinos were tireless. Walks between bohíos were often one to two hours, and although Ury, Virginia, and I were in relatively good shape, we began to huff and puff long before the locals.

The actors, Ury and Virginia, interviewed the town *espiritista* (a mixture of naturalist, Spiritist, and Santería priestess), the *delegado* (local government representative or delegate), the teacher, the family doctor (Abel), *los religiosos* (religious people, members of a local Christian group), the most well-known storyteller, the *decimista* (*décima* singer), the storekeeper, the children, the self-proclaimed *cacique* (community leader), and other area campesinos (see figures 21–24). The delegado described the community's struggle for electricity, passable roads, and transportation. His was the "official" perspective on the situation, realistic yet interminably positive and optimistic, giving thanks to *el comandante* (Fidel Castro) and *La Revolución* for the progress experienced by Dos Brazos so far. Meanwhile, the storyteller explained the myth of the local ghost: a woman dressed in white who was said to haunt a particular stretch of the river called Paso de Mano, named for the handlike shape of a large rock at its ford. Local campesinos superstitiously swore that to be safe from the ghost and her destructive nature, one had to touch the rock before proceeding over the river. At this, Ury, Virginia, and I looked at each other, wondering which particular fork of the river that had been on our way up the mountain and hoping there would be no repercussions for our neglect of the ghostly homage. The older generation lamented the exodus of the young people from the countryside. With the

21. Espiritista and her altar,
Dos Brazos, Guantánamo
Province

(below) 22. Musicians preparing
to perform in *Guajiros a los cuatro
vientos*, Dos Brazos, Guantánamo
Province (Both photos by Laurie
Frederik, 2000)

23. Impromptu cockfight held before the official demonstration, Guantánamo Province

(below) 24. Virginia and Ury interviewing campesinos in Dos Brazos, Guantánamo Province (Both photos by Laurie Frederik, 2000)

flight of the young people, they said, went the promise of el campo's legacy, a reality that directly contradicted popular romanticism of the countryside.

This urban migration was reflected in the play, *Guajiros a los cuatro vientos*, that ultimately resulted from the investigation:

> *Sale el muchacho del agua. Lleva en la mano una maleta de madera. Entra Ancieta con otro mazo de leña sobre su cabeza.*

Ancieta: *¿Y para dónde vas?*
Muchacho: *Me voy al pueblo,*[5] *ya no soporto más este lugar.*
Ancieta: *¿Al pueblo? Si tú no conoces a nadie por allá.*
Muchacho: *Tengo la dirección de un primo, nunca lo he visto, pero bueno . . .*
Ancieta: *¡Que tengas suerte! y encamínate bien.*
Muchacho: *Eso quiero, dicen que en la ciudad hay muchas cosas que divierten a uno, además hay mucho adelanto y yo no quiero quedarme aquí para cargar agua.*
Ancieta: *¿Y tu madre?*
Muchacho: *Tengo más hermanos, ellos la cuidarán bien. Bueno, Ancieta, hasta un día, ahora tengo que caminar mucho para coger los camiones.*
Ancieta: *Cuídate mucho y regresa un día, antes que yo me muera. (Para sí) Es lo mejor que hace el pobre.*

> *Enter the young man who carries water, carrying a wooden suitcase. Enter Ancieta with another bundle of wood balanced on her head.*

Ancieta: And where are you going?
Young Man: I'm leaving for the city. I can't stand this place anymore.
Ancieta: To the city? But you don't know anyone there.
Young Man: I have my cousin's address. I've never seen him before, but, well . . .
Ancieta: Well, good luck with your new life! Travel safely.
Young Man: That's what I want. They say that there are a lot of interesting things to do in the city and it is very modern. I don't want to stay here and carry buckets of water.
Ancieta: And your mother?
Young Man: I have other brothers and sisters to take good care of her. Well, Ancieta, until another day. Right now I have to walk a long way to catch one of the trucks to the city.
Ancieta: Take care of yourself and come back someday, before I die. *(To herself)* That's the best thing the poor guy can do.[6]

Other residents proudly told us about the community's role in the Revolution and their experiences as *combatientes* (combatants, militants, fighters), either as actual soldiers or as protectors and helpers for rebels passing through the region. When we asked about cultural practices that they felt had died out, they mentioned a rural religious ritual (*Alumbrados* or *Altares de Cruz*), various games for adults and children, particular foods, and the absence of their amateur musical groups. They also talked with great passion about the *pelea de gallo* (cockfight). Although this practice was made illegal after 1959, the campesinos were obviously proud of it and delighted in its clandestine continuation, in what was yet another inconsistency with the official image of the ideal campesino culture.

When we asked all our questions about lost traditions, the locals became excited and nostalgic for activities that had been suspended during the crisis, and ultimately the community was given permission (after the delegado lodged a request with the municipal and provincial authorities) to "stage" the traditions most representative of Guantánamo's campesino culture for the urban visitors. This included, first and foremost, a cockfight (see figure 23, above); on the condition that the birds would not fight to the death and that there would be no gambling. The local aficionados proudly brought along their *gallos finos* (fancy roosters) to show us this popular tradition. In this "authentic demonstration" for the artists, the roosters were preened and laced with spikes, décimas were sung in their honor, water was spat on them for luck, and the audience members smiled for the anthropologist's camera. The *gallo* would, not surprisingly, take on a primary role in telling this community's story, first appearing in one of the community member's original décimas, written and sung by a campesino named Vivenia and inserted into the opening scene of the script:

Ancieta:

Si canto kiquiriquí	If I sing cock-a-doodle-doo
es cantar de un gallo fino	it's to sing like a fine rooster
que canta en el matutino	that sings in the morning
para sentirse feliz	to feel happy

Laureano:

Con mi tonado sonora	With my thundering tune
voy anunciando la hora	I go announcing the hour
al labrado que me añora	to the land that calls me

y necesita la hora	and needs to know the time
Octaciano:	
Yo soy un gallo cantor	I am a singing rooster
que me conmueve el amor	that stirs up love
espero al amanecer	I wait for the sunrise
para cumplir mi labor.	To complete my work

Other cultural staging included the *corrida de cinta* (similar to ring jousting), where a rider on horseback held a small straight metal pin and rode as fast as he could down a track. At the end of the track were two poles with a wire line drawn across. Hung from the line were colorful pieces of ribbon tied into a loop. The rider's challenge was to get the pin through the loop while going full speed. A judge, also on horseback, waited behind the pole to assess whether or not the rider had been successful. Points were tallied. We were told that this game was also played, albeit less frequently, with live ducks or chickens, the rider having to successfully grab and hang onto or pull off the greased neck of the bird hanging by its feet from the wire. The winner won the unfortunate duck or chicken for dinner. Needless to say, I was glad this latter variation was not part of the day's festivities. Another tradition not performed for the corrida de cinta was the ritual circling of horses. Normally the event (and other important festival activities, we were told) would be preceded by men on horseback galloping in a circle around the clearing, the lead rider carrying a large Cuban flag. Although we begged them to please show us, one of the campesinos explained that there were not enough horses and riders, and thus the display would not be impressive enough to do justice to the carrying of the flag. They did finally succumb to our pleading and ran two laps, but without flag. After the corrida de cinta, the children (all boys) gathered excitedly for the *palo de grasa*. A large, smooth *palo*, similar to a telephone pole, was stuck deep into the ground. The pole was roughly ten to twelve feet tall. Pig fat (*grasa*) was then applied thickly to the pole, and a prize placed at the top. The contestants had to climb up the pole to reach the prize. The boys stripped to their shorts, rubbed dirt and sand all over their bodies from the nearby road for better traction, and attempted to climb the greased pole.

The most extensive, meticulously prepared, and anticipated part of the campesinos' cultural staging that month was the Altar de Cruz. Similar to the Alumbrados mentioned in chapters 3 and 4, Altares de Cruz were religious rituals carried out when someone had fulfilled a "promise" to their chosen saint or virgin. In Guantánamo, religion was largely *cruzado*, or mixed, even more so that than in Havana or Santiago de Cuba, a variable mélange of Catholicism, Protestantism, Santería, African religions, and Spiritism (communication with spirits of the long dead). If a woman had a sick child, she might promise an Altar of the Cross ritual to San Lazaro, or Chango and Santa Barbara, or the Virgin Mary (or whichever they worshiped) for the child to be healed. At the Altar of the Cross, the *padrino* or *madrina* (host or hostess) provided all the materials to make and put on the altar, as well as food and drink for the party to follow the ritual. The altar had to be set up in a very specific way. Religious hymns were sung, prayers were recited, and then the community divided into groups to sing in choruses, competing for the items on the altar. The judge for the singing competition was the pardrino or madrina sponsoring the *Altar* (see Vitori Ramos 1998) (see figures 25 and 26).

In Dos Brazos, only one woman, named Pilar, remembered all of the prayers and hymns, as it had been so long since an Altar de Cruz had been performed in Dos Brazos. She quickly took control of the production and gave instructions to the rest of the community, distributing tasks among them, the two actors, and the anthropologist. Interested in showing the best of campesino culture to the visitors, the Dos Brazos delegado procured enough funds from the local branch of the Ministry of Culture to buy the necessary materials. For over a week, the women sat at the table in the doctor's house, making and decorating by hand paper crosses, a Cuban flag, a boat, stars, and doves, all essential elements of the ritual setup. Boxes of candles were brought in, and locals donated sheets, wood, and religious figurines to construct the altar. Abel bought beer and rum for the party to follow, unhooking the solar panel from the medicine refrigerator and connecting it to the cassette player to play music. At the beginning of the ritual, the delegado stood up to remind everyone *comportarse bien* (to behave themselves), that this was a cultural event but also a sacred one, and that he expected discipline and control from the residents. Trained to follow lines, the actors participated in the opening prayers and hymns, turning the spotlight over to the campesinos when it was time for the singing competition, consisting of various rounds of chorus teams, trying to outdo one another in cleverness of verse and intensity of performance. Like Teatro de los Elementos, the actors of El Laboratorio saw the inherent theatricality of this ritual, its haunting music incorporated into the final product.

25. Altar de Cruz ritual, the *madrina* (godmother or ritual hostess) sits by the altar and judges the campesinos singing improvisational choruses, Dos Brazos, Guantánamo Province (photo by Laurie Frederik, 2000)

(below) 26. Altar de Cruz ritual, one of the competing choruses sings to the altar, Dos Brazos, Guantánamo Province (photo by Laurie Frederik, 2000)

After a month of living and conducting interviews in Dos Brazos, the actors returned to Guantánamo City to write the play. The artists met and brainstormed about how to narrate the campesinos' story in theatrical form. Eyes closed so that she could imagine Dos Brazos, Virginia began to improvise and tell a tale of a magical rooster and the power its song had over a small mountain town. Ury then expanded on her story, embellishing it and incorporating particular details of Dos Brazos and its actual characters into the storyline. After a discussion of various possible scenarios, a scene progression was written, and eventually, over the following weeks, a full theatrical text was completed. I gave feedback and contributed my own ideas when asked, since I had been present for the entire investigation and had formed my own relationships with the campesinos of Dos Brazos, but the storytelling and playwriting were left to the professionals. Campesinos voices were taken and poeticized, turned to fable, laden with metaphors and allusion. It had been planned that the campesinos would act out their own characters from their own perspective, but this inconsistency in the execution of the group's mission was not noted.

What began as a simple *canto de gallo* (song of the rooster) developed into a play that connected the symbol of the gallo to the notions of campesino identity and communal solidarity. It was called *Guajiros a los cuatro vientos* (Guajiro from Every Direction), borrowing a statement made during one of the informant interviews. As in the creative process of Los Elementos, the characteristics and social histories of the community's residents were inserted into the play, romanticized, exaggerated, and made either more abstract or more distinct. And also like Los Elementos, the stories told by the campesinos were adapted into a theatrical fable to be performed. The "authors," Ury and Virginia, identified themselves as campesinos, and thus claimed to be able to accurately transcribe (versus translate) the "native" voice of Dos Brazos into a play. They did not consider their own authorship of the play as problematic, nor did they see themselves in a mediating role. They did not wait for a famous writer from Havana to organize and poeticize the text, for they understood the dialogue as already bona fide *campesino*—raw and rural, complete with local accent and vocabulary—Folk Rusticity with a hint of artistic poetics, since artists were trained to add such elements and this was professional theater after all.

Once the play was typed and copied—an arduous task involving a frantic three-week and two-city search for paper, carbon, and a type-writer—we returned to Dos Brazos to mount it with the local campesinos. None of the Dos Brazos residents had ever before acted or performed theatrically, and few had even seen theater at all. Only a small handful of them had some amateur musical experience (guitar and décima singing). Although El Laboratorio had intended to mount the play using only campesino actors, difficulties emerged in recruiting cast members and also in getting the campesinos to learn the unfamiliar process of following a script, memorizing lines, blocking, and following scene sequences, not to mention performing a character in front of their family, friends, and fellow community members. Many of the older campesinos still could not read, despite the early literacy brigades and four decades of local schooling. Younger campesinos were literate at a basic level, but not comfortable with using long pages of text that had to be recited from memory. In areas like this, where books were unavailable (or long deteriorated, or their pages used for "more practical" purposes) —and one's livelihood was determined by strength, endurance, and agricultural expertise—there had been no need to develop such "literati" skills. But given the difficulty Ury and Virginia had confronted in order to find a single ream of paper and to make copies with typewriter and carbon paper, the scripts were very reluctantly abandoned (see figure 27). Several women were interested in performing, but were not allowed to by their husbands. Some were unsure what a theatrical play consisted of, and were too scared to participate. One of the local men would not allow his wife to participate without him. When it rained, the sometimes hour-long trek from their bohíos proved too tedious, and no one showed up for rehearsal. The campesino-actors also did not show up when rumors of a long-overdue meat delivery required they keep their place in line at the local bodega, lest they lose their monthly ration. They waved to us, passing on the road, and called out that they'd return when the meat had arrived. Five days later we resumed rehearsals.

These obstacles were daunting at first, threatening the success of the project. But sufficient cast members were finally recruited, and the play-making methodology was restrategized. Script reading was transformed into improvisation of themes, and the campesinos began to learn the sequence of themes in the storyline orally and by repetition, ad-libbing their lines accordingly. The chaos and inconsistency created by this innovation ultimately forced Ury and Virginia, to perform alongside the campesinos to guide the amateur actors and to "direct" the story they told. The results on stage were mixed. The local folks were certainly speaking in their own words and in their own way—rough, straightforward, improvised, and country-accented instead of the semi-poetic and enunciated verse of the written script, but in the end they were still guided by the trained imaginations and actions of the professional artists, the scenes and character relationships, not to mention the moral of the story, not fully their own. By this point in my fieldwork, I seriously doubted if Cuban campesinos could ever truly "speak" in the theatrical context, or if *anyone* could, for that matter. Regardless of intended author, the conversion from improvised dialogue to rehearsed script necessitated mediation, editing, rearrangement, and theatricalizing. The "emotional truth" might be maintained in this process, yes, but with a sacrifice of detail, accuracy, and candor. The transformation of campesino to campesino-actor inevitably changed the nature of their words, the consciousness of a performer

27. El Laboratorio de Teatro Comunitario director, Ury Rodríguez, directs Rey, a campesino actor, the soon-to-be-abandoned script in Ury's hand, Dos Brazos, Guantánamo Province (photo by Laurie Frederik, 2000)

identity making utterances even less singular, rather heteroglossic: "another's speech in another's language, serving to express authorial intentions but in a refracted way" (Bakhtin 1984:324), and also less "sincere" (cf. Austin 1965 on theater and performatives).

The Story Told and Its Performative Consequences

The play debuted on June 27, 2000, the audience sitting on the grass and leaning against their horses, laughing and clapping without restraint, even directly addressing the actors, responding to a line, making jokes about their appearance or actions as they recognized particular characters modeled on local personalities and idiosyncrasies. The set consisted of a facade of a bohío, wooden planks nailed vertically (wood and nails borrowed from several of the area residents; some even taken off of their own dwellings, later to be extracted and returned) with palm leaves constructing the roof. The front door was functional, revealing the expanse of the open field and hills and the occasional grazing goat behind it when an actor passed through (see figures 28–30).

The story opens with a scene in a small caserío with a husband and wife. It is obvious they are in love, showing their affection most visibly in the literal shaking of the bohío at the start of the play, moaning and cooing heard from offstage. The doctor of the community is introduced on a routine house call, along with neighbors, all of whom are happy and cooperative. There is comic bantering back and forth. The conflict in the play is introduced when the women are depicted washing clothes in the river and gossiping about the seductive singing of the magical rooster that wakes them every morning. One of their husbands overhears the conversation and misinterprets the rooster to be an adulterous man. The rooster is symbolically important as a symbol of masculinity, of *cubanía*, and of Dos Brazos. When the men turn against the women and begin to distrust them, the rooster flees, taking the well-being of the people along with it. Drought follows and the crops die, neighbors put up fences to keep others off of their property, and the men fight in a dance-like pelea de gallo, circling around each other, ready to attack. There is ultimately a happy ending, of course, when there is a search, the rooster is found, and social order is restored. The live band of local musicians begin to play a *guaracha*, and the audience is invited to dance on "stage" with the actors.

28. *Guajiros a los cuatro vientos* set and rehearsal,
Dos Brazos, Guantánamo Province

(below) 29. During the performance of *Guajiros a los cuatro vientos*,
with the El Laboratorio co-director, Virginia, acting in the scene,
Dos Brazos, Guantánamo Province
(Both photos by Laurie Frederik, 2000)

After the performance, a discussion was held and the campesinos were invited to talk about what the play meant to them, their experience with the visiting theater group, and their culture and local identity. The campesinos conveyed their perceptions of what "culture" consisted of, and what they believed El Laboratorio had done for and brought to their community. However, the only ones to engage in dialogue with the professional actors were the state delegado, the teacher, and several other community leaders, all male. The delegado was especially animated in his intervention, telling the Dos Brazos audience that culture was not only theater and music, but also the way they dressed, how they presented themselves, how they greeted each other and visitors to the community. He stressed that this play should remind them to never act as *maleducados* (badly educated, badly behaved). He went on with much

30. *Guajiros a los cuatro vientos*, full cast, Dos Brazos, Guantánamo Province (photo by Laurie Frederik, 2000)

animation for ten minutes. After this, I imagine that some folks who might have spoken out thought better of it. Those remaining silent also did so, perhaps, from habit, allowing the leaders and what they perceived as the "educated" (or perhaps just the more powerful) to voice opinions first, fearful that their own critical opinions would not be well received or would be judged inappropriate. Thus, cultural authority was established within the local community along a predetermined set of standards. Official storytellers in the countryside did not include all campesinos in their narratives any more than those with the power to define cubanía included all Cubans in their essentializations.

Ultimately, the campesinos were told (as they had first supposedly told the artists) that *el gallo*—the guiding trope and "metaphoric predication" of the play (see Fernandez 1986:199)—represented their community and that its "song" was their song of unity and cultural identity; that "el gallo somos todos" (the rooster is all of us). They were told that they should not lose the song of el gallo, which represented community identity and pure Cuba, for doing so would jeopardize their happiness (the "performative consequence" of this experience; see ibid.). The play's message was that if they let go of el gallo there would be conflict, illnesses, discontent, and decay, and their youth would abandon the land and go to the cities. This was an exaggeration, as artistic performance and narrated fables often are, but the underlying message was clearly understood nonetheless. It was an already socially acceptable critique of the Cuban situation and appropriately "revolutionary" in its presentation.

The campesinos of Dos Brazos seemed content with this analysis and accepted the story told as accurate, since it was, after all, their own. Nodding and smiling, they listened respectfully to the aggressive delegado and to the artists, then rode their horses back home. In conversation, the play's conclusions were repeated, validating the "actionable identity" of the metaphor used in the play (Fernandez 1986:199) as well as in the Teatro Comunitario movement. But did the campesinos truly believe that they were, in fact, losing their culture and that it needed to be rescued? Did they fully understand the political import of professional artists visiting their isolated caserío to teach them the importance of "saving" their campesino-hood? Or had they not yet recognized their own cultural authority? If these campesinos were, indeed, the soul of the Cuban nation, why weren't they traveling to the cities to educate the urban dwellers instead? Why didn't they put on their own play?

The obstacles to this possibility had less to do with the actual potential of campesino educators than it did with the probable cool reception of an urban audience. Although Julio Baratute of Grupo Lino Álvarez de Realengo 18 developed a growing consciousness of his cultural authority as an artist and the power of his group's *nueva fama* (new-found fame) (interview with Julio Baratute, El Lechero, 2000), he was not granted equal authority in Havana. Urban teatristas snickered at the rudimentary and amateur acting skills of the campesinos from Oriente, the simplicity of the play's story structure. And they laughed at their Folk Rusticity. Some audience members (mostly conference-attending artists and intellectuals) even walked out before the end of the performance. While members of Teatro de los Elementos were considered artistic elites in the Cienfuegos and Villa Clara regions for their poetic representations of the beauty and mystique of the countryside and its traditions (and authors like Atilio Caballero certainly advanced this reputation), their plays still went largely misunderstood in Havana (too rural, or perhaps not rural enough), were rarely reviewed in-depth, and were not well attended by the general public. The group was awarded national prizes for their commitment to communitarian theater and community enhancement, but not usually for the aesthetics or artistry of the performance itself. The plays were actually beautiful, highly theatrical and poetic, but sometimes so abstract or specific or both (depending on the audience member interpreting them), that they were difficult for the average Cuban, urban or rural, to understand without inside context. More communicable were their short-form, solo, and clown pieces, and their plays for children.

La Cruzada's mission was to bring theater to isolated and neglected areas, not the other way around. The goal of the project was cultivation and education of campesinos. It was a cultural crusade into the culture-deficient mountains, not an expedition into an already culture-saturated (and thus already *culto* city). El Laboratorio de Teatro Comunitario was a new project featuring only two actors. Traveling to Dos Brazos required an entire day and took the actors away from their families and other professional commitments in Guantánamo City. Rehearsing a play to be repeated and presented outside of Dos Brazos would have demanded even more time in the countryside, especially given the slow pace of rural play making. Neither could the campesino-actors have left their homes, farms, and animals for the time necessary to travel around Cuba if invited to perform. Furthermore, El Laboratorio had few resources and scant funding, since it was not yet an established and nationally recognized *proyecto* (unlike La Cruzada and Los Elementos). The purpose of all of these Teatro Comunitario groups was to embrace the creative process, not the final product. To perform on a national scale would require the transformation of the rural groups, as well as the campesinos, into something altogether different—into something less comunitario and less campesino.

The division of local, regional, and national in Cuba was significant, and despite the degree to which the central communist system was successful in attempting to level the playing field, there remained a particular idea of what was top versus down, urban versus rural, and professional versus amateur. Cultural repertoires varied even within rural regions, especially given the lack of communication between the areas.[7] One might conclude that certain types of Claudio Lomnitz's "intimate cultures" were created, although not based on class per se (see Lomnitz 1991 and 1992; cf. Herzfeld 1997 on cultural intimacy). Lomnitz explains that "In fact, a regional culture will always have a degree of systematic variation in the meanings attached to the signs of even the regionally 'shared' cultural domains: meaning is produced within preexisting symbolic contexts, and since these symbolic contexts differ by cultural group, and even between different persons occupying different positions within a group, the interpretation of regionally shared signs will tend to vary accordingly. One would expect an especially rich set of multivocal symbols in the cultural domain that is 'shared' within a region" (1992: 24). The admiration of the *imagery* of the countryside, its people and traditions, was shared among all regions. But the actualities of these regions differed markedly, the national imagination largely uninformed and inaccurate.

Within the rural areas, the distinction between differing "symbolic contexts" was especially evident during social investigation and playmaking. Although the rural campesinos and the rural artists seemed to share cultural domains, their worldviews and language ideologies came together in a slippery juxtaposition. The rural artists believed they were seeing the same reality and speaking the same language as the campesinos and that their intralingual communication was mutually compatible. The artists sincerely believed they were talking intimately to the campesinos, representing their real-life situation and presenting their voices on country stages. Meanwhile, the campesinos clearly understood that the artists were using their poetic, "artistic" language to portray elements of their rural culture in a particular way. The campesinos knew the plays were not "real," although they appreciated the attention and recognition by what they considered a cultural elite. The performances were entertaining and struck a chord for audiences, but were not necessarily "authentic" by campesino standards. But "realness" in the theater world is differently understood than realness in everyday life. The plays were real rural culture for the actors and were real campesino theater for the campesinos. Both agreed on its realness and accuracy in the genre of theatrical performance. Part of the artists' assumed familiarity with rural "folk" was partly due to an ongoing dialogue about peasantry, guajiros, and campesinos in Cuba and in Latin America more broadly. Certainly there was no shortage of textual and oral renditions of rural lands and their customs (referred to as *campesino, guajiro, jíbaro, paisano, agrarista, gaucho, llanero,* etc.).

An important thing to specify in both of my examples—that is, from Cumanayagua and Guantánamo—was that the staging of campesino traditions, both by the campesinos themselves and by the actors, was not "folklorization" (Olson 2004). It was not the selective and opportunistic editing of a particular tradition for profit and distribution in the market. Although Compay Segundo and Polo Montañez had their moments in the spotlight, they did not represent an entire population in their folksy and so-called traditional country crooning. Unlike Russian folk music (ibid.), ghosts of Taíno Indians (Dávila 2001), or Afro-Cuban Santeros in Havana, the development of the rural Cuban *Hombre Novísimo* was cultivated for the intellectual realm, for the community of artists who made their living off of their imaginative ability. Creative license was thus expected and welcomed. Rawness and Folk Rusticity were embraced, but only up to a point, and only insofar as this symbol of the *pura cepa* could be integrated into something transcending the harsh reality of Cuba's latest crisis. It was a unique (or perhaps "extra-ordinary" or "paradoxical," according to Bourdieu 1991:129) artistic narrative, separate from discourses of the state and those created by the Cuban people.

Compositions of Folk Identity

I have used the term *folk* here and in other sections to include all forms of rural people and to broaden the concept beyond the rural Cuban. When using *folk* instead of *campesino* I mean to include peasants, *paisanos, jíbaros*, *agraristas*, and any other term used to describe them around the world. When using *campesino* I refer specifically to rural people in Cuba, both as images and actual people. The endurance of the campesino image in modern Cuba relates to a broader and lengthier historical discourse about rural peasants and farmers that is found in Europe and throughout Latin America, as they have been mythological characters in much of European and Latin American history. In many cases, rural folk —celebrated by José Martí in his famous cry for "our" unified "America"—remain champions, not only of history, but also of contemporary struggles to define national identity and cultural distinction (see Martí 1891; Wolf 1966, 1969, 1972).

The writer and Cuban patriot José Martí desired to unite the "disinherited Spaniard, the Argentine *gaucho*, the Chilean *roto*, the Peruvian *cholo*, and the Venezuela *llanero*," who all "were touched where their common affections lay" (Martí [1893] 1967:183). These common affections were also shared by the disenfranchised Cuban campesino. All the rural folk of Latin American countries—those who worked the land and fought for it—symbolized the soul and the backbone of their respective nations. Martí claimed that America was the land of heroes who were wrapped in Indian, mixed-blood, and white (and in Cuba's case, African) souls, "merged into a single flame" which was "constant and inextinguishable." This conversation has been especially prevalent in Spanish-language literature around the world, due in part to a growing anthropology of the postcolonial subject in Latin America and the Caribbean.[8]

After Cuban independence in 1898 and the death of José Martí, Pan-American sentiments remained strong and the intellectual community began to utilize the poetic and patriotic words of the martyred "Father," the "Apostle," or "El Maestro" (teacher) of Cuban nationalism in their work. Some Cuban scholars have traced the beginnings of an identifiable popular and "genuinely Cuban" culture to what has been called the critical decade of 1923–33, during which a now-familiar trend was taking place: intellectuals were responding to the corruption and *desnacionalización* (denationalization) of Yankee values by turning away from European elitism and toward the Cuban "folk," sometimes also including the imagery of the indigenous Cuban Indian as part of the same land-loving group. Intellectuals began to identify with the popular masses, and the *pensamiento* (philosophy and thought) of José Martí was rekindled through prominent writers of the time: Julio Antonio Mella,

Rubén Martínez Villena, Pablo de la Torriente Brau, Juan Marinello, and Raúl Roa García, among others. "And thus the national-popular culture reappeared" (Segrera 1985:9–10). Martí's "America" was kept in the national repertoire and the idea of the Latin American "trunk" (Martí 1891) was passed on to modern-day Cuba, becoming especially evident, and again revived in popular discourse after 1990. Cuba and Cubans remain fundamentally Latin American, their national spirit stemming from Latin American rural folk and Martí's *hombres sinceros*: the poor, most powerless masses of peripheral rural regions, revolutionary fighters with nothing to lose and everything to gain, willing to sacrifice everything and die for their nation (cf. Anderson 1983; Lomnitz 2001).

In nineteenth-century Spain, nostalgia and admiration rang out for the *segadores* (harvesters) after colonial power was lost and high society fell into a perceived state of decay. The intellectual generation of 1898 published romantic renderings of the countryside and the resultant literary tradition of *costumbrismo* (study of folklore, approved traditional customs) was absorbed into the educational systems and consciousness of many Latin American countries (see Azorín 1917, 1919, 1990; Baroja 1920, 1927, 1946; de Unamuno 1903, 1916, 1944; and other writers from the Generation of 1898). Indeed, the Cuban campesino entered into the Cuban imaginary largely through the writings and artistic representations of Spanish-speaking artists and writers who had been and continued to be part of every Cuban's education. Many of the early twentieth-century campesinos were of Spanish descent. Cuba's very own patriotic father figure, José Martí, was the son of Spanish immigrants, as were many first-generation Creoles in the nineteenth century. In Mexico, the *agraristas* (agrarians) gained a place in national consciousness in the revolution of 1910–20.[9] And in Puerto Rico, the *jíbaros* (rural peasants) had been, for many years, the prototypic "folk" that defined the nation and every individual's sense of Puerto-Ricanness. The jíbaro is invoked as the "symbolic habitus of the Puerto Rican soul," writes Lillian Guerra (1998:5, cf. Dávila 1997) and in deference to the work of Edgar Martínez Masdeu (1975), she comments that "the *jíbaro* has become no more than an abstraction in which Puerto Ricans have invested the whole of their collective consciousness. When one wants to emphasize that one is Puerto Rican through and through, one only need say '*soy jíbaro*' (I am a *jíbaro*)" (Guerra 1998:5–7). Such depictions have crossed borders and bodies of water, and this rural image, by whatever name, was part of the shared understanding of many

Latin American identities. Inevitably, this essential rurality was also reflected in and was influential upon the society's art, music, literature, and
performance. In the 2000s, the Cuban campesinos and their artistic
spokespersons joined the segadores, agraristas, and jíbaros in the drive
to maintain the noble elements of their homeland's past, the nostalgic
yearning for and defense of what Bourdieu would call the "protodoxa" or
symbolic "naturalization of the social order" (Bourdieu 1991:132–33).

The Exotic and the Familiar

In contrast to the *indigenistas* (indigenous movements) of Central and
South America, the cultural battle in Cuba was not a class struggle or
separatist movement; nor was it an ethnic or blood distinction. The national promotion of the campesino was inclusive of Cuban citizens as a
whole and did not attempt to highlight or empower a previously marginalized segment of society (cf. Dávila 2001). Cuba was, after all, still socialist, and equality and unity were still part of the master narrative. From an
urban perspective on class and race conflicts, campesinos stood outside;
they transcended pesos or dollars, they were de-racialized, exoticized, and
romanticized (and usually male). In reality, the "race" of the campesino, if
a distinction was forced, varied according to region and population. During my research, I encountered campesinos with skin color from very pale
to very dark, although it was true that the latter were less numerous. In
Escambray, the populations were light skinned. In Guantánamo, the campesinos of Dos Brazos were also relatively light skinned, while those in the
pueblo of El Lechero (the home of Grupo Lino Álvarez) were darker
mulatto. During La Cruzada Teatral, we encountered communities of
campesinos with a distinctly Indian look: shorter in stature, with ruddier
skin tones and straight black hair. The Cuban actors claimed that these
were the last descendants of the otherwise-massacred native Indians, such
as the Arawak and Taíno, and that they had only survived given their
extreme isolation living in the mountainous areas. Considering the extreme "más allá-ness" of these particular populations, I could believe this
hypothesis. Other famous historical rural folk (though specialized in time
for their political task), the Mambises, were insurgent groups during the
wars for independence made up of mostly dark-skinned ex-slaves, along
with indigenous Cubans and Asian Cubans. Elpidio Valdés, a famous

mambí cartoon character, is depicted as a white peasant. In general, however, most Cubans imagined the typical campesino as light skinned or "white," regardless of the historical or contemporary realities.

The exoticization of the campesino occurred in two ways: first, through a geographic mystification of remoteness and second, through romantic visions of man living in harmony with nature: *el hombre y la naturaleza.* Campesinos in this mythic imagery were simple folks tilling their fields in the morning mist and telling stories at night by low-burning kerosene lamps as crickets chirped softly in the shadows. Cubans understood that one had to go out and "search for" true campesinos, which created a sense of distance and mystery. The fact that they were endangered created a sense of urgency and intensity. The campesinos were made familiar by the stories told about them, folk dancing in festivals and cultural *espectáculos* (variety shows), plays about campesino culture, and scholarly conferences. Universally recognized campesino musicians like Compay Segundo and Polo Montañez, "El Guajiro Natural" (the Natural Guajiro), were heard blasting on radios and sound systems in apartments in Havana, Santiago de Cuba, and even Miami. Made famous abroad, these rural artists returned home as quintessentially Cuban, even though, paradoxically, their CDs were sold for hard currency, even on the island.[10]

Polo Montañez (Fernando Borrego Linares) was an especially interesting example of the more recent commercialization of rural music and the Cuban imaginary. He was a poor campesino (referred to as the usually more derogatory, but in this case, more charming *guajiro* in public biographies and promotions) living in rural Pinar del Río. As the story goes, he was sitting under a tree for shade while playing his guitar one fine day in 1999 when he was "discovered" by a foreign musical producer passing along the road. His discovery was followed by an award-winning CD (*Guajiro Natural*) and a DVD documentary of his life, *El Guajiro* (2005, LUSAFRICA, EU). Montañez's humble and romantic rural upbringing was romanticized throughout the documentary, which was distributed after he was killed in a car accident in Havana in 2002.

I have shown how the "old ambivalence" between city people and country folk (Williams 1973) was alive and well in Cuba in the twenty-first century. Many city-dwelling Cubans had developed a sort of love–hate relationship with their resident rural folk. These people were referred to as guajiros when they were being made fun of, and as campesinos when the commentary was one of respect and admiration. Those I knew, artists or not, used the terms nostalgically and metaphorically to describe their roots: "Yo sí soy guajiro de verdad, y no lo niego" (I am a real *guajiro* and I don't deny it), sung the famous Cuban musician, Beny Moré in 1950. Yet in the same breath they laughed at rural "primitiveness" and *atraso* (backwardness). The landlord of my little garage apartment in Havana was originally from Camagüey, a small city in the center of the island. He would ask me about my work in el campo and sigh nostalgically when I showed him photographs. "Sabes, Laura, soy campesino" (You know, Laura, I am a campesino), he would remind me, establishing his authority on the topic of my study. But then he would shake his head, raise his eyebrows, and laughingly thank God he had become more modern and educated. Those I encountered in urban areas, as well as periodic individuals in rural areas, often repeated this sentiment. One young *campesina* said to me in El Lechero, Guantánamo: "Soy una bruta. ¿Porqué quieres hablar conmigo?" (I am a brute. Why do you want to interview me?). In light of such, we could ask how these two seemingly antithetical images might be reconciled, but such contradictions were often inseparable and co-dependent—just as many Cubans often cited the *doble moral* (literally double moral, hypocrisy of action in relation to one's discourse about it) to explain the illogical yet fragile balance of the Special Period (see Palmié 2004; Wirtz 2004), reminding me directly of the ubiquitous circumstance of "me complique." Sujatha Fernandes, analyzes hip-hop music and film in contemporary Cuba, and writes about how the doble moral was once used in the pejorative sense, people publicly espousing their loyalty to the collectivist and egalitarian ideology while privately acting in contrary ways. "But today it is posited as a form of resistance to a politics that tries to confine people within boundaries. Rather than conform to the official culture, you need to adopt a doble moral: if you are to continue believing what you do believe, you have to dissemble" (Fernandes 2006:67).

History is part and parcel of the mimetic faculty, yet interpretations of history are not uniform, and once they enter the flow of artistic interpretation, the resultant images take on a new "reality." This new reality is perpetuated by reproduction in performance for an audience. What became apparent from the theatrical representation of the campesino, whether by professional urban artists or amateurs in the mountains, was that this was an image laden with contradictions. Campesinos were pure and sincere, but also *inculto*: their way of life was "primitive," or *atrasado*; they were not in tune with the outside world; and they were ignorant about urban life and modern technology. The romantic illusion of the good, hardworking, land-loving revolutionary became privileged; conspicuous by their absence were the more negative characteristics of campesino life, such as drinking, violence, theft, and gambling. The very people who defended the campesinos, worked with them, lived with them, and devoted their art to rescuing and reestablishing their traditions and values—even going so far as to assert "Yo soy campesino" in the appropriate contexts—were also keen to distinguish themselves as different, as having artistic talent, being intellectuals, and being *culto*. "Mimesis registers both sameness and difference," says Michael Taussig (1993:129), and in this case, performing artists simultaneously registered their identification *with* the campesinos, as well as their distinction *from* them, depending on the situation. The ways in which professional artists assumed the role of campesino were inconsistent, both on and off the stage, their pronouns alternating between "we" and "them." What was artistically reproduced was a mixture of historical referencing, individual beliefs and experiences, and the official images put forth by the state. The campesinos, however, did not share this confusion. Although local residents appreciated the fact that the professional actors were often "from" rural areas and had chosen to return to do theater, the actors were still considered relative outsiders, not even as culturally close as the *nuevos campesinos* of Escambray. Most campesinos living in these mountain bohíos expressed no desire to move to the noisy, dirty, and crowded city, to talk or dress "fancy," or to be taken in by what they considered to be its materialism. They did not identify with urban people at all. A campesino was a campesino. In this respect, the play's title, *Guajiros a los cuatro vientos*, was completely accurate, and they did not seem to see their own lack of discursive agency. Various comments led me to believe that they though that it was better the artists speak on their behalf, since they were *bruto* (brutish, rough) in comparison. So did the campesino "speak"? Looking at my ethnographic data, it really depended on perspective and definition of agency.

In the early twenty-first century, the idealized campesino—exotic and familiar, modern and traditional—exhibited the most desirable attributes of humility, sincerity, simplicity, and collective cooperation, all aligned with socialist philosophy. This campesino did not desire expensive items or money and did not criticize the state. He (the ideal campesino image was primarily masculine) was faithful to the Revolution, willing to fight to defend its honor and to continue to embody its social-ist values. This campesino still tilled the land with an ox-driven plow and lived in a small modest house made of wood, palm leaves, and dirt floors, without electricity or running water. He was geographically isolated. Many of the traditions still existing in the mountain regions of both Escambray and Guantánamo were, in fact, representative of the roman-tic rural traditions that have persevered for generations. The woeful songs of Altares de Cruz rituals echoed throughout the night, fulfilling promises to the Virgin Mary and Chango (and in 2000, to Elián Gonzá-lez) followed by festive *guateques*. Corridas de cinta tested the horseman-ship skills of the adults, while palo de grasa games entertained the chil-dren. In these zones of silence, campesinos strummed their guitars on the front porch of their bohíos after the *malanga* and *boniato* had been planted,[11] improvising décimas about their everyday lives.

Not surprisingly, the official narrative ignored darker sides of rural tradition, such as alcoholism, wife beating, gambling, livestock stealing, and the not-so-romantic physical hardships of rural life in Cuba, such as the lack of medical facilities and supplies, electricity, running water, and transportation. In Dos Brazos, Ury, Virginia, and I discussed the fre-quency of stories told to us by local women admitting to beatings received at the hands of their husbands or boyfriends and about feeling trapped in their social roles and gendered household obligations. Whether or not to include this negative element of rural life in the play was heavily debated, since it would mean publicly presenting a serious problem in a commu-nity the actors hoped to instead unify, invigorate, and inspire. Ultimately, there was a scene of wife beating in the play, which, to our surprise, elicited laughter, even by the women in the audience. Here we are re-minded of Handler and Gable's "celebratory narratives" (see introduc-tion), Susan Gal's and Judith Irvine's theorization of the "erasure" or the rendering invisible of some persons or activities (2000), Trouillot's "si-lencing the past" in the retelling of official history or the construction of national identities, and Michael Herzfeld's concept of "cultural intimacy," familiar but uncomfortable, connected to a "deep sense of cultural and political vulnerability" (2005 [1997]:14). Lucky for Ury and Virginia, the artistic narrative and the magic of the theatrical lens were able to make these otherwise unseemly elements comical and thus socially acceptable, or at least negotiable.

Some Cubans perceived campesinos as counter-revolutionaries who fought against Fidel Castro and the guerrilla fighters in the 1950s and as rebel "bandits" who terrorized the Escambray Mountain region in the 1960s (but see Alroy 1972). In the early 1990s, campesinos were perceived by city dwellers as greedy capitalists who sold produce at high prices in urban areas during the most desperate years of the Special Period—driven by the desire for profit more than compassion, communal cooperation, or national solidarity. But as time passed and food became more plentiful in the late 1990s, the resentment and anger softened and rural images (through theater, television, music) once again conveyed nostalgia for the human value of the humble man. In Dos Brazos, the brutish side of the campesino was represented through humor in a nonaestheticized theatrical performance, filled with local characters and colloquialisms, Folk Rusticity at its best. Most of the actors were inexperienced and imperfect, their self-representation earnest and vulnerable. The story told of the magical gallo—told by the campesinos, interpreted and translated by the actors, and retold by both campesinos and actors (a process James Fernandez might consider a "manipulation in mutuality" 1986:99) —was romantic and symbolic, serving to encourage and unify. The inherent contradictions of the production were syncretized and coherent. It seemed that I was the only one perturbed by the dramatic irony of these storytellers and their story told.

Unlocked Identity, Danger, and the Campesino Chronotope

As economic and political configurations transform Cuban society, narratives of national identity are also changed. I found definitions of Cuba and Cubanness to be "wavering between vocabularies" (Bhabha 1994:2), hovering in a sort of eternal conceptual liminality (or hybridity), between language and history, geography and politics, and more recently, between renditions of campesino-ness. Homi Bhabha's discussion draws on the writings and ideas of Hannah Arendt (1958), who says that modern society is a "hybrid realm where private interests assume public significance"; and on Benedict Anderson's imagined communities, the simultaneous "unisonance" of the modern nation embodied in narrative culture. The Cuban teatrista Magaly Muguercia also recognizes the narrative liminality in Special Period Cuba and labels it the experience of "Ser Precario" (Dangerous Being), a time of precariousness, of identity in vacillation:

Desde que se inició la presente década, la sociedad cubana vive sometida a una situación de crisis extrema y asombrosa resistencia. En ese lapso, la conciencia nacional ha fraguado, entre otros, un poderoso referente. Hacia él confluyen disímiles interpretaciones de nuestro presente; en torno a él gravita la actividad de un imaginario hipersensible. En el punto en el que una pluralidad de explicaciones, códigos y ansiedades se intersectan, se configura el Ser Precario. Al Ser Precario lo constituye su propia oscilación, un vaivén incesante entre lo que cohesiona y lo que dispersa, entre lo Idéntico y lo Otro. (Muguercia 1997:9; see also 1996a and 1996b)

Since the beginning of the present decade, Cuban society has been subject to a situation of extreme crisis and astounding resistance. In this interval, national consciousness has forged, among other things, a powerful point of reference. Different interpretations of our present converge, creating a hyper-sensitive imaginary. At the point where the plurality of explanations, codes, and anxieties intersect, the Precarious Being is configured. The Precarious Being constitutes its own oscillation, an incessant sway between what coheres and what disperses, between the Same and Another.

Muguercia explains that the experience of the Ser Precario activated a field of virtuality, of desires, utopias, fantasies, and illusions and that it evoked magnetic representations of destruction and growth. She was optimistic (in 1997), proposing that the "disintegration" of identity had the potential to break down what was rigid and fixed, that identity could finally be "unlocked" or opened under the social and ideological conditions of the 1990s (ibid.:9–10).

However, if the narration and definition of cubanía had been unlocked and opened up to diverse perspectives, who was telling the official or most "authentic" story? Who was deciding which details went in and which were left out? What was being celebrated, cleaned up, or erased? Who had the authority to tell the story, and why did the Cuban people listen to them? How was this new (or reconfigured) story being written into history? Although those who have written about Cuba within its watery borders may have displayed Bhabha's "temporality of culture and social consciousness" (Bhabha 1994:2), they also evidenced the country's enduring link to a Pan–Latin American history. The nation's narration has relied, in part, on legends, myths, and heroes who yell "¡Viva!" It has relied on those who have had a shared understanding of the nation's symbols and images and have collectively recognized the sources of cultural authority. Cuba's national story, however unsteady it appeared, was still rooted in and was integral to the bigger picture of the postcolonial world, of the anti-imperialist struggle against mighty Goliath. Artists and intellectuals who read and were taught about the legends, myths, and heroes of this struggle went on to reinterpret and write about them anew and make them their own. National symbols and images were imagined, re-created, and popularized. They were set into national consciousness through art and popular culture. What was "authentic" or "real" was interpreted on what Fredric Jameson calls a "Homeric battlefield," where interpretative options are in constant conflict (1981:13). "Any approach to the history of these conflicts and to the Real itself necessarily passes through prior textualization, its narrativization in the political unconscious" (ibid.:35).

The precarious "virtuality" of Cuban identity and the role of the campesino might also be considered in the light of Bakhtin's chronotope—a place allowing movement through space and time—"the intrinsic connectedness of temporal and spatial relationships that are artistically expressed in literature" (1981:84), or in this case, expressed in dramatic performance. The legends of Fidel Castro and Che Guevara as guerrilla rebels during the Revolution were retold in "adventure-time," where the action sequences lay outside of the historical, quotidian, biographical, and "even biological and maturational," and where ultimately nothing could be changed (ibid.:91). In this way, Fidel and Che would never grow old and never die—an idea that perhaps changed only after Fidel Castro's 2006 emergency intestinal surgery and speculations about his imminent physical death. Bakhtin explains that this is where rules are generated and "the measure of a man" is defined: "In this kind of time, nothing changes: the world remains as it was, the biographical life of the heroes does not change, their feelings do not change, people do not even age" (ibid.). In contrast, the campesino as chronotopical hero resided in the adventure of "everyday life," in a "special sort of everyday time" that depicted a sinful, decrepit life, followed by crisis and rebirth (ibid.:111). The metamorphosis of the campesino in Cuba was one of the key elements of the revolutionary success story concerning national development and empowerment. The crisis of peasant illiteracy, poverty, and exploitation—followed by revolution, transformation, and progress—was the fulfillment of both a Marxist socioeconomic model and a Cuban utopian ideological model. The prerevolutionary *latifundistas* (large landowners) and the urban bourgeois were also part of this scenario, as sinful capitalists changed into loyal and humble socialists, taken "down" from their socioeconomic pedestals. Meanwhile, the campesinos became educated and "cultivated," and pulled "up" to play an equal role in society. In the Cuban socialist art world, the goal was to synthesize elite forms of "high" culture with peasant "low" or popular culture, urban with rural, modernity with tradition. The desired result was a raceless, classless, and continuous society, firmly set on the road to communism. Spatially, the joining of the two Cuban cultural worlds was supposed to create an indissoluble link. Temporally, an "exceptional, utterly unusual moment" happened in 1959, largely in the countryside, and shaped the "definitive image of the man, his essence, as well as the nature of his entire subsequent life" (ibid:116). Yet this story of transformation continued beyond the length of the story told, a new cycle having begun in the 1990s (see also Fabian 1998).

So how are the worlds joined? And how are the seams between them hidden? The rules and the "measure of a man" (and woman) may be defined in the space of narration and representation, but how does it work in real life? In Cuba, artists and intellectuals were supported by the socialist state, and thus their cultural products had political power. They were separated from "the masses" at the same time that they were, under socialist philosophy, an inseparable part of them (Marx, Castro, Guevara). They were reflective and engaged in discussions about how they believed they should represent the people and the nation. The professional artists of Teatro Comunitario (such as Los Elementos and El Laboratorio) shared their work nationally, with Communist Party members and cultural critics in Havana, with other rural artists, and also with the most remote and sometimes illiterate campesinos in Cuba's isolated zones of silence. These narrators and actors reenacted Cuba's story for everyday Cubans, inviting their open participation and free spectatorship. Some of these artists shared their experiences with national and international scholars through publications, conferences, and festivals, usually in Havana, Camagüey, or Santiago de Cuba. Artists, especially live performing artists, were ideological liaisons between the state, urban citizens, artists, intellectuals, and rural "folk." Communication was not simply top-down. Dialogue was dynamic, and interpretations of "Cuba" were in constant, often intense negotiation, in a circular, back-and-forth motion in space and over time. The Massification of Culture (by 2001 renamed the *Batalla de Ideas*, or Battle of Ideas) and the reopening of the marginal and rural Escuelas de Instructores de Arte (Schools for Art Instructors) helped to ensure the endurance of this dialogue and created a growing network of state-trained cultural specialists.[12] In a 2002 speech, Fidel Castro proudly spoke of "tens of thousands of art instructors who [were] already in training, the explosion that [would] take place in the arts in general and in other intellectual fields, and the rapid advances of our people toward an ever-higher degree of comprehensive general culture" (Castro 2002). Claudio Lomnitz summarizes the distinction between organic and traditional intellectuals and asked "whether [Mexican] intellectuals were synthesizing intimate culture for the internal use of their group; whether they were creating coherence about a group on external demand; or whether they were invested in both an internal and articulatory function" (1992: 221–24). After looking at how culture was hierarchically organized, he concludes that "intellectuals, too, must be located in the spatial dialectics of cultural production" (ibid.:221–23). Cuban intellectuals were part of the same dialectical processes as their Mexican neighbors. Although their search for identity was not focused on *mestizaje*, the same "nostalgia for cultural coherence" versus a "global cultural incoherence" (ibid.) drove their desire to distinguish a common cultural thread. The perception of global cultural incoherence has led some to label certain cultural productions as examples of "pseudo-culture" or "anti-culture." In the early 2000s, one antidote was the set of characteristics embodied by the humble and noble Cuban campesino. In Cuba, pseudo-culture, bought with dollars in commercial spaces, threatened to disrupt the very foundations of socialist ideology and morality.

Writing the Modern Campesino into Art and History

In 1977, the well-known Cuban intellectual Graziella Pogolotti wrote about the new value system developed in Cuba after the Revolution. She looked at how the new Cuban citizen, especially the campesino, was becoming more aware of her or his role in the nation and society, which transcended the actual place inhabited on a daily basis. "Therefore, what is important is not necessarily the survival of the community in its actual form, but rather the link between its existence, its interests, and a wider transforming social current" (Pogolotti 1977:111). This growing awareness was occurring without nostalgia, she claimed, for the past was an epoch of misery, struggle, repression, and constant threat. The campesinos would learn and be "cultivated" through social practice and would eventually undergo a permanent deepening of conscience. She explained that writers of her era (the 1960s), specifically the Cuban storyteller Onelio Jorge Cardoso, had written about their campesino characters as if they still lived in a past that no longer existed, a past the structures of which had been destroyed by the Revolution. In 1977, Pogolotti felt the new campesino reality had not yet made its way into literature and artistic creation, but that ultimately it was destined to form the basis of Cuba's new culture.

Revisiting Pogolotti's projection in the early 2000s, one could consider whether or not campesinos had, in fact, been transcendent in their social awareness, and also whether such phenomena were accurately represented in intellectual and artistic discourse. I answer yes to both questions, although the campesinos themselves were not (yet) their own artistic interlocutors. During the crisis of the Special Period, the campesinos reentered scholarly discussion on new terms: *culto*, socially responsible, and nationally aware (an aging Pogolotti must now be content to note), although they were still not entirely free agents of their own storytelling. As Cuban consciousness was transformed by the Special Period, the image and symbolic role of the campesino changed with it under the guidance of the official keepers of culture. Literature and drama have proven to be a strong base for "the new culture" since 1977, and they will continue to be instrumental vehicles that both reflect and influence the place of Cuba in Latin America and the twenty-first-century world. Pogolotti's essay was still relevant thirty years after publication, as the role of the campesino entered yet another phase of reinterpretation and transformation following the breakdown of old value systems.

Critics have claimed that such "folk" (proletariat or peasants, oppressed or colonized) do not have the "luxury" of making myth or using metalanguage; nor do they have the necessary "accredited" or "delegated" speech, so they are unable to perform when called upon (Barthes 1972:148; Bourdieu 1991; Ching and Creed 1996; see also Verdery 1991). The case study of Dos Brazos suggested that there was some truth to this assertion, but its universality has been refuted by the experience of other rural groups around the world that have been more successful, including the projects of Paulo Freire and Augusto Boal in Brazil and South America, the Mayan Women's Theatre Collective LA FOMMA (Fortaleza de la Mujer Maya) in Mexico, and Teatro Campesino in the United States, just to name a few of the most well-known examples.

Given continued opportunities in a revolutionary communist society, I believe the campesinos (educated, computer literate, and classically "cultured") in Cuba will ultimately take control of their own historical representation, especially if Cuba's reopened Schools for Art Instructors continue to grow and prosper. But when they do take control, the current campesino image embedded in the development of the Hombre Novísimo will necessarily change, as will the campesinos' own cultural identity. They will no longer be "what they used to be." Will the national narrative still be culturally coherent with Cuba's socialist history if taken out of the hands of the artists, intellectuals, and cultural institutions? Or will a future "illuminating" moment of creativity ultimately steer it in a different direction altogether? Given the strength of the international market for particular types of Cuban cultural products, we will have to wait and see if official policy and perceptions of "pseudo" versus "pura cepa" change with popular demand.

The next and final chapter will look deeper into the inconsistencies of this creative process in Cuban society. I describe a trip I took with the Teatro Comunitario artists into the "belly" of one of the world's "capitalist beasts" (J. Martí 1891), and I look at how the noblest rural revolutionary artists were seduced by opportunity, new adventures, and profit.

7

DRAMATIC IRONY AND
JANUS-FACED NATIONALISM

or, the triumphant stage return of el negrito
and míster Smith

What is required is a historical conception of culture. What is also required is a contemporary idea of culture, of the opposition between the different artistic movements. [. . .] Memory must be recuperated, because one of the things that the triviality of pseudo-culture does, is it kills culture.—CARLOS MARTÍ (2001)

Unlike the form, the concept is in no way abstract: it is filled with a situation. Through the concept, it is a whole new history which is implanted in the myth.
—ROLAND BARTHES, *Myth Today* (1957)

The game is over when people start wondering if the cake is worth the candle.
—PIERRE BOURDIEU, *Language and Symbolic Power* (1983)

Who had the authority to say what was really and authentically Cuban and who was a pure Cuban at the turn of the millennium?[1] I have shown how "culture workers" began to reinterpret and contest the notion of true Cuban culture during the Special Period. Wanting to counter the increasing threat of pseudo-culture (e.g., Afro-Cuban rituals reproduced in hotels for *divisa*-wielding, sunburned, and rum-sipping Europeans), these official keepers of culture were intent on rescuing the authentic *pura cepa* of Cuba. This once and future hope, this *preemptive nostalgia*, inspired the ongoing battle towards *la victoria*, a victory that ultimately symbolized never giving in to the imperialist North. Such a move toward the rural man in times of national crisis was by no means a unique historical phenomenon in the world. Examples of similar movements have been documented throughout Latin America (Boyer 2003; Dávila 2001; Lomnitz 1992, 2001), the Caribbean (Guerra 1998), Hawaii (Desmond 1999), Asia (Ivy 1995), Europe (Badone 1991; Williams 1973), and North America (Handler 1988; Handler and Gable 1997) to name just a few. But Cuba was different in that it was still socialist and still governed by a strict Communist Party. Therefore, this fierce *batalla* against capitalist culture, which at the same time was tolerated and even embraced, posed a particularly interesting paradox, ironic in its implications.

Marketing Cubanía: National and International Audiences

The theatrical narrative has come full circle. The original Cuban national characters introduced in chapter 1 (*negrito, mulata, gallego*) weathered independence, social revolution. and the implementation of communist ideology that resulted in an official banishment from performance and the media. And then they were finally allowed back on stage during the Special Period. This chapter exposes the dramatic irony of Cuba's two faces—one of which was marketed internally with the traditional socialist rhetoric of humility, sacrifice, and loyalty, and the other sold for dollars in marble-floored, air-conditioned hotels that were off limits to Cuban citizens. In the midst of this battle between old and new, real and pseudo, there was a distinct difference in how Cuban identity was being marketed on the national as opposed to international level. The government double-played this identity by simultaneously promoting and condemning so-called pseudo-culture; in other words, Cuban nationalism in the early 2000s was Janus faced. Foreign tourists and international cultural consumers were fed different images of Cuba than the Cubans themselves received, and even though Cubans recognized that both faces were viable parts of their living culture, they scorned and sometimes even resented the reproductions created for the tourist industry. This was especially true of performing artists. While the state attempted to combat the spread of cultural banality, it was coincidentally ensuring its endurance. While needing to feed the Cuban economy, the state was also trying to sustain a revolutionary, anticapitalistic ideology that supported the nation's political philosophy. This ideological control was maintained through the fully state-supported cultural system and an apartheid-like separation of the resident population from the tourist industry. State-trained professional artists performing within Cuba were paid by the Ministry of Culture, and most were encouraged to work in their local communities (including neighborhoods of Havana). Those who left the inner circle to perform in places of consumption for foreigners may have jeopardized their intellectual authority and reputation, but also became privy to an entirely new and powerful "other" world. They lost symbolic capital within the cultural institutions, and amongst their peers, but they gained actual capital profits instead that made their lives easier and more comfortable.

The situation in Cuba fit Fernandez's and Huber's (2001) description of "true irony," which "dwells in uncertainty, with a kind of comic sense of the finitude and impermanence of all things human," an irony that shares the "generic sense of the discrepant [and] sees no easy solutions" (ibid.:22). These authors also evoke Kenneth Burke's "classic irony," which is based upon "a sense of fundamental kinship with the enemy as one needs him." Burke explains that this enemy is not "merely outside him as an observer but contains him within, becoming consubstantial with him" (quoted ibid.). And, indeed, Cuba was "consubstantial" with the *divisas* brought in by their ideological and moral enemies in North America and Europe. As a visitor ruminating (spectating) upon a set of relationships that appeared inherently incongruous, I saw the situation as truly, classically, and also "dramatically" ironic. Dramatic irony (also called tragic irony) in the theater world refers to an incongruity between a situation and the accompanying words or actions, when the audience is aware of the incongruity but one or more of the characters is not. The action and dialogue of the play reflect this disconnect of knowledge between the characters and the spectators, which is often comic but also tragic. Of course, many were aware of the discrepancies in Cuban society, but this ironically aware "audience" lived mainly in urban areas where they had the clearest possible view of the multitude of live actors and discrepant actions on the contemporary stage: Cuban *militantes* and foreign tourists; popular media and state censors; pesos, dollars, and *convertibles*; white, Afro-Cuban, mulatto, and Chinese people; purity and contamination; communism and capitalism.

The Return of El Negrito

As seen in the previous chapters, one of the major issues in the contemporary Cuban artistic and intellectual scene was the question of what was "truly" or "authentically" Cuban, and as my research has demonstrated, campesino traditions held strong symbolic value for those making this assessment. So how was it, then, that *el negrito* from the nineteenth-century Teatro Bufo reentered the public sphere, inadvertently riding a wave of black consciousness brought in partly by academics and artists from the United States? In the late 1990s, Teatro Bufo characters began to sneak back onto the public stage, sometimes one at a time, inserted into other non-Bufo plays, sometimes as a full Bufo cast (*negrito*, *gallego*, *mulata*, *chino*, *guajiro*, and Míster Smith). Compared to the campesino's public makeover and welcome party, the negrito's return was more surreptitious, but it was not censored or castigated, especially after the successful 1997 debut and extended run of a Bufo play called *El Tío Francisco y Las Leandras* (Uncle Francisco and the Leandras) in Havana's well-respected Hubert de Blank theater. The modern negrito was played by an Afro-Cuban in blackface instead of a white man in blackface, and la mulata was played by a *mulata* woman (*mulato/a* is one of the more than thirteen recognized racial categories in Cuba). El gallego, originally a Spanish colonist, was merged with "míster Smith" (the American), and the combination was represented more generally as the archetypal *extranjero* (foreigner)—here the Spanish colonist evolved into the imperialist or capitalist. Contemporary political references were inserted into the new comic monologues, but the actors in these productions prided themselves most on being able to perform their roles with as much faithfulness as possible to the original versions from the nineteenth century and early twentieth. Many actors and theater critics considered the Teatro Bufo plays part of their heritage and cultural patrimony; although there were Cuban *teatristas* and general audiences who still considered the Bufos racist and were aghast at their return (interview with Esther Suárez Durán, Havana, 2006). In 2004, La Cruzada Teatral performed a Bufo play on its annual trip to the mountains. The negrito was played by Ury Rodríguez, who told me with conviction that maintaining the original texts, character mannerisms, and costuming had been very important to the text. According to other Cruzada members, it was the most popular and well-received performance of the trip that year.

Such performances, previously deemed racist by many but still one of the more popular and successful theater styles of prerevolutionary Cuba, were once more allowed, along with a growing number of conferences on the distinctiveness of Afro-Cuban identity and black consciousness, and other events highlighting Afro-Cuban religion, music, and dance. These new (or renewed) public voices about distinct racial groups in Cuba were permitted, partly due to the growing demand in the tourist sector for Afro-Cuban cultural demonstrations, and also due to what Cubans informally called the "flexibilization of culture." Although José Martí and Fidel Castro believed that the essential Cuban was *more* than black or white, after 1990 Afro-Cubans asserted that they, as Cubans, were *also* black.

The Flexibilization of Culture

Responding to a need for hard currency and the demands of foreign tourists, the public display of *cubanía* was diversified, especially in major tourist areas such as Havana and Santiago de Cuba. Restrictions on individual expression, sexuality, and religion were relaxed. State officials stopped actively repressing Afro-Cuban religions, particularly their accompanying ritual music and dance, when the growing commercial sphere showed high demand for these performances. New freedoms and new social priorities, which were connected to the ominous economic crisis, gave rise to new creative motivations. This subtle yet powerful cultural shift or flexibilization directly affected cultural production as artists recognized and enjoyed a widening of parameters. The Cuban state realized the need to allow its suffering residents to let off steam, and was forced to reduce social restrictions lest the population explode (revolt) from pent-up frustration and despair. Social critique in urban performances still relied heavily on analogy, but referential associations became more daring and direct. Cuban theater and film productions were never conformist or blatantly propagandistic, and being a *conformista* was criticized in the artistic industries. The socialist realism of the Soviet Union had not taken hold in Cuba the same way it did in Eastern Europe. But artists in the theater and film, and especially in music, took several steps further during the Special Period, toes a few inches over the line instead of on it.[2]

The economic crisis divided the allegiances of once-devoted revolutionaries, and soon ideological strategists realized that the key to maintaining calm and compliance was to redirect focus from the ideal of a homogeneous population of khaki-clad *Hombre Nuevos* to permit and, what's more, celebrate cultural, religious, and racial diversity. The development of small private businesses was allowed in the late 1990s, although very heavily taxed and regulated ones. My friends and informants joked that during the crisis, the state was too busy trying to fix the economy and restore the integrity of the political infrastructure to worry about the daily activities of the people. And artists (especially artists in rural areas outside of Havana) joked that gasoline and working automobiles were not available to send out the censors to assess their pieces or shut down their productions.[3] The opening up of religious practice had a direct effect on trends in performance and the theater. In 1997, the first Rito y Representación (Ritual and Representation) conference was held in Havana. Afro-Cuban "ritual theater" was analyzed in the papers presented, and plays dedicated to themes from African and syncretic religions were performed. Included in the lineup in 2000 were *Oshún y las cotorras* (Oshun and the Parrots) by Grupo Teatro Caribeño, directed by Eugenio Hernández Espinosa; *Comunión al monte* (Communion on the Hill) by Grupo Teatro Palenque, directed by Agustín Quevedo; *La esclava Elena* (Elena the Slave) by Grupo Espacio Abierto, directed by Xiomara Calderón; and *Noche de Satín Regio* (Night of Royal Satin) by Grupo Rita Montaner, directed by Gerardo Fulleda León. Miguel Barnet, president of the Fundación Fernando Ortiz, opened the conference, and Rogelio Martínez Furé, general director of the Conjunto Nacional Folklórico, gave closing remarks. Most of the conference—including its roundtables, workshops, conference papers, and demonstrations—was devoted to Afro-Cuban themes.[4] Many new professional theater groups had emerged in the late 1990s and early 2000s, adopting plays written by Afro-Cuban playwrights and performed by Afro-Cuban actors. During this period of flexibilization, Afro-Cuban religious ritual and ceremony became prevalent and popular, not only in closed conferences and theaters, but also on public streets for interested passersby and *divisa*-paying tourists.

People Tourism and the Nature of Folkloric Bodies

Jane Desmond analyzes the construction of the "ideal native" in tourism as a form of "soft primitivism": "Contemporary cultural tourism replaces talk of race with talk of culture but retains the earlier notions of particular races' giving rise to particular cultures. Race becomes the authenticating ground of cultural specificity, sold in cultural tourism through the live performance of real (fill in the blank: Hawaiian, Native

American, Amazonian) 'culture' by 'real' inhabitants" (1999:xxiii). In Hawaii it was the brown "hula girl," or the *hapa-haole* (half-white, half-native), that became the most desired figure in local cultural or "people tourism." Desmond stresses that such figures served the tourists' need to identify the other-ness of the host culture with people who are different —in other words, natives who did not appear to be middle-class and white. Desmond's work sheds light on the Cuban situation, for "naturally" the bodies considered appropriate for folkloric and authentic Cuban performance were marketed as brown or black. Beginning in the 1990s, dark-skinned priests and priestesses of the Afro-Cuban religion Santería were dressed in white clothing with necklaces made of shell and beads, colored symbolically for particular *orishas* (red and white for Chango, yellow and gold for Oshun, blue and white for Yemeya). These practitioners (and performers) were placed conspicuously in Havana's central tourist areas, where they sat with smoke swirling upward from their cigars, offering spiritual *consultas* (consultations) for divisas. One particular Santera (Santería priestess) seated in front of Old Havana's cathedral became famous once her photo appeared in Cuba's *Rough Guide*, *Lonely Planet*, and *Frommer's*. Dance groups and musicians performed in hotel lobbies and for private group tours, while others were labeled "national" companies and considered part of Cuba's folkloric patrimony.[5] Sex tourism, an informal sector, and once characteristic of pre-Castro Cuba, increased in urban areas, the Afro-Cuban *jineteras* becoming the most successful of the sex workers. Older white male tourists were often seen walking down the street or dining in hotel restaurants with their much younger black Cuban "girlfriends" (see Cabezas 2009; Fusco 2002; Smith and Padula 1996).

While trips out to real *campesino casas del campo* (*campesino* houses in the countryside) were periodically promoted by Cuban tour agencies, such visits were more often bonus parts of tours with other destinations (Cienfuegos, Trinidad, Varadero, Pinar del Río). The visits were purposely scheduled into the itinerary in order to break up the tedium of a long trip. Lunch was served in fake campesino structures that had relatively credible palm-leaf thatched roofs, but were, however, shading very inauthentic rectangular cement floors and painted picnic tables. Male servers were dressed in *guayaberas* and straw hats, the women outfitted in long white ruffled dresses and red-checkered aprons with ribbons in their hair. The fake campesinos, spoke English, French, or Italian and lived in nearby cities, not in the supposedly authentic casa del campo. They were costumed in this "country" clothing so that they resembled rural folk from many parts of the world—a folkorization of what producers considered a rural semblance. Thus, their image "provided a potential bond of sameness, rather than difference" (Desmond 1999:xvi). This sameness or apparent "normality" is perhaps a central reason campesinos were not as marketable as the trance-inducing drumbeats, sultry rumba, and exotic rituals of Afro-Cuban folklore. There was a perceived sense of universality to rural folk, at least among European and North American tourists. Although the poetics of the *folk* were more ideologically valuable to Cuban artists, intellectuals, and representatives of state institutions who wished to promote the national pura cepa, the rituals of the *folkloric* supplied the country with money and resources and were rescuing it from economic collapse.

In a book published in Cuba on the "actuality, tendencies and perspectives on tourism," the results of a conference on the commercialization of culture are summarized:

> *Estas consideraciones, implican la obligación de elaborar diseños de programas de marketing del destino a partir de una imagen y definir los rasgos fundamentales de la identidad. En este sentido, hay que tomar en consideración, en dependencia del mercado al que nos estamos dirigiendo, entre otros, los aspectos siguientes:*
>
> *—Las manifestaciones y toda la riqueza de las tradiciones culturales, incluyendo la religiosidad popular, como expresión de la cultural y singularidad de un destino.*
> *—Las tradiciones culinarias [. . .]*
> *—La idiosincrasia y el carácter de la población.*
> *—Los valores sociales como parte del patrimonio del país.*
> *—Las tradiciones históricas como atractivo turístico.*
> *—El patrimonio arquitectónico como valor turístico.*
> *—Las posibilidades que brinda la naturaleza y el ecoturismo [. . .]*
> *—Los demás recursos turísticos existentes.*
> *—Las variadas ofertas extra hoteleras de alta calidad y novedosas.*

These considerations oblige us to develop destination-marketing programs based on an image that defines the fundamental features of [Cuban] identity. In this way, one must consider our dependency on the market that we are addressing and the elements driving it, including:

—Demonstrations of all the richness of cultural traditions, including popular
   religion, as expressions of the cultural singularity of the destination.
—Culinary traditions [. . .]
—The idiosyncrasy and character of the population.
—Social values as part of the country's patrimony.
—Historical traditions as tourist attractions.
—Architectural patrimony as tourist-worthy.
—The possibilities that nature and eco-tourism offer [. . .]
—Other existing tourist resources.
—A variety of original and high-quality offers outside the hotels.

This passage (Rodríguez Millares 2001:35) shows that the top priority in
the tourism industry at the beginning of the twenty-first century was the
inclusion of "popular religion" as an expression of Cuba's cultural singularity, and as a way to market it. Yet this celebration of Afro-Cuban
religious tradition followed decades of persecution and castigation.

The personality and "character" of the population is third on Rodríguez Millares's list, although policy prohibited most Cubans from publicly associating with foreign tourists during this era. "Social values" or
socialist morality is fourth on the list, while "nature" and the countryside
fall near the bottom. Whether campesino culture as a tourist attraction
was to be paired with popular religion and the "richness of cultural
traditions," or with "nature" and the countryside is left unclear and
unspecified. Those concerned with developing the "professionalism" of
the Cuban tourist industry lamented the popular perception of the island as a destination characterized only by its excellent beaches and
beautiful exotic women. They asserted the need to create a new image,
which they proposed to do by "modify[ing] the folkloric and exotic
image" to create a "higher level of professionalism," and "protect ourselves from the current process of globalization" (Rodríguez Millares
2001:38–39).[6] This discourse on tourism and the extent to which Cuba
had to "compete" to make itself culturally distinct (and be marketed as
such) was kept separate from institutional dialogues about nationalism
in the intellectual and artistic spheres, where cultural identity was supposedly unconscious and unmanipulated and was to be protected from
the outside, not sold to it.

Qualified (and selected) Cubans began to enroll in a school for the
promotion of tourism, called the Escuela de Altos Estudios de Hotelería
y Turismo de FORMATUR (School of Higher Studies for the Tourism and

Hotel Industries). Tourism, touted as the "business of the future," became a more frequent theme of international conferences and academic scholarship. Fidel Castro himself made speeches on the importance of tourism to the economy, while at the same time attempting to keep the rapidly growing industry within the parameters of the socialist value system. Although Fidel Castro stated that Cuba should project itself as the most attractive, diverse, and unique tourist destination in the Caribbean and Latin America, he also stressed that "no somos ni seremos competidores sino socios y colaboradores estrechos" (we are not, nor will we be competitors, rather friends and close collaborators) (Castro 1998). Cubans working in the tourist industry—especially waiters, bartenders, bellhops, and tour guides—had the best-paying jobs on the island, their tips in one day exceeding the monthly salary of doctors, lawyers, and other highly respected professionals. When taking taxis in Havana, both state-controlled and *particulares*, I discovered that the drivers were former engineers, teachers, lawyers, and company presidents who had left their original jobs to work as highly paid chauffeurs, bringing tourists to and from the airport, and driving them around to see the city's most popular attractions. English and French language classes routinely filled up and had waiting lists, replacing the once mandatory, but now useless, Russian once taught in school.

Extranjeros: The Ironies of Foreignness

Oye compa'y, no te hagas el extranjero, coño.
—Conversation in the street, Havana (July 2000)

After 1995, the legalization of the U.S. dollar, and doors opening to foreign visitors, Cubans became especially ambivalent about the extranjero—the foreigner, the tourist. Since then, the image of the extranjero has become part of a national discourse, almost divorced from the entity itself.[7] "No te hagas el sueco" (literally, don't act so Swedish), a popular expression to tell someone he or she is acting stupid or clueless, turned into "No te hagas el extranjero" (don't act like a foreigner) as the number of foreigners in Cuba increased, along with the number of nationalities represented. Even after two years living in Cuba and after four years working with the same cultural institutions, I was still referred to as *la extranjera* (or *la americana* at best) by people I did not know well. A foreigner walking down the streets of Havana, Cienfuegos, Trinidad, Cumanayagua, or Guantánamo often heard both soft murmurs and loud exclamations of "¡extranjero!" Depending on the context and who was present in the conversation, *extranjero* was sometimes replaced by the more ambivalent slang word *yuma*. There is no direct translation for *yuma*, but it was originally understood as something or someone "American." In the late 1990s and early 2000s, the word came to refer to the quality and desirability of a certain foreign product or one that just appeared foreign: "Ay, amigo, ¿esa camisa es cubano? ¡Pero parece yuma!" (Hey, buddy, this shirt is Cuban? But it seems foreign-made!). The word *yuma* was also used in a more negative way, to call out to a foreigner on the street, or to point out an extranjero to one's buddies: "Oye, yuma, ¿dónde vas?" (Hey yuma, where are you going?) or "Mire ese yuma caminando por la calle" (Check out that yuma over there). It was often spoken with cynicism or sarcasm, revealing its truly equivocal nature (for more on *la yuma*, see Ryer 2006).

While this commentary was mostly curious and positive (or at least neutral) in nature, its constancy was sufficient to establish a firm consciousness of "us" and "other," and the state did its best to ensure that this social separation remained clear and strong, so much so that it was unofficially referred to as "Cuban apartheid." Cubans were not allowed in tourist hotels or at tourist hotspots (clubs, bars, beaches) without a residence or working permit (this law was finally loosened in 2008 by Raúl Castro). Police officers and officials working at the Ministry of Foreign Relations were not allowed to fraternize with extranjeros on a personal level, and Communist Party members were discouraged from having intimate relationships with foreigners. After 2000 restrictions on Cuban and extranjero "fraternization" became even more rigid, and couples or groups of people appearing to be composed of both Cubans and extranjeros were often stopped, asked for identification, and interrogated before allowing people to continue on their way. I would periodically be stopped while walking along familiar streets in Havana with Isnoel, Ury, or any of my other friends and informants, especially if they were mulatto or Afro-Cuban. When they saw my Cuban ID they would let us go without a hassle, but the incident would never go without comment by my companions.

Most Cubans were interested in learning about other countries, practicing their English or French, and making new friends, but many I knew were simultaneously repelled by and attracted to "places of consumption." Artistically representing and performing their own culture for extranjeros was exciting and instilled a sense of national pride and distinction (not to mention profitability), but it was also criticized as "selling out" and corrupting pure cultural memory. Artists who still worked exclusively for the Ministry of Culture (state supported) proudly declared that they were not interested in money and that they preferred to work for "the people," yet in the same conversation they sighed with jealousy about a cousin or colleague invited abroad by an individual, university, foreign company, or organization. For over fifty years, Cuban identity had been constructed as the inverse of everything Americans and other capitalists represented. Cuban integrity and strength were defined, in part, on the ability to be the virtuous David and fight off the world's evil Goliath. Once Cuba's nemesis had been let in the door, contradictory and confusing messages were sent to the general population, creating anxiety about what would happen next. The Cuban state defended its actions as desperate and temporary (even after more than ten years), while attempting to divert attention from the socioeconomic crisis by taking its customary offensive stance.

It was difficult to be a foreigner in Cuba. Foreignness suggested access to and accumulation of U.S. dollars. Even after living in some of the most isolated areas of Cuba for two years, I found myself speechless or defensive whenever my companions offhandedly remarked that something was yuma or morally contaminated by capitalism. Although they assured me that I was different, I remained sensitive to their comments, especially since I was usually the only extranjera in the area. "Contamination," I was told, referred to the state of the soul, the spirit, and the underlying essence of a person. A contaminated individual was one who had succumbed to the materialist influence of capitalist culture (most often implying American culture). This was considered highly negative and many Cubans did not like to admit they enjoyed so-called *lujos* (luxuries), such as nice clothing, furniture, appliances, and jewelry. They condemned them as unnecessary items desired only by those who had lost faith in the socialist values put forward by Fidel and the Cuban state.

The irony of my own situation in Cuba as both an extranjera (and yuma) and an anthropologist was compounded by the "special" liminal phase in history within which I was working. I was a symbol of Muguercia's Ser Precario (see chapter 6), but I was also a fellow teatrista and a sympathetic *compañera* who had lived with them for two years. As a spectator I had a particular view of the dramatically ironic situation unfolding before me, but as a participant I was also another actor on the political stage, perhaps not always fully aware of how my own role was influencing or would ultimately affect the scene.

The Boat to Europe: Ideological Compromise

In the spring of 2001, I traveled to Belgium and France to participate in the first international tour of the Teatro de los Elementos. In Europe, I fully expected the group to present its traditional repertoire depicting la naturaleza and the culture of the Cuban campesino still living in remote mountain regions, especially since the trip had been sponsored by a Belgian ecological organization called Quinoa, which supported development projects around the world. For six years, Quinoa representatives had been spending summers in Teatro de los Elementos' base of Cumanayagua, but finally, in 2001, the theater group had been invited to work with Quinoa in Brussels and to perform in various locations around Europe. I met the Los Elementos in the city, spent a couple of days with them in meetings and social excursions, and from there we traveled to a small town approximately two hours outside of Brussels. The actors lugged crates filled with scenery and props into a small community hall and began to prepare for the evening's performance. Having known this Teatro Comunitario group and its work for four years, my expectations were that they would perform something from their repertoire with themes of the romantic countryside, the campesino, and the poetic beauty of the land. Their play, *Ten mi nombre como un sueño* (see chapters 3 and 4) had only recently been debuted in Cuba, and thus, it was rehearsed and ready for performance. However, in Europe, this community group was suddenly demonstrating a Haitian fire ritual. Nego, the group's only Afro-Cuban actor, wielded knives and torches and danced in a circle while three other actors played drums and chanted. A bottle of rum was passed around. The performance climaxed as Nego sprayed his mouthful of liquor over the audience, which squealed in a combination of dismay and excited delight. After the exotic ritual, the actors brought out *batá* and conga drums, guitars, and a set of maracas, and they began to play salsa so that the audience could dance. Melodies made famous by

Buena Vista Social Club and Celia Cruz filled the hall and several nervous, yet brave Belgian couples arose to try out their salsa steps.

Disconcerted, I watched the spectacle. Los Elementos' European performance was in stark contradiction to what they had stood for as Teatro
Comunitario, but here they were forced to conform to what the foreign
public expected from them, which was the side of Cuba reserved for
tourists, for extranjeros, for the "outside." Gone were those humble
campesinos tending their crops, wearing straw hats, and reciting poetry
under the moonlight. Gone were those militant revolutionary actors
who had conversed for hours about the loss of traditional values and had
lamented the contamination of modern youth. Had there been an invisible line of pura cepa around the Caribbean island outside of which
anything was allowed? Did the rules apply only in Cuba? Blatant contradictions had been plentiful in Havana, surely, but I had shrugged them
off as an urban phenomenon. Yet now one of the most respected Teatro
Comunitario groups had crossed the forbidden line into "pseudo."

Between 2001 and 2009 I returned to Cuba annually, checking in with
Los Elementos, La Cruzada, and El Laboratorio, documenting changes in
society generally, group compositions, and individual artists' lives. In
2009, Teatro Comunitario groups persevered, but without their original
Option Zero characteristics. Themes of nature, tradition, authenticity,
purity, scarcity, and sacrifice—which began as artistic premises and points
of creative departure—were later used for political and economic gain, in
response to the same stressful factors of the Special Period that had initially inspired these groups' drive towards a nonmaterialistic purity. The
return to the pura cepa had become a marketing tool for soliciting additional state funds, or to lure foreign groups or rich extranjeros who could
help them fulfill their dreams. Ecological groups and third world development organizations from Canada and Europe continued to be interested
in the sustainable agriculture of Los Elementos' farm project and their
focus on la naturaleza, but after a second European tour in 2003, several
members of the group were inadvertently enticed into emigrating. "Somos
un barco" (we are a ship), José Oriol said, smiling sadly, after most of his
original group had "sailed abroad" (personal communication, 2003). The
group's fame, which they owed to their devotion to humility and socialist
principles, had led to personal opportunities that tested the members'
political convictions. Using the authentic native as a national tool of resistance was proving a precarious project in Cuba. Ironically, the very

thing that Option Zero Theater represented—the local culture and the pura cepa—landed them national *premios*, initiations to travel abroad, and commercial market opportunities.

The Comedy and Tragedy of Twenty-First-Century Cubanía

Cuban political ideology and the national imaginary has been saturated with the classic dichotomy of rural and urban, purity and contamination, past (traditional) and present (modern), yet it was, in fact, much more complicated than it first appeared, a scenario rich in paradox. What was once the Hombre Nuevo—progressive and modern—was obsolete by 2000, never fully realized, while the new ideal, the Hombre Novísimo, was a challenging fusion of humble austerity and cosmopolitan refinement. Theater groups like Teatro Escambray, that first crusaded into the countryside to enlighten "primitive" and illiterate peasants, bringing modernity and progress in its wake (Teatro Nuevo), later reformulated their mission as a modern crusade (Teatro Comunitario and Option Zero Theater) to preemptively nostalgize and rescue a dying past, the same past the Revolution had once struggled to transcend.

Cuban artists struggled for professional and personal survival. Although they attempted to avoid politics, they were inescapably caught up in it, trapped within the discourse their craft was supposed to provoke. They cherished campesinos as virtuous and humble, but also criticized them as backward and brutish—in the end, still *inculto*, even as they represented contemporary Cuban nationality. The preservation of this particular heritage was partly in the hands of these official producers of culture, and although they strove for innovation and individuality in their work, they also felt some degree of responsibility and loyalty to the national collective. Néstor García Canclini states that "the dramatization of the patrimony is the effort to simulate that there is an origin, a founding substance, in relation with which we should act today." Yet, he continues: "What that patrimony *is* will inevitably change over time in any social context: The world is a stage, but what must be performed is already prescribed. [. . .] To be cultured implies knowing that repertory of symbolic goods and intervening correctly in the rituals that reproduce it" (Canclini 1995:110). In Cuba, the actual dynamic of this process became evident on closer examination. True patrimony and its "repertory of symbolic goods" were openly negotiated in intellectual circles. Modernizers and traditionalists combined forces during the Special Period to teach the noble, and then famous, campesinos the contemporary version of campesino-hood so that they could fulfill their new national role. Successful theater groups had to prove that they had played a part in the campaign for national cultivation—a cultivation based on a kind of preemptive nostalgia for a figure supposedly dying out, but one which never really existed. The potential misstep resulted from attempting to rewrite the archive but misinterpreting the repertoire (see Taylor 2003).

Teatro Comunitario, or more specifically, Option Zero Theater, was considered a theater that was born out of crisis, but Cuban artists could not unveil the regime's political pretense or undermine its rhetoric without risking their livelihood and even their freedom.[8] Instead, the theater and its teatristas appropriated politics and used it to their own ends in a subtle and sometimes unconscious act of subversion. Artists took advantage of the official and popular appeal this form of theater enjoyed. The state welcomed its apparent revolutionary loyalty and dedication to maintaining the integrity of socialist morality, while the population wanted to believe that such a simple form of beauty and humility still existed given the hardships everyone endured almost twenty years after the onset of the Special Period. There was both a public and private mask that had to be maintained. What remains to be seen in 2012 and beyond is where the next *batalla* will lead the Cuban people and the Cuban artists who represent them. When nostalgia can no longer bolster (or hold back) the troops, where will Cuba turn? And how will its artists respond? Perhaps the preemptive battle to save cubanía will be victorious ("la victoria siempre"), and the crisis will someday end, but it is also possible that *hasta* (until) will be forever incorporated into Cuba's nationalist battle cry.

Cubans were proud and sure, never doubting for long the strength and longevity of their cubanía in whatever form it might appear. Although the state believed that globalization, the dollar, and the influx of foreigners were threats to national identity and solidarity, the opposite was actually true. The state was undeniably losing the power it once held through the socialist illusion of a utopian future, but Cuba was not losing its national culture. Its representations were changing over the years as Cuban society slowly wrestled its way out of the long and wearisome Special Period, but all the original national characters continued to reappear in new guises. In the twenty-first century, the illiterate and backward guajiro grew into the educated and noble campesino, the shifty negrito became the powerful (and dollar-earning) Afro-Cuban Santería practitioner, and the colonialist gallego turned into the imperialist (and dollar-spending) extranjero. La mulata diversified into over thirteen variations but held onto her status as the ultimate symbol of the Cuban *ajiaco*. The ajiaco was a well-known culinary metaphor originally used by Fernando Ortiz in the 1930s and 1940s to describe the heterogeneity of Cuba's racial heritage: a stew of different ingredients that agglutinate but do not synthesize or lose their original flavors. In the 2000s, the notion of ajiaco was not just racial; it was also defined culturally and economically.

Ortiz stresses that Cuban culture was produced by cultural contact, "transculturation," and the continuous "translation" of foreign elements. The indigenous population of Cuba was wiped out by the Spanish conquest, and subsequent residents included settlers, slaves, and travelers. Thus Cuban culture has always been fluid and changing, Ortiz explains, characterized by mutability, uprootedness, and change: "Hombres, economías, culturas y anhelos, todo aquí se sintió foráneo, provisional, cambiadizo, "aves de paso" sobre el país, a su costa, a su contra y a su malgrado" (Ortiz 1991:23 [1940]). (Men, economies, cultures, and yearnings [in Cuba] have all been perceived as foreign, provisional, changeable, "birds of passage" over the country and its coasts, against opposition and in spite of it.) The Cuba scholar Gustavo Pérez Firmat agrees with Oritz that Cuba's "distinctive feature [was] its imperfective, processual aspect" (Firmat 1987:7–8). As I have stated in this book, I also favor the idea of cultural liminality and the need to analyze Cuban culture processually. Although Ortiz could be describing the construction of any set of traditions and identities around the world, Cuba was, indeed, unique in the degree to which its perceived "uprootedness" impacted national identity over the years. Perhaps it was the absence of a firm surviving category of "indigenous native" that so unsettled scholars of Cuba, just as it unsettled Cuban intellectuals and artists during this period of uncertainty and crisis in national identity. Methodologically, the ethnography of Cuban theater "reveals the very processes of assembling and disassembling a frame" (Martin 1994:17 in a discussion of Irving Goffman's frame analysis) more than the shifting nature of Cuban culture. What was distinctive about Cuba was precisely *how* its social and ideological frames were constructed, broken down, and rebuilt in the context of socialism and the Special Period, not just the already understood fact that culture and national identity were ever-dynamic and flowing. In twenty-first-century Cuba the constitutive role of the "native" was again in flux. Roberto Fernández Retamar's Caliban character persevered, but was adapted to the modern Cuban scene where artists attempted to merge the spiritual enlightenment of Ariel with the uncultivated earthiness of the Calibanesque masses, perhaps also linking these to the indigenous "Carib" from which Retamar drew his metaphor.[9]

I have illustrated in previous chapters how the sequential periods of crisis, struggle, and transformation in Cuba have been consistent and enduring; another element to add to our "stew" of ironies. The revolutionary Hombre Nuevo, although no longer really "new" in 2000, was still one of the strongest-flavored ingredients in the modern ajiaco and will surely be a long-term member of the national cast, standing, if not for socialism, for cooperation, loyalty, humility, for the never-ending struggle for justice and equality, and standing against imperialist domination. Our cosmopolitan campesino-like Hombre Novísimo was also moving up on the recipe list, although his exact proportions had not yet been fully determined. To continue with the metaphor—there were just too many cooks in the kitchen. Official, foreign, and popular conceptions may ultimately merge in new ways, and culturally and historically coherent (and generationally accepted) theatrical representations of cubanía will be realized. Yet the question for me has remained, what would the current process of "agglutination" hold in store for Cubans living in Cuba? Although I believed in the forces of cultural consistency and coherence, I had no set predictions for the immediate future of Cuba's political economy or for how Cubans would react to the volatile changes in official policy that seemed to occur on a monthly basis. Loyal party members were certain that "the Revolution" would continue after the death of Fidel and Raúl Castro and that Cuban socialism would survive, while "reformers" or closet counter-revolutionaries were equally convinced that the system was about to collapse. Either way, the Revolution and the revolutionary were firmly entrenched in the population's consciousness, but the definitions of *when* or *how* to be a "good" revolutionary loosened during the Special Period and will continue to change, variably defined according to the situation at any particular moment. As Barthes has said, "It is a whole new history which is implanted in the myth" (1972:19), for certainly Cuba's younger generation was beginning

31. Teatro de los Elementos actors walk thorough Cuban countryside en route to Siguanea, Escambray Mountains (photo by Laurie Frederik, 1999)

to understand the revolutionary myth in a way that suited its own contemporary situation.

One thing we may be sure of is that the theater will continue to act as a "sensitive representational barometer" of political ideology (Martin 1994:23), the creativity of the artistic community representing and taking an active role in the critical discourse of the times. What is really "real" as opposed to what is considered "pseudo" are conceptions that waver in living memory and in people's consciousness, a consciousness that is effectively represented in live performance but that is open to reinterpretation once it is placed in the historical archives. Whether Cuba ultimately comes "back from the future" (Eckstein 1994), looks to the "future of nostalgia" (Boym 2001), is "forever until it was no more" (Yurchak 2005), or acts preemptively to defend a metaphysical idea of cubanía that "once-was" and "could-be" are questions that will be increasingly open to negotiation in the next several years, especially as the nation's most vivid icon ages and weakens and a post-Castro Cuba changes the trajectory of cubanía yet again.

NOTES

Introduction

1. There was much written during the 1990s on the perceived transition of Cuban society, mainly in political science, but also in anthropology. Some of these include Sandor Halebsky and John Kirk 1992, Carmelo Mesa-Lago 1993, Jean Stubbs 1989, and Jorge Dominguez 2003, 2004.

2. One exception is Mona Rosendahl's ethnography of a small town outside of Santiago de Cuba called *Inside the Revolution: Everyday Life in Socialist Cuba* (1998). Rosendahl's book was based on fieldwork carried out in the late 1980s.

3. The term *cubanidad* was coined by José Antonio Saco, a political scientist and philosopher, who used the term to distinguish Cuban identity from that of Spain and the United States. Saco's definition was created from the *criollo* perspective, leaving out the centrality of African and indigenous cultural presence. José Martí also used the term cubanidad when discussing its role in the unity of *Nuestra America* (Our America) and the struggle against colonialism. According to Antoni Kapcia, cubanidad is Cubanness while cubanía refers to ideology and the teleological belief in cubanidad. It is generally accepted that the use of the term cubanidad emerged from a white intellectual discourse on nationalism, which then turned into a broader ideology of dissent and rebellion, *cubanía rebelde*, from the late nineteenth century to the 1950s (2000:6). After 1959, rebellion became "revolutionary"; thus, *cubanía revolucionaria* was akin to revolutionary consciousness. According to Kapcia, *cubanía revolucionaria* was "a hegemonic ideology of dissent that became fundamental in guiding the revolutionary process through the maelstrom of the first decade and the competing orthodoxies of the more recognizably socialist years to the critical 1990s, where it became a vital element in guaranteeing survival, in balancing the demands for continuity and change, stability and adaptation, and in searching for yet another identity of the *nación*" (ibid.:6–7). There are other debates about which term to use—cubanidad, cubanía, or even cubaneo (see Firmat 1997), but throughout this book, I choose to use the more contemporary cubanía.

4. Fidel Castro, speech to the Union Nacional de Escritores y Artistas de Cuba (UNEAC), June 9, 2000, reprinted in *Juventud Rebelde*, June 10, 2000:1.

5. *Martiano* refers to the philosophies of Cuban intellectual José Martí, who is considered the father of the Cuban nation and Cuban identity.

6. Various anthropological texts have been adapted for performance on the formal theatrical stage. These include two plays by Hilda Kuper, who did fieldwork in Swaziland and South Africa in the 1950s; Colin Turnbull's *The Mountain People*, which was converted to a stage play in 1972 by Peter Brook and called *The Ik*; and Ruth Behar's *Translated Woman*, which was performed in 1997 by a New York Latino theater group called Pregones. A less theatrical example of performed ethnography includes Professor McKim Marriott's Hindu "Samsara," a cultural simulation game played at the University of Chicago from the late 1960s to the late 1990s. Samsara reenacted (or "realized") certain social aspects of an Indian Hindu community through a very complex game-type simulation (see Marriott's handbook, n.d.). Both Victor Turner and Marriott described their respective simulations as "tests" of textual ethnographies—either proving or disproving the anthropological knowledge about the cultural mechanisms of a particular group of people as presented in ethnography. See Edith and Victor Turner on techniques they used in their university classes, Victor Turner 1987, and Peter Brook 1968, 1987, for further reflections on this technique.

7. I use the Spanish term *Oriente* instead of "Oriental" to distinguish the east–west relationship in Cuba from the "Orientalism" of Edward Said's influential work. Although the historical premise and general argument is quite different, the relationship of Cuba's East with its *Occidente* (Occidental, or western region) shows similar signs of western dominance and identity through contrast with an eastern "backward" culture.

8. The closer a theater performance was to the capital, the easier it was for cultural institutions and officials to monitor and censor. But at the same time, these performances could be more experimental and confrontational since they enjoyed greater exposure to international culture and media, and artistic critics expected the big city's performances to be "edgy."

9. In *Dictionary of Theatre Anthropology*, a book Barba and Savarese coauthored, and in an explanation of the ISTA, they state: "The distinction is repeatedly emphasized that the term 'anthropology' is not being used in the sense of cultural anthropology, but that ISTA's work is a new field of study applied to the human being in an organized performance situation. The only affinity between ISTA's work and cultural anthropology is the questioning of the obvious (one's own tradition). [. . .] By means of a confrontation with what appears to be foreign, one educates one's way of seeing and renders it both participatory and detached" (1991: preface). They continue: "Theatre anthropology is thus the study of human beings' socio-cultural and physiological behavior in a performance situation" (ibid.: introduction).

1. Revolutionary Performance

1. Assertions that the three characters were representative of the groups comprising the new Cuban nation is often a blanket statement about the historical impor-

tance of Teatro Bufo in general. However, Jill Lane insists that it was "simply not true until the twentieth century" (personal communication, July 2010). Lane explains that during the nineteenth century the characters only sometimes appeared in the same play, but that the idea of the triad was formed later, during the Republic. An important piece of evidence for this argument is that the mulata character did not appear on stage until 1882 (see Lane 2005).

2. Commedia dell'arte (Comedy of Art) is a form of theater that began in fifteenth-century Italy. The performances were mainly improvised using a cast of "types," or stock characters, that have continued to appear in modern performances of Commedia.

3. This increased comprehension was probably also due to the fact that the *bozal* language of the original Bufos was not being used so extensively. *Jerga bozal* literally means "muzzled slang." The bozal dialect was a mixture of "proper" and "corrupted" Spanish, which was thought to represent the ignorance and incivility of African slaves, other Cuban blacks and mulattos, as well as uneducated and poor *guajiros* of the countryside. This dialect confused grammatical gender (e.g., *el casa*), mispronounced words, misplaced accents, mixed tenses (*tuvía, teno*), and used nonsensical words. See Frederik 2001a and Lane 2005. Kristina Wirtz writes about the linguistic structure of bozal.

4. For further discussion of the role of music in Teatro Bufo, see Rine Leal 1967, and 1975b; and Robin Moore 1997, 2006.

5. For more on the banning and increasing censorship of Teatro Bufo and other stage productions in Cuba at this time, as well as the police harassment of writers and performing artists, see R. Moore 1997:43–44; Leal 1980:75; and Enrique Arredondo 1981:77, 120.

6. Artists who later became powerful figures under Castro included writers such as Alejo Carpentier, Juan Marinello, Miguel Barnet, and Carlo Rafael Rodríguez, and a group of actors including Sergio Corrieri, Roberto Blanco, Lillian Llerena, Hermina Sances, and Helmo Hernández.

7. As a result of this taboo and dearth of self-analyses of race in revolutionary Cuba, academics were forced to rely on the personal accounts of foreigners, such as John Clytus and Elizabeth Sutherland. Although the perspectives were undeniably North American, there was little else to draw on until very recently. With growing tourism and a commercial interest in Afro-Cuban culture, the literature has massively increased. Conferences on race and identity are also increasingly being held on the island. Intellectual and popular debates are hot topics of discussion. Hip-hop and rap music have been important elements of this changing racial consciousness and politicization.

8. Tomas Fernández Robaina's *El Negro en Cuba* was one of the first to emerge after a thirty-year lapse in discussion (1994). Although *afrocubano* has reemerged as a separate identity and is discussed in terms of popular culture, the issue of racial inequality has remained a sensitive subject. Between 1994 and 2004, a growing num-

ber of foreign scholars of Cuba began studying racial identities (Shawn Alfonso Wells, Paul Ryer, Nadine Fernandez), Afro-Cuban religion (Katherine Hagedorn, Ivor Miller, Lisa Maya Knauer, Kristina Wirtz), and music (Robin Moore, Ariana Hernandez-Reguant, Sujatha Fernandes, Marc Perry).

9. But although such discussions were publicly silenced, they certainly continued in the private sphere. In spite of the hopes of José Martí and the new government, racial prejudice was never fully abolished, even after legal discrimination was officially stopped.

10. These techniques included the widespread nationalization of private property and business, and the centralization of power and political control. See Louis A. Pérez 1988 and Marifeli Pérez-Stable 1999.

11. For analyses of cultural change and the development of revolutionary consciousness in the 1960s, see especially Denise Blum 2011, Julie Marie Bunck 1994, Richard Fagen 1969, and Tzvi Medin 1990.

12. One of the best-known examples demonstrating the complexity of the copyright issue has been Alberto "Korda" Gutiérrez's famous photograph of Che Guevara (called *Guerrillero Heróico*, or Heroic Guerrilla), reproduced en masse around the world without one penny going to Korda. He did not claim the rights to any profits from the photo, nor did he protest against its reproduction until Absolut Vodka attempted to market its product with the Che image on it. It was only at this point that Korda used his virtual ownership and authority as an artist to stop the production of what he considered to be disrespectful use. See Ariana Hernandez-Reguant's 2004 article, "Copyrighting Che: Art and Authorship under Cuban Late Socialism."

13. See also Fidel Castro [1961] 1980; Magaly Muguercia 1981; Anne Petit 1977; and Laurette Séjourné 1977.

14. Corrieri later went on to become a famous film actor. He is best known for his role as Serigio in *Memorias del subdesarrollo* (Memories of Underdevelopment) as well as the lead in *El hombre de Maisinicu* (The Man from Maisinicu), among others. Corrieri was politically active as a member of the Cuban Communist Party serving in various leadership positions including as the vice president of the National Institute of Radio and Television, and as president of the Instituto Cubano de Amistad con los Pueblos (Cuban Institute for Friendship among Nations).

15. See the writings of Bertolt Brecht, Erwin Piscator, Jerzy Grotowski, Peter Weiss, and Peter Brook. In Latin America, see writings of Augusto Boal, Enrique Buenaventura, Santiago García, and Leonel Menéndez Quiroa. In the United States there are histories of groups such as the Federal Theater Project, Teatro Campesino, and The Living Theater, just to name a few. Particularly informative compilations include Loren Kruger 1992; Adam Versenyi 1993, 2005; and Judith Weiss 1993.

16. "La Vitrina" (The Showcase), play script by Albio Paz, in Laura Prieto Ruiz 1992:38–41. Performed by Teatro Escambray. The *décima* continues: "*Aprende Pancho a leer, sus hijos van a la escuela, ya no piensan en la espuela. Empieza Pancho a*

tener; empieza Pancho a creer, que a aquella caballería, esta vez sí le daría, todo una vida mejor, que él solo, con su sudor, con el tiempo alcanzaría [. . .]."

17. *Por primera vez* is a nine-minute film by Octavio Cortázar, shot in 1967.

18. Unfortunately, Cano does not list the specific plays he refers to in this passage, although this representation of the guajiro was not uncommon in art, theater performances, or everyday jokes on the street or around the kitchen table. Part of what he was referring to was the repertoire of *bufo–campesino* plays from the 1800s and their descendants. Rine Leal writes that although there were a few plays that, in fact, idealized the guajiro—or at least honored their passions and conflicts (Juan Cristóbal Nápoles Fajardo's "*Consecuencias de una falta*" 1858 and José Fornaris's "*La hija del pueblo*" 1865 and "*Amor y sacrificio*" 1866)—most playwrights produced derogatory, distorted, and false images, especially the playwrights Juan José Guerrero, Zamora, and José Socorro de León (the plays are referred to in Leal 1980:47, but no publication information is provided). Esther Suárez Durán also mentions Guerrero in this latter group and says that a guajiro character named Idelfonso appeared with his wife and daughter in a less frequent appearance of *guajiras* (female guajiros; personal communication, 2009).

19. For detailed histories and descriptions of Teatro Escambray and its plays, see Séjourné 1977; Rine Leal 1978, 1980; Alma Villegas 1994; Omar Cedre Valiño 1994; and a compilation on the group, edited by director Rafael González, n.d. There are also analyses of Teatro Escambray contained in larger works about Teatro Nuevo and Latin American popular theater; see especially Judith Weiss 1993.

20. Flora Lauten later became a professor of theater at the Instituto Superior de Arte (National Arts University, or ISA) and began a new company called Teatro Buendía (Good Day Theater), a very provocative and successful group in Havana.

21. For more on the persecution of homosexuals, see Reinaldo Arenas 1994 and Ian Lumsden 1996. On religious discrimination see Juan Clark 1998; Margaret Crahan 1989; John Kirk 1989; and Roger Reed 1991.

22. Immediately following the Revolution, leading up to and after the attack at the Bay of Pigs by the United States in 1961, a new guerrilla movement had formed, primarily in the mountains of Escambray. These *bandidos* (bandits) consisted of Cuban counter-revolutionaries, American soldiers, and, it is said, CIA agents. The fight against these counter-revolutionaries became part of official propaganda, with thousands imprisoned as a result. Many campesinos in the Escambray region were forcefully moved to a town called Sandino in Pinar del Río Province to separate them from the rebels.

23. Juan Carlos Martínez, *Tablas*, February 1985, no. 3.

24. For more on literary writers and the Cuban Revolution, see José B. Alvarez 2002.

2. Artists in the Special Period

1. *Opción Cero* script, Teatro de los Elementos 2002: 2. Written and produced in 2001 in Cumanayagua.

2. See Fidel Castro speeches, published in Cuba's national newspaper, *Granma*, 1990 and 1991.

3. *Opción Cero* script, Teatro de los Elementos 2002:3.

4. Ibid.:2–4.

5. The relationship between city and country dwellers has been complicated over the last several decades. Farmer's markets were initially opened in 1980 as part of a "material incentives" plan to increase production, then closed down in 1986 during the state's attempt at "Rectification," including the rectification of morals. Urban Cubans resented the high prices charged by the campesinos even though the country was not yet suffering the severe economic straits as in the Special Period soon to follow. In the early 1990s, and especially after 1994 when farmer's markets were legally reopened, resentment against the campesinos continued, for many believed they were profiting from the hardships and hunger of the rest of the population.

6. For more on Teatro Campesino, see Luis Valdez 1990 and Yolanda Broyles-González 1994.

7. The word *máquina* translates literally as "machine" or "engine." In Cuba the word is popularly used to refer to old American cars (mostly from the 1940s and 1950s) used as collective taxis.

8. By 2009, almost every state organization had an email account, and cybercafés were emerging in Havana, charging $6–$15 an hour for very slow Internet access. Most local residents did not have access to e-mail unless working with an educational or cultural organization in an official position. In 1999, students at the University of Havana could purchase a connection if they were able to spend $5 a month—way beyond the means of most Cubans in the 1990s (roughly a two-week salary). And the phone company, ETECSA (Empresa de Telecomunicaciones de Cuba S.A.), also provided dial-up e-mail access to those given permission, but the fees were still often beyond the means of Cubans earning a salary in pesos.

9. Until 2008, many hotels in Cuba were for foreigners only, at prices set in divisas, while others charged in Cuban pesos and were only open to Cuban citizens.

10. But see James Fernández on the movement of metaphors in expressive culture (1986, 1991).

11. See also Rachel Weiss (2007:14), who mentions a similar phenomenon among painters and other plastic artists denying an association with the "official" after 1990.

12. Armando Hart Dávalos was the minister of culture from 1976 to 1997.

3. Creative Processes and Play Making

1. Symbols, on the other hand, can be disassociated from the Cuban context or parts of society, even while they have particular meaning. Examples include the prerevolutionary Mambí fighter, the bearded revolutionary, the ubiquitous CDR (*Comités de Defensa de la Revolución*, Committees for the Defense of the Revolution), or the number 26 (the date in July when Fidel Castro attacked the Moncada Fort). Fernandez explains that "symbols are abstracted sign-images which have lost their direct link with the subjects on which they were first predicated in specific contexts" (Fernandez 1974:120). Certainly in the Cuban context, "[social] movement is obtained by the use of metaphor for purposes of persuasion and performance" (ibid.:122; see also Fernandez 1972). Metaphors of guerrilla warfare, the Revolution, and the United States as the evil Goliath are used to mobilize the masses, to build national unity and establish social order "for purposes of classification" (ibid.). An example of metaphoric classification: a loyal Cuban is a revolutionary fighter or a brave, selfless "David" while a dissident counter-revolutionary is officially called a *gusano* (worm).

2. *Devised theater* is a term used mainly in England and Europe, also known as "collective collaboration" in the United States. It is what the group Teatro de los Elementos was doing to create new plays during my stay in Cumanayagua. See Alison Oddey 1996 and Dierdre Heddon 2005.

3. "Blocking" refers to the physical placement and movement of actors on stage throughout the scenes of a play; stage direction, such as "walk stage left" or "stand downstage center." Blocking also includes the placement and use of scenery and props in particular scenes.

4. "Caballero, Atilio, and Grupo Teatro de los Elementos 1999 (hereafter, *Ten mi nombre como un sueño*):34.

5. Ibid.:6–8.

6. Ibid.:4, 32.

7. El Rápido was a Cuban version of McDonald's, and was the first fast food restaurant in Cuba, selling hamburgers and pizza in *divisas*.

8. These sorts of concepts are taught as exercises in Western theater and as part of the creative process in a variety of improvisational performance genres. I have learned different versions of them in workshops I have taken over the years, including sketch comedy (Second City Chicago), theatrical clown (500 Clown), improvisational comic theater games (the Futurists), and improvisational storytelling enactment (Playback Theater). For exercises that include these concepts, see especially Spolin 1983 and Boal 1992.

9. The "fight against bandits" referred to the fight against counter-revolutionaries in the Escambray Mountain region during the 1970s.

10. Although, among those interviewed, we found more young campesinos in the Escambray region who wished to move to urban areas than we did in Guan-

tánamo Province, probably due to the former province's relative proximity to Havana. In the mountains of the Oriente, the largest cities were Guantánamo and Santiago de Cuba, which did not offer the same economic and cultural possibilities as Havana. Also, Havana seemed much farther away to them than Haiti or the Dominican Republic—as if Havana were a foreign country: unreachable.

4. Inundation of Siguanea and Cuba

1. Caballero, Atilio, and Grupo Teatro de los Elementos 1999 (hereafter, *Ten mi nombre como un sueño*):16.

2. By 2006, the hotel was routinely accepting foreigners paying in *divisas* in an attempt to maintain itself in the midst of its crumbling and deteriorating condition.

3. *Ten mi nombre como un sueño*:3–4.

4. Fulgencio Batista was Cuba's military leader from 1933 to 1940, and president from 1940 to 1944. He became president again, after staging a coup from 1952 to 1958, and was finally ousted by Fidel Castro and his guerrilla rebel army in 1959.

5. *Ten mi nombre como un sueño*:17.

6. Ibid.:36–37.

7. Ibid.: 10.

8. Ibid.:8–9.

9. Ibid.:13.

5. Cultural Crusades of Guantánamo

1. The certificate of appreciation that is the source of this chapter's second epigraph was given to all Cruzada members for their tenth anniversary by the Municipal Culture Board, Popular Power of Maisí, on February 22, 2000.

2. Not every Cuban was allowed to have a telephone line in his or her house in 2000, and success often depended on the "importance" of the individual's social role, and/or personal connections with ETECSA officials. One telephone line was inevitably shared by neighbors and friends, and often a telephone number was given out with the addendum *vecino* (neighbor's phone) to warn potential callers that they will have to wait while their neighbor went out to find them. The call center required your Cuban carrné (identification) number, name, address, and the number to be called. Once connected with the designated individual, you were directed to a numbered booth and then charged by the minute. Phone calls to the United States in 2000 were approximately $1.50 per minute.

3. GaGá was a type of music and dance originating from the fusion of the traditions of Haitian immigrants with those of rural Cuba.

4. By 2003 the Guantánamo theater board (the municipal Consejo) decided to reduce the number of separate projects to better distribute dwindling state support, and the four groups were merged into two: Teatro Dramático de Guantánamo (adult Dramatic Theater) and Teatro Güiñol (children's puppet theater). By then,

Tío Tato had left the country and was rumored to have married a foreigner, and El Mago had joined Teatro Güiñol.

5. The Casa de Joven Creadores, or House of Young Artists, provided space and additional support for artists under thirty-five years of age. Painters, sculptors, actors, writers, and dancers shared the two-story house, once an elegant mansion, using small open patios for rehearsals, performances, and *peñas*. A small dance studio complete with wood floor allowed up to six dancers to practice at a ballet barre. By 2003, Ury Rodríguez was too old to continue as a *joven* artist. He and Virginia lost the space and had to store their costumes and sets in their own homes.

6. See Espinosa's compilation of Teatro La Yaya and Boudet's introduction, 1981. See also Magaly Muguercia 1981, 1988; and Randy Martin 1994 for analyses of Flora Lauten's plays and her role in the Cuban theater world.

7. See Raquel Carrió 1997:3–6 ("Otra tempestad: De la investigación de fuentes a la escritura escénica").

8. *La Cruzada* brochure, 2000, statement by Antonio Fernández Seoare, general coordinator of LA BARACA (professional organization of Teatro Comunitario in Cuba, comprised of its directors and supporters).

9. In 2000 a small boy was the only survivor of a group of Cuban rafters attempting to reach the United States. His mother, along with the others, died when the raft overturned. The boy, Elián González, had relatives in Miami, who decided to take him in and keep him in the United States. The affair became highly politicized, the custody of Elián Gonzalez symbolically representing and played out the struggle between Cuba and the United States. In Cuba, the media referred to the issue as a kidnapping. T-shirts with the boy's photo and the words *Salvamos a Elián* (Save Elián) were printed and distributed by the thousands. Protest marches and demonstrations were held in alternating towns around the country and televised nationally every evening. In the most isolated areas of rural Oriente, signs calling for the rescue of Elián were arranged in shells or in rocks along small embankments, and schoolchildren were also taught special jingles to sing. Elián González became an international figure, his symbolism theorized in scholarly articles and journalistic publications. See Sarah Banet-Weiser 2003; and L. Valdés 2000.

10. A *jinetera* in Cuba is considered a "hustler" rather than a prostitute who attempts to attract the attention of foreign men, and there are also male *jineteros* hustling women. They exchange companionship or sex and romance or both for nice dinners in divisa-charging hotels and restaurants, clothing, jewelry, and cash. Some jineteras and jineteros also try to seduce foreigners into marrying them and bringing them to North America or Europe. During the most extreme years of the Special Period crisis (1990–95) jineteras were said to work for seemingly simple things that were most lacking, such as soap, pens, cooking oil, or new shoes.

11. Herrero Beatón, *La muerte juega el escondido* script, n.d.:14–15.

12. Ury Rodriguez, Virginia Lopez, and Cristina Gonzalez 1995.

13. In the attempt to reach United States territory around the base, many are drowned or eaten by sharks in the water, or killed by land mines when trying to

make a run for it on land. Once on dry land, however, they are free from Cuban law and taken in as refugees under the Cuban Adjustment Act of 1966, better known as the "wet foot dry foot" policy. The Cuban state and especially revolutionary Cuban citizens refer to these people as traitors, as gusanos.

14. Fidel Castro's most recent campaign for the "Battle of Ideas" and the implementation of a new specialized group of "social workers" hired to enforce the movement was also likened to China's Red Guard. Alberto, personal communication, Havana, 2006.

15. Any trip abroad must still be funded by outside sources in divisas. Trips to distant cities within Cuba are sometimes funded by the Ministry of Culture, La Fundación Hermanos Saíz, or UNEAC, but only in alliance with a particular conference, symposium, or festival, and often without providing housing or other expenses.

6. Storytellers and the Story Told

1. Miguel Barnet is a scholar and writer, best known for *Biografía de un cimarrón* (Biography of a Runaway Slave), first published in 1968. Waldo Leyva is a well-known and respected Cuban poet who has published several collections, some set to music by Nueva Trova artists (see Leyva 2002). Jesús Guanche is a highly respected anthropologist and professor at the University of Havana. He has written widely on Cuban ethnicity and culture (see Guanche 1980, 1983). Natalia Bolívar is also an anthropologist and writer, specializing in Afro-Cuban culture. She is best known for her book *Los Orishas en Cuba* (The Orishas in Cuba) (1990).

2. See Pablo de la Torriente-Brau 1962. There was a film, *Realengo 18*, made in 1961 about the land struggles of the peasants of Realengo 18.

3. Rogelio Baratute was still alive in 2000 but only occasionally performed with the group. Due to Parkinson's disease, his ability to speak was limited, although he still remembered all of his lines from previous roles and recited them while I transcribed several of the group's unwritten scripts. His grandson, Julio Baratute, had taken over the direction of the group. Interview with Rogelio Baratute, El Lechero, 2000.

4. In spite of the criticisms by Havana intellectuals, Grupo Lino Álvarez members were greatly affected by this trip to the capital and their confidence increased significantly through their recognition as "actors" in the history of Cuban theater. One year after the conference, the director, Julio Baratute, left El Lechero and moved to Guantánamo City to attend one of the newly opened Schools for Instructors of Art. As of 2010 he continued to live in the city as a professional theater instructor.

5. The use of *pueblo* in this segment referred to a "city" more than a town, but the actors decided, in collaboration with participating campesinos, that *ciudad* did not "flow" well in the text, and the idea of a town was just as intimidating to residents in this zone of silence as a city.

6. Ury Rodríguez Urgelles and Virginia López 2000, *Guajiros a los cuatros vientos* script.

7. In the zones of silence there was no way to pass messages through modern technology since there is no radio signal or electricity. Communication between campesinos had to be either face to face or via another individual—a courier carrying a verbal message. In my experience, messages were sent with the tractor driver, who passed by every second or third day; through a child willing to walk or run the distance to the recipient; or through friends visiting or trading in another location.

8. For example, Sidney Mintz 1974, 1985a, 1985b; Michel-Rolph Trouillot 1988, 1993, 1995; Roberto Fernández Retamar 1971, 1997; R. Price 1990; David Scott 1999; Arlene Dávila 1997, 2001; Kevin Yelvington 2001.

9. See Christopher Boyer 2003 for more on the history of the agraristas. He also describes the importance of the writer and artist in the perpetuation of popular representations of Mexican campesinos.

10. For a detailed account of the Cuban popular music industry in Havana and the international market, see Ariana Hernandez-Reguant 2004. For classical Cuban *trova, nueva trova,* and other early musical forms, see Robin Moore 1997, and for contemporary Cuban hip-hop and rap, see Sujatha Fernandes 2006.

11. Malanga and boniato were root vegetables found in Cuba that made up a large part of the rural diet. Both were prepared like potatoes, boiled and seasoned with butter and salt. In the countryside, where there was little food variety, they were also grated and made into a sugary porridge for breakfast or dessert.

12. The Schools for Art Instructors were developed in 1961 in order to staff the Casas de Cultura around the country and to direct the amateur musical, dance, and theater groups in each location. The majority of these schools were closed in late 1980s, and any remaining were closed in the early 1990s. With the Massification of Culture (later, the Battle of Ideas) and the national campaign to redevelop the cultural traditions of the country, they were reopened in 2001, with record numbers of new teacher graduates sent out into marginal urban neighborhoods and rural areas to reinvigorate dying or defunct artistic groups and programs.

7. Dramatic Irony and Nationalism

1. In this chapter's first epigraph, Carlos Martí was president of UNEAC, when he spoke alongside the minister of culture, Abel Prieto, on cultural contamination and pseudo-culture at a UNEAC symposium in Havana in 2001.

2. Some particular examples I witnessed in Havana between 1997 and 1999 were *Mama* at Teatro Brecht (Brecht Theater House); *Mar nuestro* (Our Ocean) by Teatro Mío (My Theater Group); and an adaptation of *Caligula* by Teatro Público (Public Theater). The mother character in *Mama* was suggestive of Fidel Castro. In the play she has two daughters, one of whom is obedient and stays close to Mama while the other is argumentative and rebellious. In the end, the second daughter packs a suitcase and jumps over a symbolic river to get free from Mama. *Mar nuestro* is a play about three women stranded on an island after a shipwreck ("the damned circumstance of water on every side"). The characters are white, mulatto,

and black and racial tensions are played out in the scene progressions. The question of whether to "wait and see" or take action and try to escape is the primary organizing theme of the play. The Cuban *Caligula* was the traditional play about power and corruption, with direct hints that the narrative could be applied to the local situation. One of the most popular examples of metaphoric and analogous critique was a play by Alberto Pedro called *Manteca* (Pig Fat), which was banned until the early 1990s for its suggestions that the pig was actually Fidel Castro. The story is about a family who must decide whether to kill the pig for food during the worse years of the Special Period or to keep it alive since it had accompanied them for so many years as a companion. Comedy sketches were also very popular events in the 1990s. Put on by young actors and attended by younger crowds at Havana's Teatro Brecht on Tuesday nights, they were fast paced and provocative. The jokes that were the most dangerous politically were delivered rapidly and buffered by more benign humor, the audience's collective gasp barely perceptible before it was blunted by the next vignette.

3. For a history and discussion of the flexibilization of religion, see Margaret Crahan 1989 and John Kirk 1989; on sexuality, see Ian Lumsden 1995; on racial identity, see Robaina 1994; and on small business practices, see Jorge Corrales 1994.

4. See *Tablas*, no. 4, 1996 for various articles on the conference, as well as a discussion of Ortiz's "transculturation," syncretism, possession, and *ritualidad* in Cuban theater. See also Inés María Martiatu 2000.

5. Katherine Hagedorn 2001 discusses the division between sacred and secular performance in Afro-Cuban religious rituals, focusing on the Conjunto Folklórico Nacional (National Folkloric Dance and Music Group) in Havana. See also Robin Moore's 2006 chapter "Afro-Cuban Folklore in a Raceless Society" for a full history of how Afro-Cuban music, drumming, and dance were perceived by society both before and after 1959.

6. See R. Moore (2006:185–96), who describes how such concerns about professionalizing Afro-Cuban traditions or "folklore" have been part of official discussions of acceptable cultural production under socialism since the 1960s and the creation of the Conjunto Folklórico Nacional in 1964.

7. This process is analogous to the ways in which the phrase "9–11" (referring to the September 11 attacks on the World Trade Center) became a phenomenon in its own right, divorced from the actual event and the date on which it occurred.

8. Various accounts claim that there are still over two hundred political prisoners, or "prisoners of conscience," in contemporary Cuba. In 2003 alone, seventy-five suspected dissidents were imprisoned for engaging in "treasonous activities" and given sentences of up to twenty years.

9. Roberto Fernández Retamar 1971.

GLOSSARY

Altar de Cruz: Altar of the Cross, a religious ritual performed in the eastern regions of Cuba by practitioners of *cruzados*—crosses or mixes of Catholicism, Santería, and Spiritism. *Los cruzados* and Altar of the Cross rituals are considered "folk religion." See *Alumbrados*.

Alumbrados: Literally "illuminations." Another name for Altar of the Cross rituals, the term is used in the Escambray region.

Los Años Gris: The Gray Years, also known as "The Dark Years" and sometimes Cuba's "Cultural Revolution" (when compared to China). Spanning the years from approximately 1968 to 1976, the Gray Years was a period of heightened censorship and control over artistic expression. See *UMAP* camps.

area of consumption: Areas where goods and services were sold in *divisas*, or hard currency: U.S. dollars until 2004, "convertibles" (convertible Cuban currency) afterward.

batalla: Battle or struggle.

Battle of Ideas: One of Fidel Castro's most recent campaigns to end corruption. "Social workers" were recruited to monitor and report back on any potential corrupt behavior in *divisa* industries, such as fuel sales and *shopping* stores, and in other services sold in hard currency. Critics likened the movement to China's Red Guard. However, many Cuban people saw it as a positive and necessary measure.

bodega: State-run store where rationed goods were distributed, sold in Cuban pesos or rationed by *libreta*.

campesino: Farmer. In Cuba *campesino* referred broadly to someone who lived in the rural areas and works on or lives off the land. The definition of the modern Cuban campesino was discussed at length by the theater group in Cumanayagua (Teatro de los Elementos). Campesinos in post-1959 Cuba were not peasants, and some scholars argued that they never were, even before the Revolution. Sidney Mintz (1985), for example, distinguishes between peasant and rural proletariat in prerevolutionary Cuba. (See also *nuevo campesino*.)

el campo: The countryside or the rural areas.

Carné de Identidad: Cuban identity card.

caserío: Small scattered groupings of campesino dwellings (*bohíos*, or rural huts).

Although they are often named as a "community" (such as Dos Brazos) and have a government-built "center" with state *bodega* (store), *campesinos* in *caseríos* often live an hour's walk away from their neighbors in the next closest dwelling. The closest English translation might be "hamlet."

Consejo Nacional de Artes Escénicas: The National Cuban Board of Theater Arts, under the Ministry of Culture and based in Havana, had organizational and economic control over all the professional performance groups in Cuba. There were regional (provincial) theater boards in each of the provinces.

(peso) convertible: The Cuban convertible peso (CUC) was introduced in the mid-1990s to replace the U.S. dollar, and became the currency that tourists used in areas of consumption. Until 2004 the convertible Cuban peso was equivalent in value to the U.S. dollar (according to the Cuban state) and was circulated along-side the Cuban peso (CUP). During my fieldwork, change given for cash payment at a farmers market or street vendor was often given in a combination of pesos, convertibles, and dollars. The convertible became the only legal substitution for foreign currencies when the dollar was pulled from public circulation on November 8, 2004. As of 2011, there was an extra 10 percent commission charged to change U.S. dollars into convertibles, but no added commission for euros, Canadian dollars, or British pounds.

creative process: The process by which a play or other artistic endeavor is created. In the theater this process includes the conceptualization of the play to be produced, discussions and debates about the chosen theme or script, adaptation, improvisation, rehearsal, production, performance, and reception. Participants include all members of the theater world, including actors, directors, playwrights, musicians, dancers, producers, technical and lighting design artists, audiences, and any community members who take part in the process in some capacity.

La Cruzada Teatral: The theater company that toured through rural Guantánamo every year, beginning on José Martí's birthday in January and lasting for one month.

cruzados: Mixed religions of Catholicism, Santería, and Spiritism, existing mostly in the rural eastern regions of Cuba. See *Altar de Cruz.*

cubanía: Currently, the more popular term for Cuban-ness and Cuban identity. The term cubanidad is also used to refer to Cuban-ness, although it is criticized for being a term used primarily by white intellectuals (including Fernando Ortiz).

culto: Cultivated or culturally educated.

décima: Literally "tenth," musical stanzas consisting of ten octosyllabic lines. This form of rural music originated in Spain, and is now heard mainly in rural Cuba. The lines of Cuban décimas are often improvised by two singers. Décimas are also often called *controversias* (controversies, debates).

divisa: Hard currency, or foreign currency used and exchanged mostly in areas of consumption. The word *divisa* was usually used to refer to U.S. dollars until

2004, when they were taken out of legal circulation. After 2004, all foreign currencies had to be changed into pesos convertibles in order to be used in officially sanctioned stores.

dollarization: The legalization of U.S. dollars in 1993 and the changes in society that resulted. This term often refers to how the change itself affected society, culture, and ideology throughout the Special Period.

extranjero: Foreigners or strangers. This word became politically loaded during the late 1990s and into the early 2000s as increasing dollarization and global culture entered Cuban society. See also *yuma.*

flexibilization of culture: The unofficial perception that the rigid control on artistic expression, religious practice, and popular style was loosened after the crisis of the Special Period began in 1990.

gallego: The male character representing the white Spanish colonist in prerevolutionary Teatro Bufo plays.

guajiro: Rural peasant or hillbilly, used either to refer to someone with affection or with disdain, depending on the context, though *campesino* is the more respectful word used in revolutionary Cuba.

Hasta la victoria siempre: "Ever onward until victory," Che Guevara's famous declaration.

Hombre Novísimo: "The Even Newer Man." My own way of referring to the transformation of political and cultural identity in Cuba after the mid-1990s. It was a twenty-first-century ideal that moved away from the *Hombre Nuevo,* seen as outdated and old-fashioned in the early 2000s.

Hombre Nuevo: The New Socialist Man, a Marxist idea used in socialist rhetoric and philosophy.

hombre sincero: The "sincere man" from José Martí's famous poem "Yo soy un hombre sincero," which reads in part: "Yo soy un hombre sincero / De donde crece la palma, / Y antes de morirme quiero / Echar mis versos del alma" (I am a sincere man / from where the palm trees grow, / and before I die I want to / share the verses from my soul).

ideology: A system of beliefs and ideas that a group (class, sphere, population) of people has about their social and political world. In the United States there are class-based ideologies. When discussing Cuba I refer mainly to national or political ideology, and socialist ideology in particular.

intellectual: A person who does some kind of mental (vs. physical) work, often producers in the artistic sphere, reflecting upon ideology, culture, and identity. My use of the word *intellectual* is usually joined with *artist* (literary writer, poet, essayist, social theorist, art critic), although someone may be an artist without necessarily being an intellectual.

la lucha: Struggle or fight. In Cuba *la lucha* is a key metaphor for many of the struggles of everyday society and in the socialist ideology of sacrificing for the good of the nation.

más allá: Farther out, beyond. The *campesino de verdad* is always said to live farther out or deeper into the mountains than the speaker.

Masificación de Cultura. Massification of Culture. The phrase, referred to a cultural movement introduced in 1998 by Fidel Castro and Minister of Culture Abel Prieto to spread "culture" to the masses, especially to the most isolated areas in the country. It was discontinued by 2000 after repeated criticisms by Cuban artists who felt it deflated the valuation of individual creativity and did not want their art "massified."

me compliqué: Meaning generally, "Things got complicated for me," or "I was hindered." Used especially frequently during the Special Period as an excuse for not being prepared, being late, or not showing up at all. Usually implying that the bus never arrived, there was a blackout and they were not able to work, there was a family emergency, or just a phrase to describe generally the way things were in Cuba during the 1990s.

la naturaleza: Nature. Teatro de los Elementos considered la naturaleza transcendent of politics.

el negrito: The ex-slave black character in prerevolutionary Teatro Bufo plays.

nuevo campesino: New campesino. A term I heard only by resident campesinos in small Escambray Mountain region communities to refer to city people who had been allotted a plot of land from the state after 1990 and had moved out to the countryside after having grown up in urban areas. The term used was, in fact, "nuevo campesino" instead of the more grammatically correct, "campesino nuevo." It referred to new farmers who were commercially corrupt, who did not have the same integrity, humility, and honesty of "real" campesinos who had been brought up "on the land."

Occidente: "Occident" or the western region of Cuba, usually referring to Havana and Matanzas.

Opción Cero: Option Zero. The last-resort strategy unofficially proposed and circulated largely by myth and rumor among the people in Cuban society after 1990 about what to do if a total blockade or attack were to ensue. As a military and survival strategy, citizens were to be evacuated from the urban and coastal areas and moved to the interior of the country (*el campo*), food rations totally collectivized, and people to live completely off the land.

Option Zero Theater: A term I use to refer to a form of *Teatro Comunitario* that emerged in the rural areas in 1990 with groups such as Teatro de los Elementos and La Cruzada Teatral. These theater groups performed in spite of the extreme scarcity of resources (and became famous as a result). Artists vowed to sacrifice time and energy to bring theater to new audiences and to bring beauty and art to the most isolated rural regions.

Oriente: "Orient" or the eastern region of the island, such as Guantánamo Province, Granma Province, and Santiago de Cuba. Before 1976, Oriente was itself, a large province that included Guantánamo, Granma, and Santiago de Cuba.

premio: Prize or award. Premios were very important for artists and intellectuals living in socialist societies, since recognition and reward for high-quality work were normally not given in material form. Such premios and other certificates were kept in a portfolio that Cubans proudly showed upon request.

pueblo: Small town or village. The term was also often used to refer to the nation or "the people."

pura cepa: Pure stock or pure root (of Cuban culture). Although *pura cepa* was interpreted more broadly as "pure blood," similar to *la raza* in other parts of Latin America and claims to indigeneity, pura cepa in Cuba was cultural and political rather than biological. In Cuba the *pura cepa* did not refer to the most primitive "natives" of the past, or to the prerevolutionary campesino who subsisted totally off the land. Rather, *pura cepa* referred to all that positively symbolized the socialist campesino and the successes of Revolution. The term *pura cepa* suggested a socialist morality: unity, cooperation, loyalty, and sacrifice for the good of the whole. It rejected individualism, materialism, imperialism, inequality, and the moral contamination that were thought to be connected to capitalism.

revolucionario: Revolutionary. In Cuba "revolutionary" referred to those people or attitudes loyal to the ideals put forth by Fidel Castro and the 1959 Revolution (and later socialism). Those who attempted to fight against the "revolutionary government" were referred to as *bandidos* (bandits or outlaws), counter-revolutionaries, dissidents, or *gusanos* (worms).

shopping: Pronounced "choping" in Spanish, *shopping* stores (also called "dollar stores") sold goods in hard currency. Initially, these stores were open only to those with foreign passports, but they eventually opened to anyone with *divisas* to spend. Many of the essential goods once rationed by the state could only be found and purchased at these stores after 1990.

Special Period ("The Special Period in Time of Peace"): The economic crisis of the 1990s and early 2000s. Whether or not the Special Period had ended depended on where one lived, one's profession, and access (or not) to hard currency. Scholars working in urban areas, along with relatively affluent Cubans, felt the Special Period ended in the early 2000s. Many rural residents I met, especially in the zones of silence, believed that nothing had improved since the beginning of the crisis in 1990.

teatrista: "Theater people," including actors, playwrights, technical workers, designers, musicians, theater critics, etc. A teatrista was anyone whose work contributed to the production or assessment of theater and considered himself or herself part of the theater "world."

Teatro Bufo: Theater of the Buffoon or Comic Theater of the late nineteenth century and early twentieth. Considered the first national theater of the independent Cuban Republic, its main characters included *el gallego*, *el negrito*, and *la mulata*.

Teatro Comunitario: The communitarian theater or "theater of/for/by the community" that revived the investigative methodology of the *Teatro Nuevo* of the 1960s.

Teatro Escambray: Escambray Theater. The first example of Teatro Nuevo in Cuba, developed in 1968 by Sergio Corrieri. Teatro Escambray was considered the epitome of Revolutionary theater and was modeled after Augusto Boal's Theater of the Oppressed and other forms of "theater for the people" around the world—even as it became the model for much Latin American theater. Methods of playmaking were very anthropological in nature; living with and interviewing local campesinos to then devise or create and write the play. Plays were ultimately performed back to the local people for debate and discussion.

Teatro Nuevo: The "New Theater" of the Revolution, beginning with Teatro Escambray.

UMAP **camps:** *Unidades Militares de Ayuda a la Producción* (Military Units to Help Production). From 1965 to 1968, they were known as concentration camps, which functioned to sequester those opposed to the Marxist-Leninist ideology established by the Revolution. Along with dissident artists and intellectuals, the persecuted included homosexuals and devout religious believers. Thousands (some estimates reach 25,000) were transported on buses to several stadiums in the province of Camagüey, separated into groups, and transferred to mills to work. At night they were watched under guard.

UNEAC: *Unión Nacional de Escritores y Artistas de Cuba* (National Union of Writers and Artists in Cuba). An elite association of artists and intellectuals, based in Havana.

Velvet Prison: A term coined by writer Miklós Haraszti (1987) to explain the situation of artists and intellectuals living in a socialist system. Although they were censored and thus imprisoned in terms of free expression, that prison was lined in velvet, in that they were fully supported by the state to produce their art full time, and were often granted special perks, especially if their art was ideologically supportive of socialism.

yuma: Foreign, often North American, a slang word used either as an adjective to describe an item, or as a noun to label an individual.

zonas de silencio: Zones of silence. Isolated rural areas without radio signal or electricity, these were also called "areas of difficult access," since there were no direct roads or means of transportation into them.

SOURCES CITED

Newspapers and Journals

Adelante, Havana, 1867–1940
Bohemia, Havana, 1910–68
Carteles Revista, Havana, 1958
Conjuntos, Casa de las Américas, Havana 1965–2006
Cuba Contemporánea, Havana, 1913–23
Diario de la Marina, Havana, 1867–1938
La Discusión, Havana, 1867–1924
La Gaceta, Havana, 1848–1902
El Mundo, Havana, 1910–60
Granma, Havana, 1980–2006
Juventud Rebelde, Havana, 1997–2006
Venceremos, Guantánamo, 1999–2006
Tablas, Havana, 1968–2006
TEMAS, Havana, 1997–2006
Unión, Havana, 1997–2006

Cuban Essay Volumes, No Editor, Collective Authorship

Cooperativismo y colectivismo. Biblioteca popular de orientación económica y Social.
   Havana: Editorial LEX, 1960.
Los cubanos rezamos a Dios: Devocionario popular: Conferencia de Obispos
   Católicos de Cuba. Mexico City: Obra Nacional de la Buena Prensa, 1997.
Teatro y Revolución. Havana: Editorial Letras Cubanas, 1980.
Universidad de las Villas. *Teatro bufo: Siete obras.* Santa Clara: Universidad de las
   Villas, n.d.

Formal Interviews, 1997–2006

Teatro de los Elementos

Lexis Pérez, May 1999
Kirenia Macias Días, May 1999

Freddy Pérez, June 1999
Isnoel Yanes González, June 1999, December 2000, January 2006
Héctor Luis Castellanos Sobrino, June 1999
Joel Ramón Pérez Ruiz, June 1999
Antonio Ramón Ojeda Pozo ("Lolo"), June 1999
José Oriol González Martínez, December 1998, June 1999, February 2000
Juan Bautista Castillo Poll ("Nego"), February 2001

Consejo Nacional de Artes Escénicas

Alexis Abreu Báez, December 2000

Centro Nacional de Cultural Comunitaria

Rene Cardona, September 1999

Centro Nacional de Investigación de Artes Escénicas

Haydee Sala Santos, January 1999, November 2000
Miguel Sánchez León, December 1999, February 2001
Esther Suárez Durán, December 2000, February 2001, January 2006

La Cruzada Teatral, El Laboratorio de Teatro Comunitario

Virginia López, March 2000, June 2000
Gertrudis Campo Bernal ("Tula"), July 2000
Maribel López Carcassés, June 2000, July 2000
Ury Urgelles Rodríguez, June 2000, December 2000, February 2001, January 2006

Grupo Lino Álvarez de Realengo 18

Regino Baratute Pinera, May 2000
Rogelio Baratute, May 2000
Julio Baratute Páez, May 2000
Graciano Baratute Márquez, May 2000
Ernestina Baratute Romero, June 2000
Luis Baratute Omar, June 2000

Teatro Escambray

Rafael Gonzalez, September 2000

Secondary Sources

Alonso González, Gladys, ed. 1998. *Fiestas populares tradicionales cubanas*. Centro de Investigación y Desarrollo de la Cultura Cubana Juan Marinello. Havana: Editorial de Ciencias Sociales.
Alroy, Gil Carl. 1972. "The Peasantry in the Cuban Revolution." In *Cuba in Revolution*. Edited by Rolando E. Bonachea and Nelson Valés. New York: Anchor Books.

Álvarez, José B. 2002. *Contestatory Cuban Short Story of the Revolution*. New York: University Press of America.

Anagnost, Ann. 1997. *National Past-Times: Narrative, Representation, and Power in Modern China*. Durham: Duke University Press.

Anderson, Benedict. 1983. *Imagined Communities: Reflections on the Origin and Spread of Nationalisms*. New York:Verso.

Angert, Erica. 2006."Hybrid Networks and Urban Spaces in Post-socialist Cuba. Ph.D. diss., University of Southern California, Los Angeles.

Appadurai, Arjun. 1990. "Disjuncture and Difference in the Global Cultural Economy." *Public Culture* 2:2 (Spring): 1–24.

——. 1996. *Modernity at Large: Cultural Dimensions of Globalization*. Minneapolis: University of Minnesota Press.

Arblaster, Anthony. 1991. "The Death of Socialism—Again." *The Political Quarterly* 62:1 (January–March): 35–44.

Arenas, Reinaldo. 2000. *Before Night Falls*. New York: Penguin Books.

Arendt, Hannah. 1958. *The Human Condition*. Chicago: University of Chicago Press.

Arredondo, Alberto. 1936. "El negro y la nacionalidad." *Adelante* 10:6.

——. 1937a. "Dos palabras más sobre el negro y la nación." *Adelante* 20:7–8.

——. 1937b. "El arte negro a contrapelo." *Adelante* 26:5–20.

Arredondo, Enrique. 1981. *La vida de un comediante*. Havana: Editorial Letras Cubanas.

Arrufat, Antón, ed. 1998. *La isla en peso: Virgilio Piñera*. Havana: Ediciones Unión.

Artaud, Antonin. 1958. *The Theater and Its Double*. New York: Grove Press.

Artiles, Freddy. 1988. *Teatro y dramaturgia para los niños en la Revolución*. Havana: Editorial Letras Cubanas.

Austin, J. L. 1965. *How to Do Things with Words*. Gloucestershire: Clarendon Press.

Ayala, Cristóbal Días. 1994. *Discografía de la música cubana*. Vol. 1: *1898–1925*. San Juan: Fundación Musicalia.

Azorín. 1917. *El paisaje de España visto por los españoles*. Madrid: Renacimiento.

——. 1919. *El alma castellana*. Madrid: Caro Raggio.

——. 1990. *Los pueblos: Ensayos sobre la vida provinciana*. Alicante, Spain: Instituto de Cultura "Juan Gil Albert."

Badone, Ellen. 1991. "Ethnography, Fiction, and the Meanings of the Past in Brittany." *American Ethnologist* 18:3:518–45.

Bakhtin, Mikhail. 1981. *The Dialogic Imagination: Four Essays*. Translated by Michael Holquist and Caryl Emerson. Austin: University of Texas Press.

——. 1984. *Rabelais and His World*. Translated by Hélène Iswolsky. Bloomington: Indiana University Press.

Banet-Weiser, Sarah. 2003. "Elian Gonzalez and the Purpose of America: Nation, Family, and the Child-Citizen." *American Quarterly* 55:2 (June): 149–78.

Barba, Eugenio. 1995. *The Paper Canoe*. New York: Routledge.

Barba, Eugenio, and Nicola Savarese. 1991. *A Dictionary of Theatre Anthropology: The Secret Art of the Performer*. New York: Routledge.

Barber, Karin. 2000. *The Generation of Plays: Yorùbá Popular Life in Theater*. Bloomington: Indiana University Press.

Barmé, Geremie. 1999. *In the Red: On Contemporary Chinese Culture*. New York: Columbia University Press.

Barnet, Miguel, and Esteban Montejo. 1966. *Biografía de un cimarrón*. Havana: Instituto de Ethnología y Folklore.

Baroja, Pío. 1920. *Divagaciones sobre la cultura*. Madrid: Caro Raggio.

———. 1927. *La sensualidad pervertida: Ensayos amorosos de un hombre ingenuo en una epoca de decadencia*. Madrid: Caro Raggio.

———. 1946. *El mundo es ansí*. Buenos Aires: Espasa-Calpe.

Barral, G. 1932. "Una nueva embajada de arte cubano." *Bohemia* (February): 38.

———. 1954. "Recuerdos de Alhambra en la Muerte de Villoch." *Bohemia* (February): 66–76, sup. 10, 76.

Barthes, Roland. 1972 [1957]. *Mythologies*. New York: Hill and Wang.

Bassnett-McGuire, S. 1979. "El teatro campesino: From actos to mitos." *Theatre Quarterly* 9:34 (Summer): 18–20.

Bauer, Rainer Lutz. 1992. "Changing Representations of Place, Community and Character in the Spanish Sierra del Caurel." *American Ethnologist* 19:3:571–88.

Bauman, Richard. 1984 [1975]. *Verbal Art as Performance*. Prospect Heights, Ill.: Waveland Press.

———. 1986. *Story, Performance and Event: Contextual Studies of Oral Narrative*. New York: Cambridge University Press.

Bauman, Richard, and Charles Briggs. 1990. "Poetics and Performance as Critical Perspectives on Language and Social Life." *Annual Review of Anthropology* 19:59–88.

———. 1992. "Genre, Intertextuality, and Social Power." *Journal of Linguistic Anthropology*. 2:2 (December): 131–72.

———. 2000. "Language Philosophy as Language Ideology: John Locke and Johann Gottfried Herder." In *Regimes of Language: Discursive Constructions of Authority, Identity, and Power*." Edited by P. Kroskrity. Santa Fe: School of American Research, 139–204.

———. 2003. *Voices of Modernity: Language Ideologies and the Production of Social Inequality*. Cambridge: Cambridge University Press.

Bauman, Zygmunt. 1991. "Living without an Alternative." *Political Quarterly* 62:1 (January–March): 35–44.

Beckett, Samuel. 1956. *Waiting for Godot: A Tragic Comedy in Two Acts*. Devonport, Auckland, N.Z.: Evergreen Books.

Behar, Ruth. 1993. *Translated Woman: Crossing the Border with Esperanza's Story*. Boston: Beacon Press.

Benjamin, Walter. 1969. *Illuminations*. New York: Schocken Books.

Bennett, Susan. 1996. *Performing Nostalgia: Shifting Shakespeare and the Contemporary Past*. New York: Routledge.

———. 1997. *Theatre Audiences: A Theory of Production and Reception*. New York: Routledge.

Berezin, Mabel. 1994. "Cultural Form and Political Meaning: State-Subsidized Theater, Ideology, and the Language of Style in Fascist Italy." *American Journal of Sociology* 99:5 (March): 1237–86.

Berlant, Lauren. 1993. "National Brands / National Body: Imitation of Life." In *The Phantom Public Sphere*. Edited by Bruce Robbins. Minneapolis: University of Minnesota Press.

Bernstein, J. M. 1991. *Theodor W. Adorno: The Culture Industry. Selected Essays on Mass Culture*. New York: Routledge.

Betancourt, Juan Rene. 1940. *Doctrina negra: La única teoría certera contra la discriminación racial en Cuba*. Havana: P. Fernandez y Cía.

Betancourt y Garcia, Ramón. 1936. "Igualdad de derechos." *Adelante* 1 (January): 8.

Bhabha, Homi. 1990. *Nation and Narration*. New York: Routledge.

———. 1994. *The Location of Culture*. New York: Routledge.

Blau, Herbert. 1990. "Universals of Performance; or Amortizing Play." In *By Means of Performance: Intercultural Studies of Theatre and Ritual*. Edited by Richard Schechner and Willa Appel. Cambridge: Cambridge University Press.

Blum, Denise, 2011. *Cuban Youth and Revolutionary Values: Educating the New Socialist Citizen*. Austin: University of Texas Press.

Boal, Augusto. 1975. *Técnicas latinoamericanas de teatro popular: Una revolución copernicana al revés*. Buenos Aires: Corregidor.

———. 1979. *The Theatre of the Oppressed*. Translated by Charles McBride. New York: Urizen Books.

———. 1992. *Games for Actors and Non-Actors*. London: Routledge.

Bode Hernández, Germán. 1997. *Décimas rescatadas del aire y del olvido: Estudio y selección de 140 décimas cubanas improvisadas (1940–1944)*. Fundación Fernando Ortiz, Havana, Cuba.

Bolívar, Natalia. 1990. *Los orishas en Cuba*. Havana: UNEAC.

Boudet, Rosa Ileana. 1981. "Prólogo" to *Teatro La Yaya* by Flora Lauten. Havana: Editorial Letras Cubanas.

———. 1983. *Teatro nuevo: Una respuesta*. Havana: Editorial Letras Cubanas.

———. 1994. "El Teatro de la Comunidad: ¿Otra Utopia Compartida? In *Tablas*, 1–2:2–7.

Bourdieu, Pierre. 1991. *Language and Symbolic Power*. Cambridge: Harvard University Press.

———. 1993. *The Field of Cultural Production: Essays on Art and Literature*. New York: Columbia University Press.

Boyer, Christopher. 2003. *Becoming Campesinos: Politics, Identity, and Agrarian*

Struggle in Postrevolutionary Michoacán, 1920–1935. Stanford, Calif.: Stanford University Press.

Boyer, Dominic, and Claudio Lomnitz. 2005. "Intellectuals and Nationalism: Anthropological Engagements." *Annual Review of Anthropology* 34:105–20.

Boym, Svetlana. 2001. *The Future of Nostalgia.* New York: Basic Books.

Brenner, Philip, et al., eds. 1989. *The Cuba Reader: The Making of a Revolutionary Society.* New York: Grove Press.

Brook, Peter. 1968. *The Empty Space: A Book about Theatre: Deadly, Holy, Rough, Immediate.* New York: Atheneum.

———. 1987. *The Shifting Point: 1946–1987.* New York: Harper and Row.

Broyles-González, Yolanda. 1994. *El Teatro Campesino: Theater in the Chicano Movement.* Austin: University of Texas Press.

Brundenius, Claes, and John Weeks, eds. 2001. *Globalization and Third World Socialism: Cuba and Vietnam.* New York: Palgrave.

Buchowski, Michal, et al., eds. 2001. *Poland beyond Communism: "Transition" in Critical Perspective.* Fribourg, Switz.: University Press.

Buckser, Andrew. 1999. "Modern Identities and the Creation of History: Stories of Rescue among the Jews of Denmark." *Anthropological Quarterly* 72:1: 1–17.

Bunck, Julie Marie. 1994. *Fidel Castro and the Quest for a Revolutionary Culture in Cuba.* University Park: Pennsylvania State University Press.

Butler, Judith. 1997. *Excitable Speech: A Politics of the Performative.* New York: Routledge.

Caballero, Atilio, and Grupo Teatro de los Elementos. 1999. "Ten mi nombre como un sueño." Unpublished play manuscript. Cumanayagua, Cuba.

Cabezas, Amalia. 2009. *Economies of Desire: Sex and Tourism in Cuba and the Dominican Republic.* Philadelphia: Temple University Press.

Calá, Romilio A. Portuondo. 1940. "Sobre el problema negro." *Adelante* 25:12.

Calhoun, Craig, ed. 1993. *Habermas and the Public Sphere.* Cambridge: MIT Press.

Camnitzer, Luis. 1994. *New Art of Cuba.* Austin: University of Texas Press.

Camus, Albert. 1991 [1942]. *The Myth of Sisyphus.* Translated by Justin O'Brien. New York: Vintage Books.

Cañellas, Miguel R. 1996. "Grupo Teatro de los Elementos: A Proposito de un Estreno." In *Tablas,* 2:92–94.

Cano, Osvaldo. 1992. *Antologia de Teatro Cubano, tomo 6.* Havana: La Editorial Pueblo y Educación.

Carlson, Marvin. 1992. "Theater and Dialogism." In *Critical Theory and Performance.* Edited by Janell Reinelt and Joseph Roach. Ann Arbor: University of Michigan Press.

———. 1996. *Performance: A Critical Introduction.* New York: Routledge.

Carrió, Raquel. 1997. "Otra tempestad: De la investigación de fuentes a la escritura escénica." In *Tablas* 3–4:3–6.

Carrió, Raquel, and Flora Lauten. 2000. *Otra tempestad.* Havana: Ediciones Alarcos.

Casal, Hernani. 1890. "Teatro de variedades." *La Discusión*. January 24.

Casal, Lourdes. 1984. "Race Relations in Contemporary Cuba." In *The Cuba Reader: The Making of a Revolutionary Society*. Edited by Philip Brenner et al. New York: Grove Press.

Castellanos, Jorge and Isabel. 1988. *Cultural Afrocubana*. Vol. 2.

Castells, Ricardo. 1995. "Fernández Retamar's 'The Tempest' in a Cafetera: From Ariel to Mariel." *Cuban Studies* 25:165–82.

Castillo Bueno, Maria de los Reyes. 2000. *Reyita: The Life of a Black Cuban Woman in the 20th Century*. Durham: Duke University Press.

Castro, Fidel. [1961] 1980. "Palabras a los Intelectuales." In *Revolución, Letras, Arte*. Havana: Editorial Letras Cubanas.

——. 1961. "Discurso pronunciado por el comandante Fidel Castro Ruz, en el act de clausura de la primera conferencia regional de plantaciones de la America Latina." March 6. http://www.cuba.cu/gobierno/discursos/1961/esp/f060361e.html (accessed January 8, 2012).

——. 1968. *Major Speeches*. London: Stage One.

——. 1969. *Fidel Castro Speaks*. Edited by Martin Kenner and James Petras. New York: Grove Press.

——. 1972. *Discursos. Tomo 2*. Havana: Editorial de Ciencias Sociales.

——. 1976. *Obras escogidas. Tomo 1: 1953–1962*. Madrid: Gráficas Elica.

——. 1981. *Fidel Castro Speeches: Cuba's Internationalist Foreign Policy 1975–1980*. Edited by Michael Taber. New York: Pathfinder Press.

——. 1983. *Fidel Castro Speeches*. Vol. 2: *Our Power Is That of the Working People Building Socialism in Cuba*. Edited by Michael Taber. New York: Pathfinder Press.

——. 1987a. *Por el camino correcto*. Havana: Editora Política.

——. 1987b. *Ideología, conciencia, y trabajo político / 1959–1986*. Havana: Editora Política.

——. 1989. *In Defense of Socialism: Four Speeches on the 30th Anniversary of the Cuban Revolution*. New York: Pathfinder Press.

——. 1990. *Salvar la patria, la Revolución, y el socialismo*. Havana: Editora Política.

——. 1999. *Una revolución solo puede ser hija de la cultura y sus ideas*. Discurso pronunciado en el Aula Magna de la Universidad Central de Venezuela. February 3. Havana: Editora Política.

——. 2000. Speech to the Unión Nacional de Escritores y Artistas de Cuba (UNEAC). Havana: Reprinted in *Juventud Rebelde*, June 10, 1.

——. 2002. Official Inauguration of the 2002–2003 School Year Revolution Square, Havana, September 16. Speech reprinted in *Granma* newspaper.

Cepero, Graciela Montero, et al. 1987. *La educación estética del Hombre Nuevo*. Havana: Editorial de Ciencias Sociales.

Cespedes, Benjamin. 1888. "¿Qué quieren?" *La Fraternidad*. Nov. 10, 1.

Chanan, Michael. 2004. *Cuban Cinema*. Minneapolis: University of Minnesota Press.

Ching, Barbara, and Gerald W. Creed, eds. 1996. *Knowing Your Place: Rural Identity and Cultural Hierarchy*. New York: Routledge.

Chueg, Raimundo Despaigne. 1939. "¿Cómo debe resolverse el problema racial cubano en la nueva constitución?" *Adelante* 64–65:11–20.

Clark, Juan. 1998. *Religious Repression in Cuba*. Cuban Living Conditions Project. Unknown binding. 1985 publication, Piscataway, N.J.: Transaction Publishers.

Clark, Katerina. 1995. *Petersburg: Crucible of Cultural Revolution*. Cambridge: Harvard University Press.

Clifford, James. 1988. *The Predicament of Culture: Twentieth Century Ethnography, Literature, and Art*. Cambridge: Harvard University Press.

Clifford, James, and George Marcus, eds. 1986. *Writing Culture: The Poetics and Politics of Ethnography*. Berkeley: University of California Press.

Clytus, John. 1970. *Black Man in Red Cuba*. Coral Gables: University of Miami Press.

Cockrell, Dale. 1997. *Demons of Disorder: Early Blackface Minstrels and Their World*. Cambridge: Cambridge University Press.

Cohen-Cruz, Jan. 2005. *Local Acts: Community Based Performances in the United States*. New Brunswick: Rutgers University Press.

——. 2006. "Introduction: The Ecology of Theater-in-community." In *Performing Communities: Grassroots Ensemble Theater*. Edited by Robert Leonard and Ann Kilkelly. Oakland: New Village Press.

Conquergood, Dwight. 1988. "Health Theatre in a Hmong Refugee Camp: Performance, Communication, and Culture." *Drama Review* 32:3 (Autumn): 174–208.

——. 2002. "Performance Studies: Interventions and Radical Research." *Drama Review* 46:145–53.

Corbitt, Duvon. 1939. "Mercedes and Ralengos: A Survey of the Public Land System in Cuba." *Hispanic American Historical Review*, 19:3:262–85.

Coronil, Fernando. 1996. "Beyond Occidentalism: Toward Nonimperial Geohistorical Categories." *Cultural Anthropology* 11:1:51–87.

Corrales, Jorge. 2004. "The Gatekeeper State: Limited Economic Reforms and Regime Survival in Cuba, 1989–2002." *Latin American Research Review* 39:2 (June): 35–65.

Crahan, Margaret. 1989. "Catholicism in Cuba." *Cuban Studies* 19:11–18.

Daniel, Yvonne. 1995. *Rumba: Dance and Social Change in Contemporary Cuba*. Bloomington: Indiana University Press.

Dávila, Arlene. 1997. *Sponsored Identities: Cultural Politics in Puerto Rico*. Philadelphia: Temple University Press.

——. 2001. "Local/Diasporic Taínos: Towards a Cultural Politics of Memory, Reality, and Imagery." In *Taíno Revival: Critical Perspectives on Puerto Rican Identity and Cultural Politics*. Edited by Gabriel Haslip-Viera. Princeton: Markus Wiener Publishers.

de Costa, Elena. 1992. *Collaborative Latin American Popular Theatre: From Theory to Form, From Text to Stage*. New York: Peter Lang Publishing Group.

de la Fuente, Alejandro. 1995. "Race and Inequality in Cuba, 1891–1981." *Journal of Contemporary History* 30:131–68.

de la Fuente, Jorge. 1992. *Arte, ideología y cultura*. Havana: Editorial Letras Cubanas.

de la Torriente-Brau, Pablo. 1962. *Realengo 18 y Mella, Rubén y Machado*. Havana: Edición Popular.

de Leuchsenring, Emilio Roig. 1969. "Participación de Martí en La Guerra Chiquita." *Bohemia* (January): 132–35.

De Marinis, Marco. 1993. *The Semiotics of Performance*. Translated by Áine O'Healy. Bloomington: Indiana University Press.

Desmond, Jane. 1999. *Staging Tourism: Bodies on Display from Waikiki to Sea World*. Chicago: University of Chicago Press.

de Unamuno. 1903. *De mi país: Descripciones, relatos y artículos de costumbres*. Madrid: Librería de Fernando Fe.

——. 1916. *Ensayos*. Madrid: Publicaciones de la Residencia de Estudiantes.

——. 1944. *Paisajes de alma*. Spain: Revista de Occidente.

de Velasco, Carlos. 1913. "El Problema Negro." *Cuba Contemporánea* 1:2 (February): 73–79.

Dilla, Haroldo. 1999. "The Virtues and Misfortunes of Civil Society." NACLA (North American Congress on Latin America) *Report on the Americas* 32:5 (March–April): 30–36. Reprinted in *The Cuba Reader: History, Culture, Politics*. Edited by Aviva Chomsky, Barry Carr, and Pamela Maria Smorkaloff. Durham: Duke University Press.

Domenech, Agustín Pupo. 1995. *El gallo fino cubano*, 15–16. Havana: Editorial SIMAR, S.A.

Domínguez, Jorge. 2003. "A Constitution for Cuba's Political Transition: The Utility of Retaining (and Amending) the 1992 Constitution." Miami: Transition Project, Institute for Cuban and Cuban-American Studies, University of Miami.

——. 2004. Cuba's Economic Transition: Successes, Deficiencies, and Challenges. In *The Cuban Economy at the Start of the Twenty-First Century*. Edited by Jorge I. Domínguez, Omar Everleny Pérez Villanueva, and Lorena Barberia. Cambridge: President and Fellows of Harvard College, 17–47.

Domínguez, Jorge, Omar Everleny Pérez Villanueva, and Lorena Barberia, eds. 2005. *The Cuban Economy at the Start of the Twenty-First Century*. Cambridge: David Rockefeller Center for Latin American Studies at Harvard University.

Dominguez, Virginia R. 1986. *White by Definition: Social Classification in Creole Louisiana*. New Brunswick: Rutgers University Press. Reprinted 1994.

Douglas, Mary. [1966] 2003. *Purity and Danger: An Analysis of Concepts of Pollution and Taboo*. New York: Routledge.

Durán, Esther Suárez. 1995. "Otra mirada al teatro bufo cubano; sin prejuicios, con amor." In *Tablas* 1:23–27.

——. 1999. "El teatro vernáculo: Trayectoria de la cubanidad." In *De las dos orillas:*

Teatro cubano: *Vervuert—Iberoamericana*. Madrid and Frankfurt: Edited by la Sociedad de Teatro y medios de América Latina, 131–37.

———. 2006. "El ciervo encantado en la selva oscura del teatro cubano." In *Como un batir de alas: Ensayos sobre el teatro cubano*. Havana: Editorial Letras Cubanas.

Eckstein, Susan Eva. 1989. "The Debourgeoisement of Cuban Cities." In *The Cuba Reader: The Making of a Revolutionary Society*. Edited by Philip Brenner et al. New York: Grove Press, 419–29.

———. 1994. *Back From the Future: Cuba under Castro*. Princeton: Princeton University Press.

Engels, Friedrich. 1978. "Socialism: Utopian and Scientific." In *The Marx-Engels Reader*. Edited by Robert C. Tucker. New York: W. W. Norton and Company.

Enríquez, Carlos. 1938. *Campesinos felices*. Painting, oil on canvas.

Espinosa, Carlos. 1981. *Teatro La Yaya*. Havana: Editorial Letras Cubanas.

Espinosa Mendoz, Norge, and Marilyn Garbey Oquendo. 1999. *Yorick: ¿Teatro joven en Cuba?* Havana: Casa Editora Abril.

Esslin, Martin. 1991. *The Theatre of the Absurd*. 3rd ed. Harmondsworth: Penguin Books.

Estrada, Gabriel Llanes. 2001. *Con la décima a cuestas*. Camagüey: Editorial Ácana.

Fabian, Johannes. 1998. *Moments of Freedom: Anthropology and Popular Culture*. Charlottesville: University Press of Virginia.

Fagen, Richard. 1965. "Charismatic Authority and the Leadership of Fidel Castro." *Western Political Quarterly* (June): 265–84.

———. 1969. *The Transformation of Political Culture in Cuba*. Stanford, Calif.: Stanford University Press.

Faubion, James, and George Marcus, eds. 2009. *Fieldwork Is Not What It Used to Be: Learning Anthropology's Method in a Time of Transition*. Ithaca: Cornell University Press.

Feijoo, Samuel, ed. 1965. *Sabiduría Guajira*. Havana: Editora Universitaria.

Fermoselle, Rafael. 1974. *Política y color en Cuba: La Guerrita de 1912*. Uruguay: Ediciones Géminis, Montevideo.

Fernandes, Sujatha. 2003. "Fear of a Black Nation: Local Rappers, Transnational Crossings, and State Power in Contemporary Cuba." *Anthropology Quarterly* 76:4 (Fall): 575–608.

———. 2006. *Cuba Represent!* Durham: Duke University Press.

Fernandez, James. 1972. "Persuasions and Performances: Of the Beast in Every Body and the Metaphors of Everyman." *Daedalus* 101:1 (Winter): 39–60.

———. 1974. The Mission of Metaphor in Expressive Culture." *Current Anthropology* 15:2 (June): 119–45.

———. 1986. *Persuasion and Performance: The Play of Tropes in Culture*. Bloomington: Indiana University Press.

Fernandez, James, ed. 1991. *Beyond Metaphor: The Theory of Tropes in Anthropology*. Stanford, Calif.: Stanford University Press.

Fernandez, James, and Mary Huber, eds. 2001. *Irony in Action: Anthropology, Practice and the Moral Imagination*. Chicago: University of Chicago Press.

Fernandez, Nadine. 2010. *Revolutionizing Romance: Interracial Couples in Contemporary Cuba*. New Brunswick, N.J.: Rutgers University Press.

Ferrer, Ada. 1991. "Social Aspects of Cuban Nationalism: Race, Slavery, and the Guerra Chiquita, 1879–1880." *Cuban Studies* 21:37–56.

———. 1999. *Insurgent Cuba: Race, Nation and Revolution*. Chapel Hill: University of North Carolina Press.

Firmat, Gustavo. 1987. "From Ajiaco to Tropical Soup: Fernando Ortiz and the Definition of Cuban Culture." University Park: Latin American and Caribbean Center, Florida International University, LACC Occasional Papers Series, Dialogues, no. 93.

———. 1997. "A Willingness of the Heart: *Cubanidad, Cubaneo, Cubanía*." Cuban Studies Occasional Papers Series 2: 7. Miami: University of Miami.

Foucault, Michel. 1984. "What Is an Author?" In *The Foucault Reader*. Edited by Paul Rabinow, 101–20. New York: Pantheon Books.

Fraser, Nancy. 1996. "Rethinking the Public Sphere: A Contribution to the Critique of Actually Existing Democracy." In *Habermas and the Public Sphere*. Edited by Craig Calhoun. Cambridge: MIT Press, 1993: 109–42.

Frederik, Laurie. 2000. "Una mirada dentro del trabajo colectivo de Teatro de los Elementos." *Conjunto* 117:58–71.

———. 2001a. "The Contestation of Cuba's Public Sphere in National Theater, and the Transformation from Teatro Bufo to Teatro Nuevo." *Gestos: Teoría y práctica del teatro hispánico* 16:31 (April): 65–97.

———. 2001b. "Una experiencia antropológica: El guajiro a los cuatro vientos." *Tablas* 2:73–74.

———. 2005. "Cuba's National Characters: Setting the Stage for the Hombre Novísimo." *Journal of Latin American Anthropology* 10:2:401–36.

———. 2009. "Preemptive Nostalgia and La Batalla for Cuban Identity: Option Zero Theater." In *Cuba in the Special Period: Culture and Ideology in the 1990s*. Edited by Ariana Hernandez-Reguant. New York: Palgrave.

Frederik Meer, Laurie. 2007. "Playback Theater in Cuba: The Politics of Improvisation and Free Expression." *Drama Review* (TDR) (December): 106–20.

Freire, Paulo. 1970. *The Pedagogy of the Oppressed*. Translated by Myra Berman Ramos. New York: Seabury Press.

———. 1973. *Education for Critical Consciousness*. New York: Seabury Press.

Friedrich, Paul. 1989. "Language, Ideology, and Political Economy." *American Anthropologist* 91:2 (June): 295–312.

Fusco, Coco. 2002. *The Bodies That Were Not Ours*. New York: Routledge.

Gable, Eric, and Richard Handler. 2004. "Deep Dirt: Messing up the Past at Colonial Williamsburg." In *Marketing Heritage: Archaeology and the Consumption of the Past*. Edited by Yorke Rowan and Uzi Baram. Walnut Creek, Calif.: Alta Mira Press.

Gal, Susan. 1989. "Language and Political Economy." *Annual Review of Anthropology* 18:345–67.

———. 1991. "Bartok's Funeral: Representations of Europe in Hungarian Political Rhetoric." *American Ethnologist* 18:3:440–58.

———. 2005. "Language Ideologies Compared: Metaphors of Public/Private." *Journal of Linguistic Anthropology* 15:1:23–37.

Gal, Susan, with J. I. Irvine. 2000. "Language Ideologies and Linguistic Differentiation." In *Regimes of Language: Ideological Politics, and Identities*. Edited by P. Kroskrity. Santa Fe: School of American Research.

Galarreta, Luis L. 1913. "Concepto de la beneficencia pública." *Cuba Contemporánea* (March): 66–72.

———. 1914. "Caracteres del teatro francés contemporáneo." *Cuba Contemporánea* 4:4 (April): 370–71.

Ganga, Creto. 1847. "Un ajiaco o la boda de pancha jutia y canuto raspadura."

García, Canclini, Néstor. 1995. *Hybrid Cultures: Strategies for Entering and Leaving Modernity*. Minneapolis: University of Minnesota Press.

García, Daniel, ed. 1995. *Cuba: Cultura e identidad nacional*. Havana: UNEAC.

Garzón Céspedes, Francisco. 1977. *El teatro de participación popular y el teatro de la comunidad: Un teatro de sus protagonistas*. Havana: UNEAC.

Geertz, Clifford. 1973. *The Interpretation of Cultures: Selected Essays*. New York: Basic Books.

Gellner, Ernest. 1983. *Nation and Nationalism*. Ithaca: Cornell University Press.

Gerrasi, John, ed. 1968. *Venceremos! The Speches and Writings of Ernesto Che Guevara*. New York: Simon and Schuster.

Geyer, Michael, ed. 2001. *The Power of Intellectuals in Contemporary Germany*. Chicago: University of Chicago Press.

Gilroy, Paul. 1993. *The Black Atlantic: Modernity and Double Consciousness*. Cambridge: Harvard University Press.

Goffman, Erving. 1959. *The Presentation of Self in Everyday Life*. New York: Doubleday.

———. 1974. *Frame Analysis: An Essay on the Organization of Experience*. New York: Harper Colophon Books.

Goldfarb, Jeffrey. 1998. *Civility and Subversion: The Intellectual in Democratic Society*. New York: Cambridge University Press.

Gómez, Juan Gualberto. 1873. "Cuba no es Haití." *La Igualdad*, Havana, May 30:2.

González, Waldo. 1996. "¿Crisis en el teatro cubano?" *Bohemia* 88:11:42–45.

González Freire, Natividad, ed. 1961. *Teatro cubano (1927–1961)*. Havana: Ministerio de Relaciones Exteriores.

González Rodríguez, Rafael. n.d. *Teatro Escambray*. Historical Booklet, Manicaragua.

———. 1996. "Teatro Escambray: Toward the Cuban's Inner Being." *The Drama Review* 40:1 (Spring): 98–111.

Goodman, Walter. 1873. *The Pearl of the Antilles or, an Artist in Cuba*. London: H. S. King.

Gottberg, Luis Duno. 2003. *Solventando las diferencias: La ideología del mestizaje en Cuba*. Madrid: Iberoamericana.

Grant, Bruce. 1995. *In the Soviet House of Culture: A Century of Perestroikas*. Princeton: Princeton University Press.

Grotowski, Jerzy. 1968. *Towards a Poor Theatre*. New York: Simon and Schuster.

Guanche, Jesús. 1979. "Significación de la cultura popular tradicional." *Revolución y Cultura* 1:85:26–29.

———. 1980. "Hacia un enfoque sistémico de la cultura cubana." *Revolución y Cultura* 1:90:35–40.

———. 1983. *Procesos etnoculturales de Cuba*. Havana: Editorial Letras Cubanas.

———. 1996. *Componentes étnicos de la nación cubana*. Havana: Fundación Fernando Ortiz, Ediciones Unión.

Guerra, Francois-Xavier. 1994. "The Spanish-American Tradition of Representation and Its European Roots." *Latin American Studies* 26:1–35.

Guerra, Lillian. 1998. *Popular Expression and National Identity in Puerto Rico: The Struggle for Self, Community, and Nation*. Gainesville: University Press of Florida.

Guerra, Ramiro. 1964. *Sugar and Society in the Caribbean: An Economic History of Cuban Agriculture*. New Haven: Yale University Press.

———. 1989. *Teatralización del folklore y otros ensayos*. Havana: Editorial Letras Cubanas.

Guerrero, Juan José. 1864. "Un guateque en la taberna un martes de Carnaval."

Guevara, Ernesto "Che." 1965. "El socialism y el hombre en Cuba." In *Revolucion, Letras, Arte*. Edited by Virgilio Lopez Lemus. Havana: Editorial Letras Cubanas, 1980, 34–48.

———.1968. *Socialism and Man in Cuba and Other Works*. London: Stage 1.

———. 1969. *Che: Selected Works of Ernesto Guevara*. Edited by Rolando Bonachea and Nelson Valdes. Cambridge: MIT Press.

———. 1997a. *Che Guevara Reader: Writings by Ernesto Che Guevara on Guerrilla Strategy, Politics, and Revolution*. Edited by David Deutschmann. Melbourne: Ocean Press.

———. 1997b. *Sobre Literatura y Arte*. Selected and edited by Isabel Fernández López. Havana: Editorial Arte y Literatura.

Habermas, Jürgen. 1991. *The Structural Transformation of the Public Sphere: An Inquiry into a Category of Bourgeois Society*. Translated by Thomas Burger. Cambridge: MIT Press.

Hagedorn, Katherine. 2001. *Divine Utterances: The Performance of Afro-Cuban Santería*. Washington: Smithsonian Institution Press.

Halebsky, Sandor, and John M. Kirk. 1992. *Cuba in Transition: Crisis and Tansformation*. Boulder: Westview Press.

Hallam, Elizabeth, and Tim Ingold, eds. 2008. *Creativity and Cultural Improvisation*. Oxford: Berg Publishers.

Handler, Richard. 1988. *Nationalism and the Politics of Culture in Quebec*. Madison: University of Wisconsin Press.

Handler, Richard, and Eric Gable. 1997. *The New History in an Old Museum: Creating the Past at Colonial Williamsburg*. Durham: Duke University Press.

Handler, Richard, and Jocelyn Linnekin. 1984. "Tradition: Genuine and Spurious." *Journal of American Folklore* 97:385:273–90.

Hann, C. M., ed. 1992. *Socialism: Ideals, Ideologies, and Local Practice*. New York: Routledge.

Haraszti, Miklós. 1987. *The Velvet Prison: Artists under State Socialism*. New York: Basic Books.

Hart Dávalos, Armando. 1979. *Del trabajo cultural: Selección de discursos*. Havana: Editorial de Ciencias Sociales.

——. 1990. *Identidad nacional y socialismo en Cuba*. Havana: De la Cultura Ediciones.

——. 2001. *Cultural para el desarrollo: El desafío del siglo XXI*. Havana: Editorial de Ciencias Sociales.

Haslip-Viera, Gabriel, ed. 2001. *Taíno Revival: Critical Perspectives on Puerto Rican Identity and Cultural Politics*. Princeton: Markus Wiener Publishers.

Havel, Václav. 1986. "Power of the Powerless." In *Living in Truth*. Edited by Jan Vladislav. London: Faber and Faber.

Heddon, Dierdre. 2005. *Devising Performance: A Critical History*. New York: Palgrave Macmillan.

Helg, Aline. 1991. "Afro-Cuban Protest: The Partido Independiente de Color, 1908–1912." *Cuban Studies* 2:101–22.

——. 1995. *Our Rightful Share: The Afro-Cuban Struggle for Equality, 1886–1912*. Chapel Hill: University of North Carolina Press.

Hernández, Armando. 1936. "El Negro, la Cultura y la Revolución." *Adelante* 2 (June): 13.

——. 2004. "Copyrighting Che: Art and Authorship under Cuban Late Socialism." *Public Culture* 16:1:1–29.

Hernandez, Rafael Rodriguez. 1997. "The Paradoxes of Cubanology." *South Atlantic Quarterly* 96:1 (Winter): 143–57.

——. 2003. *Looking at Cuba: Essays on Culture and Civil Society*. Gainesville: University Press of Florida.

Hernández, Rosa María, ed. 1993. *José Martí: Versos sencillos*. Havana: Letras Cubanas.

Hernández Menéndez, Mayra, ed. 1986. *Repertorio de teatro para el movimiento de aficionados*. Ministerio de Cultura, Dirección de Artistas Aficionados. Santiago de Cuba: Editorial Oriente.

Hernández-Reguant, Ariana. 2002. "Radio Taíno and the Globalization of the Cuban Culture Industries." Ph.D. diss., University of Chicago.

Herrero, Ramiro, ed. 1983. *Teatro de relaciones*. Havana: Editorial Letras Cubanas.

Herrero Beatón, Ramiro. n.d. "La Muerte Juega al Escondido: Una Leyenda Guajira." Unpublished script.

Herzfeld, Michael. 1982. *Ours Once More: Folklore, Ideology, and the Making of Modern Greece*. Austin: University of Texas Press.

———. 2005 [1997]. *Cultural Intimacy: Social Poetics in the Nation State*. 2nd ed. New York: Routledge.

Hill, Jane, and Judith Irvine. 1993. *Responsibility and Evidence in Oral Discourse*. New York: Cambridge University Press.

Hobsbawm, Eric, and Terrance Ranger, eds. 1983. *The Invention of Tradition*. Cambridge: Cambridge University Press.

Holton, Kimberly DaCosta. 2005. *Performing Folklore: Ranchos Folclóricos from Lisbon to Newark*. Bloomington: Indiana University Press.

Horowitz, Michael, ed. 1971. *Peoples and Cultures of the Caribbean*. Garden City, N.J.: Natural History Press.

Huidobro, Matías Montes. 1973. *Persona: Vida y mascara en el teatro cubano*. Miami: Ediciones Universal.

———. 1982. *Teoría y práctica del catedratismo en los negros catedráticos de Francisco Fernández*. Madrid: Editorial Persona.

Hulme, Peter. 2012. *Cuba's Wild East: A Literary Geography of Oriente*. Liverpool: Liverpool University Press.

Irvine, Judith T. 1989. "When Talk Isn't Cheap: Language and Political Economy." *American Ethnologist* 16:2:48–267.

Ivy, Marilyn. 1995. *Discourses of the Vanishing, Modernity, Phantasm, Japan*. Chicago: University of Chicago Press.

Jameson, Fredric. 1981. *The Political Unconscious: Narrative as a Socially Symbolic Act*. Ithaca: Cornell University Press.

Kapcia, Antoni. 2000. *Cuba: Island of Dreams*. New York: Berg.

Kearney, Michael. 1996. *Reconceptualizing the Peasantry: Anthropology in Global Perspective*. Boulder: Westview Press.

Kertzer, David I. 1988. *Ritual, Politics, and Power*. New Haven: Yale University Press.

Kirk, John M. 1989. "Between God and the Party: Religion and Politics in Revolutionary Cuba." Tampa: USF Press.

Knapp, Steven. 1989. "Collective Memory and the Actual Past." *Representations* 26:123–49.

Kroskrity, Paul V., ed. 2000. *Regimes of Language: Ideologies, Politics, and Identities*. Santa Fe: School of American Research Press.

Kruger, Loren. 1992. *The National Stage: Theatre and Cultural Legitimation in England, France, and America*. Chicago: University of Chicago Press.

———. 1995. "That Fluctuating Movement of National Consciousness: Protest, Publicity and Postcolonial Theatre in South Africa." In *Imperialism and Theatre: Essays on World Theatre, Drama and Performance*. Edited by J. Ellen Gainor. London: Routledge.

———. 1999. *The Drama of South Africa: Plays, Pageants and Publics Since 1910*. New York: Routledge.

——. 2001. "'Wir treten aus unseren Rollen heraus': Theater Intellectuals and Public Spheres." In *The Power of Intellectuals in Contemporary Germany*. Chicago: University of Chicago Press.

——. 2004. *Post-Imperial Brecht: Politics and Performance, East and South*. New York: Cambridge University Press.

Kumaraswami, Par. 2009. "Cultural Policy and Cultural Politics in Revolutionary Cuba: Re-Reading the *Palabras a los intelectuales*." *Bulletin of Latin American Research* 28:4:527–41.

Kuper, Hilda. 1993. *A Witch in My Heart, Short Stories and Poems*. Madison: African Studies Program, University of Wisconsin.

Kutzinski, Vera M. 1993. *Sugar's Secrets: Race and the Erotics of Cuban Nationalism*. Charlottesville: University Press of Virginia.

Lakoff, George, and Mark Johnson. [1980] 2003. *Metaphors We Live By*. Chicago: University of Chicago Press.

Lampland, Martha. 1995. *The Object of Labor: Commodification in Socialist Hungary*. Chicago: University of Chicago Press.

Lane, Jill. 1998. "Blackface Nationalism, Cuba, 1840–1868." *Theatre Journal* 50 (1998): 21–38.

——. 2005. *Blackface Cuba, 1840–1895*. Philadelphia: University of Pennsylvania Press.

La Rosa Corzo, Gabino. 2003. *Runaway Slave Settlements in Cuba: Resistance and Repression*. Chapel Hill: University of North Carolina Press.

Lauten, Flora. 1981. *Teatro La Yaya*. Havana: Editorial Letras Cubanas.

Lavie, Smadar, Kirin Narayan, and Renato Rosaldo, eds. 1993. *Creativity/ Anthropology*. Ithaca: Cornell University Press.

Leal, Rine. 1967. *En primera persona (1954–1966)*. Havana: Instituto del Libro.

——. 1975a. *La Selva Oscura: Historia del teatro cubano desde sus orígenes hasta 1868*. Tomo 1. Havana: Editorial Arte y Literatura.

——. 1975b. *Teatro bufo del siglo XIX, antología*. Tomos 1–2. Havana: Editorial Arte y Literatura.

——. 1980. *Breve historia del teatro cubano*. Havana: Editorial Letras Cubanas.

——. 1982a. *La selva oscura: De los bufos a la neocolonia (Historia del teatro cubano de 1868–1902)*. Tomo 2. Havana: Editorial Arte y Literatura.

——. 1982b. *La cultura en Cuba socialista*. Havana: Editorial Letras Cubanas.

——. 1984. *La dramaturgia del Escambray*. Havana: Editorial Letras Cubanas.

Leal, Rine, ed. 1978a. *Teatro mambí*. Havana: Editorial Letras Cubanas.

——. ed. 1978b. *Teatro escambray*. Havana: Editorial Cubanas.

Lemon, Alaina. 1996. "Indic Diaspora, Soviet History, Russian Home: Political Performances and Sincere Ironies in Romani Cultures." Ph.D. diss., University of Chicago.

——. 2000. *Between Two Fires: Gypsy Performance and Romani Memory from Pushkin to Postsocialism*. Durham: Duke University Press.

León, Argeliers. 1991. "Del eje y la bisagra," or "Of the Axle and the Hinge: Nationalism, Afro-Cubism, and Music in Pre-Revolutionary Cuba." In *Essays on Cuban Music: North American and Cuban Perspectives*. Edited by P. Manuel. Lanham, Md.: University Press of America.

León Rosabal, Blancamar. 1997. *La voz del Mambí: Imagen y mito*. Havana: Pinos Nuevos.

Leonard, Pamela, and Deema Kaneff, eds. 2002. "Post-Socialist Peasant?" In *Post-Socialist Peasant? Rural and Urban Constructions of Identity in Eastern Europe, East Asia and the Former Soviet Union*. New York: Palgrave.

Lesnick, Henry. 1973. *Guerilla Street Theater*. New York: Bard Books.

Lewis, Oscar, Ruth Lewis, and Susan Rigdon. 1977a. *Four Men: Living the Revolution. An Oral History of Contemporary Cuba*. Urbana: University of Illinois Press.

———. 1977b. *Four Women: Living the Revolution. An Oral History of Contemporary Cuba*. Urbana: University of Illinois Press.

———. 1978. *Neighbors: Living the Revolution. An Oral History of Contemporary Cuba*. Urbana: University of Illinois Press.

Leyva, Waldo. 2002. *La distancia y el tiempo*. Havana: Ediciones UNION.

Llanes Estrada, Gabriel. 2001. *Con la décima a cuestas*. Camagüey: Editorial Ácana.

Lockwood, Lee. 1967. *Castro's Cuba, Cuba's Fidel: An American Journalist's Inside Look at Today's Cuba in Text and Pictures*. New York: Macmillan.

Lomnitz-Adler, Claudio. 1991. "Concepts for the Study of Regional Culture." *American Ethnologist* 8:2 (May): 195–214.

———. 1992. *Exits from the Labyrinth: Culture and Ideology in the Mexican National Space*. Berkeley: University of California Press.

———. 2001. *Deep Mexico, Silent Mexico: An Anthropology of Nationalism*. Minneapolis: University of Minnesota Press.

———. 2005. "Mexico's Race Problem. And the Real Story behind Fox's Faux Pas." *Boston Review*. November/December.

López Lemus, Virgilio, ed. 1980. *Revolución, Letras, Arte*. Havana: Editorial Letras Cubanas.

———. 1997. *Décima e identidad: Siglos XVIII y XIX*. Havana: Editorial Academia.

———. 2004. *Décimas para La Historia: La controversia del siglo en verso improvisado. Indio naborí y ángel valiente*. Havana: Editorial Letras Cubanas.

López Segrera, Francisco. 1985. "Notas para una historia social de la cultural cubana." TEMAS: *Estudios de la cultural* (Havana), no. 5:28–37.

Lowenthal, David. 1985. *The Past Is a Foreign Country*. Cambridge: Cambridge University Press.

———. 1996. *Possessed by the Past: The Heritage Crusade and the Spoils of History*. New York: Free Press.

Lumsden, Ian. 1995. *Machos, Maricones, and Gays: Cuba and Homosexuality*. Philadelphia: Temple University Press.

Machado, Antonio. 1957. *Cartas de Antonio Machado a Miguel de Unamuno.* Mexico City: Ediciones Monegros.

———. 1974. *Campos de Castilla.* Madrid: Ediciones Cátedra.

Manach, Jorge. 1969. *Indagación del choteo.* Miami: Mnemosyne Publishing.

Mannheim, Karl. 1936. *Ideology and Utopia: An Introduction to the Sociology of Knowledge.* San Diego: Harcourt.

Marcus, George, and Michael Fisher. 1999. *Anthropology as Cultural Critique: An Experimental Moment in the Human Sciences.* Chicago: University of Chicago Press.

Marriott, McKim. n.d. "Samsara: A Realization of Rural Hindu Life." Course materials project, Social Sciences Collegiate Division, Handbook updated March 31, 1997. Chicago: University of Chicago.

Martí, Carlos. 2000. "Nation, Identity, and Culture in Cuba." A conference held at the National Union of Writers and Artists of Cuba (UNEAC), Havana, Cuba, November 20–23. Discussion led by Minister of Culture Abel Prieto and UNEAC President Carlos Martí. Personal audiorecording and transcription, 1–17.

Martí, José. 1891. "Our America." In *José Martí Reader: Writings on the Americas.* Edited by Deborah Shnooka and Mirta Muñiz, 111–20. Melbourne: Ocean Press, 1999.

———. 1893 [1967]. "Mi Raza," *Patria,* April 16.

———. 1971 [1891]. "Nuestra América" (reprint), *Casa de las Américas* (Havana) 12:68 (September–October), 6–12.

Martiatu Terry, Inés María. 2000. *El rito como representación: Teatro ritual caribeño.* Havana: UNEAC.

———. 2008. *Bufo y nación: Interpelaciones desde el presente.* Havana: Letras Cubanas.

Martin, Randy. 1987. "Nicaragua—Performance after the 'Triumph': Two Views." *The Drama Review* 31:4: 60–72.

———. 1988. "Democratic Features of Socialism's Two Cultures." *Socialism and Democracy* 7 (Fall/Winter): 121–37.

———. 1994. *Socialist Ensembles: Theater and State in Cuba and Nicaragua.* Minneapolis: Minnesota Press.

Marx, Karl. 1978. "Contribution of the Critique of Hegel's Philosophy of Right: Introduction," 1844. In *The Marx-Engels Reader.* Edited by Robert Tucker. New York: W. W. Norton, 53–65.

Marx, Karl, and Friedrich Engels. 1964. *The Communist Manifesto.* New York: Simon and Schuster.

Matas, Julio. 1971. "Theater and Cinematography." In *Revolutionary Change in Cuba.* Edited by Carmelo Mesa-Lago. Pittsburgh: University of Pittsburgh Press, 427–46.

Mazzarella, William. 2004. "Culture, Globalization, Mediation." *Annual Review of Anthropology* 33:345–67.

Mbembe, Achille. 1992. "The Banality of Power and the Aesthetics of Vulgarity in the Postcolony." Translated by Janet Roitman. *Public Culture* 4:1–30.

———. 2001. *On the Postcolony.* Berkeley: University of California Press.

McGrath, John. 1979. "The Theory and Practice of Political Theatre." *Theatre Quarterly* 9:35 (Autumn): 43–54.

McKibben, Bill. 2005. "The Cuba Diet: What Will You Be Eating When the Revolution Comes?" *Harper's Magazine* 310 (Apri11859): 61–69.

Medin, Tzvi. 1990. *Cuba: The Shaping of Revolutionary Consciousness.* Translated by Martha Grenzback. Boulder: Lynne Rienner Publishers.

Mendoza, Norge Espinosa, and Marilyn Garbey Oquendo, eds. 1999. *Yorick ¿Teatro joven en Cuba?* Havana: Casa Editorial Abril.

Menéndez Quiroa, Leonel. 1977. *Hacia un nuevo teatro latinoamericano: Teoría y metodología del arte escénico.* San Salvador: UCA Editores.

Mesa-Lago, Carmelo, ed. 1971. *Revolutionary Change in Cuba.* Pittsburgh: University of Pittsburgh Press.

———. 1993. *Cuba after the Cold War.* Pittsburgh: Univeristy of Pittsburgh Press.

Milián, José. 2000. *Si vas a comer, espera por Virgilio.* Havana: Ediciones Unión.

Miller, Ivor L. 2000. "Religious Symbolism in Cuban Political Performance." *The Drama Review* 44:2 (Summer): 30–55.

Ministerio de Relaciones Exteriores (MINREX). 1965. *Cuba, Country Free of Segregation.* Havana.

Mintz, Sidney. 1974. *Caribbean Transformations.* New York: Columbia University Press.

———. 1985. *Sweetness and Power: The Place of Sugar in Modern History.* New York: Viking Penguin Books.

Mintz, Sidney, and Sally Price, eds. 1985. *Caribbean Contours.* Baltimore: Johns Hopkins University Press.

Monleón, José. 1978. *América Latina: Teatro y revolución.* Caracas: Editorial Ateneo de Caracas.

Moore, Carlos. 1988. *Castro, the Blacks, and Africa.* Los Angeles: Center for Latin American Studies, University of California.

Moore, Robin. 1997. *Nationalizing Blackness: Afrocubanismo and Artistic Revolution in Havana, 1920–1940.* Pittsburgh: University of Pittsburgh Press.

———. 2006. *Music and Revolution: Cultural Change in Socialist Cuba.* Berkeley: University of California Press.

More, Beny. 1996. "Guajiro de verdad." *Canto a mi Cuba.* Audio CD. Havana: Estudios de Grabaciones (EGREM).

Mosse, George. 1975. *The Nationalization of the Masses: Political Symbolism and Mass Movements in Germany from the Napoleonic Wars through the Third Reich.* Ithaca: Cornell University Press.

Muguercia, Magaly. 1981. *Teatro: En busca de una expresión socialista.* Havana: Editorial Letras Cubanas.

———. 1988. *El teatro cubano: En vísperas de la Revolución*. Havana: Editorial Letras Cubanas.

———. 1996a. *El escándalo de la actuación*. Havana: Editorial Caminos.

———. 1996b. "The Gift of Precariousness: Alberto Pedro Torriente's *Manteca*." *The Drama Review* 40:1 (Spring): 49–60.

———. 1997. *Teatro y utopía*. Havana: Ediciones Unión.

———. 2002. "The Body and Its Politics in Cuba of the Nineties." *Boundary 2* 29:3. Durham: Duke University Press.

Nagengast, Carole. 1991. *Reluctant Socialists and Rural Entrepreneurs: Class, Culture, and the Polish State*. Boulder: Westview Press.

Negt, Oskar, and Alexander Kluge. 1993. *Public Sphere and Experience: Toward an Analysis of the Bourgeois and Proletarian Public Sphere*. Minneapolis: University of Minnesota Press.

Núñez, Jiménez, A., and Agustín Souchy, eds. 1960. *Cooperativismo y colectivismo*. Havana: Editorial LEX.

Oddey, Alison. 1996. *Devising Theatre: A Practical and Theoretical Handbook*. London: Routledge.

Olson, Laura. 2004. *Performing Russia: Folk Revival and Russian Identity*. London: RoutledgeCurzon.

Orihuela, Roberto, ed. 1983. *Lucha contra bandidos*. Havana: Editorial Letras Cubanas.

Ortiz, Fernando. 1906. *Negros brujos: Apuntes para un estudio de etnología criminal*. Reprint. Miami: New House Publishers, 1973.

———. 1939a. "La cubanidad y los negros." *Estudios afrocubanos* 3:1–3:4:3–15.

———. 1939b. "Brujos o santeros." *Estudios afrocubanos* 3:1–3:4:85–90.

———. 1940. "Los factores humanos de la cubanidad." Havana: *Bimestre Cubana* 45:165–69.

———. [1947] 1995. *Cuban Counterpoint: Tobacco and Sugar*. Translated by Harriet de Onis. Durham: Duke University Press.

———. [1950s] 1981. *Los bailes y el teatro de los negros en el folklore de Cuba*. Havana: Editorial Letras Cubanas.

———. 1991. *Estudios etnosociologicos*. Compiled by Isaac Barreal Fernandez. Havana: Editorial de Ciencias Sociales.

———. 1993. *Etnia y sociedad*. Havana: Editorial de Ciencias Sociales.

———. 1996. "Essays." In *Fernando Ortiz y la Cubanidad*. Edited by Norma Suarez. Havana: Colección La Fuente Viva.

Padilla, Heberto. 1974. *Poesía y política*. Edited by Cargo de F. Calzón, Laura y Mayo, and Maria Luisa Álvarez. Washington, D.C.: Georgetown University Cuban Series.

Palmer, Gary, and William Jankowiak. 1996. "Performance and Imagination: Toward an Anthropology of the Spectacular and the Mundane." *Cultural Anthropology* 11:2 (May): 225–58.

Palmié, Stephan. 2002. *Wizards and Scientists: Explorations in Afro-Cuban Modernity and Tradition.* Durham: Duke University Press.

——. 2004. "Fascinans or Tremendum? Permutations of the State, the Body, and the Divine in Late-Twentieth Century Havana." *New West Indian Guide* 78:229–68.

Paskman, Dailey, and Sigmund Spaeth. 1928. *Gentlemen Be Seated: A Parade of the Old-Time Minstrels.* New York: Doubleday, Doran and Company.

Patrice, Pavis. 1992. *Theatre at the Crossroads of Culture.* Translated by Loren Kruger. New York: Routledge.

Paz, Albio, ed. 1982. *Teatro.* Havana: Editorial Letras Cubanas.

Paz, Albio, and Grupo Teatro Escambray. 1971. "La Vitrina." In *Teatro y Revolución.* Havana: Editorial Letras Cubanas, 1980. 335–90.

Pérez, Jorge Ignacio. 2000. "Teatro itinerante: Ruedas de vida y muerte." *Bohemia* 92:6 (March 10): 56–57.

Pérez, Louis A. 1988. *Cuba: Between Reform and Revolution.* 2nd ed. New York: Oxford University Press.

——. 1989. *Lords of the Mountain: Social Banditry and Peasant Protest in Cuba, 1878–1918.* Pittsburgh: University of Pittsburgh Press.

——. 1999. *On Becoming Cuban: Identity, Nationality, and Culture.* Chapel Hill: University of North Carolina Press.

Pérez-Stable, Marifeli. 1999. *The Cuban Revolution: Origins, Course, and Legacy.* New York: Oxford University Press.

Petit, Anne. 1977. "Théâtre et société a Cuba, une expérience: Le groupe théâtre Escambray." *Les Langues Modernes* 71:1–2:154–60.

Phelan, Peggy. 1993. *Unmarked: The Politics of Performance.* New York: Routledge.

Phelan, Peggy, and Jill Lane, eds. 1998. *The Ends of Performance.* New York: New York University Press.

Piñera, Virgilio. [1943] 1998. "La isla en peso." In *La isla en peso: Virgilio Piñera.* Edited by Anton Arrufat. Havana: Ediciones Unión.

Pogolotti, Graziella. 1977. "Para una cultura revolucionaria: Nuevos y viejos valores." *CASA* 18: (104):108–13.

——. 1990. "Prólogo" to *Teatro Escambray.* Edited by Rine Leal. Havana: Editorial Letras Cubanas.

——. 1997. "Art, Bubbles, and Utopia." *South Atlantic Quarterly* 96:1 (Winter): 167–80.

Potter, S. H., and J. M. Potter. 1990. *China's Peasants: The Anthropology of a Revolution.* New York: Cambridge University Press.

Price, Richard. 1990. *Alabi's World.* Baltimore: Johns Hopkins University Press.

Prieto, Abel. 2000a. "Nation, Identity, and Culture in Cuba." Conference talk held at the National Union of Writers and Artists of Cuba (UNEAC), Havana, November 20–23. Discussion led by Minister of Culture Abel Prieto, and UNEAC President Carlos Martí. Personal audiorecording and transcription, 1–17.

——. 2000b. "Vanguardia artística y masividad." *Cuba Socialista* 23:18:2–9.

Prieto Ruiz, Laura, ed. 1992. *Antología de teatro cubano*. Tomo 6. Havana: Ministerio de Cultura and Editorial Pueblo y Educación.

Quintero, Héctor. 2000. *Te sigo esperando*. Havana: Editorial Letras Cubanas.

Rabinow, Paul, ed. 1984. *The Foucault Reader*. New York: Pantheon Books.

Rapport, Nigel. 1997. "The Contrarieties of Israel: An Essay on the Cognitive Importance and the Creative Promise of Both/And." *Journal of the Royal Anthropological Institute* 3:4 (December): 653–72.

Reed, Roger. 1991. *The Cultural Revolution in Cuba*. Geneva: Latin American Round Table.

Retamar, Roberto Fernández. 1971. "Caliban" in *Calibán y otros ensayos: Nuestra América y el mundo*. Havana: Editorial Arte y Literatura.

——. 1989. *Caliban and Other Essays*. Translated by Edward Baker. Minenapolis: University of Minnesota Press.

——. 1997. "Cuba Defended: Countering Another Black Legend." In "Bridging Enigma: Cubans on Cuba." Special issue of *South Atlantic Quarterly* 96:1 (Winter): 95–116.

Ripoll, Carlos. 1985. *Harnessing the Intellectuals: Censoring Writers and Artists in Today's Cuba*. Washington: Cuban American National Foundation.

Risk, Beatriz. 1987. *El Nuevo Teatro Latinoamericano: Una lectura histórico*. Minneapolis: Prisma Institute.

Robaina, Tomas Fernández. 1994. *El Negro en Cuba: 1902–1958. Apuntes para la historia de la lucha contra la discriminación racial*. Havana: Editorial de Ciencias Sociales.

Robreño, Eduardo. 1961. "Historia de teatro popular cubano." *Cuadernos de Historia Habanera* (Oficina del Historiador de la Ciudad de la Habana) 74:11–88.

——. 1979. *Teatro Alhambra: Antología*. Havana: Editorial Letras Cubanas.

——. 1985. *Como lo pienso, lo digo*. Havana: Ediciones Unión (UNEAC).

Rodríguez, Franklin. 1994. *Poética del teatro latinoamericano y del Caribe*. Quito: Abrapalabra Editores.

Rodríguez Millares, Eulogio. 2001. *Actualidad, tendencias y perspectivas del Turismo de Eventos: El negocio del futuro*. Havana: Editorial Academia.

Rodríguez Urgelles, Ury, and Virginia López. 2000. *Guajiros a los cuatro vientos*. Unpublished play manuscript. Guantánamo, Cuba.

Roland, L. Kaifa. 2010. *Cuban Color in Tourism and La Lucha: An Ethnography of Racial Meaning*. New York: Oxford University Press.

Rolon, Rosalba. 1996. *Translated Woman*. Unpublished working manuscript based on the book by Ruth Behar.

Rona-Tas, Akos. 1997. *The Great Surprise of the Small Transformation: The Demise of Communism and the Rise of the Private Sector in Hungary*. Ann Arbor: University of Michigan Press.

Rosendahl, Mona. 1998. *Inside the Revolution: Everyday Life in Socialist Cuba*. Ithaca: Cornell University Press.

Rowe, William, and Vivian Schelling. 1991. *Memory and Modernity: Popular Culture in Latin America*. New York: Verso.

Royce Peterson, Anya. 2004. *Anthropology of the Performing Arts: Artistry, Virtuosity, and Interpretation in a Cross-cultural Perspective*. Lanham, Md.: AltaMira Press.

Ryer, Paul. 2006. "Between La Yuma and Africa: Locating the Color of Contemporary Cuba." Ph.D. diss., University of Chicago.

Saco, José Antonio. 1881. *Colección póstuma de papeles científicos, históricos, políticos y de otros ramos sobre la isla de Cuba, ya publicados, ya inéditos*. Havana: M. De Villa.

———. 1974. *Contra la anexión: José Antonio Saco*. Havana: Editorial de Ciencias Sociales, Instituto Cubano del Libro.

Sala, Haydée, and Miguel Sánchez. 1986. "Aproximaciones a un método sociológico para la valoración de repertorio teatral." *Temas* 10:113–27.

Samuel, Raphael, Ewan MacColl, and Stuart Cosgrove. 1984. *Theatres of the Left 1880–1935: Workers' Theatre Movements in Britain and America*. Boston: Routledge and Keegan Paul.

Sánchez, Luis Alberto. 1936. "Sobre el desdén del negro y por el negro." *Adelante* 5:5.

Sánchez León, Miguel. 2001. *Esa huella olvidada: El Teatro Nacional de Cuba (1959–1961)*. Havana: Editorial Letras Cubanas.

Schechner, Richard. 1985. *Between Theater and Anthropology*. Philadelphia: University of Pennsylvania Press.

———. 1988. *Performance Theory*. New York: Routledge.

———. 1993. *The Future of Ritual: Writings on Culture and Performance*, New York: Routledge.

———. 1998. "What is Performance Studies Anyway?" In *The Ends of Performance*. Edited by Peggy Phelan and Jill Lane. New York: New York University Press.

Schieffelin, Bambi, Kathryn Woolard, and Paul Kroskrity, eds. 1998. *Language Ideologies: Practice and Theory*. Oxford: Oxford University Press.

Schmidt-Nowara, Christopher. 1995. "'Spanish' Cuba: Race and Class in Spanish and Cuban Antislavery Ideology, 1861–1868." *Cuban Studies* (Pittsburgh: Center for Latin American Studies, University of Pittsburgh Press) 25:101–22.

Scott, David. 1991. "That Event, This Memory: Notes on the Anthropology of African Diasporas in the New World." *Diaspora* 1:3:261–84.

———. 1999. *Refashioning Futures: Criticism after Postcoloniality*. Princeton: Princeton University Press.

Scott, James. 1985. *Weapons of the Weak: Everyday Forms of Peasant Resistance*. New Haven: Yale University Press.

———. 1990. *Domination and the Arts of Resistance: Hidden Transcripts*. New Haven: Yale University Press.

Séjourné, Laurette. 1977. *Teatro Escambray: Una experiencia*. Havana: Editorial de Ciencias Sociales.

Seleny, Annamaria. 1994. "The Long Transformation, Hungarian Socialism." Ph.D. diss., Massachusetts Institute of Technology.

——. 2006. *The Political Economy of State-Society Relations in Hungary and Poland: From Communism to the European Union*. New York: Cambridge University Press.

Silverstein, Michael, and Greg Urban. 1996. *Natural Histories of Discourse*. Chicago: University of Chicago Press.

Smith, Lois, and Alfred Padula. 1996. *Sex and Revolution: Women in Socialist Cuba*. New York: Oxford University Press.

Smith, Paul Christopher. 1984. "Theatre and Political Criteria in Cuba: Casa de las Americas Awards, 1960–1983." *Cuban Studies* 14:1 (Winter): 43–47.

Smorkaloff, Pamela Maria. 1987. *Literatura y edición de libros: La cultura literaria y el proceso social en Cuba*. Havana: Letras Cubanas.

——. 1999. *Cuban Writers on and off the Island: Contemporary Narrative Fiction*. New York: Twayne Publishers.

Sommer, Doris. 1991. *Foundational Fictions: The National Romances of Latin America*. Berkeley: University of California Press.

Spivak, Gayatri Chakravorty. 1988. "Can the Subaltern Speak?" In *Marxism and the Interpretation of Culture*. Edited by Cary Nelson and Lawrence Grossberg. Urbana: University of Illinois Press.

Spolin, Viola. [1983] 1999. *Improvisation for the Theater: A Handbook of Teaching and Directing Techniques*. 3rd. ed. Chicago: Northwestern University Press.

Stallybrass, Peter, and Allon White. 1986. *The Politics and Poetics of Transgression*. Ithaca: Cornell University Press.

Stanislavsky, Constantin. 1936. *The Actor Prepares*. New York: Theatre Arts.

States, Bert O. 1996. "Performance as Metaphor." *Theatre Journal* (March): 1–26.

Stewart, Kathleen. 1988. "Nostalgia—A Polemic." *Cultural Anthropology* 3:3 (August): 227–41.

——. 1996. *A Space on the Side of the Road: Cultural Poetics in an "Other" America*. Princeton: Princeton University Press.

Stubbs, Jean. 1989. *Cuba: The Test of Time*. London: Latin America Bureau.

Stubbs, Jean, and Pedro Pérez Sarduy, eds. 2002. *Afrocuba: An Anthology of Cuban Writing on Race, Politics and Culture*. Miami: Ocean Press.

Suárez, Norma. 1966. *Fernando Ortiz y la Cubanidad*. Havana: Colección La Fuente Viva.

Suárez Durán, Esther. 1988. *De la investigación sociológica al hecho teatral*. Havana: Editorial de Ciencias Sociales.

——. 1995. "Otra mirada al teatro bufo cubano; sin prejuicios, con amor." *Tablas* 1:23–27; *La Gaceta de Cuba* no. 1.

——. 1998. *Baños Públicos S.A*. Havana: UNEAC publications (National Union of Writers, Artists, and Critics).

——. 2000. "Los escenarios de poder." Unpublished paper presented at the Encuentro Rine Leal, Centro Nacional de Investigaciones de Artes Escénicas, Havana. October.

——. 2006. *Como un batir de alas: Ensayos sobre el teatro cubano*. Havana: Editorial Letras Cubanas.

——. 2008. "El teatro bufo cubano, la vastedad de su universo." In *Bufo y Nación*. Edited by Inés Martiatu Terry, 239–97. Havana: Editorial Letras Cubanas.

Sutherland, Elizabeth. 1969. *The Youngest Revolution: A Personal Report on Cuba*. New York: Dial Press.

Swanger, Joanna. 1999. "Lands of Rebellion: Oriente and Escambray Encountering Cuban State Formation, 1934–1974." Ph.D. diss., University of Texas, Austin.

Tabares, Vivian Martínez. 1996. "Manteca: Catharsis and Absurdity." *Drama Review* 40:1 (Spring): 44–48.

Taussig, Michael. 1992. *Mimesis and Alterity: A Particular History of the Senses*. New York: Routledge.

Taylor, Diana. 1991. *Theatre of Crisis: Drama and Politics in Latin America*. Lexington: University Press of Kentucky.

——. 2003. *The Archive and the Repertoire: Performing Cultural Memory in the Americas*. Durham: Duke University Press.

Taylor, Diana, and Juan Villegas, eds. 1994. *Negotiating Performance: Gender, Sexuality and Theatricality in Latin/o America*. Durham: Duke University Press.

Taylor, Frank. 1988. "Revolution, Race, and Some Aspects of Foreign Relations in Cuba since 1959." *Cuban Studies* (Pittsburgh: Center for Latin American Studies, University of Pittsburgh Press): 18:19–44.

Teatro de los Elementos. 2002. "Opción Cero." Unpublished manuscript. Cumanayagua, Cuba.

Therborn, Goran. 1980. *The Ideology of Power and the Power of Ideology*. London: NLB.

Thiong'o, Ngugi wa. 1997. "Enactments of Power: The Politics of Performance Space." *The Drama Review* 41:3 (Fall): 11–30.

Thomas, Susan. 2008. *Cuban Zarzuela: Performing Race and Gender on Havana's Lyric Stage*. Urbana: University of Illinois Press.

Toledo, Héctor R. Castillo. 2000. "Un acto distinto." *Montañés*, Cienfuegos, 5:10:3.

Tonkin, Elizabeth. 1992. *Narrating Our Pasts: The Social Construction of Oral History*. Cambridge: Cambridge University Press.

Trouillot, Michel-Rolph. 1988. *Peasants and Capital: Dominica in the World Economy*. Baltimore: Johns Hopkins University Press.

——. 1993. "The Caribbean Region: An Open Frontier in Anthropological Theory." *Annual Review of Anthropology* 2:19–42.

——. 1995. *Silencing the Past: Power and the Production of History*. Boston: Beacon Press.

——. 2003. *Global Transformations: Anthropology and the Modern World*. New York: Palgrave Macmillan Press.

Turnbull, Colin. 1992. *The Mountain People*. New York: Simon and Schuster.

Turner, Edith. 1994. "Reenactment of Traditional Rites of Passage." In *Crossroads: The Quest for Contemporary Rites of Passage*. Edited by Christopher and Meade Mahdi. Chicago: Open Court.

Turner, Victor. 1957. *Schism and Continuity in an African Society: A Study of Ndembu Village Life*. Manchester: Manchester University Press.

———. 1969. *The Ritual Process: Structure and Anti-Structure*. Chicago: Adine Publishing Company.

———. 1974. *Dramas, Fields and Metaphors: Symbolic Action in Human Society*. Ithaca: Cornell University Press.

———. 1982. *From Ritual to Theatre: The Human Seriousness of Play*. New York: PAJ Publications.

———. 1987. *The Anthropology of Performance*. New York: PAJ Publications.

Twine, France Windance. 1998. *Racism in a Racial Democracy: The Maintenance of White Supremacy in Brazil*. New Brunswick: Rutgers University Press.

Ueland, Brenda. [1938] 2007. *If You Want to Write: A Book about Art, Independence and Spirit*. Minneapolis: Graywolf Press.

Urrutia, Gustavo, E. 1932. "Cuba, el Arte, y el Negro II." *Adelante* (November): 9–20.

———. 1935. "Cuba, el Arte, y el Negro III." *Adelante* (September): 9.

Valdés, Nelson. 2000. "Milagros, delfines, orishás y la derecha cubano-americano: La significación de Elián González." *Nueva Sociedad* 168:14–22.

Valdez, Luis. 1990. *Luis Valdez Early Word: Actos, Bernabe and Pensamiento Serpentino*. Houston: Arte Publico Press.

Valiño Cedre, Omar. 1994. *La aventura del Escambray: Notas sobre teatro y sociedad*. Havana: Pinos Nuevos.

———. 1997. "La cruzada teatral: Otra ventana al universo." *Revolución y Cultura* 36:5/97:18–21.

———. 1999. *Trazados en el agua: Un mapa del archipiélago teatral cubano de los 90*. Santa Clara: Ediciones Capiro.

Valladeres, Octavio Pérez. 2000. "Siguanea: ¿Atlántida en el Escambray?" *Montañés* (Cienfuegos) 5:10:4.

van Erven, Eugene. 2001. *Community Theatre: Global Perspectives*. New York: Routledge.

Verdery, Katherine. 1991. *National Ideology under Socialism: Identity and Cultural Politics in Ceauşescu's Romania*. Berkeley: University of California Press.

———. 1992. "Ethnic Relations, Economies of Shortage, and the Transition in Eastern Europe." In *Socialism: Ideals, Ideologies, and Local Practice*. Edited by C. Hann. New York: Routledge.

———. 1994. "Beyond the Nation in Eastern Europe." *Social Text* (Spring): 1–19.

———. 1996. *What Was Socialism and What Comes Next?* Princeton: Princeton University Press.

Versenyi, Adam. 1993. *Theatre in Latin America: Religion, Politics, and Culture from Cortes to the 1980s*. New York: Cambridge University Press.

Versenyi, Adam, ed. 2005. *Latin American Dramatists*. 1st. ser. Detroit: Thompson Gale.

Villegas, Alma. 1994. "The Origin, Development, and Processes of Teatro Escambray in Cuba 1968–1985." Ph.D. diss., New York University.

Villoch, Frederico. 1938. "Teatros que fueron." *Adelante*. August 28–September 25 (Sundays).

Vitier, Cintio. 1997. "Martí and the Challenge of the 1990s." *South Atlantic Quarterly* 96:1 (Winter): 213–20.

——. 1999. *Resistencia y libertad*. Havana: Ediciones Union (UNEAC).

Vitori Ramos, Maria del Carmen. 1998. "Fiestas tradicionales campesinas." In *Fiestas populares tradiciones cubanas* by "Collective Authors." Havana: Editorial de Ciencias Sociales.

Vološinov, V. N. 1973. *Marxism and the Philosophy of Language*. Translated by L. Matejka and I. R. Titunik. Cambridge: Harvard University Press.

Wagner, Roy. 1981. *The Invention of Culture*. Chicago: University of Chicago Press.

Weinreb, Amelia Rosenberg. 2009. *Cuba in the Shadow of Change: Daily Life in the Twilight of the Revolution*. Gainesville: University Press of Florida.

Weiss, Judith. 1977. *Casa de las Américas: An Intellectual Review in the Cuban Revolution*. Madrid: Estudios de Hispanófila, Editorial Castalia.

——. 1993. *Latin American Popular Theatre: The First Five Centuries*. Albuquerque: University of New Mexico Press.

Weiss, Mark, trans. 2010. *La Isla en Peso: The Whole Island*. Translation of Virgilio Piñera's *La Isla en Peso*. Exeter: Shearsman Books.

Weiss, Rachel. 2007. "After the Storm in Cuba: A Case of Withdrawal." *Social Identities* 13:2:183–99.

Wells, Shawn Alfonso. 2004. "Cuban Color Classification and Identity Negotiation: Old Terms in a New World." Ph.D. diss., University of Pittsburgh.

Willett, John, ed. 1957. *Brecht on Theatre: The Development of an Aesthetic*. New York: Hill and Wang.

Williams, Raymond. 1973. *The Country and the City*. Oxford: Oxford University Press.

——. 1977. *Marxism and Literature*. Oxford: Oxford University Press.

——. 1987. *The Sociology of Culture*. New York: Schocken Books.

Willis, Susan. 1986. "Caliban as Poet: Reversing the Maps of Domination." In *Reinventing the Americas: Comparative Studies of Literature of the United States and Spanish America*. Edited by Bell Gale Chevigyn and Gari Laguardia. Cambridge: Cambridge University Press, 92–105.

Wilshire, Bruce. 1982. *Role Playing and Identity: The Limits of Theatre as Metaphor*. Bloomington: Indiana University Press.

Whitfield, Esther. 2001. "Fiction(s) of Cuba in Literary Economies of the 1990s: Buying in or Selling Out?" (Guillermo Cabrera Infante, Zoe Valdes, Daina Chaviano, Pedro Juan Gutierrez). Ph.D. diss., Harvard University.

——. 2008. *Cuban Currency: The Dollar and "Special Period" Fiction*. Minneapolis: University of Minnesota Press.

Whitten, Norman, and Arlene Torres, eds. 1998. *Blackness in Latin America and the Caribbean: Social Dynamics and Cultural Transformation*. Bloomington: Indiana University Press.

Wirtz, Kristina. 2004. "Santería in Cuban National Consciousness: A Religious Case of the Doble Moral." *Journal of Latin American Anthropology* 9:2:409–38.

Wolf, Eric. 1966. *Peasants*. Foundations of Modern Anthropology Series. Englewood Cliffs, N.J.: Prentice Hall.

——. 1969. *Peasant Wars of the Twentieth Century*. New York: Harper and Row.

——. 1972. *The Human Condition in Latin America*. New York: Oxford University Press.

Woolard, Katherine. 1998. "Language Ideology as a Field of Inquiry." In *Language Ideologies: Practice and Theory*. Edited by B. Schieffelin, K. Woolard, and P. Kroskrity. Oxford: Oxford University Press, 3–47.

Yelvington, Kevin A. 2001. "The Anthropology of Afro-Latin America and the Caribbean: Diasporic Dimensions." *Annual Review of Anthropology* 30:227–60.

Yun, Lisa. 2009. *The Coolie Speaks: Chinese Indentured Laborers and African Slaves in Cuba*. Philadelphia: Temple University Press.

Yurchak, Alexei. 2005. *Everything Was Forever until It Was No More*. Princeton: Princeton University Press.

INDEX

Page numbers in italics refer to illustrations or tables.

Abreu, Alexis, 89–90, 115
acting, 29, 119, 203; technique, 22, 142, 242. *See also* improvisation
Afro-Cuban, xxii, 3, 26, 29, 36, 45–46, 65–66, 79, 127, 172–73, 187, 259–71, 282n8, 314nn5–6. *See also* culture
agricultural reforms, 15, 54, 58, 63–64, 71
Agüera, Nisia, 211
Amistad del los Pueblos (Friendship among [Socialist] Nations), 212, 282n14
Anderson, Benedict, 22–23, 252
Años Dorados (Golden Years), 49
Años Gris (Gray Years), 8–9, 49, 75, 212
anthropology, 6, 29–30, 37–39, 130, 221, 245; author's role in theater groups and, 31–32, 98, 142–43, 156, 209, 233; methods of, used in theater, 24, 63; of theatre, 142; works of, made into plays, 280n6. *See also* ethnography
Arenas, Reinaldo, 75
Arendt, Hannah, 252
artes plásticas (visual arts), 86, 284n11
artist, artists, 4, 8, 60; author as, 28–29; campesinos and, 5–6, 243–44; collaboration and, 30–31
La Asociación Nacional Hermanos Saíz (National Association of the Saíz Brothers), 207
audience, audiences, xx, 36, 113, 120, 183, *208*; colonial, 45; funding and, 116, 207, 214; international, 187, 260–61; laughter of, 7, 44, 204, 251; in performances, 24–25, 27, 30–31, 199–200, 271; rural, *136*, 167–71, 189–91, 198; success of performance determined by, 7, 105; Teatro

Escambray and, 63–64; Teatro Nuevo and, 61; urban, 167–71, 242; virgin, 89
authenticity, 2, 6, 139, 195, 212, 231; campesino identity and, 35, 63, 244; national identity and, 5, 15, 253–54, 259, 261, 272; race and, 264–65; theater groups and, 89–92, 110, 221
authority, xxi, 242; Cuban national identity and, 2, 13, 63, 255; during Años Gris (Grey Years), 9, 49–50; during Batista regime, 47; in Special Period, 9, 20–21, 34, 76–110; Massification of Culture campaign and, 188, 209–10; plastic artists and, 284n11; punishment of, 49–50, 69–75; in Revolution, 11–12, 17–19, 56, 58–59, 213–14; state funding of, 27, 101, 111, 116, 118, 260–61; urban artists vs. rural, 84, 182–83, 186, 190–92, 215–16

Bakhtin, Mikhail, 23, 254
Baratute, Julio, 222, *223*–24, 242, 288n3, 288n4
Baratute, Rogelio, 221, 288n3
Barba, Eugenio, 30, 142
Barber, Karen, 112
Barceló, Tomás, 177
Barnet, Miguel, 29, 219, 264, 281n6, 288n1
Barthes, Roland, 276
Batista, Fulgencio, 47, 152, 156, 220, 286n4
Battle of Ideas, 26, 255–56, 288n14, 289n12. *See also* Massification of Culture campaign
Bauman, Richard, 25–26, 49, 112. *See also* emergence
Bautista Castillo, Juan (Nego), 107, 120, 271

Beckett, Samuel, 35, 111, 139, 170–73
Behar, Ruth, 30, 280n6
Bennett, Susan, 169
Bertolt Brecht Political Theater, 60
Bhabha, Homi, 252–53
blackface, 5, 34, 43–44, 262. *See also* Teatro
  Bufo
Blanco, Roberto, 281n7
Boal, Augusto, 22, 31, 60, 210, 223, 258. *See
  also* Theater of the Oppressed
Bolívar, Natalia, 219, 288n1
Borrego Linares, Fernando. *See* Montañez,
  Polo
Boudet, Rosa Ileana, 8, 21, 26, 56–59; on
  Teatro Nuevo, 67, 84–85
Bourdieu, Pierre, 18, 55, 211, 247
Brazil, 22, 258
Brecht, Bertolt, 22, 60–61
Briggs, Charles, 25–26
Brook, Peter, 280n6
Buenaventura, Enrique, 22
Burke, Kenneth, 261
Bush, George W., 176

Caballero, Atilio, 115, *145*, 156, 165; as
  author, 123, 170, 242; in play production,
  149, 152, 158; waiting for, 130, 138–41, 171
Cabildo Teatral (Cabildo Theater), 65–66,
  185
Cabrera, Guillermo Infante, 75
campesino, campesinos, 108–10, 168, 193,
  235, 247–52; as actors, 221, 223, 225–26,
  236–37; constructions of, 19–20, 35,
  124–27, 153–55, 173, 175; education campaigns and, 54–55, 66, 100, 102; genera-
  tional differences among, 91, 137,
  285n10; images of, *109*, *126*, *148*, *194*, *196*,
  229; interviews with, 31–32, 122, 135, 143,
  170–71, 218; land politics and, 98–99,
  151–52, 219–20; racialization of, 246–48;
  relation of, to artists, 241–44; in Revolution, 15–17, 22, 89, 128; in Special Period,
  83–86; studies of, 26; Teatro de los Elementos and, 104; Teatro Escambray and,
  63–65; theater and, xix–xxi, 199–200; in
  tourism industry, 265–67; traditions of,
  80, *228*, *229*, 231–32; urban verses rural
  identity and, 1–2, 13. *See also* guajiro

Camus, Albert, 172
Cano, Osvaldo, 63, 283n18
capitalism, 81, 165, 167, 172, 270; campesino
  identity and, 6, 108, 252; capitalist theater characters and, 35, 155–58, 161, 262;
  capitalist vs. socialist theater, 69, 114;
  Hombre Novísimo and, 14; race and, 52;
  in revolutionary ideology, 135, 152, 215,
  255; in Special Period, 2–3, 12; in theater
  production, 36; transition to socialism,
  56, 58–59, 260
Cardoso, Onelio Jorge, 198, 257
Caribbean, xxi, 4, 181, 245, 260, 268; racial
  identity, 41–42. *See also under names of
  individual countries*
Carpentier, Alejo, 282n6
Carrío, Raquel, 189
cartoons, 108, *109*, 247–48. *See also* Elpidio
  Valdés; Liborio
Casa de Joven Creadores (House of Young
  Artists), 184, 287n5
Casa de las Américas (House of the Americas), 101–2, 189
Casas de Cultura (Houses of Culture), 66,
  99, 121, 124, 181, 212, 289n12
Castillo, Nelda, 189–90
Castro, Fidel, 15, 75, *109*, 110, 174, 177; on
  campesino figure, 89; Cuban Revolution
  and, 5, 47–51, 53, 55, 151; declaration of
  Special Period by, 3, 8; Fidelismo and,
  11; health of, 254; Massification of Cul-
  ture campaign and, 187; on Option
  Zero, 34, 77–78; "Palabras" speech of,
  50, 68–69; on race and Cuban identity,
  52, 263; reputation of, 140; on tourism,
  268; use of culture by, 12, 56, 103, 118,
  213–14, 256; visit of, to Teatro Escambray, 66
Castro, Raúl, 15, 36, 134, 180, 269
censorship, 26, 68, 121, 143–44, 280n8;
  Great Purge and, 75; self-, 18, 56, 70, 114,
  116, 215; of state artists, 69, 118
Centro de Antropología (Anthropology
  Center), 29
Centro Nacional de Cultural Comunitario
  (National Center for Community Culture), 212
Cervantes, Miguel de, 201, 203

Chekov, Anton, 22

China, 42, 56, 212, 261, 288n14

Cienfuegos, Camilo, 53

Cienfuegos (city), 1, 19, 104, 242; audiences in, 28, 31, 167; tourism in, 7, 95, 265

citizens, citizenship, 23, 44, 46; revolutionary, 5, 49, 72; rural vs. urban identity and, 3, 63, 85, 89, 247, 255–56. *See also* Hombre Novísimo; Hombre Nuevo; nationalism

class (socioeconomic), 60–62, 125, 243, 247, 265; in Cuban Revolution, 34, 41–43, 51–54, 255. *See also* capitalism; socialism

Clifford, James, 24

Clinton, Bill, 176

Clytus, John, 52, 281n7

cold war, 36, 79, 172, 178

Colombia, 22

colonialism, 6, 38, 44–47, 189; anti-colonial struggle and, 41–42, 279n3; colonial theater characters and, 34, 262, 275. *See also* imperialism; postcolonialism; Ten Years' War; Wars for Independence

commedia dell'arte, 43, 46, 281n2

Committed Theater, 22

Communist Party, xxi, 55, 71, 134, 255, 260; relation of, to foreigners, 269; in Special Period, 9; theater people as members of, 118–19, 124; tourism and, 14

Congreso de la Cultura y Desarrollo (Culture and Development Conference), 110, 209

Congreso de Rito y Representación (Ritual and Representation Conference), 264

Congreso Iberoamericana y Caribeño de Agentes del Desarrollo Socio-cultural Comunitario (Ibero-American and Caribbean Congress of Agents for Socio-Cultural Community Development), or "Communidad" (Community), 88, 110, 209, 211, 219, 222–23

Conjunto Folklórica Nacional (National Folkloric Dance and Music group), 187, 264, 290n5, 290n6

Conjunto (journal), 101, 103

Conquergood, Dwight, 37–39

Consejo Nacional de las Artes Escénicas (National Theater Board), 1, 86, 185, 213; adjudicating authenticity by, 89, 91, 187; censorship and, 114, 169; funding artists by, 183, 186

Corrieri, Sergio, 59, 82, 84, 212, 281n6, 282n14

costumbrismo (literary genre dealing with customs), 246

Cremata, Carlos, 211

criollos, 41, 279n3

La Cruzada Teatral Guantánamo-Baracoa (Theater Crusade Guantánamo to Baracoa), xix–xxi, 1, 20, 35, 175–217, 242, 247; comparison of, to other theater groups, 91; *El tío Francisco y Las Leandras* (Uncle Francisco and the Leandras) and, 262; images of, *184*, *185*, *194*, *196*, *202*, *208*; *La muerte juega el escondido: Una leyenda guajira* (Death Plays Hide and Seek: A Hillbilly Legend), 200–203; research with, 32, 90

Cuadra de Comedias (Comedy Sketch Theater Group), 220

Cuban Adjustment Act (1966), 287n13. *See also* United States: embargo/blockade by

cubanía (Cuban identity), xxi, 1, 32, 160, 214, 270, 277; artists and, 12, 82; "cubanidad" vs., 279n3; definition of, 241; history of, 41–42; race and, 53; in Special Period, 13, 17, 20; symbols of, 238; theatrical characters and, 48, 51; in tourism industry, 260–61, 263

Cuban Revolution (1959), 177–78, 213–14, 231, 254, 283n22; art and, 9, 12, 55–62, 68–69, 99–103; campesinos and, 15, 128, 135, 151, 251–52; definition of, 49–50; gender and, 137; ideology of, 156; race and, 51–55; religion and, 198; representation during Special Period, 16–17, 84, 89, 276; revolutionary consciousness and, 10–11, 34, 55–56, 215–16; symbols, 117; theater and, 18, 21–23, 26, 47–48, 66, 90–92; violence of, against artists, 69–72, 74–75. *See also* citizens, citizenship: revolutionary citizen

cultural imperialism, 13–14

cultural revolution, 55–56. *See also* Años
　Gris
culture, 5, 36, 52, 100, 243, 240; Afro-
　Cuban, 29, 46, 79; anthropological stud-
　ies of, 30, 38–39; of campesinos, 122, 124,
　137, 154, 168, 271; capitalist, 270; cultural
　crusades and, 32, 54, 101, 175–217, 242;
　cultural elites and, 7, 244; cultural iden-
　tity and, 16–19, 23; cultural imperialism
　and, 12, 14; cultural mixing and, 42; cul-
　tural revolution and, 55–56; cultural
　tourism and, 264–68; in Early Cuban
　Republic, 44; flexibilization of, 263–64;
　globalization and, 170; high, 255; loss of,
　225, 231, 241; Massification of Culture
　campaign and, 26, 35, 98, 160, 187–92,
　255–56; national identity and, 50, 62–63,
　275; official, 68, 249; politics of, 72, 212;
　popular, 13, 45, 246, 254–55, 282n8;
　pseudo-, 2, 14, 35, 256, 259–60; rural,
　137, 219, 244; urban, 4
Cumanayagua, 20, 34–35, 91, 97–98, 215;
　research in, 27, 31; Teatro de los Ele-
　mentos in, 111–74, 211

Damas de Blanco (Ladies in White), 1
dance, dancing, 5, 21, 119, 135, 144, 287n5;
　Afro-Cuban, 44, 98, 187, 262–63, 290n5;
　by audiences, 238, *238*; author and, 4, 28,
　33, 203; Haitian, 181, 286n3; rural folk, 2,
　45, 219; study of, 88; on television, 17; in
　tourism industry, 14, 265
Danza Libre (Free Dance), 185
Década Negra (Black Years). *See* Años Gris
décimas (songs), 17, 148, 158–59, 173, 251;
　examples of, 62, 144–45, 231–32; Poetic
　Fantasy and, 85; in *Ten mi nombre como
　un sueño*, 163, 167
Desmond, Jane, 264–65
devised theater, 34, 104, 112, 118, 285n2
dissidents, 1, 75, 285n1; persecution of, 9–
　10, 70–71, 290n8
divisas (hard/foreign currency), 95, 191,
　213, 216, 261; definition of, 92–93; shop-
　ping and, 97; tourism industry and, 259,
　264–65, 284n9. *See also* peso convertible
Dominican Republic, 181, 286
Dos Brazos, 20, 225–42, 247, 251–52, 257;

images of, *136, 194, 228–29, 234, 237,
　239–40*
Douglas, Mary, 19
Dragún, Osvaldo, 60

Elpidio Valdés (cartoon character), 108, 247–
　48. *See also* mambises; Padrón, Juan
emergence, 112, 122
emotional truth, 24, 143, 237
Enríquez, Carlos, 5–6
Escambray region, 21, 26, 36, 62–67, 96–
　97, *126*, 190; Cuatro Vientos, 134–38, *136*,
　163; traditions in, 251; violence in, 252.
　See also Cumanayagua; Siguanea; Teatro
　Escambray
Escuela de Altos Estudios de Hotelería y
　Turismo de formatur (School of
　Higher Studies for the Tourism and
　Hotel Industries), 267–68
Escuela Nacional del Arte (ena; National
　School of Art), 72, 105
Escuelas de Instructores de Arte (Schools
　for Art Instructors), 66, 256, 258, 288n4,
　289n12
ethnography, 2–4, 14–15, 20–33; of actors,
　21–24, 27, 35, 64, 83; meta-, 23; partici-
　pant observation and, 24, 32, 90, 143;
　performance studies, 38–39, 275. *See
　also* anthropology; methodology
ethnomusicology, 43
Europe, 41, 45, 71, 245, 260–61; Eastern
　Europe, 3, 68, 70, 263; emigration to, 75,
　192; performance tours in, 27, 46, 271–
　73
extranjero (foreigner), 74, 95, 102, 137, 177,
　268–72. *See also* gallego

Fabelo, Rigoberto, 211
Fagen, Richard, 54–55
Faubion, James, 24
Federación Estudiantil Universitaria (feu;
　University Students Federation), 71–72
Federal Theater Project, 282n15
Fernandez, James, 252, 261; on metaphor,
　50, 112, 117, 241, 284n10, 285n1
film, films, 56, 86, 127, 182, 249, 263; for-
　eign, 216; *Lista de Espera* (2000), 94;
　Realengo 18 (1961), 288n2; research pro-

cess and, 37, 75; stars of, 282n14; *Strawberry and Chocolate* (1994), 173; *Titanic* (1997), 201; video recordings of performances, 31, 119, 159; video salons and, 88

flexibilization of culture, 160, 263–64

folk culture, 36; Folk Rusticity and, 85–86, 170, 203, 235, 242, 244; rural folk and, 54, 125, 255; theater and, 60, 62. *See also* Poetic Fantasy

folk identity, 2, 171, 244–48, 257; campesinos and, 6, 219; of city folk, 190, 206; definition of, 26

folklore, 26, 36, 187, 246; Afro-Cuban, 6, 290n6; folklorization/folkloricization and, 2, 244; in tourism industry, 264–68

Fornaris, José, 283n18

Fornet, Abrosio, 9

Foucault, Michel, 139, 206

Freire, Paulo, 223, 258

Fulleda León, Gerardo, 264

Fundación Fernando Ortiz (Fernando Ortiz Foundation), 29–30, 264

Gable, Eric, 6, 251

Gal, Susan, 49, 251

gallego: after Cuban Revolution 48, 51; in Teatro Bufo, 34, 43–46; in twenty-first century, 36, 260, 262, 275. *See also* Teatro Bufo

García, Raúl Roa, 246

García, Santiago, 60

García Canclini, Néstor, 273

gender, 247, 250, 251, 283n18; in campesino communities, 135, 236, 240; in literary crusades, 54; machismo and, 137; in Teatro Bufo, 5; in theater groups, 119, 133; in tourism industry, 265–67

globalization, 2, 14, 170, 187, 267, 274; fight against, 5, 12–13

Goldsmith, Oliver, 81

Gómez, Luis, 135

González, Elián, xxii, 197, 215, 251, 287n9

González, Julián, 1

González, Nidia, 211

González, Rafael, 66, 82, 90–91, 101, 283n19

Grupo Andante (Traveling Theater), 91

Grupo Espacio Abierto (Open Space Theater Group), 264

Grupo Lino Álvarez de Realengo 18 (Lino Álvarez Theater Group of Realengo 18), 33, 90, 219–24, 222, 242, 288n1

Grupo Rita Montaner (Rita Montaner Theater Group), 264

Grupo Teatro Caribeño (Caribbean Theater Group), 264

Grupo Teatro Palenque (Arena Theater), 264

guajiro, 162, 181, 248–49, 275; campesino and, 5, 7, 15; constructions of, 63, 81, 198; in *Don Quixote*, 200–203, *202*; hillbilly and, 5, 15, 63, 81, 124, 127, 156, 165, 200; Liborio cartoons and, 108–9, *109*; music and dance of, 153; in Teatro Bufo, 48, 262, 283n18; in *Ten mi nombre como un sueño*, 163, *166*. *See also* campesino, campesinos

Guanche, Jesús, 219, 288n1

Guantanamo Bay Naval Base, 177, 181, 186, 206, 287n13

Guantánamo City, 1, 27, 32, 176–77, 193, 220, 235

Guantánamo Province, xix, xxii, 14, 175–258; images of, *136*, *184–85*, *194*, *196*, *202*, *208*, *222*, *228–29*, *234*, *237*, *239–40*; race and, 42; religious rituals in, 127; theater groups in, 19, 31–33, 35, 90–91. *See also* Dos Brazos

Guelman, Alexander, 22

La Guerilla de Teateros (Theater Guerrillas), 91

Guerra, Lillian, 246

Guerrero, Juan José, 283n18

Guevara, Ernesto "Che," 57, 59, 91, 97, 255, 282n12; on art, 11; constructions of, 254; on Hombre Nuevo, 10, 21, 49, 53; on utopia to come, 170–71

Guitiérrez, Alberto. *See* Korda

Hagedorn, Katherine, 187, 290n5

Haiti, 106–8, 120, 181, 285n10, 286n3

Handler, Richard, 6, 251

Haraszti, Miklós, 48, 67–69, 117

Hart Dávalos, Armando, 56, 105, 212, 284n12

Havana, 22, 35, 48, 186, 263, 284n8; constructions of campesinos and, 7, 133;

Havana (*cont.*)
ethnography in, 3–4, 28–29, 31, 33, 167–68; Grupo Lino Álvarez de Realengo 18 and, 219, 221–23, 288n4; La Cruzada Teatral Guantánamo-Baracoa and, 213; migrants and, 81, 120; Oriente and Guantánamo vs., 176–79, 195, 215; as "real" Cuba, 1, 13; religion in, 244; Teatro Bufo and, 262; Teatro Comunitario and, 255; Teatro de los Elementos and, 92, 104–5, 108, 170, 242; Teatro Escambray and, 21, 63; Teatro Nuevo and, 82; theater in, 57, 59, 86–87; theater world and, 116, 190–91; tourism in, 14, 172, 182, 187–88, 265

Hawaii, 260, 265; hula and, 265

Hernández, Helmo, 281n6

Hernández, Pepillo, 152, 155–58, 161, 163

Hernández Espinosa, Eugenio, 264

Hernández Lorenzo, Maite, 210–11

Herzfeld, Michael, 251

history, 6, 36, 102, 187, 259, 266–67; campesinos in, 26, 219, 245–48, 256–58; of Cuban Revolution, 15, 48–50; Fredric Jameson on, 254; gender and, 137; José Martí on, 47; Karl Marx on, 41; Katherine Verdery on, 214; memory and, 123, 164; national narratives and, xxi–xxii, 46, 141; Pan–Latin American, 253; Raymond Williams on, 80–81; regional, 128, 144, 148–52, 158, 168; religious, 3; staging of, 106, 249; of Teatro Escambray, 211; theater in, 18

Hombre Novísimo (Even Newer Man), 13–14, 16, 173, 258, 273; constructions of, 191, 244; nostalgia for, 19, 77

Hombre Nuevo (New Man), 13–15, 55–59, 82, 172, 263; Che Guevara on, 10; replacement of Teatro Bufo characters and, 48–53; in Special Period, 17; Teatro Nuevo and, 21, 34, 65

Hombre Viejo (Old Man), Fidel Castro as, 15

Huber, Mary, 261

Hubert de Blank Theater, 261, 262

ideology, xxi, 55–56, 254–55, 260, 279n3; in Años Gris, 8–9, 70; art as ideological weapon and, 80, 212–13, 216; campesino image and, 6, 91, 266, 273; changes of, during Special Period, 13–14, 16, 50, 276; culture and, 2, 58; diversity and, 263; ideological education and, 43, 48, 54; of language, 49, 243; racial, 52–53; revolutionary, 11–13, 22–23, 156; Teatro Estudio and, 59; Teatro Nuevo and, 65; theater and, 24–26, 36–37, 117, 277

imperialism 12, 54, 259, 275; anti-imperial struggles and, 5, 14, 23, 53, 254, 276; capitalism and, 35, 172; counter-revolutionary art and, 49–50; theater as tool against, 26. *See also* cultural imperialism

improvisation, 112, 161–65, 234, 285n8; in commedia dell'arte, 281n2; by El Laboratorio de Teatro Comunitario, 235–37; in music, 2, 251; by Teatro de los Elementos, 101, 122, 130–33, 140, 157–58

indigeneity, xxi, 29, 244–45, 247; Cuban racial identity and, 41–42, 275–76; indigenismo and, 45; in tourism industry, 264–65

irony (dramatic), 35–36, 151, 252, 260–61, 171, 176

Instituto Superior del Arte (ISA; National Arts University), 22, 28, 66, 185, 189, 190

interdisciplinarity, 26, 37–39

Irvine, Judith, 49, 251

Jamaica, 106

Jameson, Fredric, 254

jíbaro (Puerto Rican peasant/farmer), 244–47

jineteras, jineteros (prostitutes, hustlers), 81, 201, 203, 265, 287n10

Juárez, Edilberto, 185

Kapcia, Antoni, 279n3

Korda (Alberto Guitiérrez), 282n12

Korimacao (theater), 91

Kuper, Hilda, 280n6

El Laboratorio de Teatro Comunitario (Communitarian Theater Laboratory), 20, 32, 90, 217, 224–42, 237, 255; giving voice to campesinos, 35; *Guajiros a los cuatro vientos* (Guajiros of the Four

Winds) and, 32, *228*, 230–41, *239*, *240*, 250

Lane, Jill, 43, 281n1

language ideology, xii, 48–49, 243. *See also* ideology

Latin America, 14, 71, 101, 181, 253, 257; "folk" figure in, 219, 244–47, 260; nationalisms in, 35; race in, 41–42; theater in, 22, 34, 61, 82, 200; tourism in, 268. *See also* Martí, José; Nuestra America; *and under names of individual countries*

Lauten, Flora, 65, 84, 188–89, 223, 283n20

Leal, Rine, 43, 57–58, 102–3, 283n18

Lenin, Vladimir, 11, 13, 15, 70, 172

Leyva, Waldo, 212, 219, 288n1

Liborio (cartoon character), 108, *109*, 110

Lima, Lezama, 75

literacy campaigns, 15, 54–55, 65, 103, 236

Living Theater, 282n15

Llerena, Lillian, 281n6

Lomnitz, Claudio, 242, 256

López, Virginia, 184, 203, 225, 227, 235–36, 251, 287n5; images of, *229*, *239*

López Carcassés, Maribel, 182–83

Loredo, Rómulo, 198

la lucha (the struggle), xxi, 10, 16–20, 80, 151–52, 174; art and, 79–80, 104

Mackandal, François, 106–7

El Mago (the magician), 183, 286n4

mambises, 247

Manteca (1993) ("Pig Fat"), 289n2. *See also* Pedro, Alberto

Mao Tse-tung, 56

Marcus, George, 24

Marinello, Juan, 246, 281n6

Martí, Carlos, 212, 289n1

Martí, José, 47, 172, 192, 205; martiano and, 14, 280n5; on Nuestra América, 279n3; poetry by, 135, 175, 197; on race and Cuban identity, 52, 245, 263

Martin, Randy, 25, 47, 57, 82, 275, 277

Martínez Furé, Rogelio, 264

Martínez Masdeu, Edgar, 246

Marx, Karl, 11, 13, 15, 22, 60, 70, 172; on history and comedy, 41, 45

más allá (farther out, beyond), 181–87, 192,

219, 223, 247; art and, 9, 35; campesinos and, 122, 125, 133, 170, 175–76, 226

Massification of Culture campaign, 32, 97, 187–92, 207, 214, 289n12; impact of, on La Cruzada, 209–10; pseudo-culture and, 35; renaming of, 255–56. *See also* Battle of Ideas

Mayakovsky, Vladimir, 22

Mayan Women's Theater Collective LA FOMMA, 258

Mella, Julio Antonio, 245

methodology, 2–4, 20–36, 113, 167–68, 275; interdisciplinarity and, 38; theater production and, 63, 83, 104, 142–43, 171. *See also* ethnography

Mexico, 46, 181, 246, 256, 258

mimesis, 249–50

Ministry of Culture, 89, 106, 204, 209, 233, 270; awards given by, 207, 213; in Cuban Revolution, 56; ethnography and, 28; Teatro Comunitario and, 86; Teatro Nuevo and, 88

minstrelsy. *See* blackface; Teatro Bufo

Montañez, Polo, 244, 248

Moore, Robin, 43, 45–46, 290n5, 290n6

Moré, Beny, 249

Muguercia, Magaly, 252–53, 270

mulata, 34, 281n1; after Cuban Revolution, 48, 51; in Teatro Bufo, 43–45, 262; in twenty-first century, 260, 275. *See also* Teatro Bufo

music, 20, 28, 80, 91, 97, 238, 265; Afro-Cuban, 46, 262, 290n5; black popular, 44; campesino, 142, 144, 148, 233, 248; Dominican, 181; in Grupo Lino Álvarez de Realengo 18 productions, 221; guajiro, 45, 153; Haitian, 181, 286n3; hip-hop, 2, 249, 281n7; in La Cruzada Teatral Guantánamo-Baracoa productions, 198; under Ministry of Culture, 86; musicians and, *228*; in Option Zero Theater productions, 90; rap, 14; Russian folk, 244; salsa, 2, 6, 131, 187, 271–72; in Teatro de los Elementos productions, 105; on television, 17. *See also* décimas

Nápoles Fajardo, Juan Cristóbal, 283

nation, 1–2, 49–50, 174, 212, 243; artists in

nation (*cont.*)
  politics of, 63, 70, 214; campesino as
    icon of, 5, 32, 35–36, 83, 108–10, 245–46;
    culture in building of, 9, 12, 103, 188,
    210; foreigners and, 268–69, 274; as
    imagined community, 22–23, 252;
    national memory and, 38, 77, 125;
    national narratives and, 113, 172, 218–19,
    258; national theater and, 59, 64–65;
    race and, 42–44, 46, 51–55. *See also*
    nationalism
national identity, 50, 62–63, 275. *See also*
  culture
National Institute of Culture, 47. *See also*
  Ministry of Culture
nationalism, 5, 13–14, 37, 53, 205, 267; artistic, 46; during crisis, 26, 260, 275–76;
  gender and, 137; in literacy campaigns,
  54; national symbols and, xxi–xxii, 10,
  254, 285n1; popular culture and, 17–18.
  See also cubanía; Massification of Culture campaign; pura cepa
National Theater, 57, 189
National Theater Board. *See* Consejo
  Nacional de las Artes Escénicas
negrito, 34, 43, 45; after Cuban Revolution,
  48, 51; in twenty-first century, 36, 260–
  63, 275; *See also* Teatro Bufo
neoliberalism, 12. *See also* capitalism
nostalgia, 91, 103, 152, 195, 246, 256; in
  anthropology, 6; campesino figure and,
  5, 107, 173; for campesino traditions,
  198, 231; preemptive, 19, 170, 259, 273–
  74, 277; rural spaces and, 81; in theater,
  84–85
Nuestra América (Our America), 245–46,
  279n3. *See also* Martí, José

Obraztsov, Sergey, 22
Occidente (western Cuba), 14, 180, 214,
  280n7; definition, 179. *See also* Havana
Opción Cero (Option Zero), 34, 76–80,
  192, 205, 272
Option Zero Theater, 32, 90, 221, 273–74
Orientalism, 179, 280n7
Oriente (eastern Cuba), 26, 35, 91, 176, 188,
  280n7; definition of, 179; mocked by
  western and urban people, 81, 242

Orientistas (people studying in the Oriente of Cuba), 26
Oriol González Martínez, José, 91–92,
  103–5, 272; in Cumanayagua, 98–99;
  Lexis Pérez Hernández and, 110, 119; on
  Los Elementos's hiatus, 115; national
  connections of, 211; performance of,
  165; personal history of, 71–72, 120; play
  production and, 124–41, 149, 158–59,
  163; research process and, 31; son of, 107
Ortiz, Fernando, 29, 42, 173–74, 275

Padilla, Heberto, 67, 73–75
Padrón, Juan, 108. *See also* Elpidio Valdés
Palomita (Little Dove Theater), 183–84
Pavonato (Gray Years). *See* Años Gris;
  Pavón Tamayo, Luis
Pavón Tamayo, Luis, 9
Paz, Albio, 62, 65–66
peasants. *See* campesino, campesinos
Pedro, Alberto, 289n2. See also *Manteca*
Pérez, Carlos, *185*, 186, 203. *See also* Tío Tato
Pérez, Esther, 211
Pérez, Jorge Ignacio, 177, 201
Pérez Firmat, Gustavo, 275
Pérez Hernández, Lexis, 98–99, 124–25,
  132, 138, *157*, 162, 173; collaboration with
  José Oriol, 110, 119
Pérez Peña, Carlos, 102
performance, performances, 55, 101, 114–
  15, 170, 200, 271; access to, xix, 83, 221;
  campesino figure and, 19, 254; by campesinos, 65, 217, 225–26; censorship of,
  167; definition of, 24; in Early Cuban
  Republic, 44; ephemerality and, 7–8, 21;
  of ethnography, 23, 143, 280n6; of folk-
  dance, 219; gender and, 236; marketability and, 27; nontraditional, 4; performative consequences and, 117; production process of, 34, 120–74; race and,
  262; religious, 3, 233, 263–64; rural, 7;
  significance of audiences at, 30–31, 64,
  89, 113, 242; spaces of, 46, 48, 56–57, 87,
  98, 107; state funding of, 17–18; studies
  of, 37–39; in tourism industry, 187–88,
  265. *See also* theater
peso convertible, 84, 186, 261. *See also* peso
  (cubano)

peso (cubano), 92, 128, 147, 155, 261, 284n9; campesinos and, 206, 247; exchange rate of, with dollars, 95; shopping and, 97, 153. *See also* divisas; peso convertible

photography, 66, 80, 135, 156, 177, 265, 282n12

Pinar del Río, 28, 95, 169, 248, 265

Piñero, Virgilio, 75, 159–60, 173

Plan Turquino Manatí, 97, 138

Playa Girón, 91

Poetic Fantasy, 85–86, 100, 107, 170, 203, 220

poetry, 67, 73–75, 118, 122, 159–60; in performance, 145–46, 152–53, 156, 162–63, 242; poets and, 24, 28, 30, 47, 119, 128–29, 135; Raymond Williams on, 80–81

Pogolotti, Graziella, 256–57

Pong, Alfredo, 109

postcolonialism, 245, 254

Prieto, Abel, 187, 212, 289n1

propaganda, xxi, 5, 11, 55, 65, 103, 283n22; relation of, to art, 69, 215–16. *See also* Massification of Culture campaign

pseudo-culture, 2, 14, 35, 256, 259–60

Puerto Rico, 246

Punta de Maisí, xix, *196*, 200

puppetry, xx, 182–84, 193, 198, 204, 207, 210–11

pura cepa (pure stock/root), 5, 173, 203, 258–59, 266; campesino figure and, 6, 108; Hombre Novísimo and, 14, 244; rural spaces and, 1, 35, 83; in Special Period, 13, 19; in theater, 82, 197, 272–73. *See also* cubanía

Quinoa (organization), 271

Quinquenio Gris. *See* Años Gris

race, 2, 60, 106, 189; academic studies of, 281n7, 282n8; Afro-Cuban identity and, 26, 65–66, 269; ajaico and, 275; Asian-Cuban identity and, 247; campesinos and, 247–48; Chinese-Cuban identity and, 42, 261; in Cuban Revolution, 34, 49–54, 255; gallego and, 34, 36, 260–63, 275; gender and, 289n2; José Martí on, 245; mulatas and mulattos and, 34, 41–43, 48, 260–63, 275, 281n1; negrito and, 34, 48, 260–63, 275; perceptions of

Guantánamo and, 179; racial nationalisms and, 46; in Special Period, 260–63; in Teatro Bufo, 43–48; whiteness and, 26, 289n2. *See also* blackface; criollos; cubanía; gallego; indigeneity; mulata; negrito; pura cepa; racism; slavery

racism, 262; anti-discrimination legal reforms and, 49–54, 282n9

religion, religions, 13, 118, 215, 275, 290n5; Afro-Cuban, 2–4, 36, 262, 265; altar photographs and, *228, 234, 244*; Alumbrados/Altares de Cruz and, 79–80, 127, 197, 231–33, 251; campesino figure and, 35; censorship of, 70; Christianity, 172, 227, 233; espiritismo (spiritism), 2, 233; Judaism, 172; language of, 18; religiosos and, 198, 227; Santería, xxii, 14, 149, 173, 183, 187; spirituality and nature and, 82, 89, 103, 105; in tourism industry, 263–67; voodoo, 106

Retamar, Roberto Fernández, 276

revolutionary consciousness, 11, 34, 50, 54–56, 65, 215–16, 279n3. *See also* Cuban Revolution

revolutionary theater, 23, 49, 57, 61, 66. *See also* Cuban Revolution

Risk, Beatriz, 61

Robaina, Tomas Fernández, 52, 53, 282n8, 290n3

Rodríguez, Carlo Rafael, 281n6

Rodríguez, Ury, 192, *229, 237*, 251, 269; acting, 201, 262; directing El Laboratorio de Teatro Comunitario, 32; on shortages during Special Period, 205–6; storytelling project and, 224–27, 235–37; in Teatro Rostro, 184, 217

Rodríguez Millares, Eulogio, 267

Rosendahl, Mona, 279n2

Russia, 22, 244, 264. *See also* USSR

Saco, José Antonio, 279n3

Said, Edward, 179, 280n7

Sances, Hermina, 281n6

Santa Clara, 3, 28, 95, 97, 104, 144

Santamaría, Haydee, 101

Santiago de Cuba, 2, 86, 177, 233, 248, 255; research in, 3, 28; tourism in, 179, 186–87, 263

Savarese, Nicola, 30, 280n9

Schechner, Richard, 23–25, 39

Segarra, Teresita, 211

Segundo, Compay, 244, 248

Séjourné, Laurette, 29

sexuality, 203, 263; gender norms and, 133, 137, 236; heterosexuality, 99, 119, 133, 162, 238; homosexuality, 9, 70, 147, 160, 173; marriage and, 99, 137, 236, 251; sexy mulata figure and, 34, 173; in tourism industry, 187

sex work, 265, 287n10. *See also* jineteras/ jineteros; tourism: sex

shopping, 3, 81, 97, 125, 153, 216

Siguanea, 35, 128, 142–74, 220, 227; images of, *148, 154*

slavery, 42–43, 106, 247, 264, 275

socialism, 5, 12, 49, 215; artists under, 25, 27, 29, 68–70, 114–17; bureaucracy and, 28, 191; campesino figure and, 17, 101; in Eastern Europe, 3, 78–79; moderniza- tion under, 11, 18, 34; parasocialist society and, 13–14, 172; racial politics of, 52; socialist education and, 66, 103, 216; socialist ideology and, 10, 23, 110, 125; socialist morality and, 65, 108, 256, 267, 274; in Special Period, 16, 20, 276; the- ater and, 55–59, 64; waiting under, 169– 72

socialist realism, 22

Spain, 36, 169, 246, 279n3; emigration to, 75, 201. *See also* Ten Years' War; Wars for Independence

Special Period in Time of Peace, 18, 26, 133, 176, 263; ambivalences during, 50, 249; artists during, 34, 76–110, 192; campe- sino figure and, 252, 257, 274–75; Cuban identity during, 15, 20, 225, 259; declara- tion of, 8–9; definition of, 3; Hombre Novísimo and, 13, 17; political economy and, 10–12, 186; shortages and, 205; Tea- tro Bufo and, 48; waiting during, 169– 71. *See also* Massification of Culture campaign

Spivak, Gayatri Chakravorty, 20, 143

Stanislavsky, Constantin, 22

storytelling, 2, 35, 113, 207, 218, 257; national, 13, 18, 36; Option Zero Theater

and, 90; play production and, 149, 161, 225–44, 253–55; Teatro Rostro and, 184. *See also* emotional truth

Suárez Durán, Esther, 8, 43, 283n18

subaltern, 20, 143, 216, 219

Sutherland, Elizabeth, 281n7

Tabío, Juan Carlos, 94

Taussig, Michael, 218, 250

Taylor, Diana, 37–38, 274

Teatro Acero (Theater of Steel), 65. *See also* Paz, Albio

Teatro Brecht (Brecht Theater), 60, 289n2

Teatro Buendía (Good Day Theater), 188– 90, 197, 283n20

Teatro Bufo (Theater of the Buffoon), 5, 34, 43–48, 50–51, 282n1, 282n5; *El Tío Francisco y Las Leandras* (Uncle Fran- cisco and the Leandras, 1997), 262

Teatro Campesino (Farmworker's The- ater), 86, 258, 282n15

Teatro Comunitario (Communitarian Theater), 27–29, 80–92, 121; award for, 207; changes to, 217, 272; goals of, 243, 255; as Option Zero Theater, 34, 273–74; rhetoric of, 204, 225. *See also* La Cruzada Teatral Guantánamo-Baracoa; Grupo Andante; La Guerilla de Tea- treros; Korimacao; El Laboratorio de Teatro Comunitario; Option Zero The- ater; Teatro de los Elementos

Teatro de la Comunidad (Theater of the Community), 84. *See also* Lauten, Flora; Teatro La Yaya

Teatro del Este (Theater of the East), 72. *See also* Oriol González Martínez, José

Teatro de los Elementos (Theater of the Ele- ments), 20, 98–100, 104–7, *131,* 227, *277,* campesino revival and, 108–11; compared to El Laboratorio de Teatro Comunitario, 233, 235; compared to La Cruzada Teatral Guantánamo-Baracoa, 206, 209–12; crit- icism of, 101–3; devised theater and, 285n2; European tour of, 271–73; *Opción Cero* (Option Zero, 2001), 76–79; process of theater production of, 30–32, 34–35, 113–16; reputation of, 91–92, 242; *Ten mi nombre con un sueño* (Remember My

Name as if it Were a Dream, 1999), 101, 120–74, *157*, *166*

Teatro de Relaciones (Theater of Relationships), 66

Teatro Dramático de Guantánamo (Adult Dramatic Theater), 286n4

Teatro Escambray (Escambray Theater), 62–67, 72, 98, 212, 221; changes to, 91, 273; criticism of, 99–103; formation of, 59; goals of, 21–22; Hombre Nuevo figure and, 50; as model for other groups, 82–84, 90, 104; studies of, 26, 211

Teatro Estudio (Studio Theater), 59–60, 188

Teatro García Lorca (García Lorca Theater), 57

Teatro Guaso (Guaso Theater), 188

Teatro Güiñol (Puppet Theater), 183, 286n4

Teatro Karl Marx (Karl Marx Theater), 57

Teatro La Yaya (Theater of La Yaya), 65, 189, 223. *See also* Lauten, Flora; Teatro de la Comunidad

Teatro Los Doce (Theater of the Twelve), 188–89

Teatro Mella (Mella Theater), 57

Teatro Mío (My Theater), 289n2

Teatro Nuevo (New Theater), 27, 61, 65–67, 273; in Cuban Revolution, 34, 49, 59–60; in 1980s, 82–83, 85, 88. *See also under names of relevant theater groups*

Teatro Público (Public Theater), 289n2

Teatro Rostro (Face Theater), 183–85, 217. *See also* Ury, Rodríguez

Teatro Tierra Roja (Red Earth Theater), 72. *See also* Oriol González Martínez, José

Teatro Tomás Terry, 57. *See also* Cienfuegos (city)

Teatro Trianon, 183, 185

television, 17, 53, 150–51, 181–82, 209–10

Ten Years' War (1868–78), 42

theater, 4, 7–8, 18, 243–44, 277; anthropological, 29–30, 32; campesino figure in, 15; children's, 183, 204; circuits, 190–91; comic, 43, 48; critics, 103–4, 114, *114*, 210–11, 262; devised, 112, 285n2; disciplinarity and, 37–39; during Batista regime, 47–48; ethnography of, 27, 275; exhibition contexts of, 87–89, 144; experimental, 100, 185; history of, 22, 43, 100, 104–5, 166–67; Latin American, 60–62; people of, 28, 30, 110, 274; people's, 21, 31, 60, 65; political, 21–26, 55–60, 101; production process of, 120–74; race and, 53; revolutionary, 11, 49, 72, 90–92, 102; ritual, 264; rural, 17, 19–20, 66, 85, 221; Russian, 22; in Special Period, 82; street, 91, 105; in tourism industry, 98; in United States, 200. *See also* acting; audience, audiences; blackface; commedia dell'arte; improvisation; irony; performance, performances; Option Zero Theater; Poetic Fantasy; puppetry; *and under names of individual theater groups*

Theater of the Absurd, 172. *See also* Beckett, Samuel

Theater of the Oppressed, 22, 60. *See also* Boal, Augusto

Tío Tato (Carlos Pérez), xx–xxi, 183, *185*, 186, 203

Torriente, Ricardo de la, 108, *109*. *See also* Liborio

Torriente Brau, Pablo de la, 246

tourism, 36, 95, 146–47, 216, 260; in Guantánamo Province, 177–79, 182; marketing of campesino and, 5–7; performances and, 33, 99, 172–73, 187–88, 263–69; sex, 265, 287n10; in Special Period, 12, 14. *See also* jineteras, jineteros

Trinidad (Cuban city), 7, 95, 179, 265, 269

Trouillot, Michel-Rolph, 251

Turnbull, Colin, 280n6

Turner, Edith, 280n6

Turner, Victor, 25, 39, 117–18, 280n6

UMAP labor camps (Unidades Militares de Ayuda a la Producción), 9, 70–71

Unión de Jóvenes Comunistas (UJC; Union of Young Communists), 71–72, 118

Unión Nacional de Escritores y Artistas de Cuba (UNEAC; National Union of Writers and Artists of Cuba), 73–74, 185, 187, 212–13, 288n15, 289n1; Castro's address to, 12. *See also* Martí, Carlos

United States, 12, 32, 183, 201, 262; Cuban
identity and, 279n3, 285n1; embargo/
blockade by, 16, 36, 158; emigration to,
169; national symbols and, xxi, 285n3;
performances in, 46; theater movements in, 121, 282n15; war with Cuba,
47. *See also* Gonzalez, Elián
University Theater (of Havana), 47
USSR, 8, 16, 77, 263. *See also* Russia

Valdés, Elpidio. *See* Elpidio Valdés
Valdez, Luis, 86
Valiño, Omar, 210–11, 213
Varadero, 7, 95, 265
Velvet Prison, 67–72, 74, 117, 214
Verdery, Katherine, 3, 35, 211–12, 214
Villena, Rubén Martínez, 246
visual culture. *See* artes plásticas; cartoons;
dance, dancing; film, films; perfor-

mance, performances; photography;
puppetry; television; theater

Wallis, Graham, 114–16
Wars for Independence (1868–78, 1879–80,
1895–98), 46–47, 247
Weiss, Judith, 21, 41, 25–26, 75, 102
Williams, Raymond, 37, 80–81

Yanes, Isnoel, xvi, 99, 118, 124, 157, 162
yuma (slang: foreign or American), 269–
70

zonas del silencio (zones of silence), xix,
35, 179–80; campesinos in, xxi, 152;
Cuban identity and, 26; remoteness of,
2, 193, 224–26, 289n7; theater groups in,
88–90, 191, 209–10

LAURIE FREDERIK IS AN ASSISTANT PROFESSOR
OF PERFORMANCE STUDIES AND ANTHROPOLOGY
AT THE UNIVERSITY OF MARYLAND.

Library of Congress Cataloging-in-Publication Data

Frederik, Laurie Aleen.
Trumpets in the mountains : theater and the politics of
national culture in Cuba / Laurie A. Frederik.
p. cm.
Includes bibliographical references and index.
ISBN 978-0-8223-5246-4 (cloth : alk. paper)
ISBN 978-0-8223-5265-5 (pbk. : alk. paper)
1. Theater—Political aspects—Cuba.
2. Traveling theater—Cuba.
3. Cuba—Rural conditions.
4. National characteristics, Cuban. I. Title.
PN2401.F74 2012
792.097291—dc23   2011053295